Retailing, Consumption and Capital:

Towards the New Retail Geography

Edited by Neil Wrigley and Michelle Lowe
University of Southampton

Longman Group Limited
Longman House, Burnt Mill, Harlow
Essex CM20 2JE, England
and Associated Companies throughout the world

First published 1996

British Library Cataloguing in Publication Data
A catalogue entry for this title is available from the British Library.

ISBN 0-582-22824-7

Library of Congress Cataloging-in-Publication data
A catalog entry for this title is available from the Library of Congress.

Set by 7 in 10/11 Palatino
Pruduced through Longman Malaysia, ETS

Contents

List of Contributors

Editors

Neil Wrigley is Professor of Geography and Head of the Department of Geography at the University of Southampton. He was previously Editor of *Transactions of the Institute of British Geographers* and Professor of City and Regional Planning at the University of Wales, Cardiff. His research interests and the geography of retail restructuring; retailing and the regulatory state; and the internationalization of retail capital.

Michelle Lowe is Lecturer in Geography at the University of Southampton. She is co-editor with Peter Jackson and Frank Mort of the UCL Press Series *Consumption and Space*. Her research interests are the new cultural geographies of retailing, fashion retailing, and gender and consumption.

Contributors

Nicholas Blomley is Associate Professor in the Department of Geography, Simon Fraser University, Vancouver, Canada

Sophie Bowlby is Senior Lecturer in Geography at the University of Reading

Susan Christopherson is Associate Professor in the Department of City and Regional Planning, Cornell University, USA

David Clarke is Lecturer in Geography at the University of Leeds

Louise Crewe is Lecturer in Geography at the University of Nottingham

Christine Doel is a Research Student in the Department of Geography, University of Cambridge

Mona Domosh is Associate Professor in the Department of Geography, College of Liberal Arts, Florida Atlantic University, USA

Jo Foord is Senior Lecturer in Geography at the University of North London

Paul Freathy is Lecturer in the Institute of Retail Studies, University of Stirling

Ray Hudson is Professor of Geography at the University of Durham

Alex Hughes is Lecturer in Geography at the University of Aberdeen

Paul Glennie is Lecturer in Geography at the University of Bristol

Terry Marsden is Professor of City and Regional Planning, University of Wales, Cardiff

David Sadler is Lecturer in Geography at the University of Durham

Ruth Shackleton is a Research Student in the Department of Geography, University of Southampton

Leigh Sparks is Professor in the Institute of Retail Studies, University of Stirling

Nigel Thrift is Professor of Geography at the University of Bristol

Christine Tillsley was formerly ESRC Research Assistant in the Department of Geography, University of Reading

Alan Townsend is Reader in Geography at the University of Durham

Acknowledgements

Chapter 3
The research for this chapter was undertaken during the course of an ERSC research studentship.

Chapter 4
The authors' research reported in this chapter was undertaken with the support of a grant from the ESRC ('Changing retailer–manufacturer links: a study in the geography of employment' No. R–00231588).

Chapter 8
The research for this chapter was partially supported by a grant from the US Department of Labor, Employment and Training Administration. The author would like to thank Beth Redfield and Beth Sheehan for research assistance and Neil Wrigley for comments.

Chapter 13
The author would like to thank Bev Pitman, Felix Driver, Neil Wrigley, Michelle Lowe, Liz Bondi and Peter Jackson for their supportive and critical comments.

Chapter 16
The author would like to thank Graham Clarke, Adam Tickell and Marcus Doel for thoughts which have influenced this chapter. Especial thanks to Adam Tickell for his immense practical help. This work relates to the ESRC Fellowship Consumption, Lifestyle and the City (Award No: H52427002294).

Part 1

Introduction

CHAPTER 1

Towards the new retail geography

Michelle Lowe and Neil Wrigley

During the 1980s, what came to be called 'the political-economy perspective' emerged as both the cutting edge and new orthodoxy of conceptual analysis in human geography, and debate within that broad perspective was fundamental to the reformulation of geography's place within the social sciences (Massey, 1989). When combined with the major structural/spatial transformations occurring in industrial capitalism, the political-economy perspective resulted in a remarkable flowering of theoretically inspired work in geography concerning uneven development and regional change, spatial divisions of labour, industrial restructuring, the inconstant geography of capitalism, the territorial organization of production, and the transition from 'Fordism' to 'flexible accumulation'. Indeed, a 'new' economic geography was in many senses born. This new approach focused on the manner in which the 'territorial foundations of capitalism operate, are reproduced, and transformed through time' (Scott and Storper, 1986), and was rooted in the belief that 'political economic processes . . . are profoundly shaped by their geography, and that any theoretical apparatus in the social sciences which ignores the geographical dimensions of these processes . . . does so at its own peril' (Storper and Walker, 1989).

Rich and many faceted as this new literature became, it contained, however, remarkably little discussion of circulation and consumption activities preferring instead to centre its emphasis on 'production' and the 'productive sphere'. In addition, it offered relatively few insights into the innovatory aspects of what Christopherson (this volume, Chapter 8) terms 'consumption work'. Partly in consequence, but partly in cause, neglect of *retailing* as a sector of economic activity worthy of attention in the 'new' economic geography was profound. In addressing this issue Ducatel and Blomley (1990) advanced the view that the root of this neglect lay as much with the traditions of retail geography as with the curiously myopic oversight of circulation and consumption activities within the 'new' economic geography. Ducatel and Blomley's view was that a 'wholly inadequate analysis' of retailing and retail change lacking a 'systematic account of *retail capital*' (1990: 207) had characterized the traditional literature of retail geography. As a result, retail geography, potentially 'one of the most interesting of sub-disciplines, given the subtlety and importance of retail capital, consumption and space' had 'been made into one of the most boring of fields' (Blomley, this volume, Chapter 13). While we do not dissent from this view, we choose in this book not to labour such controversy. Rather we wish here to suggest that a 'new retail geography' *is* in the process of creation. The 'new retail geography' which has emerged during the 1990s is characterized – above all else – by theoretical engagement and by a shared perspective among its adherents that 'retail capital, and its transformation, is a vital and relevant topic for research and demands urgent attention' (Ducatel and Blomley, 1990: 225).

The early 1990s, as this book will demonstrate, was a period then when retail geography began to take its economic geographies seriously and began to explore such issues as: the geography of retail restructuring; the interface between retail and financial capital; the complex and contradictory relations of retailing with the regulatory state; the interrelations of corporate strategy, corporate culture and market structures in the industry; the social relations of 'production' in retailing; the structure of channel relations (notably retailer–supplier relations); the spatial switching of retail capital; and the configuration of retail spaces to induce consumption. However, as Blomley (this volume, Chapter 13) argues, heartening as these new economic geographies of retailing were, they coincided with a time at which the theoretical high ground of critical human geography was experiencing a rapid and significant 'cultural turn' (Crang, 1993; McDowell, 1994). No sooner had a theoretically embedded new economic geography of retailing, focusing upon retail capital and its transformation and upon the extent to which 'the transformation of the retail sector and of consumption work represents a second wave of industrial restructuring' (Christopherson, this volume, Chapter 8), begun to be embraced, than there were calls for 'a cultural perspective on retailing' and consumption spaces to be adopted (Dowling, 1993: 297). Such analysis of the cultural logic of retailing was to be focused centrally upon retail spaces 'as contexts where the meaning of commodities is produced and negotiated' (Dowling, 1993: 297), and upon the 'construction of femininity and the creation of a sense of place [as] central attributes of the retail enterprise' (1993: 296). Moreover, it was to be elaborated by a tradition of cultural perspectives on consumption, and a concern with the shift from production to consumption spaces, as seen in the work of writers such as R Bowlby (1985; 1987), M Morris (1988), Abelson (1989) and Zukin (1991), and paralleled in the sociological work on consumption sites and consumption cultures represented in the edited volume of Shields (1992a).

The emerging consensus, as Blomley (this volume, Chapter 13) notes, is that 'a retail geography worthy of its name . . . must (therefore) take *both* its economic and cultural geographies seriously', and it is that philosophy which underpins this volume. Our aim is to provide a collection of studies by a small number of the many geographers who have begun to develop such a reconstructed retail geography. As we shall show, they have done this via theoretically informed accounts of the transformation of retail capital and the manner in which retailers are 'more and more actively mediating the producer–consumer relation' (Sayer and Walker, 1992: 91), and via the larger project of combining 'an exploration of the economic structures of retail capital with an analysis of the cultural logic of retailing' (Blomley, this volume, Chapter 13). Our view then is that retailing, conceived either in terms of the traditional maxim of 'location, location, location' (Jones and Simmons, 1990), or in terms of the unique position which retail capital occupies between production and consumption – 'mirroring its struggles with productive capital in its relations with consumers' (Ducatel and Blomley, 1990: 225), or alternatively in terms of being uniquely suited to analysis of the links between femininity, masculinity, place and consumption (Dowling, 1993; Blomley, this volume, Chapter 13; Domosh, this volume, Chapter 14), is an inherently *geographical* phenomenon. As a result, it is, we suggest, of central importance both to the broader progress of critical human geography and to the wider study of circulation and consumption in the social sciences, to have a vibrant reconstructed retail geography positioned at the cutting edges of theoretical debate. We offer this book as one step along that journey.

A reconstructed retail geography as discussed above demands then that the economic and cultural are enmeshed and mutually constituted. Notwithstanding this, the form of those interconnections remains one of the central problematics in attempts to move debate forward (Crewe and Lowe, 1995; Jackson, 1994; Jackson and Thrift, 1995; Marsden and Wrigley, 1995). Recognizing, therefore, that it is artificial to draw out separate economic and cultural geographies of retailing, we propose, nevertheless, to address key themes in each area and to show how these are played out in this collection. In so doing, however, we attempt to maintain – as an underlying theme – this central economic/cultural problematic.

Themes in the new economic geographies of retailing

In detailing the various ways in which retail geography began to take its economic geographies seriously in the early 1990s, we have already outlined a series of issues which began to be explored. All were rooted, as we have seen, in an attempt to develop a systematic account of the transformation of retail capital and its geographical expression. In the following sections we draw together such issues under three headings: retail capital and retail restructuring; retailing and the transition to flexible accumulation debate; and retailing and regulation. While these themes clearly present only a partial view of what is a complex and developing field, we see the topics we have selected as important markers in the construction of the new economic geographies of retailing and, as such, worthy of further attention.

Retail capital and retail restructuring

At the heart of the political-economic retheorization of retail geography that got underway in the early 1990s was a concern with retail capital and its transformation. As Clarke (this volume, Chapter 16) demonstrates, there were essentially two main strands of that work. First, a form of 'meso-level' theory centred upon the rise of corporate retail power, the capital logic that drives the process of retail accumulation, the competitive strategies and corporate restructuring processes that transform the industry, and 'a more sophisticated understanding of the *reciprocal* nature of the relations between space and corporate retail activity' (Clarke, this volume, Chapter 16). Much of this work was couched in terms of 'retail restructuring' (Wrigley, 1987; 1988b; 1989). Second, attempts to identify an abstract category of 'retail capital', and to lay the foundations of a Marxist interpretation of the position and function of retail capital within the wider circuits of capital (Ducatel and Blomley, 1990).

A central feature of Ducatel and Blomley's important paper was their attempt to define the form, function and logic of retail capital as a subform of commercial capital 'located between production and final consumption', having 'as its function the realization of the surplus value locked up in consumer commodities', and as its primary logic 'the accumulation of capital through repeated acts of exchange' (Ducatel and Blomley, 1990: 218). More recently, Fine and Leopold (1993b: 274) have argued that this attempt ultimately fails and that 'retail capital does *not* emerge as an appropriate abstract category to develop within Marxist theory'. Fine and Leopold's view is that retail capital should not be treated analytically as an undifferentiated category but instead as heterogeneous, falling within separate vertically interconnected systems of commodity provision. That is to say, retail capital should be considered within a vertical *'chains* of provision' framework, and that the nature of retail capital is likely to be sector specific. (Fine (1993) has also argued this case more generally in respect of geographical studies of consumption – see the later section of this chapter on 'consumption chains'.)

Although important, the Fine and Leopold critique of the ultimate level and character of abstraction on which Ducatel and Blomley pinned their hopes is, in many senses, of only technical significance when set against the wider impact of the Ducatel and Blomley paper. Both the broader objectives of that paper (namely, their rejection of orthodox retail geography and their plea for a theoretically informed analysis of retail capital in the widest sense), and its secondary objectives (an attempt to bridge the gap between the abstract and the concrete by investigating, within a broad political-economy perspective, 'the spatial expression and manifestation of retail restructuring') were undoubtedly realized. If one of the end points of attempts to rethink retail capital relates, therefore, to an ability to address issues of the spatial expression of retail restructuring, how then was the framework of a meso-level theory centred on the 'geography of retail restructuring' to be organized?

Initial attempts to develop such a framework were rooted to a greater or lesser extent in the industrial restructuring debates of the 1980s, and inevitably drew upon Massey and Meegan (1982). As a result, Wrigley (1988b) focused his discussion of the restructuring of the UK retailing industry in the mid-1980s on four interrelated themes: the concentration of retail capital; the intensification of 'production' within retailing; the spatial switching of retail capital; and technological change within retail distribution. Ducatel and Blomley (1990), in turn, drew attention to: the concentration of retail capital; the associated shift in power at the productive-commercial interface to the advantage of retail capital; and the attempt by retail capital to reduce circulation costs. Explicit or implicit in these attempts was, however, the view that processes of retail restructuring were *not* directly analogous to those in the manufacturing sector, and that any framework must remain sensitive to the fact that the 'character of production organization in services presents a specific set of analytical problems and an emerging division of labour which differs from that in manufacturing' (Christopherson, 1989: 131). In no sense, therefore, were these attempts to adopt what has been referred to as the 'strong version of restructuring theory' (Lovering, 1989). Rather, they were attempts to use restructuring concepts, particularly the crucial notion of restructuring as 'a process of deliberate or planned structural reconfiguration in response to changing market conditions' (Clark, 1993: 5) – that is to say, a *re*making of the inherited configuration of production and relocation of industries, firms, etc to new, higher trajectories of accumulation (Webber *et al*, 1991) – merely as heuristic devices or useful analytical tools.

More generally, Wrigley has adopted a framework for the discussion of retail restructuring in which six themes are given prominence:

1 reconfiguration of corporate structures in retailing
2 reconfiguration of retailer–supply chain interfaces (e.g. shifts in retailer–supplier power balances)
3 organizational and technological transformations in retail distribution
4 reconfiguration of labour practices and social relations of 'production' within retailing
5 the spatial penetration, manipulation and switching of retail capital
6 the regulation of retail restructuring.

Several of these themes are discussed in more detail in this introductory chapter and/or elsewhere in the volume: see for example, Doel (Chapter 3), Foord, Bowlby and Tillsley (Chapter 4) and Hughes (Chapter 5) on the retailer–supplier interface, and Christopherson (Chapter 8), Freathy and Sparks (Chapter 9), and Lowe and Crewe (Chapter 10) on labour practices and the social relations of 'production' in retailing. At this stage it is sufficient, therefore, to take just one of these themes – for example, that relating to the way corporate retail capital 'actively explores and penetrates specific spaces at a number of scales' (Ducatel and Blomley, 1990: 225), the way it manipulates spatial layout and design to induce consumption, and the way it often remakes the inherited configuration of 'production' via a process of capital switching (i.e. via a reconfiguration of the locus of profit extraction) but sometimes gets locked into (finds it difficult to abandon) existing geographies – to draw out the contrast with orthodox retail geography.

As Clarke (this volume, Chapter 16) notes, space in the new economic geographies of retailing is interpreted in a far more dynamic way. It is conceived as the product of social activity, in which the active creation and re-creation of markets, the 'grounding' of capital, the relation between spatial configuration, spatial discipline and control, and so on are viewed as central issues in both the capital imperatives facing corporate retailers and in the contested retailer–consumer relation. That is to say, the new economic geographies of retailing have brought not only a far more 'sophisticated understanding of the *reciprocal* nature of relations between space and corporate retail activity' (Clarke, this volume, Chapter 16), but also one in which retail spaces, rather than being viewed as passive surfaces 'are increasingly being cast as actively produced, represented and contested' (Blomley, this volume, Chapter 13). In this way, the spaces of contemporary shopping centres, for example, are explored against a spectrum of interpretations: as examples of the bargaining power exercised by major retail 'anchor tenants' over property developers writ large (Guy, 1994); as premeditatedly configured and segmented 'machines for selling'; as contested publicly used but privately owned and policed arenas; as stages serviced by largely invisible hands in which retail employees are cast members rather than employees (Lowe and Crewe, this volume, Chapter 10); as filtered and projected images of the urban environment and temples to the consumption of symbolic capital; as landscapes of myths and elsewhereness (J Hopkins, 1990); and as complex, socially constructed interfaces between retail capital and consumption. The arbitrary categories of the 'economic' and the 'cultural' are in this way constantly shattered, as new economic geography of retailing readings of such spaces of retail capital accumulation, blur into new cultural geography of retailing readings of 'consumption spaces' (see later sections of this chapter).

Retailing and the transition to flexible accumulation debate

As Gertler (1992: 259) noted, 'work surrounding the "flexibility thesis" has brought a prominence to spatial research' which is perhaps 'unmatched by any other idea to emanate from geography, regional science or planning'. Understood by most geographers in terms of a direct confrontation with the rigidities of Fordism, flexible accumulation rests in Harvey's (1989c: 147) view upon a startling 'flexibility with respect to labour processes, labour markets, products, and patterns of consumption. It is characterized by the emergence of entirely new sectors of production, new ways of providing financial services, new markets, and above all, greatly intensified rates of commercial, technological, and organizational innovation'. Nevertheless, despite the stress which both Harvey (1989c) and Gertler (1988) place upon consumption patterns, technological and organization innovation, and labour practices/control in their definitions of 'flexible accumulation', the core of the wider 'flexibility' debate became focused during the late 1980s to a large extent upon the transformation of manufacturing production and the geographical configuration of production systems/production complexes (Lovering, 1990; Sayer, 1989; Schoenberger, 1988; Scott, 1988a). Neglect of the service sector and circulation activities was marked (indeed Gertler (1992: 268) categorized it as forgotten sector in the 'diaspora' of debate on the flexibility thesis). This, in turn, prompted warnings, such as that of R L Martin (1990: 1280), that until the preoccupation with manufacturing and neglect of services in such debates 'is rectified our understanding of the economic landscape of post-Fordism will remain incomplete and rather one-sided'.

Despite this neglect, there were those who from the very outset of the flexible accumulation debate believed that it was to retailing and the innovatory aspects of 'consumption work', rather than manufacturing and production work, that social scientists should look to discover the essence of the transformation from the rigidities of Fordism. Outside academic geography, R Murray's (1989: 42) view that 'in Britain, the groundwork for the new system [flexible accumulation/post-Fordism] was laid not in manufacturing but in *retailing*' was influential, and was echoed by geographers such as Christopherson (1989: 131) who drew attention to the limitations of the 'manufacturing-oriented flexibility model' and argued that it was in services such as retailing that 'some of the most significant innovations in labour use, particularly the use of so-called flexible labour, are occurring'.

Embedded within this view of the centrality of retailing and consumption work to the flexibility debate were two separate but interrelated themes. The first of these stressed the position of retailing (particularly in the UK) at the cutting edge of technological and organizational innovation, and as fundamental to the greatly accelerated circulation time of capital.

Retailers (particularly the major UK food retailers) were seen to have developed during the 1970s and 1980s logistically efficient stock control systems, and quick-response centrally controlled warehouse-to-store distribution networks. These systems permitted shorter and more predictable delivery lead times, and facilitated a significant reduction in the so-called 'conversion ratio' (the ratio of warehouse to sales space) within stores. Pressure was placed on suppliers to develop *just-in-time*, fixed-performance specification, production and factory-to-warehouse distribution systems to match. The result was a significant and progressive reduction in retailer inventory holdings (and the amount of working capital tied up in those holdings) throughout the 1980s (see

Marsden and Wrigley, this volume, Figure 2.1) as more and more of the costs (including 'uncertainty' costs) of inventory holding were passed back to manufacturers/suppliers. During the 1980s these centrally controlled distribution and stock control systems provided fertile ground for the adoption of increasingly sophisticated computer-based information technology (IT) systems which, by the end of the decade, had developed into fully integrated management information systems in which EPOS (electronic point of sale) data were used to automate/control the linkage between within-store inventory levels, the warehouse/distribution network, and central administrative functions (ordering, accounting, analysis, etc). Moreover, these systems were increasingly linked back via EDI (electronic data interchange) into the computer systems of manufacturers/suppliers permitting 'paperless' supply-chain control (electronic exchange of orders, invoices, etc) with massive savings in clerical labour. EDI also facilitated computerized tracking systems (retailer interrogation of manufacturer/supplier/ contractor-distributor computer systems to discover where in the distribution chain particular orders are located) giving early warnings of possible delays and scope for contingency action. The result was not only further shortening of order cycle times but also significantly increased predictability in delivery lead times. By the end of the decade, the large UK food retailers could supply stores smoothly and predictably within 12 hours of an order being automatically transmitted, compared to 24 hours in the early 1980s and 48 hours in the late 1970s.

Sayer and Walker (1992: 174) in their discussion of 'just-in-time' (JIT) systems in manufacturing suggest that firms 'wishing to institute JIT [must] ensure that deliveries of inputs are not only just in time but are as constant in content as possible' and that this is 'quite different from the situation of retailers who demand flexible, rather than constant inputs on a just-in-time basis'. As a result, they argue that 'it is quite misleading to generalize from retailing to manufacturing' as R Murray (1989) attempted to do in arguing that, in Britain at least, the groundwork for flexible accumulation was laid not in manufacturing but in retailing. It is our view, however, that, in terms of leading-edge UK retailing, Sayer and Walker's interpretation is a misjudgement and that the spirit of Murray's argument is more accurate. Highly innovative, computerized control of the supply chain was used by the major British food retailers to ensure, above all, *predictable* cost-controlled supply. It was not so much day-to-day flexibility that these firms sought and prized from their JIT systems but control – first of inventory costs via a constant flow-line supply system geared to the demands of the large out-of-town superstores and replacing the chaotic supply/delivery patterns (with high risks of 'stock-out') characteristic of the smaller High Street supermarkets of the 1960s and 1970s and, more recently, of administration costs.

Moreover, in positioning themselves at the cutting edge of technological development, UK retailers became (almost by default) highly innovative organizations (see Doel, this volume, Chapter 3). The centralized, logistically efficient, stock-control/distribution systems put into place during the 1970s and early 1980s facilitated the development of own-label trading (which invariably required retailers to take responsibility for distribution and warehousing). In turn, this was a critical feature of the shift in power from manufacturers/suppliers to retailers in the UK; a shift which had its roots in the macro-regulatory environment (see Wrigley, 1992a, and next section). The growth (and significance in power-balance terms) of own-label trading involved retailers in making increasingly significant inputs to product innovation, product design, and specification of the manufacturing process. In this, they were aided by their access to the consumer demand, consumer preference and sales data – item-by-item, store-by-store, region-by-region – which flooded out of their EPOS systems from the mid-1980s onwards, and which continued to be enhanced in the 1990s as such scanner data were linked (via consumer card systems) to information on household demographics and socio-economic characteristics. As Sayer and Walker (1992: 91) suggest, retailers (particularly in the UK) became, as a result, more and more involved in 'actively mediating the producer-consumer relation' in an innovative way and, more generally, as Marsden and Wrigley (1995) have suggested, in delivering new and revised 'rights to consume' to particular groups in society while, simultaneously, attempting to define consumption interests around their own particular notions.

The second theme relating to the centrality of retailing and consumption work to the flexibility debate stressed the position of retailing as a leading-edge industry in terms of the transformation of labour practices and the social relations of 'production'. These transformations were seen as involving far more than 'the steady dismantling of a relatively skilled, male-dominated labour force, and its subsequent replacement by a low-skilled, lowly paid, feminized work-force, coupled with the increasing use of part-time and juvenile labour' (Ducatel and Blomley, 1990: 222). Rather they involved many innovations such as the skilled use of a multiply segmented 'contingent' labour force, and the increasingly sophisticated use of EPOS-based IT systems to monitor that workforce and to deploy workers, work hours, and work practices very precisely to temporal fluctuations in demand.

As Freathy and Sparks (this volume, Chapter 9) and Christopherson (1989, and this volume, Chapter 8) demonstrate, retail employment structures changed dramatically during the 1970s and 1980s in both quantitative and qualitative terms, with many of the tasks involved in selling commodities being 'redesigned and combined so as to decrease labour inputs or direct them to serving the most profitable market segments' (Christopherson, this volume, Chapter 8). A simple dualistic core/periphery, primary/secondary conception of the retail workforce proved increasingly inadequate to capture the emerging subtleties of a multiply segmented retail workforce. In this workforce there were fundamental divisions between voluntary 'career' part-time workers and secondary involuntary part-time workers. The proportion of the contingent workforce employed for very small numbers of hours per week rose dramatically (in the UK from 24 per cent in 1979 to 42 per cent in 1985) and 'zero hour' (i.e. no specific minimum number of hours) contracts became ever more common. However, there was also some limited evidence of countervailing tendencies, such as functional flexibility (using a full-time worker to do multiple tasks) replacing numerical flexibility, a stabilization in the long-term decline of full-time employment in the industry (see Christopherson, this volume, Chapter 8), and the rise of customer service and customer care as frontiers of competitive advantage in the 1990s (see Lowe and Crewe, this volume, Chapter 10). In turn, this 'unpacking' and problematizing of the concept of flexible labour in retailing (Christopherson, 1989; Lowe and Crewe, 1991) provided a vital and important corrective to views of labour process transformations emerging from the dominantly manufacturing-oriented flexibility debate.

The impact of, and contradictions involved in, the use of the highly innovative computer-based IT systems in retailing (discussed above) was a second area in which work on retail labour processes made a major contribution to the flexibility debate. S Smith (1988), for example, in considering the labour process implications of the introduction of EPOS systems into UK retailing, drew attention to the fact that whereas EPOS did not significantly increase checkout speeds, it did offer considerable scope for detailed monitoring of individual staff performance. 'Management can measure the average time it takes for each checkout operator to handle the average individual item, how long they take to deal with each customer, the amount of time taken between scanning the last item and taking payment for the transaction, the amount of down-time between customers, takings per hour, number of miss-scans and so on' (S Smith, 1988: 150). Nevertheless, at least initially, retailers were very reluctant to exploit this 'big brother' aspect for fear of precipitating a backlash from checkout operators (S Smith, 1988: 151). In addition, while EPOS systems automated the re-ordering process, reduced in-store inventory levels, allowed concentration on faster selling of the most profitable lines, and speeded up the feedback loop between buying and selling so that good and bad decisions by central buyers within the firm showed up more quickly, they brought in their train several new fragilities. For example, checkout operators lost their powers of mental arithmetic and ability to cope with unexpected customer requests, warehouse staff suffered from 'aisle blindness or pickers amnesia' (S Smith, 1988: 154), access to EPOS data had in some cases to be deliberately denied to certain levels of the managerial hierarchy, and there was potential for catastrophic computer system failure with the result that stores occasionally (and with considerable embarrassment) had to be cleared of all customers as there was no possibility in the bar-coded/EPOS world of pricing in the traditional manner. As Gertler (1988: 425) noted in the context of manufacturing industry, 'flexible technologies and labour processes seem to be particularly riddled with contradictory outcomes'. The innovative use of EPOS-based IT systems in retailing served to highlight both the nature of these contradictions and the increased system fragility which accompanied the enhanced potential for labour process monitoring and control.

Retailing and regulation

Orthodox retail geography was remarkably silent about regulation and the complex and contradictory relations of retail capital with the regulatory state. With the exception of a rather one-dimensional discussion concerning the constraining influence of land use planning regulation and some limited debate about shop opening hours regulation, the transformation of retail capital appeared to take place in a world devoid of a macro-regulatory environment shaping competition between firms, the governance of investment, the use of labour, and the overall extraction of profits from what Appadurai (1986) calls the 'situation of exchange'. Neither was there any attempt in orthodox retail geography to conceptualize the nature of the contemporary regulatory state, and to use such a conceptualization to inform analysis of the changing structures and geographies of channel relations within production–consumption chains.

As the politicale–conomic retheorization of retail geography began to develop in the early 1990s this lacuna fortunately began to close (though Blomley's (1986) earlier pioneering efforts should also be noted). In this section, three aspects of this concern with retailing and regulation will be highlighted. First, attempts to address the importance of forces of regulation which operate at the spatial scale of the nation-state in forming and re-forming corporate strategies and geographical market structures in retailing. Second, debates about public interest versus private interest regulation and the privileging of corporate retail capital. Third, attempts to locate debate concerning the nature of contemporary retailer–regulatory state relations in a version of state theory which places emphasis on the administrative practices of the regulatory state.

The inextricably intertwined nature of national regulatory frameworks, corporate strategies and market structures is a theme which has been considered by Christopherson (1993), Wrigley (1992a; 1995) and Gertler (1995). Christopherson (1993: 274) has argued that the 'rules' governing investment within, and competition between, firms 'constitute *environments for capital accumulation'* and produce 'quite different patterns of economic behaviour within and across national boundaries'. As a result, she has called for nuanced analysis of the divergence between national space economies 'manifested in merger and acquisition behaviour, labour market regulation and firm investment patterns', and for more definitive work exploring the relationships between states, the regulation of markets, investment regimes, corporate strategies and spatial outcomes.

One of the examples that Christopherson uses to illustrate this argument is US retailing and its restructuring as a result of the regulatory and capital market condition changes of the 1980s. However, the analysis is very brief. A much more detailed consideration of the impact of changing regulatory regimes in the USA on corporate structures and spatial organization is provided in Wrigley's (1992a;

1995) two-part comparative study of corporate restructuring in the food retailing industries of Britain and the USA.

In the first part of this study, the differential nature of the regulatory environment in which the industries had operated over a fifty-year period until the early 1980s is shown to account for the major disparities (in corporate concentration, power relations, profitability, productivity, and geographical structures) which had emerged between British and US food retailing. The hostility of the US regulatory environment during this period to the development of 'big' retail capital, and to market share being concentrated into the hands of a small number of large chains operating multi-regionally and enjoying considerable purchasing leverage, is contrasted with the benign regulatory environment in Britain which proved conducive to the development of a highly concentrated 'big capital' food retailing industry, enjoying immense oligopsonistic buying power, and to the development of an increasingly uniform spatial offering (see Marsden and Wrigley, Hughes, and Shackleton, this volume, Chapters 2, 5 and 7). In the second part of the study, the comparative analysis is extended to the period of regulatory relaxation, hostile takeovers and leveraged buyouts (LBOs) of the late 1980s (a period which Clark (1989) described as the era of the 'arbitrage economy'). Food retailers in both countries became prime targets for LBOs, hostile takeovers, leveraged acquisitions and mergers, as regulatory regimes in the two countries went through a period of convergence, and the impact of new financial instruments in deregulated securities markets became all pervasive. It is shown, however, that, despite the operation of increasingly similar 'rules' governing investment and competition, the corporate strategies and market structures which characterized the food retail industries of Britain and the USA by the early 1990s revealed both marked, and more subtly important, differences. In that sense it is argued that although market rules clearly constitute environments for capital accumulation, corporate strategies and territorial outcomes cannot simply be 'read off' from market rules. Contextual analysis sensitive to the history and geography of regulation, is clearly vital to attempts to insert national regulatory forces into studies of retail restructuring.

A second broader area of debate in economic geography which has informed the political-economic retheorization of retail geography is that concerning the distinction between *public interest* and *private interest* regulation. Rather than conceiving of regulation as simply a state function carried out in the public interest through policies which intervene in the market, 'an interpretation of regulation as encompassing public and private activities offers richer analytical possibilities' (Christopherson, 1993: 276). The view taken is that markets are always regulated, the question is merely 'by whom, in whose interest, and at what scale' (Christopherson, 1993: 275). Private interest regulation is seen, therefore, as occurring when the state empowers particular private sectional interests to act on its behalf and to regulate the activities of other sets of actors in the system. Unlike public interest regulation, such regulation is not open to public participation and scrutiny. Rather the state bestows legitimacy on particular sectional interest at the expense of others.

Marsden and Wrigley (1995, and this volume, Chapter 2) have considered how, under the neo-conservative political project of the 1980s, private interest regulation of the UK food system emerged. They argue that this increasingly privileged corporate retail capital, that the major UK food retailers were delegated by the state key responsibilities in the management and policing of the system and that, as a result, the major retailers became, in a very real sense, legitimatory agents for the state. Nevertheless, despite the reconstitution of regulatory frameworks to be supportive of retailer interests, Marsden and Wrigley demonstrate that the retailer–regulatory state relations which emerged in the UK by the early 1990s were highly complex, riven through with tensions, internal contradictions and the potential for regulatory/legitimization crisis. On the one hand, faced with pressure to justify their market power and regulatory responsibility, the major retailers were forced to become more adroit at projecting the benefits of their custodial role, at sustaining in political terms the lucrative markets created in the 1980s, and at reproducing mechanisms, arguments and ideologies which would protect their competitive space. On the other hand, the regulatory state which, in the UK at least, had become critically dependent upon the economic dominance of the retailers as the 'new masters of the food system' (Flynn and Marsden, 1992) was forced to seek periodically to control the private recipients of its delegated power, and faced the difficult task of balancing the dual pressures involved in sustaining corporate retail capital accumulation while maintaining a divergent public interest.

Inevitably such considerations of the tensions and contradictions in retailer–regulatory state relations must result in attempts to locate discussion of retailing and regulation within a broader theorization of the nature of the contemporary regulatory state. In attempting to do this, Marsden and Wrigley (this volume, Chapter 2) draw attention to the inadequacy of many of the generalized conceptions of 'The State' which view it as a separate and functional entity capable of acting consistently in pursuit of particular class interests. As a result, they attempt to locate their analysis of retailing and regulation within a version of state theory championed by Clark (1992) which attributes a significant degree of autonomy to state apparatuses, and places emphasis upon the administrative manner, style and logic by which the state regulates society in general, and the economic landscape in particular. In this way, the socio-political practices involved in regulation become the prime focus for research, and attention is shifted to the highly contested nature of regulatory space and the powerful actors who dominate that space at any given time (Hancher and Moran, 1989: 277).

In adopting such a hermeneutical focus on institutions, however, Marsden and Wrigley stress that they do not intend to imply that broader conceptual questions about the role of the state should be neglected. Indeed, their discussion of the problems faced by the UK regulatory state when confronted with evidence of apparent anti-competitive practices in retailing, highlights the structural limitations imposed on the state by its relation to capital, and the dilemma that this poses for regulation. They are suggesting simply that an attempt is made to redress what Clark (1992) has referred to as the 'privileging of economic metaimperatives over institutional interests', with sensitivity to the institutional cultures of regulation, to the web of complex contingencies involved in regulation, and to the spatial differentiation of regulation. Their analysis of retailer–regulation state relations in the UK suggests that corporate reorganization – particularly in a sector such as retailing in which the boundaries of competition and accumulation are constantly being tested but in which the regulatory state has become critically dependent upon the economic dominance of the major corporations – needs contingent state practices to help construct and legitimize, on a continuous basis, these conditions at national and international levels. The ability of the regulatory state to retain a certain amount of adaptability, creativity and capacity for action within its administrative practices in these circumstances reinforces a variable and contingent interpretation of the nature of the state.

Themes in the new cultural geographies of retailing

As we have already argued, the 'new retail geography' which has emerged during the 1990s is characterized – above all else – by theoretical engagement and by a shared perspective among its adherents that 'retail capital, and its transformation, is a vital and relevant topic for research and demands urgent attention' (Ducatel and Blomley, 1990: 225). But, in parallel with more general accounts of capitalist restructuring that have emerged during the 1990s, we suggest here that a *cultural logic* as well as an *economic logic* is significant to such a project. In this we support Jackson's (1993: 207) observation that

> understanding processes, of uneven development, spatial divisions of labour and the transition to more flexible modes of capital accumulation [or for that matter, in the context of this volume, a consideration of retail capital and retail restructuring] involves much more than a simple mapping of the contours of consumption change, narrowly conceived.

There is an increasing recognition that 'these apparently rational "economic" forces are culturally encoded' (Jackson, 1993: 207). Reflecting their origins (in feminist and cultural theory) analyses of this cultural logic of retailing were at the outset, and as we have already suggested, focused centrally upon retail spaces 'as contexts where the meaning of commodities is produced and negotiated' and upon 'the construction of femininity and the creation of a sense of place [as] central attributes of the retail enterprise' (Dowling, 1993: 296–7). But as the new cultural geography more generally began to take shape and began to influence even the most hardened economic theorists, and as critical cultural geography began to envelope the large majority of contemporary human geography, the arena of this cultural logic of retailing also extended. The new cultural geographies of retailing we describe here reflect this broader perspective. Here then we examine these emergent new cultural geographies of retailing under three headings. First, 'consumption sites, spaces and chains'; second, 'the consumption experience', and finally, in an attempt to bring move the project forward, 'new landscapes of consumption'.

Consumption sites, spaces and chains

In what they characterize as a survey of the literature on 'Geographies of Consumption', Jackson and Thrift (1995) have usefully suggested that it is possible to divide such studies into work on: (a) the changing *sites* of consumption; (b) the *chains* that link consumption's multiple locations, and (c) the *spaces* and *places* of contemporary consumerism. They include in their review 'studies by those who identify themselves as geographers and studies which emphasise questions of space and place, irrespective of their authors' disciplinary affiliations' (Jackson and Thrift, 1995: 3). While we have some difficulty with a clear definition of the distinction between 'sites' and 'spaces and places' we find this framework instructive in thinking through the new cultural geographies of retailing which are beginning to emerge. Here then we shall focus on those sites which have been given particular attention in that work – specifically the department store and the mall; on the chains that link consumption's various sites – specifically those constructed between retailers and manufacturers and those which have latterly been seen to comprise the 'consumption process'; and finally the spaces and places of contemporary consumerism – specifically their gendered nature and the ways in which their geography facilitates consumption. In this we choose to follow Blomley (this volume, Chapter 13) who defines spaces not only as planes upon which the new cultural geographies of retailing take shape but also as arenas which are actively formed, reformed and contested. Running the risk of parochialism we focus here solely on research work in geography which has concentrated on – or is emerging on – these themes, paying special attention to the various ways in which such issues are tackled in this collection.

Consumption sites

As we have already suggested there have thus far been two main focuses for research on consumption *sites* within what might be characterized as the new cultural geographies of retailing. The first, the department store, has occupied a great deal of attention as a historical site of consumption. The second, the mall (probably as the contemporary equivalent of the department store) has also commanded much academic commentary. Outside these two central sites studies have been rather underdeveloped although, as we shall see shortly, this myopia looks set to change.

The department store

As Glennie and Thrift (this volume, Chapter 12) suggest, 'accounts of consumption skills and practices prior to the department store are particularly sketchy'. Thus although they (along with other writers) refer to the important consumption sites of the past such as the street, marketplace or fair, there has been little detailed geographical work on these themes (except Glennie and Thrift, 1992; 1993). Rather, it is the department store as the quintessential consumption site of the late nineteenth and early twentieth centuries which has occupied a central position in the new cultural geographies of retailing. As Domosh (this volume, Chapter 14) comments 'the nineteenth century witnessed the development of department stores, arguably the most visible, urban representations of consumer culture and the economics of mass production and selling'. Domosh's work on nineteenth-century New York City focuses on the role of the city's major department stores and their place in shaping the consumer landscape, and is complemented by Blomley's (this volume, Chapter 13) reading of Emile Zola's 1883 novel *Au Bonheur des Dames* (*The Ladies' Paradise*) a book modelled on the rise of the famous Parisian department store, *Bon Marché*. As Blomley demonstrates, that novel has, at its heart, the constant tensions/ambivalences between the department store as a 'machine' for retail capital accumulation in which the spatial configuration of the store is the first weapon in the induction of consumption and the department store as a 'cathedral of consumption' in which the meaning of commodities is established and in which the construction of both feminity and masculinity occurs within its highly gendered space. As is clear, these studies of the nineteenth-century department store, plus related work such as that of Dowling on Woodward's department store in downtown Vancouver from 1945 to 1960 (Dowling, 1991; 1993), are historical/cultural in nature. In contrast, geographical work on contemporary consumption sites has tended to centre on the mall.

The mall

In many ways the twentieth-century mall may be viewed as the contemporary equivalent of the nineteenth-century department store. Indeed, by the end of the nineteenth century the framework for the establishment of the shopping mall could be viewed in embryonic form as 'department stores began to function almost as home parlours, with tea rooms, restaurants, art galleries and grand architectural displays [while] outside the stores, wide sidewalks enabled those fashionable dresses to stay clean' (Domosh, this volume, Chapter 14). Today the department store acts as an essential 'anchor' tenant in shopping mall design. Contemporary retailing as Domosh (this volume, Chapter 14) suggests is then 'rooted in the eighteenth and nineteenth century, and the new retail geography should help us detect and delineate how these transformations of two centuries ago continue to shape contemporary retailing activity and design'. In this regard it is perhaps surprising then that the mall as a site of consumption has been consistently viewed as an entirely separate entity from the department store. Indeed there are clear possibilities for cross-fertilization in these areas. Until, now, however, the mall has been the focus of work in its own right. A significant amount of this research, as Jackson and Thrift suggest, has been focused on the West Edmonton mega mall in Canada which has 'drawn geographers like moths to a flame' (Jackson and Thrift, 1995: 7). Shopping malls in the UK have – with the exception of the Merry Hill Centre (Lowe, 1991; 1993) – received less attention. A criticism of much of this work on the mall has been its emphasis on the 'spectacular' and its ignorance of 'the more mundane places where most people routinely shop' (Jackson, 1994). While we have some difficulty with a clear distinction between 'the spectacular' and 'the everyday' as it is characterized in the developing literature, we welcome research which extends beyond 'the tyranny of the single site' (Jackson and Thrift, 1995: 9). In this respect Jackson, Thrift, and Holbrook's ongoing research on Brent Cross and Wood Green shopping centres is exemplary. Notwithstanding this, however, there still appears to be some reluctance to carry out research on the (relatively) 'everyday' sites of the High Street or the supermarket (although, for an exception see Judd, 1994). Again we see this as an arena rich in potential.

Consumption chains

In Jackson and Thrift's (1995) characterization of work on 'geographies of consumption', consumption chains are given considerable emphasis. From our perspective this aspect of geographical work on retailing and consumption is the least developed. The majority of the literature that does exist focuses explicitly on the food system and the vertical channels linking the consumption process through to the study of agriculture, food manufacturing and food retailing (Arce and Marsden, 1993). The work of Cook (1994) is particularly interesting in this respect. His study of the incorporation of 'exotic' fruits (such as papaya and mango) into the 'everyday' landscapes of the British supermarket demonstrates processes of cultural transformation across the food chain. Such issues are also beginning to be examined in the clothing sector by Lowe (1995) who considers the form of the relationship between designers, manufacturers and retailers. More specifically, Lowe is concerned to illuminate the ways in which partnerships between UK fashion clothing manufacturers, retailers and designers are formed and encouraged by intermediaries such as the British Fashion Council. The cultural construction of fashion and the linkage between 'exotic' designer/high fashion and 'everyday' street/High Street fashion are central to this analysis. Jackson and Thrift have also extended work on consumption chains via their study of consumption as a social process, which begins with a single 'isolated act of purchase' (Jackson, 1994), in Brent Cross and Wood Green shopping centres. Their view of consumption as a dynamic socially constructed activity is one which is increasingly being addressed under the rubric of 'the spaces and places of contemporary consumerism' (Jackson and Thrift, 1995).

Consumption spaces and places

As we have already suggested, consumption spaces and places, 'rather than passive surfaces – are increasingly being cast as actively produced, represented and contested' (Blomley, this volume, Chapter 13). Within this framework it is possible to see two specific sub-themes. The first focuses on the gendered nature of these spaces and places. The second relates to the various ways in which the geographical organization of such spaces facilitates consumption.

Gender and consumption

We have already mentioned the department store as a central consumption site of the nineteenth century and touched briefly upon the way in which the key contributions in this area pay specific attention to the various ways in which such sites are gendered spaces. For Domosh (this volume, Chapter 14) and Dowling (1991; 1993) 'consumption . . . is central to the lives of women and the constitution of femininity' (Dowling, 1993: 295) and 'the cultural landscape of retailing, the very spaces in which it operates, is fundamentally shaped by the relationship between gender, ideology and the development of modern consumer culture' (Domosh, this volume, Chapter 14).

Indeed, and as we have already suggested (reflecting their origins in feminist and cultural theory), such studies of retail spaces as central sites, for the construction of femininity comprised some of the original work within the new cultural geography of retailing and it is from this starting-point concerned with 'the implication of retail spaces in the reproduction of femininity and . . . masculinity' (Blomley, this volume, Chapter 13) that much subsequent work has developed. In particular such concerns have led to a consideration of retail spaces as contested sites where the identities of individuals and commodities are given meaning.

Given the origins of the new cultural geographies of retailing in such matters it is perhaps surprising then that (until the mid-1990s) there has been little consideration of contemporary retail spaces as socially/culturally constructed and actively contested (although see Goss, 1993). Such questions are beginning to be given the attention they deserve both within (e.g. Jackson and Holbrook, 1995) and outside the discipline (e.g. Mort, 1995). Mort, for example, examines the ways in which a variety of masculine identities were formulated in relation to the shifting consumer culture of Soho in the 1980s and, critically, how sexuality and consumption were interlinked. However this work – on the gendered nature of twentieth-century consumption spaces – is still embryonic. Rather what literature there is that has developed out of this frame has tended to focus upon the ways in which the geographical organization of such spaces facilitates consumption.

The geographical organization of consumption spaces
A consideration of the various ways in which retail space is organized in order to facilitate consumption takes us back to Ducatel and Blomley's concerns with what they term the 'premeditated configuration of retail space in an attempt to induce consumption' (Ducatel and Blomley, 1990: 223). The work of Goss (1992; 1993) is some of the most exemplary of research in this field, focusing as it does on the ways in which 'developers and designers of the retail built environment exploit the power of place . . . to facilitate consumption'. This line of work has been followed by Crewe and Lowe (1995) who – in their attempt to move towards a 'geography of consumption and identity' – consider the creation of 'differentiated spaces of consumption', how 'retailing and consumption create and re-create place specific identities and how cultural attributes and capital gain are intrinsically bound together'. Critically here is a consideration of the 'consumers as dupes' versus 'consumer sovereignty' debate. Are consumers hapless passive victims being conned into conspicuous consumption by an environment designed to increase what shopping mall architects call 'dwell time' in the centre, or rather are consumers clearly aware of and sensitive to the use of shopping centre design to induce consumption to such an extent that they deliberately attempt to subvert this interconnection? For example acting out the role of 'post-shoppers' – hanging out in the mall with no intent to purchase. These questions concerning the ways in which the organization of space mediates 'the materialist relations of mass consumption' and disguises 'the identity and rootedness of the shopping centre in the contemporary capitalist social order' (Goss, 1993: 19), have been addressed in later accounts which attempt to fuse cultural studies of the spaces of the shopping mall/High Street with more economic readings of consumption places as essential sites of profit accumulation for retailers. Work on the experience of consumption, which we shall now discuss, also tends to focus around these themes.

The consumption experience

With reference to the 'consumers as dupes'/'consumer sovereignty' debate outlined above, and signalling their own developing work on Brent Cross and Wood Green shopping centres, Jackson and Thrift (1995) bemoan the fact that 'geographers have tended to ignore the active role of consumers in shaping contemporary consumer cultures. Consumers rarely get a look in in geographical accounts as living, breathing complexes of subject positions with myriad concerns' (Jackson and Thrift, 1995: 9). While we obviously acknowledge this viewpoint – and whilst we agree with Jackson and Thrift's contention that, at least in part, this omission reflects geography's concerns with a few specific consumption sites (see above) – we note the following. First, some work *has* centred on the consumer – albeit rather narrowly conceived thus far in terms of the consumers' leisure experience in the consumption site itself. Second, the people who *work* in the various consumption landscapes have been, until recently, equally hidden from geographical enquiry. We shall examine each of these topics in turn.

At play in consumer landscapes

The association between consumption and leisure is a long standing one. Indeed, shopping as a social activity is explored in Glennie and Thrift's analysis (this volume, Chapter 12) of early modern shopping in which they view 'sociality [as] . . . an integral part of "going shopping" ', while Blomley (this volume, Chapter 13) in considering Zola's *The Ladies' Paradise* centres on 'the dream like consumer paradise' which is constructed within the department store. In this setting shopping as seduction takes place 'women are made to revel in . . . commodities, losing themselves in their sexuality'. Despite these early connections between shopping and leisure/pleasure it is in the late twentieth-century that the boundaries between retailing and leisure have become increasingly blurred (Newby, 1993). Such blurring owes much to the advent of the large out-of-town retail (and leisure) centres which have arguably lured consumers away from the dispiriting retail experience that comprised much of Britain in the 1970s. As Newby (1993: 208) has suggested, the enjoyment of consumption was – and still is – 'frequently frustrated by a retail system that removed the "pleasure" element from shopping'. Taking their cue from North American malls designed specifically (by Victor Gruen, pioneer of the shopping mall) as 'more than just a place where one may shop' (Goss, 1992: 165–6) centres like Merry Hill in the West Midlands and Metrocentre in Gateshead have cleverly conflated retailing/leisure and tourism. Like the examples cited by Goss (1992; 1993), such centres have become tourist attractions in their own right, typically housing 'fun fairs and fashion shows . . . [hosting] community dances and concerts . . . [and providing] fitness classes . . . food and drink' (Goss, 1992: 160). 'There are 22 million shoppers . . . who visit Merry Hill every year, spending an average of £42' (Joseph, 1993). Echoing the experiences that Blomley describes in Zola's *Ladies' Paradise*, 'they stroll through the warm, clean, glassy arcades, spared by the rain . . . [and] like the fashion shows in the amphitheatre' (Joseph, 1993). In this framework the mall becomes an essential site for communication and interaction, a place for 'hanging out', for 'tribalism', where adolescent subcultures are formed and where key lifetime experiences take place. Such issues, while tackled extremely successfully by several authors in Shields (1992a) have – as Jackson and Thrift (1995) correctly acknowledge – yet to be centred on by geographers. Notwithstanding this however, and following the lead taken in historical work by Glennie and Thrift (1992; 1993, and this volume, Chapter 12), there have been some attempts to explore such themes via both the study of 'consumption and identity' (in developing work by Crewe and Lowe, 1995; Jackson and Holbrook, 1995) and through a consideration of 'alternative spaces of consumption', notably the car boot fair. In this latter work Gregson and Crewe (1994: 6) view the car boot sale as a 'quintessential postmodern consumption site, one which synthesises leisure with consumption . . . in a new spatial form. . . . A place for buying and selling and a site for pleasure, somewhere to look, to wander, to rummage'.

In considering the consumers' experience as one of *'play'*, however, it is important not to lose sight of the fact that for many consumers such activities are not so simply defined. For example Domosh (this volume, Chapter 14) in her account of the activities pursued by women of nineteenth-century New York (many of whom spent significant amounts of their time shopping) views shopping as 'a major part of womens' *work*' and hence, once again, echoes the 'consumers as dupes/consumer sovereignty' debate. Likewise, in her study of the 'spaces of the supermarket', Judd (1994: 91) suggests that such shopping is perceived as an extension of domestic labour with working women, in particular, contesting 'the production of the image of the supermarket space as a pleasant, efficient and covertly seductive environment'. Of course, the 'everyday' space of the supermarket – and its shopping experience as work – is often contrasted with the more pleasurable activities associated with more 'spectacular' shopping developments where leisure shopping takes place. But as Jackson and Holbrook (1995) have discovered, even these latter landscapes include within them aspects of skill, anxiety and complexity more often associated with the world of work. It is from this consideration of 'shopping as work', to the work required in stores and shopping centres to sustain the consumption experience, that we shall now turn.

At work in the consumer landscapes

As Christopherson (this volume, Chapter 8) suggests, 'while the culture of consumption has received increasing attention in the 1980s, consumption workplaces . . . have been relatively neglected'. Paralleling research on 'workplace geographies' (Crang, 1994), which themselves owe much to the 'cultural turn' within the discipline, concern has shifted away from accounts of the restructuring of retail employment (see Freathy and Sparks, this volume, Chapter 9) and towards a consideration of 'qualitative elements of the transformation of consumption work which are often ignored in more traditional empirical surveys of retail employment' (Lowe and Crewe, this volume, Chapter 10). The social relations of consumption work have become a central theme of these enquiries such that it is no longer sufficient to consider the numbers and types of jobs provided in retailing. Rather, it is now important to focus upon the *types of people* employed in consumption landscapes, as well as the various ways in which consumption work is particularly demanding of its employees. Both of these aspects of retail employment are in line with Sayer and Walker's (1992: 85) contention that 'the division of labour has shifted more towards work done in support of the immense social process of selling'. We shall examine each of these in turn.

In their consideration of the neglect of retail employment in human geographical enquiry, Lowe and Crewe (1991: 346) begin to address the issue of 'image' in retail employment, suggesting that 'consumers want to be served by people who are like them and hence there are certain [retail] employers who consider youth or ethnicity, for example, to be important attributes' (see also Christopherson, 1990b; Crang and Martin, 1991). Research at Merry Hill in the West Midlands has confirmed these suspicions. Here employers are selecting employees on the basis of their appearance over and above their aptitude or retail experience, with black workers being particularly concentrated in high fashion stores with a strong image-consciousness (Lowe, 1991). Such connections have also been made by Christopherson (this volume, Chapter 8) who suggests that 'the employment of young people . . . can be seen as a clear marketing strategy'. A consideration of the role of the retail employee as a marketing tool for the retail organization leads us on then to a discussion of the ways in which retail employment – like other forms of 'consumption work' – is particularly demanding of its employees.

Unlike the labour forces of many large industrial corporations, retail sales assistants are constantly 'on display' to purchasers of their products. Hence 'the ability to communicate, be polite, smile and have a great appearance' (Hudson *et al*, 1992) is of critical importance to such workers and, as we have seen above, the employment of particular types of individuals to 'front' the retail store is essential. However, in the increasingly competitive retail environments of the 1990s such strategies are no longer enough to ensure continued competitive advantage. Rather, the retail sales assistants, like Crang's (1994) employees at Smoky Joe's restaurant, increasingly comprise the actual product on sale. This 'selling of the staff' is at its most pronounced in the use of 'customer care' strategies which focus upon customer service as the key determinant in contemporary strategies of retail competition. At their most advanced in North American companies like The Gap, Inc. where 'staffers' are instructed how to operate in the store via the 'Gap Lexicon', and in large out-of-town shopping/leisure complexes like Meadowhall in Sheffield, such trends look set to have a much broader impact (Lowe and Crewe, this volume, Chapter 10).

New landscapes of consumption

Readers of this volume will no doubt recognize that the consumption sites and spaces (and associated consumption experiences) under consideration here are increasingly ubiquitous aspects of contemporary (western and often non-western) societies. Indeed the omnipresence of such new consumption landscapes has led Knox (1991) to the view that western societies are being transformed into a landscape which is like a supermarket writ large in which the whole of the landscape is geared towards consumption. We have much sympathy with this viewpoint and would like here to consider the various ways in which this is the case. Here then we shall examine these 'new landscapes of consumption' paying specific attention to the ways in which consideration of such landscapes may direct our 'new cultural geographies of retailing' in the future. We do this under two main headings. First, we reconsider consumption sites and spaces that have been the subjects of academic attention in the past. Second, we examine new consumption sites and spaces which are, in our estimation at least, likely to prove important in the future. We confine our discussion to the examples we know best. Hence we focus on examples of these new landscapes in the UK. Readers will doubtless recognize, however, that the themes that emerge here have much broader applications.

Reconsidering consumption sites and spaces

As we have already noted the primary consumption sites and spaces that have thus far been considered by geographers have been 'the department store' and 'the mall' with some secondary (largely historical) research work being directed at 'the street'. Here we would like to reconsider these consumption sites and spaces via an examination of their contemporary importance.

The department store

In the decade of the 1990s 'the department store' appears to be enjoying something of a revival. Such stores are no longer associated purely and simply with major retail groups such as John Lewis or House of Fraser. Rather the contemporary department store has appeared in an altogether different guise – the so-called 'flagship store'. Incorporating the 'own label' as their sole product identity, stores such as the new 'Dr Marten's Department Store' in Covent Garden, London, or the myriad of new flagship stores in New Bond Street, London takes us full circle back to the department stores of the nineteenth century considered by (among others) Blomley and Domosh in this volume (Chapters 13 and 14). Like their nineteenth-century equivalents the contemporary department stores combine within their 'spaces', designer interiors, rituals of display and leisure, sexuality and food. At Donna Karen in Bond Street, for example, DKNY mineral water, New York bagels and New England cheesecake allow the contemporary consumer to lose themselves in the ultimate 'own label' experience. At Dr Marten's Department Store the 'Doctor's Orders' Canteen/Café offers Wollaston Shepherd's Pie or Northamptonshire Bangers and Mash and even includes a children's hairdressing department, while the interior of the Dolce and Gabbana 'flagship store' in Sloane Street has been designed on a palazzo style and combines both classical and modern elements. Furniture includes gilt picture frames and baroque divans. The association in these new consumption landscapes of product and place identity is profound and offers much in the way of research potential in the future.

The mall

Crewe and Lowe (1995) suggest that it is important to shift 'the research focus away from dominant accounts of the malling of retail space and of global homogeneity and [to] . . . focus instead on the complexity and differentiation of retail spaces'. From our perspective it is also essential to move beyond a homogeneous view of shopping malls and to focus instead on the various ways in which such 'centres often strive to establish their unique identity' (Jackson, 1994). While some such matters have been considered – notably by Lowe (1993) in her examination of the 'selling' of the Merry Hill shopping centre – we suggest here that the differentiation of shopping malls is far more advanced than a reading of the literature to date would suggest. Virtually every local shopping centre has within it some version of the 1980s-built mall (or often more accurately the 1960s-built and 1980s-renovated mall). Such in-town shopping precincts stand in marked contrast to their out-of-town mega-mall equivalents, while in-town centres vary in scale and type from that at Neal's Yard in Covent Garden to the Broad Street Mall in Reading. Then there are the malls constructed – once again in the 1980s or 1990s – as part and parcel of the tourist strategies of particular towns or cities – Canute's Pavilion at Ocean Village in Southampton is a case in point. Centred mainly around fast food outlets and selling primarily Belgian chocolates, fold-up cards, candles and massage oils, such malls are an essential means by which particular localities are being reconstructed and 'sold' no longer as centres of production but of consumption. Finally, there are the 'discount malls' such as that at the 'Clarks Village' at Street in Somerset. Here the differentiation of the mall experience can be viewed at its most extreme with whole coachloads of consumers being bussed in for that extra special 'bargain'. The latest phase of the Clarks Village includes the redevelopment of the former engineering workshops and medical departments of the original Clarks footwear factory.

The street

We noted above that 'the street' as a consumption landscape has been largely neglected except in a few historical studies. However, Crewe and Lowe (1995) have begun to address this neglect via their consideration of 'pioneering retailers and their creation of differentiated spaces of consumption'. Paralleling suggestions regarding the 'remaking of the mall' discussed above, certain streets are seen to acquire particular consumption identities. Hence, Little Clarendon Street in Oxford with its mixture of coffee shops, tapas bars and charity stores, intermingled with up-market clothing retailers, becomes a central place to 'hang out' for the young (and often not so young) and trendy of Oxford. Carnaby Street in London – famed as a centre for fashion in the 1960s – still maintains a certain 'aura'. An account of such differentiated 'streets of style' leads us to a further important theme. The evolution of 'style' in public places – especially 'the street' has become the subject of much popular attention. More specifically, the reciprocal relationship between international (high) designer fashion and 'streetstyle' (Polhemus, 1994) is an inherently geographical project.

New consumption sites and spaces

During the 1990s a number of new landscapes of consumption have emerged and continue to emerge in the UK. Given the rapidity of developments it is almost impossible to mention them all. Here then we have chosen to structure our discussion of such landscapes under three main headings. First, 'the captured market' whereby individuals confined in places for other very different reasons are induced to consume. Second, 'taking consumption to the consumer' specifically in 'the home'. Finally, via an examination of consumption opportunities associated with more conventional leisure pursuits, 'the leisured consumer'. All of the above are centred on the driving mechanism of intensifying consumption and are engaged in a calculated reworking of space to ensure that such intensification takes place.

The captured market

The essential conditions for a captured market are a guaranteed throughflow of large numbers of individuals who are likely to consume, some enforced wait time, and/or a lack of locally available alternatives. At its most advanced at the airport (where security measures and air traffic controllers ensure a minimum wait time), at the railway station, or on cruise ships or cross channel ferries, such consumption sites are increasingly being targeted as essential new opportunities by retailers. 'Gatwick Village' at Gatwick Airport's South Terminal includes a vast array of High Street chains. Here the ultimate blurring of leisure and retail takes place. With vast numbers of potential 'customers' on holiday, extended 'seasons' for particular product lines can be achieved, and customer socio-economic profiles compare favourably with those in more traditional shopping centres. Moreover, anxious about their impending flights and unknown holiday locations 'travellers' are likely to spend significantly more than more conventional High Street customers. In a similar vein petrol/service stations have become 'mini markets'. Indeed, 'filling station snacking, as well as full scale shopping is the fastest growing but least predicted area in retailing today. . . . Out of hours diners . . . include late night clubbers, police patrols and lorry drivers' (Margolis, 1995).

In considering the 'captured consumer', two further examples come to mind. The first is the office development – often in a strategic new location – which includes in its 'bowels' some combination of retail facilities. The much vaunted Canary Wharf in London is a case in point, but new business centres and allied retail outlets are an increasingly common form of 'consumption landscape'. At Merry Hill in the West Midlands, for example, the latest phase of development comprises primarily offices at Waterfront East and West and – despite their locations adjacent to the Merry Hill Centre – additional retail facilities have been developed on the ground floors of the office blocks. The final example of the 'captured consumer' is the case of the hospital. In the wake of health service privatization what was once the remit of the Hospital League of Friends – selling fruit and flowers at the hospital entrance – has been broadened to include national chainstores such as John Menzies.

Taking consumption to the consumer

The 'home' as the traditional site of reproduction/consumption has been re-cast as a 'new consumption landscape' of considerable potential. This expansion of 'home shopping' has taken several forms. First, and most obviously, via the dramatic growth of mail order catalogues which allow someone who is not close to a shopping centre or prefers not to venture out to shop from home. The household names of home shopping in the UK – like Littlewoods, Kays and Freemans – have been joined by a wealth of 'niche' targeted shopping catalogues such as Next, Racing Green and Lands End. Interestingly here there is often cross-fertilization between the catalogue and the High Street/mall with Racing Green, for example, opening stores following the success of its mail order operations (Webb, 1994). Second, the advent of 'lifestyle magazines' such as those produced by Sainsbury, Marks & Spencer or Harvey Nichols have become an essential means of marketing new season product lines at the very heart of the consumption landscape – the living rooms and kitchens of the middle classes. Finally, the Internet is being investigated as a new means of taking consumption to the consumer. IBM, for example, has begun a pilot shopping service for PC Gifts and Flowers which will initially sell flowers, balloons, teddy bears and gourmet food. If successful the company proposes to add video games, watches, cameras and coffee to its product range (May, 1994).

The leisured consumer

The Walt Disney and Warner Brothers empires were the first to take a successful leisure product – film – and roll it out into a complete consumption experience (via theme park and store). The Disney Store and the Warner Brothers Studio Store can be viewed as the ultimate shopping and entertainment mix and have become increasingly popular in UK shopping centres. A less well known (but significantly growing) example of this leisure/retail blurring are the more traditional leisure pursuits of the British – football clubs. As football has become increasingly big business – and often itself moved 'out of town' – the old club shops have become superstores 'open six days a week and crammed with everything from club duvets, to gnomes, aftershave, jeans, teddy bears and mountain bikes' (Longmore, 1994). But the commercialization of this particular leisure experience does not end here. Manchester United, for example, 'plans to open stores in Tokyo and Sydney to add to its branches in Plymouth, Dublin, Belfast and the centre of Manchester'. These stores 'boast a loyalty that other retail brands would die for' (Longmore, 1994).

Conclusion

As Blomley (this volume, Chapter 13) argues, 'the problem – and the potential – of . . . retail geography is that categories such as "economy" or "culture" are constantly being shattered. The two seem mutually implicated, with both of them expressed in and mediated by the multiple geographies of retailing'. As a result, a reconstructed retail geography finds itself at the very heart of contemporary debate within critical human geography. It is our view that this opportunity must be seized and the challenge addressed.

While it is true that economic geographers have traditionally operated with 'a surprisingly uncritical, superorganic and static conception of culture' (Gertler, 1995: 2), it is equally the case that there has been a certain insensitivity within the 'cultural turn' in human geography to macro-regulatory context, to capital imperatives, and to the complex of linkages between production and consumption. Some of the most exciting work in contemporary economic geography, we would argue, is attempting to re-inject 'culture' into the lexicon of economic geography and to problematize the concept of culture when examining 'the process by which industrial cultures – whether at the level of the workplace, the region, or the nation – are themselves produced and reproduced by social practices' (Gertler, 1995: 2) – or as Gertler has put it, more informally, to 'unpack the c-word!' Work on such issues as power, identity and knowledge within the firm (Schoenberger, 1994a) which stresses the importance of the social asset structures of managers and 'the way in which corporate identity and corporate culture frame the kinds of knowledge that can be produced and utilized by the firm in the creation of competitive strategies' (1994a, 449) is symptomatic of attempts in economic geography to shatter the arbitrary categories of the 'economic' and 'cultural'. In cultural geography, there are also welcome signs of reciprocal trends; for example, of attempts to locate cultural analyses of consumption within the context of political and economic power.

As the political-economic retheorization of retail geography with its central concerns with the transformation of retail capital, a 'more sophisticated understanding of the *reciprocal* nature of the relations between space and corporate retail activity' (Clarke, this volume, Chapter 16), labour processes and the social relations of 'production', and relations with the regulatory state, blurs into analyses of the cultural logic of retailing with its concerns with consumption sites, spaces and chains, the consumption experience, and the construction of identity, we are drawn back to Blomley's view (this volume, Chapter 13) that retail geography is potentially one of the most interesting and challenging sub-disciplines 'given the subtlety, and importance of retail capital, consumption and space'. Ultimately, this volume can do little more than indicate some of the possibilities of such an integrated new retail geography which takes both its economic and cultural dimensions seriously. However, we are convinced of the significance of that task. In our view, it is of central importance, both to the broader progress of critical human geography and to the wider study of circulation and consumption activities in the social sciences, to have a vibrant reconstructed retail geography positioned at the cutting edges of theoretical debate.

Part 2

Corporate restructuring and retailer–manufacturer–regulatory state relations

CHAPTER 2

Retailing, the food system and the regulatory state

Terry Marsden and Neil Wrigley

In most advanced economies, the 1980s saw a period of considerable change in the roles and functions of the state. Deregulation of state structures, so as to cope with fiscal crises and re-establish entre-preneurial principles, became central to the neo-conservative project that was established as the dominant political process in many countries. In turn, this had a major impact upon the food procurement, production and delivery system, a system which traditionally had been viewed as a major direct and indirect state activity (see Marsden *et al*, 1993; Self and Storing, 1962). However, as several commentators have suggested (Cerny, 1991; Christopherson, 1993; Flynn *et al*, 1994), what appeared initially to be deregulation was, in reality, merely a changing form of regulation. And so it was in the food system. As the state sought to disengage, it often passed responsibility to corporate firms – particularly retail capital – giving rise to new forms of private interest regulation of the food system.

Nowhere was this process more apparent than in the UK, where the 1970s had already witnessed a progressive increase in the power of the major food retailers. The 1980s were to be characterized by a massive and sustained concentration of capital and the emergence of a small group of retail corporations whose turnover, employment levels, profitability, and sheer market and political power came to rival the largest industrial corporations in any sector of the UK economy. By the end of the 1980s, during years which have been described as the 'golden age' of British food retailing (Wrigley, 1991), the major food retailers emerged as 'the new masters of the food system' (Flynn and Marsden, 1992). They wielded immense oligopsonistic buying power and had been delegated by the regulatory state key responsibilities in the management and policing of the food system and in the social structuring of consumption.

Within this shift to a retailer-dominated, private-interest regulated, food system which took place in the UK during the 1980s, four types of relationships were profoundly changed – those between food retailers and food manufacturers, food retailers and farmers, farmers and the regulatory state, and food retailers and the regulatory state. Although these changes are intimately interconnected, it is our aim in this chapter to theorize the nature of the retail/food system/regulatory state nexus by initially separating out each of these relationships. It will soon become clear, however, that any examination of changing relations within the food system also provides an important window through which to study the nature of the contemporary regulatory state, to conceptualize regulation and the social and administrative practices of the state, and to pose questions about the adequacy of many of the generalized models of 'The State'. In the final section of the chapter, therefore, we attempt to use our analysis to pose such questions and to raise much wider issues about empowerment, consumption, class formation, and state mediation.

Setting the scene: retailer–supply chain interfaces

Food retailer–food manufacturer relations

In the words of analysts at NatWest Securities, the UK food manufacturing/processing sector 'entered the 1980s as a fragmented, inefficient, largely domestically based industry struggling to come to terms with the growing power of the major food retailers' (*The Times*, 9 February 1990). Since the 1960s and, in particular, the passage of the Resale Prices Act 1964, power had moved away from the manufacturers/suppliers and towards a group of food retailers. These were committed to building market share by passing on to their customers at least part of the volume discounts which they obtained from the food manufacturers, and the lower operating costs which they obtained from larger-scale outlets and faster stock turnover. Indeed, by the end of the 1970s there was already considerable concern being voiced that the shift in power from food manufacturers to retailers may have gone too far, and that the rapidly expanding food retailers might be receiving non-cost-related discounts from the food manufacturers of a magnitude sufficient to constitute an anti-competitive abuse of buying power (Wrigley, 1992a).

The emergence of the neo-conservative state in the 1980s simply compounded this shift in power. Concentration of capital in UK food retailing continued apace. As Table 2.1 demonstrates, by 1990, on one estimate, the top five food retailers held 61 per cent of national sales (although other estimates, calculated on different definitions of the total national food market, place the figure closer to 50 per cent). Moreover, a 'super league' of just three firms – Sainsbury, Tesco and Argyll (the operators of Safeway) had begun to separate out in terms of growth, profitability and annual capital investment. The hugely increased market share of the major food retailers endowed them with immense oligopsonistic buying power. This came to condition all aspects of food manufacturer–retailer relations. In addition, the large food retailers aggressively exploited 'own-label' trading and their ability to control the allocation of selling space in order to squeeze out the nationally advertised brands of the food manufacturers (K Davies *et al*, 1986). In combination, these two factors allowed the large food retailers to demand ever-larger discriminatory discounts, including backdated discounts from the food manufacturers, and to impose ever more stringent conditions of supply.

Table 2.1 Top five British grocery corporations: estimated shares of total grocery sales

	1982[a]	1984[b]	1988/89[c]	1990[d]
	(%)	(%)	(%)	(%)
J Sainsbury plc	9.5	11.6	14.5[f]	16.3
Tesco plc	8.7	11.9	14.8	15.7
Argyll Group plc	(3.8)[e]	5.1	9.7	11.2
Asda plc	4.6	7.2	7.9	10.4[g]
Dee Corporation/Gateway plc	n.a.	7.3	11.4	7.8[h]

[a] *Source*: AGB figures quoted in K Davies *et al* (1985: 9).
[b] *Source*: Verdict Market Research.
[c] *Source: Retail Business Quarterly Trade Reviews* 12, December 1989: 12. Figures relate to year to March 1989.
[d] *Source*: Verdict Market Research (*Supermarketing*, 18 January 1991).
[e] Crude estimate: Argyll acquired Allied Suppliers in 1982. Allied's market share on acquisition was approximately 3%.
[f] Does not include grocery sales of Savacentre, the Sainsbury subsidiary. If included, rankings of Tesco and Sainsbury are reversed.
[g] Prior to major financial and organizational problems of Asda 1991/92 (for details see Wrigley, 1991, 1992b).
[h] Following buyout by Isosceles and disposal of assets to Asda and Kwik Save.

Stringent conditions of supply were imposed on food manufacturers to match the centralized, logistically efficient, stock control and quick-response, warehouse-to-store, distribution systems developed by the retail corporations in the 1970s, and early 1980s (McKinnon, 1989; Sparks, 1986b). This allowed the major food retailers to reduce their inventory holdings progressively throughout the 1980s (Figure 2.1 shows the case of Tesco) and to pass back more and more of the costs, including 'uncertainty costs', of inventory holding to the food manufacturers. Moreover, the large food retailers typically operated on negative working-capital cycles (Norkett, 1985). That is to say, they were supplied on credit but turned over their stock well before their suppliers had to be paid. As a result, within the accelerated circuits of capital which came to characterize British food retailing, food manufacturers were obliged to pass to retail capital ever-greater proportions of the surplus value generated in the act of production. The effect of this was seen in both profitability and relative returns on capital employed in food manufacturing and retailing. As Figure 2.2 demonstrates, the return on capital in food manufacturing declined relative to food retailing in the late 1970s and early 1980s while, during the 1980s, profit levels of the food manufacturers increased at only half the rate achieved by the major food retailers. By the beginning of the 1990s, powered by

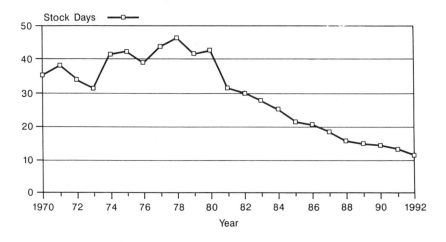

Figure 2.1   Changes in inventory holdings (measured in terms of stock days held), Tesco, 1970–92. (*Source*: redrawn from D L G Smith and Sparks, 1993)

the imposition of their oligopsonistic buying power on the food manufacturers, by massive capital investment programmes in new stores and computer-based IT systems, and by significant increases in labour productivity, the net profit margins of the major UK food retailers (Table 2.2) had risen to levels which were quite unusual in international terms.

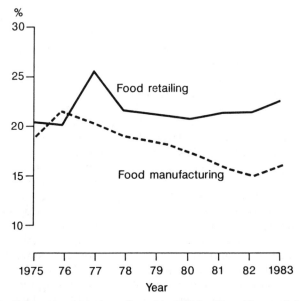

Figure 2.2   Return on capital employed in UK food retailing and food manufacturing 1975–83 (*Source*: adapted from OFT, 1985)

Table 2.2 Trends in net profit margins (%) of 'big three' grocery retailers' major operations 1985–92* (figures based on turnover exclusive of VAT)

Retailer	1985	1986	1987	1988	1989	1990	1991	1992
Sainsbury	5.25	5.53	6.09	6.54	7.31	7.61	8.32	8.71
Tesco	2.72	3.10	4.10	5.21	5.86	6.18	6.62	7.09
Safeway	3.57	3.89	4.34	4.69	5.19	5.94	6.74	7.49

Source: Adapted from Henderson Crosthwaite (1992)
* i.e. takes account of only major format/fascia of the company, *not* secondary formats/operations such as Lo-Cost/Presto (Argyll), Savecentre/Homebase/Shaw's (Sainsbury).

Although the story of the 1980s was largely one of increasing retailer dominance of the retailer–supplier interface it is important not to over-caricature those relations. As Foord, Bowlby and Tillsley (this volume, Chapter 4) and Doel (Chapter 3) demonstrate, retailer dominance did not go uncontested. Moreover, subtle shifts in the form and content of retailer–supplier relations occurred. For example, in the late 1970s and early 1980s, food retailers became very heavily involved in management of the supply chain. In particular, their input to product innovation, product design, and specification of the manufacturing process became increasingly significant as part and parcel of the growth of own-label products. Although highly successful, such involvement in product specification, quality monitoring, and so on tended to raise retailer costs. As a result, Foord, Bowlby and Tillsley suggest that during the later 1980s a shift towards less interventionist retailer–supplier 'partnerships', based on a 'preferred supplier' type model (Crewe and Davenport, 1992), took place representing an attempt by the retailers to shift back more of the product development/quality control costs to the manufacturers.

Food retailer–farmer relations

With certain minor exceptions, UK food retailers did not feel it necessary during the 1980s to vertically integrate and take an equity stake in the food production chain. Indeed, the trend, if any, over the decade was towards vertical disintegration. Rather, the major retailers relied upon their oligopsonistic buying power to achieve the market relations which they desired.

Essentially, what the major food retailers sought in their relations with the farming community was reliability of supply, at consistently high quality levels, at price levels acceptable to the retailers, and with sufficiently flexible production control to ensure variety of product – in particular, consistency of supply of the 'new' food products which were a contributing factor in driving up the net profit margins of the UK food retailers during the decade. From the retailers' perspective, however, British agriculture often failed to respond to the supply requirements of the transformed 'big capital' nature of British food retailing. On the one hand, the traditional monopoly suppliers, the producer corporatist marketing boards (such as the former Milk Marketing Board) were viewed as obstacles to be overcome in order to promote variety and continuity of supply at a competitive price. On the other hand, the relatively de-concentrated UK farm sector was seen as lacking market orientation, particularly in terms of cooperative marketing.

The trends of the 1980s were, therefore, ones of the major UK food retailers attempting to encourage with the aid of government greater co-operative activity and market orientation among UK farmers, plus a smoothing of the contracting process, while at the same time sourcing to a substantial and growing extent from overseas. In terms of their relations with UK farmers, the public statements of the major food retailers stressed 'mutually beneficial relationships', 'close association of producers with a collaborative retailer' (see S A Shaw *et al*, 1991), technical advice offered by retailers in maintaining quality standards, support in identifying marketing opportunities, and so on. In other words, what emerged was a more interventionist form of retailer–farmer interaction, with similarities to the late 1970s and early 1980s period of retailer–food manufacturer relations noted above, in which significantly increased retailer input to product development/quality control had been part and parcel of the growth of own-label products. Running in parallel with this interventionist UK stance, however, was a much less interventionist model which was applied by the major food retailers in the context of the rapidly accelerating level of overseas sourcing. In this area, a new internationalized 'preferred supplier' type of relationship, in which UK retailers were able to shift many of the costs of quality assurance and flexible product control, on to an overseas marketing co-operative, while still exercising the burden of 'due diligence' placed upon them by the Food Safety Act 1990 (see p. 40), was typically adopted. This was particularly significant in the context of sourcing from mainland Europe. Continental European agriculture (particularly that of France and Italy), while being dominated by smaller individual producers than in the UK, is characterized by much larger and stronger cooperative marketing organizations. These organizations were often better placed to provide the competitively priced, high volume, consistent quality, produce required by the highly capital-concentrated UK food retailers, and to absorb the costs of flexible product control and quality assurance, than were equivalent UK organizations. As a result, the 1980s saw significant growth of food imports from mainland Europe into the UK and the emergence, during the late 1980s, of an alarming UK trade deficit in this sector. By 1990, the trade gap in food and drink represented 42 per cent of the total UK current account deficit, and over half of this arose from trade with northern EC countries with no climatic advantage over the UK. Such modifications in the relationships between food retailers and farmers were assisted by the changing emphasis of state (particularly nation-state) policy.

New patterns of regulation and the food system

Farmer–regulatory state relations

The 1980s witnessed a gradual decline of agricultural producer corporatism in the UK. The relationship between the state and the farmers characterized by the annual price reviews and the links between the National Farmers' Union (NFU) and the Ministry of Agriculture, Fisheries and Food (MAFF) was gradually undermined both politically and economically. The reasons for this, though, were only partly associated with the downstream food manufacturing and retailing sectors. Rather, they were related to the changing regulatory style of government.

The 1980s witnessed a declining role for agriculture in British society in a number of ways. As part of the increasingly sophisticated food chain, its economic power diminished. While the retailers were viewed by government as the embodiment of Thatcherite free-market growth, the farmers were, more embarrassingly, seen to be the recipients of large amounts of public funds and of old-style corporatist regulatory support. The strategic contribution of agriculture to the national economy had been much vaunted until the end of the 1970s (see MAFF, 1974; 1979). However, after this point, escalating costs of surplus production, and the realization that agriculture's contribution to the national balance of trade was no longer – under the conditions of growing internationalization of trade – of great political concern, led to a piece-meal retrenchment of the industry.

Moreover, in an economy suffering the periodic rigours of manufacturing recession, there developed increasing urban-based public concern about the consequences of the state support system for agriculture, particularly focused upon the detrimental environmental and food quality effects. In this regard MAFF found itself in a position of having to deal with the management of contradictions now exposed by growing public disquiet (such as with the salmonella and bovine spongiform encephalopathy (BSE) food hygiene scares) plus the political storm and interdepartmental rivalries explicit in the government's announcement of the Alternative Land Use in the Rural Economy proposals.

In the midst of these changing regulatory conflicts came a heightened, but negative visibility of farming within Britain, associated with intensive farm practices and technologies which potentially destroy environmental quality. Increasingly, by the late 1980s, despite maintaining most of the vestiges of price support, it was the *political distance* portrayed between government and farmers rather than the maintenance of a cosy producer corporatism which typified farmer–regulatory state arrangements.

Caught within a growing interest in near-market growth and consumerism, farmers were less able to rely upon many of their productionist assumptions – and concerns over the 'cost-price squeeze' – which were so much to the fore during the forty years following the Agriculture Act 1947. Central government began to place more emphasis on the improvement of farmers' marketing practices (i.e. streamlining the sector for the purposes of supplying food manufacturers and retailers with requisite inputs), rather than upon food production for its own sake. By the early 1990s farmers were increasingly enmeshed in a complex web of state regulatory relationships which had expanded to incorporate growing public concerns associated with environmental and food quality. Moreover, these relationships were made conditional upon supplying food inputs to an increasingly market based manufacturing and retail sector.

Food retailer–regulatory state relations

As the major retailers became the principal actors in the post-productivist food system, they were delegated by the regulatory state key responsibilities in the management and policing of that system. Political legitimacy for regulatory control was thus added to the economic dominance of the food system which the major retailers had achieved by the end of the 1980s; an economic dominance underpinned by an environment of competition regulation in the UK which was conducive to concentration of retail capital and retailer dominance of the retailer–supplier interface (Wrigley, 1992a).

Whereas the two major Monopolies and Mergers Commission (MMC) and Office of Fair Trading (OFT) reviews of competitive conditions in the industry during the late 1970s and early 1980s, *Discounts to Retailers* (MMC, 1981) and *Competition and Retailing* (OFT, 1985), can be viewed as providing regulatory conditions supportive of the emergence of the 'golden age' of British food retailing in the late 1980s, statutory legitimation of the leading and directive role of the retailers in that regulatory environment came with the Food Safety Act 1990. This Act can be viewed as equivalent in symbolic importance of the links between the state and a sectional interest (in this case the retailers) as that of the Agriculture Act 1947 for farmers (Flynn *et al*, 1994). The Act was a response to EC pressures and domestic concerns surrounding food hygiene, following a number of health scares in the late 1980s. More broadly, however, it attempted to secure 'the needs of an innovative and competitive food industry by avoiding unnecessary burdens and controls' (Food Safety Act 1990). In policy terms, its effect was to shift responsibility for food quality control away from the public environmental health inspectorate and towards the retailers, who were charged with demonstrating that they had shown 'due diligence' in the manufacture, transportation, storage and preparation of foodstuffs. In this way, the major retailers were delegated key responsibilities for the management and policing of the more internationalized food system, and both political and statutory legitimacy for their new custodial role within that system.

By the early 1990s, the major food retailers had, in this fashion, become enlisted as agents and promoters of public policy. Moreover, via their role in facilitating the attacks launched by the successive Thatcher administrations on corporatist type relationships and anachronistic sectoral interests, and in delivering crucially important new and revised rights to consume, they become sustainers, in the broadest sense, of the neo-conservative political project. As a result, in a very real fashion, the major UK food retailers became legitimatory agents for the state. This positioning, however, was by no means unproblematic. Indeed, despite the new roles conferred on the retailers, the retailer–regulatory state relations which emerged in the UK by the early 1990s were highly complex, riven through with tensions, internal contradictions, and the potential for regulatory/legitimization crisis.

The early 1990s, in particular, saw growing public unease about the excesses of retailer dominance and, within the industry, an increased level of challenge to a regulatory regime which was perceived as having privileged the major corporations. In the academic literature, evidence concerning the possible emergence of excess profits, in an increasingly concentrated sector subject to rather weak regulation of competitive conditions, was debated (Moir, 1990; Wrigley, 1991; 1992a), while in the popular press, articles increasingly critical of the high net-profit margins of the major food retailers, lack of real competition, and the 'scandal of Britain's high food prices' to finance 'the building of cathedral-like supermarkets' (*Sunday Times*, 25 August 1991), began to appear. Rather than alleviate such concerns, the rapid growth during this period of a 'deep discount' food retailing sector, sparked by the entry of the European discounters, Aldi and Netto (Sparks and Burt, 1993; Wrigley, 1993a), served merely to fuel public unease and to expose more starkly the privileged relations of the major food retailers with the regulatory authorities. Aldi, for example, complained to the OFT that its rights, under EC competition law, of free entry to the British market was being frustrated by the incumbent UK food retailers (*The Grocer*, 2 June 1990; 2 March 1991), while numerous cases of refusal to supply to discount retailers by food manufacturers (most notably Shoprite by Kellogg – see Wrigley, 1993b) were interpreted as an attempt by the incumbent retailers to frustrate the advance of the discounters via covert pressure on the manufacturers to police the supply system (*Financial Times*, 22 March 1993; *The Grocer*, 20 February 1993; 13 March 1993). Such concerns were reinforced in 1993 by two actions of the 'big three' food retailers (Sainsbury, Tesco and Argyll). First, they were seen to act overtly in concert in an attempt to block the planning consent granted to the US retailer Costco to build Britain's first American-style 'warehouse club' near the M25 (London's orbital motorway) in Essex. Second, they allegedly acted in concert, covertly, to initiate a secret study of prices, profits and returns on investment designed to assess and counter the threat of an inquiry by the OFT/MMC (*Sunday Times*, 8 August 1993). The result of such actions was a blistering editorial from the *Sunday Times* (22 August 1993), under the title 'Predatory Grocers', in which British food retailing was castigated as an industry riddled with 'anti-competitive practices on a grand scale', against which the OFT was reluctant to take action. Similar criticisms of the regulatory authorities were also voiced by the Labour Party's consumer affairs spokesperson (*Financial Times*, 22 March 1993).

In the face of growing public unease about the excesses of retailer dominance of the food system, changing competitive conditions in UK food retailing, and in the context of a progressive internationalization both in the supply and delivery of food and in its regulation, several questions about the retailer–regulatory state compromise that emerged in the private-interest regulated food system of the late 1980s have begun to be raised. In particular:

1   In what ways can the regulatory state, which in the UK has become so critically dependent upon the economic dominance of the retailers as the 'new masters of the food system', seek periodically to control the private recipients of its delegated power? In other words, how is the regulatory state to react to the dual pressures of sustaining private accumulation while maintaining a divergent public interest?

2   Faced with pressure to justify their growth, market power and regulatory responsibility, how are the major retailers becoming more adroit at projecting the benefits of their custodial role within the food system, at sustaining in political terms, the lucrative markets created in the 1980s, and at reproducing mechanisms, arguments and ideologies which ensure their competitive space?

3   To what extent are the retailer–regulatory state relations that have emerged in the UK likely to be unsettled by the growing internationalization of corporate activity, supply networks, and policy? In particular, what will be the impact of the proposed progressive harmonization of UK and EU food standard/competition policy legislation? Moreover, what will be the impact of increasing interaction between a British private-interest regulated food system characterized by custodial retailer power and the very differently structured food supply systems elsewhere in the EU in which producer-corporatism remains far more persistent?

What is clear is that, as part and parcel of the legitimation of their regulatory responsibilities, the major UK food retailers have had to reconcile themselves to dealing with government at a political level. Having created lucrative markets during the 1970s and, particularly, the 1980s, and having developed internationalized systems of product sourcing, the key task of the 1990s is to sustain these markets and supply systems via constant political activity within state agencies. That is to say, through growing engagement in the *politics of market maintenance*. To this end, the activities of the British Retail Consortium (Figure 2.3) are of importance. Constituted from the representatives of all major retail companies, the Consortium merged with the British Retailers' Association in 1992, enhancing the representational power of the retailers to government at both national and international levels, and allowing retailers to keep one eye on the competitive food chain and another on the Europeanization of markets and food regulation. Marsden (1993) has documented the considerable activity of the Consortium in the Westminster context across a wide range of trading,

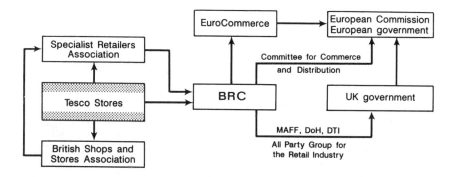

Figure 2.3   Stylized structure of British Retail Consortium links. (We acknowledge the assistance of Marion Justice in research leading to the development of this conceptualization)

land-use planning, environment, credit supply and social order issues. He has also shown how, at the European level, the Consortium operates via participation in groups such as the European Multiples Federation (GEDIS) and the European Consortium for Retailing (CECD), and via three-cornered negotiations involving MAFF, the Consortium, and the EU Directorates. In this way, the UK food retailers are attempting to maintain their competitive space by influencing and directing legislation emerging within both the UK and the EU.

Of particular importance in the retailers' attempts to sustain their competitive space and justify their broad custodial role within the food system is the way they have been allowed to construct and formally represent the 'consumer interest'. Empowerment of British retail capital in the 1980s went hand in hand with the unleashing of new and revised rights to consume; rights which Saunders and Harris (1990) have argued became more significant in sustaining the neo-conservative project than the privatization of the means of production. However, it was largely left to the major retailers to deliver those rights to consume. In doing so, they played a powerful role in structuring consumption around their own particular notions of the 'consumer interest', and began increasingly to represent that 'consumer interest' in their relations with government. Unease about the excesses of retailer dominance of the food system, and pressure to justify their custodial role, comes at a time, therefore, when the government finds itself increasingly dependent upon the retailers' ability to represent the 'consumer interest', particularly in negotiations on European wide standards of food quality, and upon the retailers' ability to deliver 'consumer rights'.

Critically dependent upon the economic dominance of the retailers in the food system, to police food quality standards and to deliver new and important rights to consume, the regulatory state in the UK finds itself, therefore, in an extremely difficult position when faced with evidence of possible anti-competitive practices in food retailing and accusations of 'paralysis' (*Sunday Times*, 22 August 1993) in its dealings with the retailers. What it must seek are opportunities, at one and the same time, for creatively sustaining the competitive space and accumulation trajectories of the major retailers, while legitimizing the process by being publicly seen to act periodically against the retailers or, at very least, to possess unambiguous deterrent powers against anti-competitive practices. Proposals to harmonize UK competition law with EU law, specifically Article 86 of the Treaty of Rome, offer exactly that possibility (Wrigley, 1993b). The UK government's preferred legislative option, put forward in the Green Paper *Abuse of Market Power* (DTI, 1992), offers the regulatory state a valuable amount of adaptability, creativity and capacity for action within its administrative practices, while providing the legitimatory authority of a general prohibition of anti-competitive practices.

Regulation and the state

Our focus on the changing relations and patterns of intermediation within the food system provides, we believe, an important window through which to conceptualize the nature of the contemporary regulatory state. Essentially, we have drawn a distinction between two emergent regulatory frameworks: public interest regulation, which from the 1980s has largely involved local forms of re-regulation (see Flynn *et al*, 1994; Marsden *et al*, 1993) and private interest regulation, whereby one set of actors, usually economic, regulate the activities of another set. Like Christopherson (1993: 276) we believe that:

> an interpretation of regulation as encompassing public and private activities offers richer analytical possibilities. An understanding of regulation as an activity carried out only by the state lends itself to a binary, on-off, conception of regulation as a form of intervention that can be eliminated, leaving a self-regulating market. This is impossible . . . where continuous regulation, by private as well as public actors, is assumed.

The public–private distinction is, of course, an abstraction. There will be inevitable tensions between these two pure forms as they attempt to serve different production and consumption interests. Consequently they are unlikely to be found in pure form, and regulatory frameworks will show a tendency to collide with one another as they are actively interpreted and re-interpreted by the participants in the regulatory structure. Nevertheless, at least initially, the distinction is worth pursuing further to highlight the changing roles of the state and of production and consumption interests.

A system of public interest regulation is one where the state has some direct involvement and which is nominally claimed to operate in the public interest, or which is at least open to some public participation and scrutiny. It is a form that is intimately associated with the

Keynesian and welfarist politics of much of the post-war period. Most often it involves the regulation of productive interests with the state acting in a benevolent manner to represent marginal interests (e.g. through the administration of wages councils to protect low-paid workers), or as an actor able to protect and promote some notion of the common public good. Most forms of public interest regulation were, at a minimum, subject to unprecedented scrutiny, and more likely to reform, during the 1980s as governments attempted to roll back the 'frontiers of the state'.

One of the clearest examples of public interest regulation in the UK is the planning system. Attempts were made to liberalize its operation through reforms at the national level during the 1980s. This created unanticipated opportunities for interest groups and professionals to develop local forms of regulation (e.g. local plans) to control private sector land development (Marsden *et al*, 1993). The practice of regulation became spatially variable, depending crucially upon the nature of the locality and its political culture. More specifically, because of the nature of the professionalized planning system, and the opportunities for public participation and impacts on public goods, the service classes were empowered and came to play a prominent role in shaping these forms of local regulation.

Private interest regulation, in contrast, occurs where the state empowers particular private sectional interests to act on its behalf and to regulate the activities of other sets of actors in the system. Such regulation is not open to public participation or scrutiny. Rather, the state bestows legitimacy on particular sectional interests at the expense of other bodies who would have wished to have been involved in policy formulation and regulation. Faced with both an overriding neo-liberal ideology and a fiscal crisis, nation states begin to make a virtue out of what seems to be a necessity. Bestowing economic power on particular private sectors means that to sustain such power, political power must also be delegated.

Private interest regulation in the UK food system is not a new phenomenon. What occurred in the 1980s is merely that private interest regulation favouring producer interests (agricultural producer corporatism) was increasingly viewed as privileging the wrong sectional interests and anachronistic corporatist relationships. It was superseded by a new form of private interest 'micro-corporatism' in which the major retailers emerged as the key actors in the post-productivist food system, and were granted political legitimacy for regulatory control which they had largely assumed already in the exercise of their considerable economic power.

As noted above, the transposing of state power on to private sector interests through micro-corporatist relations and practices occurred during a period in which the state became increasingly dependent upon retailers to deliver the new and revised 'rights' to consume unleashed by the neo-conservative project. This has broader implications, however. During the 1980s, the state became an active agent in class formation and class relations through the sphere of consumption, with class groupings becoming more clearly defined in terms of property access and ownership and consumption. The empowered groupings of service class consumers, and the new markets which they began to construct, became the constituencies and markets which the state sought, in particular, to protect. The major retailers, as we have seen, played a critical role, not only in delivering the 'rights' to consume to those constituencies, but also in defining consumption interests around their own particular notions, and in representing the 'consumer interest' in their relations with government. As a result, regulatory structures became supportive of, and sufficiently flexible to accommodate, retailer interests, and regulation became far more embedded than hitherto in consumption processes.

It is important to recognize, however, that the specific forms of micro-corporatist relations developed between retailers and the state in late 1980s Britain, must progressively confront different forms of those relations in mainland Europe, as the internationalization of corporate activity, supply networks and policy gathers pace. Given the persistence of producer-corporatism in many parts of mainland Europe, in addition to concerns about guaranteeing workers' rights and welfare (through debates about the social charter, for instance), the forms of private-interest regulation of the food system which have developed in the UK offer the potential for conflict with EU directives and the regulatory relations of *other* nation-states. National comparative analyses are needed to explore the ways in which the national regulatory structures impinge on supra-national policy making. These conflicts and their potential resolution are critical in understanding the changing geographies of regulation of both production and consumption.

It is important, therefore, to seek to understand how the major UK food retailers are attempting to manage the process of competitive and regulatory internationalization of the food system. We must ask to what extent the retailers can be regarded as more nationally embedded (because consumption practices have national characteristics, and because retailers have been delegated key regulatory functions of the state) than equivalent industrial corporations developing transnational operations. In addition, we must ask what evidence exists concerning the methods the UK food retailers are adopting to influence regulatory developments at the EU level? The need, as Marsden (1993: 24) has suggested, is to study 'the contested and contingent cross-links and matrices between international and national regulatory relations, and how these define the competitive space for retail capital'.

Finally, and perhaps most importantly, our focus on retailing, the food system, and the regulatory state – as a dynamic, competitive, and constructed matrix – draws attention we believe, to the inadequacy of many of the generalized conceptions of 'The State', in particular those which view 'The State' as a separate and functional entity capable of acting consistently in pursuit of particular class interests. Like Marden (1992: 757) we believe that the state cannot be viewed simply as representing some sort of functional integrative entity regulating the regime of accumulation, but, rather, is itself the object of struggle, and therefore cannot resolve the contradictions of capital because by its very nature it reproduces them in a political form.

As a result, we have attempted to locate our analysis in a brand of state theory championed by Clark (1992) which attributes a significant degree of autonomy to state apparatuses, and places emphasis upon the administrative manner, style and logic by which the state regulates society, and the economic landscape in particular. In this way, the socio-political practices involved in regulation become the prime focus for research, and attention is shifted to the highly contested nature of regulatory space, and to the powerful actors who dominate that space at any given time (Hancher and Moran, 1989: 277).

However, in adopting such a hermeneutical focus on institutions, we are not implying that conceptual questions about the role of the state should be neglected. Indeed, our discussion of the problems currently faced by the UK regulatory state when confronted with evidence of apparent anti-competitive practices in food retailing, highlights the structural limitations imposed on the state by its relation to capital, and the dilemma this poses for regulation. We are merely attempting to redress what Clark (1992) has referred to as the 'privileging of economic meta-imperatives over institutional interests', with sensitivity to the institutional cultures of regulation, to the web of complex contingencies involved in regulation, and to the spatial differentiation of regulation – not least between nation-states.

Our analysis of retailing, the food system, and the regulatory state in the UK suggests that corporate reorganization – particularly in a sector such as retailing in which the boundaries of competition and accumulation are constantly being tested but in which the regulatory state has become critically dependent upon the economic dominance of the major corporations – needs contingent state practices to help construct and legitimize, on a continuous basis, these conditions at national and international levels. The ability of state practices to retain a certain amount of adaptability, creativity and capacity for action in these circumstances reinforces a variable and contingent interpretation of the nature of the state. Such an approach not only needs to develop rich contemporary analyses of state–retailer–consumer relations, but also needs to seriously question how long they can justifiably persist over time and space.

CHAPTER 3

Market development and organizational change: the case of the food industry

Christine Doel

On the occasion of Lord Sainsbury's retirement from J Sainsbury plc, the Chairman of the Argyll (Safeway) Group proclaimed, '[his] name will not only go down in the history books as one of the great retailers of our time, but also as one of Britain's best businessmen' (*Super Marketing*, 6 November, 1992). Developments in the food industry during Lord Sainsbury's career have been both profound and thoroughly imbricated in the actions of the retail multiples. As a consequence, traditional distinctions between 'retailing' and 'business' have been eclipsed and retailing can no longer be regarded as innocuous shopkeeping, Arkwright-style. Britain's multiple food retailers have become major property companies and their power and influence now extend throughout the economy. One highly visible indication of this has been the proliferation of retailers' own-label products which increasingly dominate many supermarket shelves.

The ascendancy of the own-label has instigated fundamental but complex organizational changes at the food manufacturer–retailer interface. Associated causal processes have been intricate and variable. They nevertheless offer considerable insights regarding the actual process and implications of industrial organizational change. However, despite their magnitude and diversity, established theoretical literatures on inter-firm relations ultimately fail to capture the essence and dynamism of the processes that have revolutionized Britain's food industry.

Drawing largely on primary research into processes of own-label supply chain initiation and development in four product areas,[1] this chapter aims to challenge established theoretical orthodoxies by advocating a more dynamic approach to questions of industrial organizational change. After describing the character of developments within the food industry, the argument proceeds by outlining the theoretical context provided by the prevailing literatures. A number of critical empirical questions will then be raised and insights from these will be developed to suggest a fundamentally revised theoretical perspective.

The evolving British food industry

The British food system has certainly witnessed radical organizational changes since the mid-1960s. Essentially, these have reflected a complete reversal in the balance of power between manufacturers and retailers which has accompanied the development of the concept of the retailer own-label (Lang and Wiggins, 1985). Initially own-labels were regarded as inferior, 'me-too' products that competed with the leading brands on the basis of price. They were also closely allied to the 'pile it high, sell it cheap' philosophy that was advocated by several multiples during the 1970s. However, the image of the own-label has changed radically. Rather than an inferior substitute, own-labels are increasingly perceived as high quality, innovative products that are consumed by ABC1s and are no longer the preserve of the C2DE social classes (*Super Marketing*, 20 September 1992, 20). In addition to their vastly improved quality image, sales of own-label products have increased enormously. The two brands with the highest sales values in Britain are currently 'St Michael' and 'Sainsbury' (Senker, 1989) and consequently, own-label products are accounting for a rapidly increasing share of the £43.5 billion British grocery market (Economist Intelligence Unit, 1992b). Estimates of precise market share vary, but most industry analysts agree that by 1991, own-labels comprised well over 30 per cent of grocery sales (Outram Cullinan and Company, 1991; *Super Marketing*, 20 September 1992).

However, patterns of own-label growth have been far from uniform, varying along two principal dimensions. First, substantial disparities exist between different product groups with rapid own-label growth concentrated in fresh foods and highly innovative products which also, importantly, are high margin areas. Levels of own-label penetration have remained low in the staple packaged grocery sectors where manufacturers' brands have retained their franchise. A second dimension along which the degree of own-label penetration has varied significantly concerns the retailers themselves. The spectrum among the major retail multiples ranges from Marks & Spencer which sells only own-label (St Michael) products, to Kwik Save whose product range is restricted to manufacturer brands. In both cases, these extreme positions are absolutely integral to a particular retail strategy. But among the more mainstream retailers, since the late 1970s there has been a widespread, if yet unsuccessful, attempt to emulate Sainsbury and increase own-label penetration to levels of around 55–60 per cent (see Figure 3.1).

Sainsbury is Britain's most profitable retailer and in the 28 weeks to 26 September 1992, pre-tax profits increased by 19.4 per cent to £391.1 million (*The Grocer*, 7 November 1992). Many commentators have highlighted the significance of new-store development programmes adopted by Sainsbury and other retail multiples as the key to winning market share and sustaining profitable operations (Saloman Brothers Inc, 1991; Wrigley, 1991). However, as the financial difficulties of Asda

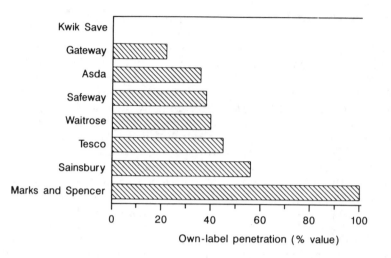

Figure 3.1 Own-label penetration levels among grocery retail multiples, 1990. (*Source*: Outram Cullinan and Company, 1991)

during the late 1980s demonstrate, the possession of large numbers of stores does not automatically mean success. While the store network certainly generates market potential and provides the physical framework for operations, the success of the organization as a whole depends critically on the efficacy of supply-chain management. Certainly, in the case of Sainsbury, the own-label product range has been integral to its success. Not only does it account for well over half of Sainsbury's total sales, but also the own-label range continues to be purposely developed in high margin product areas thereby contributing disproportionately to profit levels.

Since 1969, Sainsbury's own-label product portfolio has increased from 1500 to over 8000 different lines which by the early 1990s had generated annual sales worth approximately £6.6 billion (*Super Marketing*, 6 November 1992). When these figures are aggregated to take account of the other retail multiples' activities, the wider significance of own-label products becomes clear. But in addition to their immense quantitative importance, own-label products are integral to strategies of retailer differentiation. In a real sense therefore, the domain of horizontal competition between retailers has shifted to the efficacy of interactions across the own-label supply chain. Furthermore, the development of own-labels to some extent accounts for the demise of many well-established brand manufacturers. All of these developments are imbricated within the enormous organizational changes that have occurred in the food industry since the mid-1960s.

Own-label products are effectively supplied through a sub-contract relation which is formed as retailers select suppliers and develop products to unique specifications. So, instead of manufacturers developing their brand and then simply selling it to retailers through the medium of a wholesaler, vast sub-contract networks have emerged which now dominate and obscure the interface between the food manufacturing and retailing sectors. Correspondingly, the organizational changes that have occurred have not been restricted to the formal structures through which interactions have taken place. The tangible characteristics of the firms have altered, but in addition, governance relations have changed fundamentally, albeit differentially. In other words, the 'actual systems of co-ordination and regulation between different aspects of the production system' (Driver, 1990: 55) have undergone a radical evolution with profound and far-reaching consequences. They therefore invoke some kind of explanation.

Contrasting theoretical orthodoxies

Within the fields of economic geography and industrial organization, two influential and interrelated bodies of theory have explicitly addressed the issues surrounding sub-contracting as a mode of industrial organization. The first of these, transaction cost theory, has been principally concerned with the 'make or buy' decision. In essence, it has attempted to elucidate the circumstances under which technically separable operations are actually internalized within a particular firm in preference to coordination by the 'invisible hand' of the market. By contrast, the roots of the second body of literature may be traced to labour process analysis and theory. It therefore reflects a profound concern with the potentially adverse social implications of the sub-contracting process. These two broad schools emanate from diametrically opposed ideological premises. However, attempts have been made to synthesize their insights and thus provide some explanation for both the structure and governance of sub-contract networks. Clearly then, they should both offer considerable insights in the context of the evolving network of sub-contract relations that characterizes the contemporary food industry.

Transaction costs have been defined simply, if elliptically, as the 'costs of running the economic system' (Arrow, 1969: 48). A key insight deriving from the approach is that any mode of industrial organization will necessarily incur certain costs. However, the source of these varies and, as Oliver Williamson (1985: 4) explains, unless the factors responsible for transaction cost differences can be identified, 'the reasons for organising some transactions one way and other transactions another would necessarily remain obscured'. Williamson identifies two principal modes of industrial organization, each of which is associated with particular costs. In order to use markets, resources are used, and thus costs are incurred while discovering prices and negotiating contracts. By contrast, firms or hierarchies are subject to diminishing returns to management which in turn generate cost penalties. In both cases the existence of costs may be traced ultimately to two behavioural characteristics, namely bounded rationality and opportunism. Where the transaction costs associated with using a market are higher than those that would be incurred if production was organized through a single firm, Williamson argues that technically separable operations will be vertically integrated. More specifically, where transactions are recurrent, investment is transaction-specific and a high degree of uncertainty exists, operations are likely to be internalized as the market will seldom provide an efficient mode of governance (O Williamson and Ouchi, 1981). In his later writings, Williamson does also recognize a third, intermediate organizational form that lies between markets and hierarchies. He suggests that 'bilateral contracting' emerges as an optimal solution where both parties make transaction-specific investments and trading is recurrent yet behavioural characteristics militate against complete integration.

At one level, Williamson's transaction cost theory does appear to offer important insights into the processes surrounding the emergence of the networks of own-label sub-contract relations that have appeared across the food manufacturer–retailer interface. 'Transaction-specific investments' have certainly been made by both parties in the context of intensive product development and 'exclusivity' agreements which have been important in some food sectors. Moreover, in the relatively stable environment of the food industry, trading may be 'recurrent'. However, as the type of expertise required to manufacture and retail food differs sharply, it is certainly plausible to argue that the economies of scope accompanying complete integration would be limited. In accordance with Williamson's notions about 'bounded rationality', it is then possible that severe managerial diseconomies would result from attempts to fully integrate operations. Consequently, it could be concluded that across the food industry, bilateral exchange has emerged because it does indeed provide the most 'efficient' and effective mode of governance.

Transaction cost theory, however, says little about the wider implications of the sub-contracting process and in this context a second broad literature appears to offer important insights. Friedman (1977) for example argues that sub-contracting essentially represents a strategy of labour control that extends beyond the normal ambit of the firm. As a mode of industrial organization, it is inherently imbricated within the social relations of production and can therefore be comprehended only in terms of power differentials (F Murray, 1983; Rainnie, 1984). While large firms benefit from externalizing the costs of uncertainty through relationships 'which are designed largely to push risk and responsibility down the line' (Gertler, 1988; Rainnie, 1991, 356), sub-contractors are progressively marginalized. Delays in payment and the perpetual threat of delisting render their position one of inherent and increasing dependency.

Within the food industry, there have been persistent rumblings regarding allegations of the unfair treatment of own-label suppliers by powerful retail multiples (e.g. Skipworth, 1992). In the context of an industry in which the biggest five retailers account for around 60 per cent of sales (Verdict Research, 1991), the multitude of small suppliers individually have little countervailing power (Galbraith, 1952). Given the significance of own-label products as a critical dimension of retailer differentiation within an increasingly oligopolistic industrial structure, it is then hardly surprising that considerable pressure is exerted by the big chains. Thus insights from the labour process-based literature on sub-contracting are extremely pertinent to analyses of own-label supply chains.

Transaction cost theory may therefore be invoked to provide an interpretation of the specific organizational forms that are employed to facilitate particular transactional relations while the broad literature on sub-contracting offers some explanation of the practical implications of this form of industrial organization for the particular actors involved. In some respects the two approaches are complementary, indeed, some authors have attempted a theoretical synthesis. Scott for instance claims that viewing production as a

> complex but rationally comprehensible organizational structure rooted in the polarities of the firm and the market . . . is complementary to, and not in opposition with, those conceptions of production that strongly emphasize the tense force field of capitalist–worker relations. (Scott, 1988a; 24)

Scott pursued this argument by suggesting that firms should be regarded essentially as a series of internal and external transactions structured by the basic dynamics of the labour process. But despite the obvious appeal of such a synthesis, its validity and practical utility must be open to doubt. Scott's approach depends on the juxtaposition of theoretical arguments derived from largely incommensurable philosophical positions: while labour process-based interpretations of sub-contracting have emerged from a background of radical political economy, transaction cost theory is firmly rooted in orthodox neo-classical economics (Lazonick, 1991).

Individually, neither approach can provide an adequate explanation of the causes and implications of the sub-contract relation, and the validity of attempts at theoretical synthesis must also be questionable. But in addition, however, even the most cursory consideration of the evolution of the food industry demonstrates the failure of both approaches to address some of the central issues surrounding actual processes of organizational change. In the mid-1960s, sub-contract relations between food retailers and manufacturers barely existed; in the mid-1990s they dominate the organizational structure of the industry. More importantly, however, this transformation has not simply implied a radical change in the relations between existing firms. It has instead shared a recursive relationship with the emergence either of completely new enterprises, or of new divisions within established firms. Thus the empirical and theoretical questions with the most profound organizational implications concern the processes by which relations with own-label suppliers are initiated, the nature of subsequent developments in the structure and extent of the supply network, and the actual character of manufacturer–retailer relations. None of these issues is addressed adequately by the theoretical orthodoxies that pervade economic geography and studies of industrial organization, yet they are integral to any comprehension of the current dynamism of the food industry. The theory and the empirical reality of contemporary industrial change therefore appear to have become disengaged. Both require reconsideration.

Own-label sub-contract supply networks: modes of initiation

Transaction cost theorists and advocates of the labour process-based approach to sub-contracting alike devote scant attention to the actual mechanisms surrounding the initiation of the sub-contract relation. Both literatures have implicitly assumed that sub-contracting is always a feasible option and that the decision to adopt this organizational form will simply reflect either perceived relative efficiencies, or the implications for labour control. Empirical investigations of own-label sub-contract relations in the food industry demonstrate that the reality is far more problematic. Before the possibility of a sub-contract relation can even be considered, firms that have the capacity and the capability to fulfil that role must actually exist. In some respects this observation is banal, yet its implications are extremely damaging for both theoretical orthodoxies. Inter-firm relationships must be purposely initiated and developed. However, at least in the food industry, the actual mechanisms through which initiation occurs are themselves variegated. They essentially reflect the maturity of different food sub-sectors, the strategic significance of particular products, and the characteristics of the individual retailers involved.

In the mid-1960s, during the formative period of own-label development, brand manufacturers were still very much in the ascendancy, dominating the industry. In response to the constraints of Resale Price Maintenance, retailers developed the concept of the own-label in an attempt to weaken the manufacturers' position (Burns *et al*, 1983). This strategy was operationalized by the purchase of standard commodities from weaker brand manufacturers with surplus capacity. Early own-labels were therefore off-the-shelf products that incurred only marginal costs. As the breakfast cereals buyer from Retailer A explained, in this context manufacturers would regard own-labels simply as

> a contribution to an overhead. They have got all the machines there. If they are producing a brand one minute, why not produce an own-label the next? Although they make less margin on one product than another, it all goes towards the mix and keeps the factory going. (Personal interview, 17 July 1992)

Thus the products could be retailed at a discount while still benefiting both the manufacturer and the retailer.

Clearly, this is a very conventional argument regarding the initiation of sub-contract relations. It is also the one that implicitly informs prevailing interpretations of the sub-contract process. However, it has been fallacious to regard this as the unique, or even the most significant, mechanism underlying the initiation of own-label supply chains. The successful operation of this particular process depends on two critical assumptions: that established brand manufacturers exist, and that they are in a position to enter into a sub-contract relation. It could therefore operate only in a relatively mature product market. In practice, it has been dependent on the existence of established brand manufacturers that nevertheless occupy relatively weak positions *vis-à-vis* the market leader. So while Kelloggs and Heinz 'stoutly refuse to make copies of their prized brands' (Parkes, 1988), weaker brand manufacturers are engaged in such activities. Correspondingly, this causal process may be invoked to explain the existence of some sub-contract relations in mature product sectors such as baked beans and breakfast cereals. There are however many other own-label supply chains which have assumed far greater strategic significance but cannot be explained through this classical process of initiation.

Consider for instance the chilled ready meals sector. Writing in 1988, Parkes claimed that 'five years ago, the UK market for chilled ready-prepared meals barely existed, yet it is now worth about £130 million a year'. By 1992, its value was estimated at between £275 million and £310 million (personal interview with the ready meals buyer from Retailer A, 28 July 1992), and this phenomenal rate of growth has been forecast to continue (Key Note, 1992). Within a decade then, a completely new sector worth over £300 million has emerged. Its wider significance is far greater, however, for as Parkes (1988) explains, the sector was 'discovered, exploited and continues to be dominated not by a manufacturer but by the retailer Marks and Spencer'. Since 1988, the pre-eminent position of Marks & Spencer has been relinquished, but this has simply reflected the growing presence within the sector of other retail multiples (see Figure 3.2). Thus the situation remains that 'chilled ready meals have emerged as the first major market segment to be dominated by own-label goods' (Parkes, 1988).

The emergence of the chilled ready meals sector is of immense symbolic significance as it visibly epitomizes the changing dynamics and shifting power balance within the food industry. But more important in the current context are the processes surrounding the initiation of the associated own-label supply networks. In the early 1980s, chilled ready meals represented a completely new product sector with no brand manufacturer presence whatsoever. Thus for retailers, the appropriation of surplus capacity as the basis of an own-label supply structure was not even a possibility.

The firms that currently supply multiple retailers with ready meals are diverse in character. They include the 'convenience food product' divisions of several large, public companies, but of greater overall significance is the large number of small, specialist firms. Tracing the histories of these is instructive regarding actual processes of supply

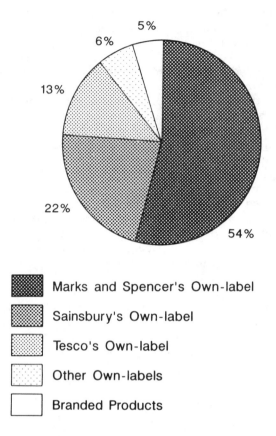

Figure 3.2 Chilled ready meals market shares (by value). (*Source : Super Marketing*, January and February 1992)

chain initiation. Manufacturer C for instance was established in 1987. Its origins may be traced to a dinner party attended by a local independent grocer who was impressed by the food and subsequently invited the host to supply his retail outlet on a very small scale. The products were spotted by Retailer E who also made contact with the dinner party host. He was then invited to supply own-label products for the national multiple. This required an enormous increase in operating capacity. As the ready meals buyer from Retailer A explained,

> [Manufacturer C] had a tiny little unit, not much bigger than the end of this office and they produced finger foods. . . . And from doing that they then started to produce the meals. When the volume started to increase, they then bought land and constructed a small factory unit. And from there, when the business had grown enough, they extended that factory unit, and now it is being extended again. . . . They only deal with [Retailer E] other than us, so they have grown on our volume. (Personal interview, 28 July 1992)

However, the initial expansion from the domestic kitchen to a small-scale factory unit required a commitment from Retailer E. As the national account manager of Manufacturer C recalled,

> basically what they said was 'we want your products. We will put an order to you in writing that you will supply us. Take that to the bank and show them that you have got an order from [Retailer E]'. I think that they gave us a contract for something like twelve months. Now that doesn't happen very often and I think that was the first time I had heard of it within the trade. I am sure that other companies have had similar help in the past, but it is very rare that that happens, very rare. But that is how we started off. (Personal interview, 20 October 1992)

The manner in which the sub-contract relation between Manufacturer C and Retailer E was initiated is unusual, but it demonstrates why 'although it will be argued that . . . supermarkets . . . ruin businesses because they suddenly pull out, at the same time they also actually create businesses' (personal interview, 19 June 1992). In addition, though, it is indicative of the types of initiatives that have had to be undertaken by the retail multiples in order to develop their own-label ready meal supply chains in the absence of organizational alternatives.

Own-label sub-contract relations may then be initiated through at least two distinct processes: the operationalization of existing brand suppliers' surplus capacity and direct intervention to develop firms with the capacity and capability to supply the retail multiples. The mechanism that is actually employed depends on a variety of factors including the maturity of different food sub-sectors, the strategic significance of particular products, and the characteristics of individual retailers. It is certainly also possible that a retailer may be able to choose between more than one mode in a given situation. The sub-contract relation between Retailer B and Manufacturer B for instance emerged through an essentially similar process to that between Retailer G and Manufacturer A (personal interview with the managing director of Manufacturer B, 12 October 1992), even though the two product markets were radically different: breakfast cereals and chilled ready meals respectively. Certainly in the case of the former, the retailer could have adopted a different strategy. However, the implications of each initiation mode are quite different. They vary in terms of the degree of mutual commitment, the possibilities for joint product development and the qualitative character of the mode of governance across the supply chain. Thus arguably the mechanism through which sub-contract links are first established is critical to any comprehension of the wider implications of this particular mode of industrial organization.

By arguing simply that a particular organizational form will exist given appropriate conditions of relative efficiency or labour control, both the transaction cost theorists and advocates of the labour process-based approach to sub-contracting assume away the whole question of how, in practice, sub-contract relations are initiated. Instead it is implicitly assumed that by making marginal adjustments, firms can effectively plug into the existing infrastructure surrounding a sub-contract network. Consequently, the wider insights, derived from understanding the implications of contrasting initiation modes, are lost. It is for instance unlikely that highly interactive and innovative relationships subsequently emerge between a retailer and an own-label supplier where the basis for that relationship was simply the appropriation of surplus capacity. By contrast, direct intervention during the firm's inception and early growth may well underpin a more dynamically interactive supply chain structure. Thus the mode of initiation has direct implications regarding the qualitative character of governance relations across the entire own-label supply chain.

The character of relations between retailers and their own-label suppliers

Multiple food retailers have persistently received adverse publicity concerning the alleged maltreatment of own-label suppliers. For instance, the practice of bidding for contracts to supply supermarket chains has been reported by Skipworth:

> One independent manufacturer . . . said the supermarket initially wanted £180 000 from him which quickly increased to £200 000. 'These guys are screwing the hell out of us. I wasn't in a position to bid at that sort of price,' he said. (Skipworth, 1992: 1)

Claims have also been made regarding substantial delays in payments to own-label suppliers. As the editor of one trade journal commented,

> That came up in the House of Commons talks[2] . . . 'Do you pay your suppliers within thirty days?'. They all said they did, but there were a lot of undercurrents that they didn't . . . You're not going to get anybody to come forward and say that. They are all worried that if they start saying that [Retailer B] doesn't pay its bills on time, for instance, they will get delisted overnight. (Personal interview, 8 July 1992)

The actual character of relationships between own-label suppliers and the retail multiples has major implications for the analysis of the sub-contracting process in the post-initiation stage. If these alleged malpractices are in fact widespread across the retailer–manufacturer interface, then the arguments of Rainnie (1991: 356) and other labour process-based theorists, that the purpose of sub-contracting is simply to 'push risk and responsibility down the line', become extremely poignant despite their neglect of initiation modes. Conversely, explanations of organizational form based only on considerations of 'efficiency' appear irrelevant, for even if the outcomes do display 'efficiency', this cannot be regarded as the primary underlying motive.

Retailer B's baked beans buyer described the governance structure characterizing his own-label product supply network:

> basically they [the potential own-label suppliers] are fighting against each other on price. It is a very competitive market. . . . So what we really tend to do is play one off against the other at the moment because they are greedy for business. (Personal interview, 26 October 1992)

Retailer A's breakfast cereals buyer gave a similar account and explained that

> we do switch suppliers . . . on cornflakes for example, I have switched my supplier three times . . . or before I joined [nine months ago] it was switched once and since I've been here I have switched it twice. (Personal interview, 17 July 1992)

In both instances then, the position of own-label manufacturing firms in their relations with particular retailers appears to be extremely vulnerable. Firms are forced into a position of low operating margins, and, even if highly efficient, continued business with a retail multiple may be terminated at short notice. As Retailer A's breakfast cereals buyer explained,

> I would personally give them four weeks working notice before we switch . . . possibly three, depending on the relationship with the supplier and the product they were packing for us. (Personal interview, 17 July 1992)

This kind of scenario does not, however, reflect the character of all own-label sub-contract relationships even within identical product markets. A senior divisional manager from Retailer B for instance claimed that

> The same suppliers would supply us cornflakes for years, perhaps twenty or thirty years. . . The business would only move if we weren't happy with the supplier or if it was an unacceptable quality, or if the price was exorbitant. We are quite well known in the trade for being very loyal to our suppliers. Unless we have got a good reason to move, then why move? We have got an established business. (Personal interview, 1 October 1992)

In addition, the national account manager of Manufacturer C admitted that throughout his firm's recent supply problems,

> [Retailer A] has been very good about it to be honest. They have understood it because they realise why it has happened. Provided you have got a good reason and they understand the reasoning, they can be very helpful. (Personal interview, 20 October 1992)

Thus there are situations in which retailers do display a degree of commitment towards particular suppliers. When problems arise they respond through the exercise of 'voice' rather than 'exit' (A Hirschman, 1970). For many own-label suppliers, the corollary of this is that the way the major multiples operate is to be very close to the private label supplier, to be dictating most things that he does and the way that he does them, to be in and out of the factory on a regular basis, to be in attendance at every new product launch and to be involved in every pack change – to be involved at every step of the way and to operate a very close policing role if you like. . . . At times it can be helpful, at times it can be too intrusive. (Personal interview with the managing director of Manufacturer B, 12 October 1992)

Retailers' 'policing role' is clearly a double-edged sword, but it does at least imply some form of commitment, for retailers are unlikely to invest time and money in the continual scrutiny of their suppliers if they have no intention of perpetuating the relationship.

The experiences of individual own-label suppliers in their interactions with the retail multiples do therefore vary. Some firms enjoy continuous, albeit exacting relationships. Other suppliers are far more likely to have their dealings with particular retailers terminated at short notice. The predictions of labour process-based approaches to sub-contracting are then poignant, particularly in the context of the experiences of this second group. Although such analyses certainly provide a 'necessary' interpretation, they do not constitute a 'sufficient' explanation. The option of terminating a relationship with a particular supplier while continuing to provide an own-label product is feasible only if alternative sources of supply are available. Thus retailers can establish this kind of arm's-length governance relation only in well-established, traditional, low-margin markets where products are essentially standardized and specifications are easily transferable. Not surprisingly then, this type of manufacturer–retailer relation will often characterize situations where the initial basis for that relationship was simply the appropriation of surplus capacity, a situation exemplified by the baked beans sector.

By contrast, other own-label manufacturers have experienced continuous relationships with particular retailers. To describe them as 'long term' in some respects would be a misnomer, for even though interactions tend to be intensive and continuous, retailers generally give no formal commitment or guarantee regarding the duration of the relationship. A senior divisional manager from Retailer B explained

I guess we have an unwritten commitment. There is nothing in writing. There is no contract sent out. We don't say 'for the next year we will take whatever . . .'. So it is very loose, just a 'gentleman's agreement'. (Personal interview, 1 October 1992)

Nevertheless, considerable emphasis is often placed on product development and the active role of retailers as effective innovators through the own-label network has been recognized, particularly in high-margin and thus strategically important product areas (Senker, 1986). In this context, the value of particular suppliers to the retailers must be immense as these will often possess unique capabilities and 'relation-specific' skills (Asanuma, 1989). Thus retailers will 'very often come to rely on subcontractors making contributions through their specialized competences, close attention to the lead firm's technology and business practices, and innovative capacity' (Sayer and Walker, 1992: 132). Moreover these are generally also the own-label sub-contract links that were initiated by direct retailer intervention during the supplier's inception and early growth (e.g. Manufacturer C). As they are concentrated in new, innovative product areas, few alternative sources of supply exist and in any case, the complexity of the products ensures that specifications are not easily transferable. But despite all of this, the retailer will not make a formal commitment to the supplier. For the national account manager of Manufacturer C, the implications of this were clear:

> You can't sit back because the business that you have today . . . you're not guaranteed it. We plan to increase our business. But unless we do our job properly and unless we do have a firm grip on everything, then we have lost it really. (Personal interview, 20 October 1992)

From the retailer's perspective, the rationale for this is obvious. The lack of any formal commitment despite the strategic significance of highly specialized suppliers means, in principle, that the discipline provided by the threat of delisting remains even if, in practice, the likelihood of this is remote because of the absence of alternative sources of supply.

In this situation, in return for even the possibility of continued patronage, the retailers' requirements are exacting. Product specifications are highly confidential and surrounded by legally binding contracts. A senior divisional manager from Retailer B explained that

> We have an own-brand specification form. It is a huge document – it was about five pages, but it is now about fifty – and it has all the details of the product. It sets out what the ingredients are, where they come from, what processes are used to make the product, what sort of checks the factories will make, whether it will do metal detection and check the quality of the food – all sorts of things. And at the end, if it is an exclusive recipe that we have worked on, we will ask that it is kept exclusive for us and the supplier will sign that – because of the time and commitment that we spend with our suppliers, and it would be very unfair if that product were to be given elsewhere. (Personal interview, 1 October 1992)

The need for such complex legal arrangements in the context of retailer–manufacturer relations that are supposedly based on 'partnerships' and 'trust' (*Super Marketing*, 17 January 1992; 6 March 1992) does appear contradictory.

To some extent though, this paradox may be legitimized by the 'due diligence' clause within the Food Safety Act 1990. This rendered retailers legally responsible for the safety of their own-label products and meant for the first time that a firm could be 'charged to prove' that it had 'taken all reasonable precautions to avoid the alleged offence' (*Super*

Marketing, 29 May 1992). Consequently, in some cases, ardent 'policing' by retailers has filtered up the supply chain as far as the ingredients suppliers. As the sales and marketing manager of Manufacturer A explained,

> manufacturers can really only use suppliers that are recommended or approved by the retailers. The 'due diligence' clause in particular now means that everything has to be vetted. . . . The advantage of dealing with an ingredient's supplier that has been vetted by the retailers is that the manufacturer has the full clout of the retailer behind it in dealing with the suppliers. (Personal interview, 15 October 1992)

The concern of the retailers about absolute product exclusivity is also indicative of the intensely competitive environment in which they operate. One manifestation of this is that retailers monitor closely the interactions between their own-label suppliers and the other retail multiples. A deputy divisional manager from Retailer B admitted

> If my suppliers start to trade with [Retailer C] I get very annoyed and say 'I can't stop you and you deal with [Retailer C] if you like, but if that is where you want to see your future then it will be with [Retailer C] and not with [Retailer B] . . .'. I won't suddenly pull everything off the shelf but I won't do any more development. 'How can I share my ideas and the expertise of my people here and my technical resources with you, if you might then share them with a major competitor?' (Personal interview, 22 October 1992)

In essence then, relations between retailers and their own-label suppliers across the food industry may assume one of two forms: arm's length, often short-term relationships that are entirely price based and usually found in mature, commodity-type product sectors, or highly interactive and exacting relationships that are effectively continuous but depend critically on continuous product innovation and stringent exclusivity agreements. Significantly though, these contrasting forms also correlate closely with different sub-contract initiation modes: the appropriation of surplus capacity and effective supplier initiation respectively.

Evolving organizational forms, evolving theoretical analyses?

Within the food industry, retailers' own-label product ranges are supplied through a vast number of overlapping sub-contract relations. Individually, these have evolved differentially from a range of starting points and with equally varying outcomes. Thus the composite character of the manufacturer–retailer interface is one of dynamic complexity. Throughout the industry there is however a widespread consensus that those own-label supply networks created by proactive retailers and characterized by intensive interaction are assuming progressively greater quantitative and strategic significance (see Figure 3.3).

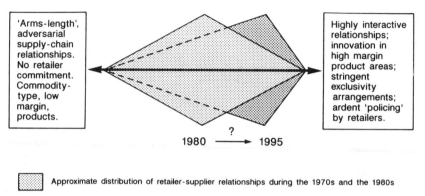

'Arms-length', adversarial supply-chain relationships. No retailer commitment. Commodity-type, low margin, products.

Highly interactive relationships; innovation in high margin product areas; stringent exclusivity arrangements; ardent 'policing' by retailers.

1980 ———→ 1995

Approximate distribution of retailer-supplier relationships during the 1970s and the 1980s

Hypothesized trend in the character of retailer-supplier relationships during the 1990s following food safety legislation, trends in consumption patterns and the emergence of retailers as innovative organizations

Figure 3.3   The spectrum of own-label sub-contract relations in the food industry

The reasons for this are multiplex. In part, they reflect the impact of the Food Safety Act 1990, which 'is probably the most important piece of legislation ever witnessed by the food industry' (Economist Intelligence Unit, 1992a: 36). A second important influence has been changing consumer tastes. Three trends variously characterize growth areas: 'convenience', 'health' and 'indulgence' (Boyle *et al*, 1990; Key Note, 1992). Products such as chilled ready meals which are perceived to meet all three criteria are complex both to manufacture and handle. The product areas that are growing most rapidly therefore tend to require intensive interaction throughout the supply chain. Nevertheless, margins are correspondingly high and thus the retailer has every incentive to foster and accentuate the directions of changing consumer demand.

A third causal factor concerns the retailers themselves. Recursively related to the changing character of own-label supply chains is the increased professionalism of the major retail multiples. The managing director of Manufacturer B reflected upon the changing balance of the nature of relations with retailers:

the way things operated ten years ago . . . it was a trading environment then. It is a much more measured and scientific kind of environment now. (Personal interview, 12 October 1992)

Not only have the retailers grown rapidly and become far more powerful, but also since the mid-1980s they have themselves developed skills and capabilities which are having a profound influence on the structure and governance of the entire food system. The actions of the dominant companies are therefore causally implicated within the immense organizational changes that have occurred. Neither of the prevailing theoretical orthodoxies that dominate studies of inter-firm relationships can fully account for this or indeed many other facets of the complexity and diversity of supply chain developments.

Labour process-based interpretations of sub-contracting are certainly poignant in the context of the actual experience of the own-label manufacturer–retailer relationship. Whether this is essentially arm's-length and ephemeral in character, or interactive and continuous, the supplier is tightly controlled and continuing retail patronage is virtually never guaranteed. Thus simply to sustain an existing retail relationship, suppliers are forced to be either highly price competitive by severely cutting their margins, or extremely proactive in product development. So, once an own-label supply chain is actually in place, this theoretical approach offers considerable insights regarding the character of inter-firm relations. However, its principal weakness rests with its failure to consider the processes by which networks of sub-contract firms come into being. Correspondingly, interpretations of the character of the inter-firm relation do also tend to be reductionist. Proponents of the approach attempt to explain every facet of this in terms of the social relations of production while other important influences, such as an evolving legislative environment and changes in the demand function, are completely overlooked.

The influence of transaction cost theory within industrial geography and studies of industrial organization has been immense (Scott, 1983). In part, its widespread appeal reflects a capacity to explain the existence of virtually any organizational form. But perhaps 'explain' is the wrong word. 'Rationalize' seems closer to the truth. Williamson's whole approach is premised on the notion that, other things being equal, perfect competition combined with the operation of the market mechanism is the key to economic efficiency. Alternative forms of organization will emerge only if the use of the market is limited by relatively high transaction costs. Thus only the most 'efficient' organizational forms survive. Therefore existing organizational forms are both 'efficient' and transaction costs economizing, or so the argument goes.

The costs of coordinating different parts of the division of labour are undoubtedly one important consideration in the organization of industrial activity. But there are also other factors which are arguably more significant. The impact of power differentials for instance is thoroughly implicated in the governance structures that currently dominate the food manufacturer–retailer interface. It is most unlikely that retailers could continually perpetuate the threat of delisting with even their most strategically important suppliers if the retail industry was not so concentrated *vis-à-vis* the manufacturing sector. While Williamson and Ouchi (1981: 364) admit that the issue of power is neither 'uninteresting or unimportant', they proceed to argue that 'power considerations will usually give way to efficiency – at least in profit making enterprises'.

This assertion itself raises a further fundamental problem with the approach. Questions of 'efficiency' are raised in an inherently static manner: given prevailing cost structures, what would be the most 'efficient' organizational form? As Auerbach (1988) argues, in a given situation, adequate markets for example may not exist and so the appearance of an alternative organizational form is inevitable irrespective of relative 'efficiency' which must therefore become a moribund concept. In order to develop the chilled ready meals sector, retailers had little choice other than to initiate the development of specialist firms and subsequently maintain an interactive relationship. Debating the relative 'efficiency' of this organizational structure is therefore meaningless. However, there is a second profound implication that arises when 'efficiency' is couched within the static axioms of neo-classical economics. Williamson's argument implies that entrepreneurs have to make organizational choices within the constraints of existing cost structures. Thus the possibility that a completely new product sector like chilled ready meals could be initiated is inconceivable within the transaction cost framework. Not only are there no pre-existing cost structures from which to derive 'efficient' organizational forms, but also the cost structures that emerge are themselves the result of the purposive actions of the actors involved (Lazonick, 1991; Sayer and Walker, 1992).

Particularly in the context of the analysis of own-label supply chains in the food industry, further problems emerge within the approach because of inadequate conceptualizations of 'firms', 'markets' and the relations between them. In the absence of any real consideration of power, firms are defined uncontroversially in terms of the extent of legal ownership, although the limitations of this are obvious (Cowling and Sugden, 1987). However, despite the importance attached to it, Williamson never provides a definition of the 'market'. He claims that 'in the beginning there were markets' (Williamson, 1975: 20), itself a highly dubious assumption which leaves the clear implication that markets are effectively regarded as 'whatever the firm is not'. This interpretation has been widely challenged. Richard Walker (1989: 54) for example argues that 'the market is an institution like any other, built of people, laws and practices, whose existence is as much in need of explanation as that of the firm'.

Hodgson (1988: 174) defines markets as 'a set of social institutions in which a large number of commodity exchanges of a specific type regularly take place' and argues further that 'the market includes a generalized mechanism to establish and publicize prices, and to promote goods and services' (1988: 177). In this context it is clear that there are in practice few real markets existing at the food manufacturer–retailer interface. One notable exception is the wholesale market for which price lists are published regularly in the trade journal *The Grocer*. But in terms of the supply of own-label products, there are no markets. Even for a mature, commodity product like baked beans where relations between retailers and suppliers are very definitely 'arm's-length' and transaction specific investments are negligible, the relation between retailers and manufacturers is still essentially one of 'non-market exchange' (Hodgson, 1988).

In his later work, Williamson (1985) does introduce the concept of 'bilateral exchange' or 'relational contracting' in recognition of this middle ground lying between markets and firms. However as Sayer and Walker explain,

> This turns out to be a vast area once we open the tight dualism of the market and the firm and cast a little light on the alternatives – so vast, indeed, that the void in the initial dualism cannot be patched over. (Sayer and Walker, 1992, 128)

In practice, at least in Williamson's use of the term, 'bilateral exchange' is certainly a 'dustbin' category. Arguably it also becomes something of a chaotic concept (Sayer, 1984) for it groups together various types of sub-contract relations that have contrasting origins and radically different implications. The manufacturer–retailer relation associated with the supply of own-label baked beans for example cannot be accommodated within the same explanatory framework as that invoked to explain the growth of the ready meals sector. While the initiation of one was associated with the appropriation of surplus capacity from an existing sector, the initiation of the second involved the creation of an entirely new product area. While relations in one remain short term, arm's-length and adversarial, those in the second, although exacting, are generally continuous and dynamically interactive, based around the imperatives of new product development. While the own-label presence has generally resulted in the demise of manufacturing enterprises in one, it has necessitated the existence and underpinned the growth of firms in the second.

Overall then, despite its influence, the transaction cost approach ultimately fails to account for the dynamism and complexity of organizational changes at the food retailer–manufacturer interface. To a large extent, its failings emanate from its grounding in a static and ahistorical economic orthodoxy. Contrary to the predictions of this orthodoxy, the basis of retailers' success has not been efficient allocation, but radical innovation both organizationally and in terms of product development (see Figure 3.4).

In this context, several writings which to varying degrees draw on the works of Schumpeter and Veblen are instructive. Storper and Walker (1989) for instance make an important distinction between 'weak' and 'strong' competition where the former is concerned with adaptation, the latter with the continual innovation that underpins industrial change. The ability to exploit this depends on firms themselves developing certain capabilities (Nelson and Winter, 1982). As Best (1992: 9) explains, 'firms that do not build into their organization the capacity to anticipate change and seize opportunities will lose out to competitors who do, no matter how efficiently they allocate resources within the pre-change conditions'. Developing this argument, Lazonick distinguishes between the 'innovative' and the 'adaptive' organization. He argues that

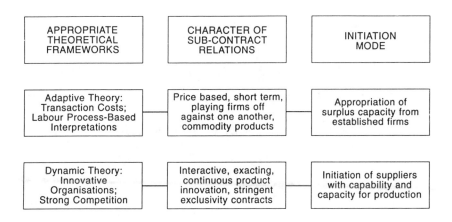

Figure 3.4 Own-label and sub-contract relations in the food industry and their theoretical implications: summary

> By overcoming constraints that less powerful productive organisations take as given, the innovative organisation escapes from equilibrium, in the process altering the economic environment that confronts its less innovative rivals. Innovative activity that creates new economic possibilities is the essence of the process of economic development. (Lazonick, 1991, 284)

Since the mid-1960s, Britain's successful multiple food retailers have certainly evolved to become 'innovative organizations' (see Figure 3.4). Not content with selling manufacturers' brands, in their quest for profit and market share they have developed new product areas within innovative and dynamic organizational structures which have radically altered the character of the manufacturer–retailer interface.

So while 'Lord Sainsbury's name will not only go down in the history books as one of the great retailers of our time, but also as one of Britain's best businessmen' (Sir Alistair Grant, quoted in *Super Marketing*, 6 November 1992), it is also valid to regard Lord Sainsbury and his peers as immensely successful innovators. For it is this innovative capacity that has essentially underpinned their ascendency.

Notes

1 Breakfast cereals, chilled ready meals, baked beans and yoghurt.
2 Evidence taken before the House of Commons Agriculture Committee's investigation of the UK Trade Gap in Food and Drink.

CHAPTER 4

The changing place of retailer–supplier relations in British retailing

Jo Foord, Sophie Bowlby and Christine Tillsley

The retail sector gained a new economic and cultural status in Britain during the 1980s. Retailing appeared to occupy a pivotal role in economic change. In part this was a consequence of the 1980s boom in which consumer demand floated on a 'magic carpet' of increasing housing equity and rising disposable incomes. This period was one of growing markets and highly competitive retailing conditions. Within retailing, responses varied with the size of the firm. There were many new births (and deaths) of small independent retailers catering to specialized markets. And while the major multiples continued to concentrate ownership through acquisition, merger and growth, they segmented and targeted their consumer base(s) more tightly.

In this chapter we argue that a key feature of retailing success in the 1980s, particularly among the major multiples, was their ability to re-shape and control supply relations. We suggest that the emphasis on interactive, flexible and stable supply *networks* was a key retailing strategy. This retail strategy was not uncontested by suppliers nor was a large retail firm guaranteed superior power in all situations. Manufacturers had counter-strategies which changed the supply relation and, in certain circumstances, limited retailers' control.

The chapter examines the (re-)shaping of the relationship between major retailers and their manufacturing suppliers in the 1980s and early 1990s by drawing on our own and others' empirical evidence. Our own research concerned the relationships between retailers and their manufacturing suppliers in the two product areas of bread, rolls and morning goods and women's hosiery. We interviewed 19 manufacturing firms and 19 retailers using intensive, semi-structured interviews during 1990 and 1991 (S R Bowlby *et al*, 1993).

In the first section we set this empirical material in the context of debates surrounding changes in the organization of the economy. In the main section we discuss changes in the *structure and governance of retail–supplier relations* and in the *relative power of* and *strategies* used by retailers and manufacturers. We conclude the main section by discussing the implications of these changes for the *spatial organization of retailer–supplier relationships*.

Retail–supply and the changing economy

It is widely agreed that there have been shifts in retail–supplier relations towards *relational contracting* in which the purchasing firm places orders with and purchases from a limited number of known suppliers on a long-term basis (Hodgson, 1988; O Williamson, 1985). These changes in retailer–supplier relations appear to be linked to the broader shifts in the economy debated by many authors (Cooke, 1988; Harvey, 1989c; R Murray, 1988; 1989; Piore and Sable 1984; Sayer 1989; K Williams *et al*, 1987). Much of this literature assumes change is either demand led or at least demand 'fed'. But, as several authors have pointed out, a major criticism of most of this work is that it fails to integrate the role of retailing into its analysis (Christopherson, 1989; Ducatel and Blomley, 1990; Gibbs, 1991; Lowe and Crewe, 1991). However, retailers play a very important role in linking production and consumption. They not only select from goods produced by manufacturers those which will be offered to consumers for purchase but also they ask manufacturers to produce specific goods for retail sale. In doing so they influence both what is produced and what can be bought. Thus, in so far as the moves towards 'flexibility' in production, identified by many researchers, are related to changes in consumer demand, retailing is likely to be a significant link in any chain of causation – however complex that chain may be. As we shall show later, retailer–supplier relations have changed significantly since the mid-1970s and these changes gathered pace during the 1980s. It appears that retailers' purchasing policies have become a more important influence on manufacturers' production strategies and hence this chapter will concentrate on retailer–manufacturer relationships.

Changes in economic organization

Three issues particularly relevant to questions of the changing form and impact of retailer–manufacturer relations, emerge from the broader economic debates: first, the significance of inter-firm relations in 'flexible' production; secondly, the nature, use and location of the 'flexible workforce'; and third, the changing geography of industrial space. Within all three the use of new technology is of particular significance.

Inter-firm relations
The significance of changing relations between firms has been raised by discussions of new sub-contracting patterns that have emerged during the 1980s. It is now widely agreed that there is a trend towards vertical disintegration rather than the earlier tendency towards vertical integration. Both existing firms and new firms are developing sub-contracting networks which are argued to promote both flexibility in response to market changes and reductions in risk for the

sub-contracting firm. These networks are often relatively stable and involve the establishment of long-term relationships between the participants. Scott (1988a) uses transactions cost analysis to demonstrate the centrality of sub-contracting to just-in-time systems and flexible production. Williamson's analysis of the role of transactions costs in leading to different organizational forms and governance structures has also been used to explain the move from market relations to relational sub-contracting (O Williamson, 1985). Cooke (1988) notes changes to both internal and external relations as firms move towards flexible production: in particular he notes that 'strategic alliances' may be formed between firms to allow product development where Research and Development (R&D) costs are high and competition fierce.

Semlinger (1991) argues that firms are increasingly taking an active role in shaping 'inter-company production networks' through relational contracting rather than market exchange. But instead of using a transactions cost analysis he proposes a 'strategic game' approach in which the outcomes are recognized as the results of 'the distribution of strategic opportunities between the parties involved' (1991, 110). Cooke and Morgan (1986) also emphasize the 'networking' aspects of large firms' organizational strategies. Despite the considerable interest in the role of inter-firm relations in competitive structures, until the mid 1990s there was little attempt to use these concepts to analyse the involvement of retail firms in strategic alliances, relational sub-contracting, or in a 'networked strategic game', and to consider the significance of cross-sectoral flexible networks in economic change. Furthermore, in most of the mainstream literature on economic change the potential role of retailers in initiating change in manufacturers' products and processes through relational contracting has been ignored.

Flexible workforce

A core element in the debate on economic change has been the reorganization of labour to achieve increased flexibility in production (S Wood, 1989). In particular, the requirements of new information technology, computer aided manufacturing or 'flexible manufacturing systems' (R Walker, 1988) have led to innovative forms of workforce planning.

The adoption of three main 'flexible labour strategies' has been discussed. These comprise strategies to enable *numerical flexibility* in workforce size; *functional flexibility* in the jobs performed by individuals; and *flexible labour practices* through the introduction of individual negotiation and performance-related reward (Morgan and Sayer, 1988). The ability to initiate change was originally strongly linked to the application of new technology (Atkinson, 1984). However, J L Morris (1988) argues that flexible labour practices are as important as the introduction of new technology in the achievement of labour flexibility. Indeed he argues that flexible labour is often independent of technical innovation. These ideas have been applied to employment in retailing (Sparks, 1987) but relatively little attention has been given to the influence of retailer–supplier relations on employment in manufacturing or wholesaling. However, Rajan (1987) has shown how shifts in the division of labour between different sectors of the economy has affected employment in services. In particular, he shows how changes in retailer–supplier relations has resulted in the decline of national employment in wholesaling and distribution.

Changing geography of industrial spaces

Tickell and Peck (1992) identify the central contradiction in current research on the geography of 'flexible accumulation' between the emergence of ' "relatively localized" new industrial spaces' and 'a deepening of global social and spatial divisions of labour' (1992: 198). On the one hand new localized industrial spaces are held to be emerging based on the agglomeration of disintegrated propulsive or leading edge industries (hi-tech; office and business services; craft/design based industries) (Piore and Sable, 1984; Scott, 1988a; Storper and Scott, 1986; R Walker, 1988). In these 'new industrial spaces' producers are claimed to be held together by shared interests in local flexible labour markets, and spatial proximity of subcontractors, suppliers and markets (Scott, 1988a).

Peck and Ticknell (1991) argue that vertical disintegration and the incorporation of flexibility strategies do not *necessarily* create the re-emergence of localized industrial areas. Sub-contracting, they argue, can and does survive over long distance because the inter-firm relationship is long-term and can tolerate distance. Amin and Malmberg (1992) also are critical of claims for the universal emergence of new regional economies based on flexible production strategies and the minimization of transport and transactions costs. Rather, they suggest, contemporary economic restructuring in Europe is part of a global extension of both old and new forms of production organization.

This literature, in conjunction with existing work on retail–supplier relations, suggests that retailer–supplier relations could play a part in creating or re-shaping industrial spaces. Indeed Totterdill (1990) has suggested specifically that encouragement of links between 'flexibly-specialized' retailers and local manufacturers should play a significant role in new local economic development strategies.

Retailing in the economy

We have suggested above that in the main body of geographical work on the changing economy little attention has been paid to the role of retailing within economic change. However, as this book makes clear, in the 1990s a new body of work on retailing has been developed which tries to set developments in retailing in the context of theories of broader economic change. We now turn, therefore, to consider some of this work. In a seminal paper Ducatel and Blomley (1990) argue that retail capital can be analysed most fruitfully as one element in the circulation of capital. They emphasize that while retailing is linked to both production and consumption it has a specific function – to realize the surplus value in commodities produced by manufacturers for consumption by the final consumer. As they put it, 'retail capital is that part of total social capital which is located between productive capital and the final consumer . . . the distinctive function of retail capital, within the wider circuit of capital, is the final exchange of commodities' (Ducatel and Blomley, 1990: 213). They also point out that a Marxist analysis concludes that retail capital cannot create value, except in so far as the retailer is involved in the movement of goods to the point of consumption and is therefore creating value through transportation (1990: 211). So, at a given moment, while retailer and manufacturer are each necessary to the other they are also competing with one another to retain as large a share of a fixed quantity of surplus value as possible. Each therefore wishes the other to bear the *costs* of realizing surplus value while retaining the lion's share of *revenue* for themselves. Thus 'while retail capital and productive capital are dependent on one another for their existence, the point of contact between these forms will be a potentially abrasive one in which retail capital will be inevitably implicated' (1990: 214). It also follows from Ducatel and Blomley's presentation of retailing as one element in the process by which the circulation of capital is achieved that changes in the retail–supply relationship are likely to have implications both for production and consumption. The act of shopping is simultaneously social and economic. Consumers purchase goods which have not only practical utility but also complex cultural meanings. Consumers' purchases are often said to send information to producers about the goods that consumers 'want' but it is important to realize that consumers select from goods presented to them by retailers. Retailers are most frequently the direct purchasers from manufacturers. Retailers thus 'mediate' between consumers and producers – but they are not neutral mediators since their selection of goods and the terms on which they buy them are shaped by the need to make a profit for themselves. Retailers therefore not only respond to but also structure consumers' desires and choice and, through their negotiations with producers, they impact not only upon what is produced but also on how it is produced. In this chapter we focus on the second set of relationships but it is important to emphasize that retailers' negotiations with manufacturers have important implications for their relationships with consumers and are strongly influenced by retailers' need to attract consumers' spending.

Research in the late 1980s and 1990s has critically examined the 'potentially abrasive' contacts between manufacturers and retailers. This work suggests that the potential conflict at the interface is mediated by a complex and increasingly long-term set of relations negotiated by individual firms through strategies and counter-strategies. This research also suggests that the changes in retailer–supplier relations in Britain during the 1990s have been shifting manufacturers towards 'flexible' forms of production and of labour organization. Retailer–supplier relations are also shown to be increasingly important in structuring manufacturers' access to consumer markets. We now move on to consider the findings of this research in more detail.

The changing place of retail–supply

During the post Second World War period in Britain, the relationships between retailers and suppliers have undergone significant change. During the 1970s and, especially during the 1980s, retail capital has become increasingly concentrated (Akehurst, 1983; Dawson and Shaw, 1989; Wrigley, 1987). This has enabled large retailers to sidestep wholesalers: for most goods they now purchase directly from manufacturers. Large retailers also have gained greater control over the physical process of distributing goods. These developments have allowed retailers to improve the speed and timeliness of goods delivery, thus reducing their costs of stock-holding and speeding up the circulation of capital (Wrigley, 1987). Although retailers have moved to gain control of distribution from wholesalers they have transferred the risk of heavy capital investment to specialist distribution firms. The distribution systems of large retailers now incorporate a network of composite warehouses, a fleet of delivery vehicles and a specialized computerized logistics operation. In most cases large retailers have now sub-contracted the building and operation of their distribution centres and road transport to specialized distribution firms although the computerized system which monitors sales and stocks remains under the control of the retailer (D L G Smith and Sparks, 1992).

In addition to the increasing concentration of ownership in the retail sector (particularly within food retailing), retailers' dominance has been further enhanced by their strategy of increasing own-label sales (K Davies *et al*, 1986; Dawson and Shaw, 1989; Grant, 1987; MINTEL, 1985/6; OFT, 1985). The result has been that a few major retailers now control a large part of the market for many products. This puts them in a potentially powerful position in their contacts with manufacturers. Manufacturers are increasingly *dependent* on retailers in the sense that retailers control access to what is for many manufacturers the only or the principal route to their major market (Emerson, 1962).

Structure and governance of retailer–manufacturer relationships

Relational contracting

Several researchers have examined the changes taking place in the retail–supply chain (S R Bowlby *et al*, 1992; Crewe and Davenport, 1992; Dawson *et al*, 1989; Doel, 1991; Chapter 3, this volume; Foord *et al*, 1992; Gibbs, 1987; 1991; Totterdill, 1990). From this varied empirical research it appears that, by the 1980s, the dominant form of retail–supplier relationship in Britain was based on a system of 'relational contracting' (Hodgson, 1988). It should, however, be noted that relational contracting is by no means an entirely new form of retailer–supplier relationship. This form of contract between large retailers and their suppliers has been in existence for many years. What is new is its increasing dominance across the retail sector; the form in which it is negotiated; and the implications of contemporary relational contracting for the division of the costs and revenues of realizing surplus value between retailer and manufacturer.

In 1986 Dawson, Shaw and Harris (1989) conducted a survey of 42 retailers and 60 manufacturers in the four product areas of fish processing, meat processing, sports and leisure clothing and house furnishings. They also did in-depth interviews with 12 major retailers, 11 manufacturers and 10 trade associations and sector analysts. They found 'there are many examples of retailers and suppliers entering into long term arrangements to do business with each other, and both parties investing heavily in the development of the relationship' (Dawson *et al*, 1989: 62). In our own research on bread and hosiery we also found that relational contracting dominated the form of interaction between all the major retailers and their suppliers. In the majority of cases the characteristic form of governance in the retail–supply relationship was *interactive*. Table 4.1 illustrates the characteristics of *relational contracting* in the case of bread. These characteristics set the boundaries within which negotiations over the allocation of costs and appropriation of revenues are carried out. Bread is interesting because its short shelf-life and perishable nature has meant that it is a difficult product to integrate into retailers' new ordering and delivery systems. However, even bread is now being absorbed into the new centralized ordering mechanisms. The case of bread can be used along with other work to summarize a number of features common to the new forms of retailer–supplier relationship.

First, *day-to-day management of contracts and product negotiations* are largely centralized. The perishable nature of bread has helped to maintain store-level ordering in most retail outlets of major chains. However, even for this product there are now moves to centralize daily ordering. For most products all orders for fresh supplies are placed by retail headquarters. For own-label products retailers check on the quality of the merchandise and the production process both through occasional (and unannounced) factory visits and, sometimes, through inspecting samples of the product in their own quality control departments.

Second, the *application of compatible IT* is critical to the evolving structure of retailer–manufacturer interaction. In the bread supply chain couriers are still used in localized areas to deliver orders to manufacturers and telephone ordering is commonplace. However, automation of this process is increasing and is dominant in most other products. Thus, retailers and suppliers are increasingly linked through compatible systems. Compatible automation increases centralized control, speed and accuracy through rapid communication of sales and

Table 4.1 Typical features of the mode of governance of retailer–manufacturer relationships for bread

Formal contracts?	Rare
Written specifications for bread recipe and packaging?	Yes
Items agreed in negotiations	Price Recipe Quality standards Hygiene Time between production and delivery Approved suppliers for manufacturer to use (only some retailers)
Frequency of product negotiations	Once or twice per year
Location of product negotiations Frequency of contacts for managing the contract	Retailer headquarters Max 1/day for quantity ordering; 1/week telephone contact between retail buyer and manufacturer; occasional factory visits
Time between order and delivery	12 to 24 hours
Orders placed BY and TO	BY Retail HQ; Stores (sometimes); TO Manufacturer HQ; individual plants (sometimes)
Methods of communication	Ordering: telephone or computer link; Retail buyer and manufacturer: telephone or meeting at retail HQ
Services from manufacturer	Quality assurance checks; Advice on production; Marketing information; Sales information/analysis; Contacting complainants (only for some retailers); Underwrite promotions; Advertising (branded goods)
Services from retailer	Design own-brand packaging; Advice on reducing costs; Advice on meeting hygiene regulations; Help negotiating with packaging and raw materials suppliers
Manufacturer sanctions	Withdrawal of business
Retailer sanctions	Withdrawal of business

stock information from retail outlets to the retail headquarters where orders to manufacturers for new production or 'call off' of existing stock are generated.

Third, *delivery* of products from manufacturer to retailers' warehouse is undertaken by both manufacturers and by third party specialist hauliers. However, specialist hauliers now dominate the final distribution of goods to individual stores. Delivery dates are specified and tightly monitored. Delivery windows at the warehouse or individual store are narrow and threats of sanctions are made by retailers to manufacturers if these are not observed. Delivery of bread is now unusual in that in almost all cases it is still made direct from manufacturer to the individual store. However, most retailers are trying to integrate bread into their own regionalized warehousing systems. We can see taking place now in the bread product area changes which occurred earlier for other products. In the past it was normal for delivery to be organized by the manufacturer. Manufacturers therefore employed salespeople to visit and sell to individual stores and drivers to deliver goods. As in the case of bread, the drivers might also be the salespeople, expected not only to deliver but also to sell the goods and to search out new potential buyers. Often such driver-salespeople would and might merchandise for the shop that they supplied. The job was therefore skilled and responsible and drivers could often earn commission through their sales activities. Many of these activities are now being moved up the retail chain. The function of selling is now carried out by the manufacturers' headquarters, delivery driving is now becoming part of the distribution sector and organized by the specialist hauliers and merchandising is increasingly being taken over by the retailer.

Fourth, *product development and specification/price* are agreed through negotiation between retailer and manufacturer headquarters. These negotiations may be short in the case of a standardized product with which the manufacturer and retailer are both familiar, for example branded baked beans. In the development of a new 'value added' retailer-brand product, the manufacturer may become involved in market research, extensive product testing, evaluation and trialling. In our research on bread we were told of examples of products which manufacturers had developed as a response to demands made by and in some type of 'partnership' with specific retailers. These could take up to two years to reach the shops.

Fifth, *establishing and maintaining the trading relationship* between individual firms requires investment of time and personnel. In our research on both hosiery and bread we found that this investment on the retail side was made through buying and merchandising teams often under the management of a senior director. Manufacturing firms often had created new posts for contract managers and/or for personnel with specific responsibility for individual retail customers. Retailers' desire to establish long-term 'partnerships' with groups of suppliers derives from the need for repeated purchase of reasonably large quantities of the same product; the need for consistency and reliability in terms of product specifications and delivery; and access to new product/process ideas and innovations. Search for new products and processes does initiate the search for new suppliers but developing these with a known and reliable supplier is less risky than total reliance on a new firm. In order to reduce the risks of over-reliance on a single partner, retailers prefer multiple sourcing for specific products and manufacturers prefer a broad customer base (Dawson *et al*, 1989).

Finally, *the location of a supplier* can be competitively important. For bread its short shelf-life and the geographical reach from a production site are factors influencing a retailer's contract. Ability to supply all the outlets of a national chain is also an important factor as retailers are increasingly trying to standardize the merchandise offered throughout the country. In our research on hosiery we found that there was a growing demand for value added products and for increased variety and quality within the volume commodity range during the 1980s. This initiated a search for new suppliers since the British manufacturers then being used by the majority of multiple retailers could not make products of the required quality. The new products were thus bought from European suppliers who were able to manufacture to the required standard. In this case distance did not hinder sourcing, but it did interrupt effective 'networking'. Custom and practice, language compatibility, familiarity with personnel in the British industry, easier control over delivery practices, loyalty of manufacturers to a particular retailer – all produced a preference for relationships with British suppliers. Once British suppliers were able to reorganize their production to supply higher quality hosiery through investment in new machinery, retailers returned to a high proportion of British sourcing for hosiery.

The close relationships developed through relational contracting both *create* and *structure* the supply market in a reflexive manner. For example, Doel (this volume, Chapter 3) suggests, in a discussion of the British food industry, that product and process innovation is interwoven with grocery retailers' creation of new supply relationships in the case of cook-chill foods (see also Doel, 1991). Here there were no pre-existing suppliers or market since it was a new product and the retailers had to create a system of supply relations. She argues therefore that supply relations should not be taken as a given: they are actively created by the firms involved. This point has general relevance to any supply situation, not just the retail–supply case.

Structure

Long-term relational contracting involves costs as well as benefits. Maintaining and servicing the relationships can be costly in time of skilled personnel and it may also involve some specific capital investment. Thus there are pressures to minimize the number of such relationships for both retailers and manufacturers. However, both retailers and manufacturers also try to maintain some choice of partners in order to avoid becoming too dependent on one another. Among the retailers we interviewed all preferred to have a choice of suppliers for their standardized products whether these were retailer own-label or manufacturer brands. Thus the same retail own-label product was often made by several manufacturers. For specialist goods retailers often were obliged to rely on a single producer. Manufacturers of standardized products supplied several retailers and manufacturers of specialized products also aimed to sell to more than one retailer – although the product sold to each one would often be slightly different. Since retailers wish own-label products to be distinctive and manufacturers want to minimize changes to manufacturing processes and labour deployment, manufacturers of own-label products have a delicate balance to maintain between differentiating the product and using similar techniques to manufacture for different purchasers and for their own branded goods.

In hosiery, for example, there was a difference in the number of suppliers used or retailers served depending on the nature of the goods being supplied. For basic standardized hosiery, sold at low prices, most retailers used six to eight suppliers whereas for more expensive value-added, standardized hosiery they used three or four suppliers. Manufacturers of basic standardized hosiery had ten to fifteen retail customers while for higher quality, standardized hosiery eight to ten retail customers was the norm. For high-value speciality hosiery, produced in very small runs, intensive relational contracting did not exist. Manufacturers served a range of retailers, the number limited only by the firm's production capacity and distribution network. Retailers were offered a choice from an existing range of products (changed annually and offered at pre-set prices). Retailers who sold such merchandise would use five to eight suppliers of such specialist hosiery, including overseas suppliers.

Our research on the bread product area showed that almost all the multiples used both of the two major plant bakers who dominate the production of bread. Multiple retailers selling to the lower end of the income scale tended to have fewer main suppliers than those with a more up-market clientele – reflecting the greater range and variety of products offered by the latter. For basic standardized bread most retailers had the major part of their turnover supplied by two to three manufacturers, two of these being the two majors. However, most also purchased the basic product in smaller quantities from independents in particular regions so that they might have a total of seven or more suppliers of standardized plant bread. For more specialized products the major multiples used between twelve and thirty small suppliers, who often supplied only those stores within a day's delivery range of the factory.

Clearly, the two major plant bakers supplied virtually all the multiples as well as major wholesalers with cheap, standardized bread. Other bakers supplying the multiples with plant bread are likely to supply three to five multiples as well as, where appropriate, their own retail outlets and major wholesalers' local depots. Manufacturers of more specialized breads are likely to supply four or five major retail customers as well as other more specialist outlets – ranging from their own retail outlets to up-market grocers and delicatessens and the catering trade.

Retailer and manufacturer strategies and power

Retailers are clearly in a powerful position in relation to their manufacturing suppliers. In this section we examine evidence about the extent of that power and the ways in which retailers have tried to exercise it.

The relative power of retailers and manufacturers in the supplier relationship is demonstrated in the form and process of contracting. In our research we found that the *written /unwritten terms of the contract* for retailers' own-label usually only specify a general intent to trade. This outlines in principle the annual/half-yearly quantities which a retailer may 'call off'. It broadly establishes a supplier's capacity and a retailer's market size. Importantly, it does not bind a retailer to the purchase of the stated amount yet, if required, a manufacturer must be able to produce this quantity. Written agreement on the process of calling-off is made only if specified technology is required. Unwritten agreements emerge through custom and practice based on the degree of familiarity between parties. Delivery windows, forms and destinations are largely dictated by the requirements of the retailer. Product specification and quality testing are negotiated and documented separately. Here some manufacturers are able to exert more control based on their superior product knowledge and production expertise. One major retailer has a compulsory Code of Conduct setting out the general standards of service and maintenance of product quality expected from all their suppliers, regardless of product. They also specify their preferred suppliers of general services such as printing and transportation.

Retailer–supplier relationships for manufacturer brands are different: there is no contract for production. There is agreement on the terms of sale, including price and discounts, size of order, and whether or not goods are supplied on a 'sale or return' basis.

The ultimate *penalty option* open to each party is the withdrawal of business. This becomes a significant factor if the retailer is particularly dependent on the supplier to supply speciality/quality/unique products (own-label or manufacturer's brand) or a supplier is overly dependent on one retailer for business. Thus, as mentioned in the previous section, the availability of *alternative* suppliers or markets becomes important to the negotiating power of both parties. Both retailers and suppliers aim to spread risk by widening their business portfolios. Prior to the withdrawal of business both retailers and manufacturers may impose minor penalties such as fines or loss of discounts.

In an increasingly competitive market the ability to provide or demand *additional services* from retailer or supplier has become part of the power play. The power of retailers is evidenced by the current trends for major retailers to demand, successfully, increased services from the manufacturers: product forecasting and design; customer trends and market analysis; technical expertise; computing services; and quality assurance. This represents a transfer of costs from retailer to manufacturer. Ability to provide such services is dependent on a supplier's capacity and/or its call on service firms from within an owning corporation. Major manufacturers of branded goods do also demand additional services from retailers including provision of promotional space, priority display and shop-floor marketing. Some costs revert to the manufacturer if 'sales consultants' for individual brands are employed.

During the 1970s two new 'models' of retailer–manufacturer relations were used by the big multiples – the 'arm's-length model' often associated with C & A and the 'marionette' model sometimes associated with Marks & Spencer. In the first, retailers specified precise price and other requirements but did not specify or monitor the methods that manufacturers used to meet those requirements. In the second, retailers specified the production methods and even the suppliers that a manufacturer should use and became involved in monitoring production methods and product quality. It was the second of these models that was most popular with the multiples by the early 1980s. Thus, using empirical evidence, taken once again from the clothing sector, Rainnie (1984) portrays an unequal power relationship between the major retailers and small clothing firms characterized by high levels of retailer intervention and control over production. Retailers were able to play a major role in determining the product itself and were in a good position to insist on low prices for the goods they purchased. However, this control involved considerable cost to retailers in monitoring production and quality. Crewe and Davenport (1992) re-examined clothing supply relationships in the late 1980s and they suggest that the pattern has now shifted to one of so-called *co-operative partnerships*. Here the retailer still holds the whip hand but works with 'preferred' suppliers to select designs and monitor quality. The contractual and long-term nature of the relationship has allowed retailers to relax their levels of intervention. It can be argued that this structure lowers retailers' costs of designing, developing and testing products by transferring these costs to the manufacturer without decreasing the retailers' revenue on each garment and still allows retailers to retain significant control of the product. However, it would seem that preferred suppliers attempt to counter retailers' transfer of costs through sub-contracting some elements of production. Sub-contracting is a central production strategy of the preferred supplier. Crewe and Davenport (1992) show how this gives rise to a hierarchical pyramid of production incorporating new spatial divisions of labour with sub-contracted employment located in low labour cost regions of Europe and the Third World. Our own findings on the contracting process also indicate a shift in sectors other than clothing towards the 'partnership' model. Thus the major multiples have been reducing the costs of exerting control over manufacturers by gaining further services from them while still retaining considerable control over the manufacturer's product.

B Belussi (1987) illustrates a very different model of retail–supply contact in a study of Benetton. This one originates in Italy and is constructed through *flexibly networked* relationships; it hinges on a close web of sub-contracted suppliers and franchised retailers. This model emerged from the manufacturing side but it is critically dependent on both a reliable group of sub-contracted suppliers and an expanding, tightly controlled, international franchised retail sector. The balance between manufacturer and franchised retailer is very different from the supply relations which dominate British retail–supply relations. The implications for the 'potentially abrasive' negotiations over surplus value in this model are located in the retail franchise-contract.

Clearly there are different possible forms of retailer–supplier relationship. Differences may stem from features of the particular product being supplied, from the characteristics of both the retailer and the manufacturer and from the regulatory regime within which the firms are operating (see Marsden and Wrigley, this volume, Chapter 2). It is also evident that, in Britain, these relationships have been changing both within the clothing sector and within the food sector. Furthermore the existing evidence shows that change in the retail–supply chain has had important consequences for the organization of production. This change has also been significant for consumption since it is through these relationships that the choice of goods available to the public is formed.

Various *strategies* are open to either retailers or manufacturers. For manufacturers, specializing in a unique and/or high-quality product can provide significant bargaining power and maintain independent status. Individual retailers and manufacturers can adopt co-operative strategies to innovate products, processes and distribution as a competitive tool.

The strategies available are likely to be affected by the size of the firms involved. Dawson, Shaw and Harris (1989) looked at the barriers faced by small Scottish local producers/manufacturers which result from the dominance of relational contracting between a limited number of major retailers and selected suppliers. They show how existing suppliers are selected on the basis of their known capabilities and capacities. As explained above, major retailers also seek to establish and maintain only enough contractual relationships to give themselves alternatives, but not so many that they become difficult to manage. The relational contracting structure can easily exclude small suppliers without the capacity to supply the whole retail chain. Thus, small suppliers must either lose some of their potential revenue to wholesalers or must incur the costs of expanding production and investing in marketing themselves in the hope (but by no means the certainty) of gaining access to the market of the multiples.

In the case of our research on bread and hosiery the increasing dominance of the own-label contract market in Britain and the size and limited number of British retailers selling own-label bread and hosiery creates general retail dominance in the supply relationship. But the relative strength of either a retailer or supplier in specific bargaining situations is significantly modified by the characteristics of the product and of the individual firms. Retailers are not always the most powerful. Nor is the larger manufacturing supplier necessarily in the best position to challenge retail power. Table 4.2 summarizes the characteristics of products and firms which alter the bargaining strength of retailers and suppliers giving examples drawn from our research on bread and hosiery. Figure 4.1 illustrates manufacturer characteristics which can offer a challenge to retail dominance.

Table 4.2 Characteristics of producers and firms influencing the bargaining power of retailers and suppliers

Characteristics	Example
Characteristics of the producing area	
1 Overall size and change in UK market	Falling bread consumption limits bargaining power of major plant bakeries
2 Size and location of alternative market segments	Up-market catering demand in London offers small bakers alternatives to multiples
3 Commodity or value-added product	Technical and product expertise in production of high quality hosiery gives specialist hosiery firms bargaining power
4 Production process(es)	Technical inability to manufacture high quality hosiery limited British producers' bargaining power in mid-1980s
Characteristics of the manufacturing supplier	
1 Relative size and position of supplying firm within its sector	Two largest hosiery firms, through ads and product presence, play major role in determining relative importance of hosiery in retailers' product mix
2 Size of product area in supplying firms' range	Some hosiery firms increased bargaining power by diversifying into lingerie and decreasing dependence on hosiery contracts
3 Sectoral organization and concentration surrounding supplying firm	Competition between two major plant bakers weakened bakers' bargaining power with retailers
4 Ownership of supplying firm	The corporate power of ABF and RHM allows Allied and British Bakeries favourable access to research and material suppliers
5 Balance of branded and own-label products in supplying firms' portfolios	Hosiery firms producing only retailer brands are in weaker bargaining position than those with strong manufacturer brand

6	Geographical location of supplying firm	Bakers who can supply all a retailer's stores have a stronger bargaining position than those who cannot

Characteristics of the retailer purchaser

1	Relative size and position of supplying firm within its own sector	Major grocery or variety multiples are in strong bargaining position for bread and hosiery respectively because of large market share
2	Total size of retailers' purchase of product	Retailers who purchase large quantities can demand lower prices from plant bread and hosiery manufacturers
3	Size and significance of product area in retailers' portfolio	Because hosiery is more significant product to variety and department stores than to grocery multiples, they take a more interventionist stance with manufacturers
4	Balance of branded and own-label products in retail firm's purchasing portfolio	Growth of sale of own-label products has increased retailers' bargaining power with producers of manufacturer brands

Clearly many of the strategies that manufacturers can adopt will involve making changes to their production processes both in order to meet the changing demands of the retailers and to try to (re)gain a larger share of surplus value. Gibbs (1987; 1991) examines the role of new technology in increasing clothing manufacturers' production responsiveness to changes in retailers' contractual demands. He shows how such demand-led change has altered the organization of production to incorporate flexible manufacturing systems and flexible labour practices. It would appear that by reducing their operational costs through capital investment certain manufacturers retain their position in contractual relationships. In our study we found that significant changes in production methods had been made in both hosiery and bread manufacturing in order to adapt to changing demands from the retailers. In the bread product area the main plant bakers were dependent on high volume production in order to gain economies of scale. During the 1970s this dependence resulted in retailers successfully bargaining with the manufacturers for lower and lower prices. This cost pressure, combined with the falling consumption of bread and the increased market share of specialist bakers during the 1980s, has resulted in extensive rationalization of production with plant closures and job losses.

Implications for the location of employment and for local economies

The changes in retailer–supplier relations involve or are involved in shifts in the spatial organization of economic activity. First, organizational centralization is reflected in spatial centralization. The move of negotiations between retailer and supplier to retailer headquarters and the growth of information processing by retailers concerning sales and products has resulted in a growth of activity at retailer headquarters. It has also resulted in declining autonomy at the store level: store managers have lost many of their decision-making functions to headquarters. A skilled headquarters workforce is required to buy products, to find or commission new ones, to maintain relationships with suppliers, to monitor markets and to organize the day-to-day and long-run stocking policies for different stores. The majority of retailers' headquarters are in the south-east of England and so the reorganization of retailers' purchasing has contributed to the growth of white collar, service employment in this region.

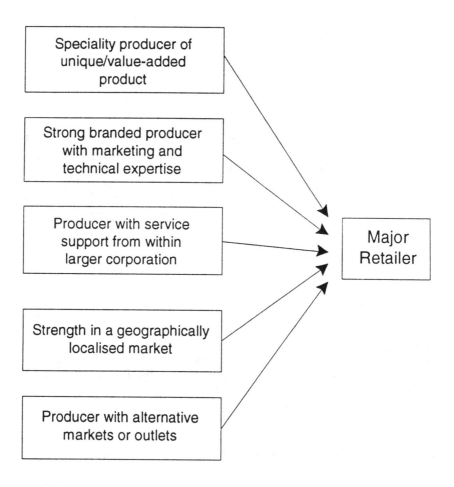

Figure 4.1 Supplier characteristics which allow a challenge to retail dominance

Second, there also has been a reorganization of selling and distribution activities at manufacturers' headquarters. Rather than these being geared to supplying a widely dispersed market of stores or wholesalers their selling activity is now focused on a few major retailers and their delivery operations are focused on the warehouses of these major retailers. The general pattern has been of a loss in employment of skilled and semi-skilled workers in manufacturing distribution. Among manufacturing headquarters staff there has been little change in the number of workers, but considerable change in the nature of the job done.

Third, the reorganization of the physical distribution of goods from manufacturer to retailer has resulted in the loss of many, widely dispersed jobs in small warehouses and wholesalers and the concentration of a smaller total workforce in fewer larger distribution centres (Rajan, 1987). Retailers must position their distribution centres to ensure efficient distribution to an existing or developing national network of their retail outlets. Figure 4.2 illustrates how this new geography of distribution is closely tied to strategic locations along the motorway network. McKinnon (1990) has estimated that such large distribution centres can have a considerable local multiplier effect and provide a range of semi-skilled and skilled jobs.

Finally, the changes in retailers' demands on manufacturers can create major shifts in manufacturing employment. Clearly, changes in the sourcing policies of large retailers can result in locally significant job losses or job gains. However, perhaps more importantly, the pressures for change in production processes created by retailers' demands for speed of response to orders and increases in quality or variety can also bring about changes in manufacturing employment. Often this change results from innovation in the technology used in production as well as in more flexible deployment of staff. Gibbs' (1987) work on the clothing industry, referred to above, and our own work on bread and hosiery demonstrate this process. Our interviews suggested that, in these industries at least, the impetus for change had come from retailer pressure rather than manufacturers' proactive innovation.

Conclusions

Relational contracting between retailer and manufacturer has been the dominant form throughout the 1980s and developed as such during the 1970s along with the growth of concentration of ownership in retailing (although such relations between a few retailers and manufacturers have existed since the turn of the century at least). A number of researchers have shown that it is a relationship in which retailers have become dominant and their data and ours confirm that for many products the contractual relationship is both intensive and centralized, in that negotiations are carried out between specialized staff at the headquarters of the retailer and manufacturer. The detailed organization of contacts between retailer and supplier and the existence of

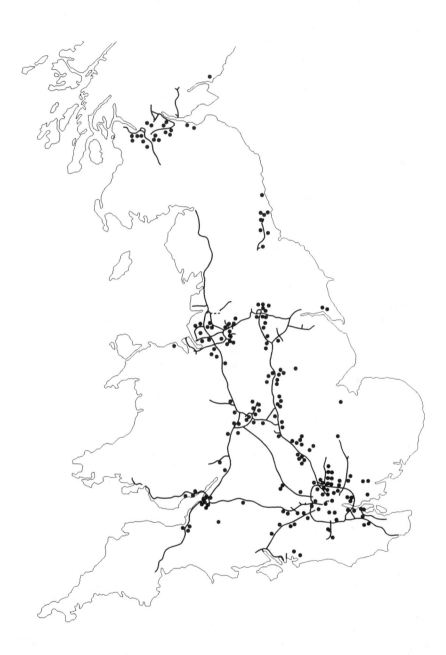

Figure 4.2 Distribution of fifty multiple retailers' central warehouses relative to the motorway network (*Source*: McKinnon, 1990)

sub-contracting relationships between 'preferred' suppliers and other manufacturers depends upon the nature of the production process, characteristics of the product and the process of consumption itself.

The research reviewed here suggests that during the 1980s the form and content of manufacturer–supplier relations altered. The changing consumption climate and competitive pressures on retailers during the late 1970s and early 1980s, allied with changes in technology, led them to give increased attention to managing the retailer–supplier chain. One element of this was the development of improved stock handling and distribution procedures that allowed retailers to transfer much of the cost and risk of stock-holding on to manufacturers. Another element was the increased retailer input into product innovation, product design and specification of the manufacturing process which was part and parcel of the growth of own-label products.

Although these developments appeared highly successful, retailers' involvement in product specification, quality monitoring and market identification involved increased costs. We suggest that the shift towards less interventionist retailer–supplier 'partnerships' that was evident by the late 1980s represents an attempt by retailers to shift some of these costs back on to manufacturers. Thus, as explained earlier, retailers demanded that manufacturers take a more active part in product development, market identification and quality control.

It is evidence of the power of retailers that they appear to have been successful in imposing these extra costs on manufacturers without any significant loss to themselves. However, it is yet to be seen whether such moves will prove entirely satisfactory to retailers – for example, not all manufacturers will be able to sustain these costs or be able to fulfil the new demands adequately. Manufacturer strategies of passing costs back to sub-contractors are not feasible in all product areas and where they are feasible may generate other problems of quality and timeliness of supply.

The recession of the early 1990s intensified pressure upon both manufacturers and retailers to cut costs and gain markets. Retailers still need to target consumers effectively, indeed this pressure is even stronger in a recession. Manufacturers need to retain not only their market but also a larger share of the revenue generated through sales. Thus, retailer– supplier relations will remain a highly significant battleground. Retailers will wish to offload more costs and risks on to manufacturers. The opportunity for manufacturers to pass these cost on down a sub-contracting chain is not available for all products. One strategy for manufacturers facing this problem is to seek to increase the sales of their own manufacturer brands to retailers. There is some evidence that this is occurring in both bread and hosiery. It is a strategy that is likely to prove successful with those retailers for whom the products in question have never been marketed as very high quality or as significant retailer brands. A number of our respondents commented that retailers would not increase the proportion of retailer-brand bread or hosiery products further and, indeed, that they were likely to reduce it slightly. These respondents suggested that this was because retailers would not gain further significant power over manufacturers or increased attraction to consumers by further growth of retailer-brand products. We would add that a further incentive to stabilize or slightly reduce retailer-brand products is the cost of specifying and monitoring their production.

The nature of the retailer–supplier relationship is of importance to the geography of industrial activity and employment. This is the case, first, because the actions of retailers can induce changes in manufacturing processes with implications for the numbers employed and the deskilling and reskilling of the workforce in those industries. Second, it is the case because employment throughout the retailer–supplier chain is shifting in both location and type. While the specific implications will vary with each product and the initial organization and geography of production, some general trends are suggested by current research. Pressures to speed up response to retailers' orders and to reduce costs but improve quality, if met successfully, tend to lead to investment in new machinery and organizational change in production involving the loss of some skilled manual jobs. Skilled and semi-skilled jobs in warehousing, distribution, and headquarters clerical work are created in new locations. There is an expansion in skilled white collar and professional jobs in headquarters locations with the largest expansion taking place in retail headquarters in the south-east of England. However, as the experience of the recession has shown, some of this latter expansion has been temporary and we suggest that it is unlikely to grow to its former size in a future upturn.

Our findings also suggest that while the exigencies of relational contracting give a small advantage to British suppliers when seeking contracts with British retailers, these retailers are happy to extend their supply chains overseas if by doing so they can find successful products. Although in the case of a highly perishable and staple commodity, such as bread, the spatial configuration of manufacturing plants and transport to retail stores or warehouses is highly significant, the location of production is, in general, only a minor element in retailers' decision to use a particular supplier. Given the existence of efficient transport and communication technology, the quality of the relationship and manufacturers' skills in negotiating with retailers are far more significant.

The move to relational contracting in retailer–supplier relations clearly parallels developments in manufacturing supply. In both it facilitates flexibility in meeting changes in demand and a reduction in the risk faced by the dominant partner in the relationship. However, it is important to emphasize that achieving such flexibility and risk reduction also involves costs and the creation of some inflexibilities – for example, the risk of excluding small firms with 'good' products. Where large and powerful firms are engaged in negotiating such relationships it is vital to any understanding of the outcome to analyse the basis of their power, their aims, the costs they incur and the benefits they achieve.

We have shown that the changes in production strategies adopted by the manufacturers of consumer goods in Britain cannot be properly understood without analysis of the aims and actions of retailers. More generally this implies that more attention needs to be paid to the processes through which production and consumption are linked. Thus, finally, we join other commentators in urging that more research effort be devoted to investigating the geography of the retail industry. Retailing is an integral element in the linkage of production and consumption and has played and will play an important part in structuring changes in both those spheres.

CHAPTER 5

Forging new cultures of food retailer–manufacturer relations?

Alexandra Hughes

One of the key features of retail restructuring in the food industry has been the emergence of new forms of retailer–manufacturer relations. In economic terms, such relations in advanced capitalist economies are types of vertical inter-firm organization which exist between two interdependent functions of capital. The character of these food retailer–manufacturer relations in the UK has been documented in various ways by both economic geographers and business economists, largely with respect to an imbalance in power relations which tends to favour the retailers and which appears to be associated with the execution of retailer power and innovation within the supply relationships, particularly those concerning retailers' own-label products (Doel, this volume, Chapter 3; Foord *et al*, 1992; this volume, Chapter 4; Grant, 1987; Senker, 1989). In contrast to the UK, as this chapter will show, the qualitative character of retailer–manufacturer relations in the US food industry, centring around both manufacturers' brands and retailers' own-labels, appears to be less retailer-led and to be organized in different ways. This appears to reflect a balance of power relations which has not yet moved towards the retailers to the extent that it has in the UK. Such differences between the food retailer–manufacturer relations in the UK and USA are complex, and the variances are at once politically, economically, socially and culturally constructed. The recognition that the 'social' and the 'cultural' are a fundamental part of the production of supply relationships is implicit within the work by economic geographers concerning UK retailer–manufacturer relations. Here the aim is to make such a recognition more explicit through a cross-country comparison of the 'cultures' of supply relationships in the UK and USA.

Central to an understanding of the role played by culture in producing new forms of food retailer–manufacturer relations is Gertler's (1995) view that 'industrial cultures – whether at the level of the workplace, the region, or the nation – are themselves produced and reproduced by social practices'. In addition, the critical theorization presented in this chapter uses Gertler's further proposition that 'workplace practices, attitudes and norms . . . do themselves *constitute* a distinctive industrial culture – but one which is actively shaped by macroregulatory context'. Gertler suggests that the range of literature which has tackled the issues surrounding business organization and inter-firm relations utilizes abstract, static notions of culture which are viewed as being inherited by firms, regions or nations rather than being continually reproduced through business relations. He then problematizes cultural aspects of business relationships through the suggestion that they are shaped by the macro-regulatory environment of the nation-states in which they operate. This chapter, then, uses these notions in the context of food retailer–manufacturer relations in the UK and USA. Gertler's ideas are further advanced through an appreciation of the relationship between retailer–manufacturer relations and the logic of capital. It is suggested that the nation-state plays a role in shaping the power relations between the retailers and manufacturers in both economies. These power relations condition the competitive logic used within the supply relationships which, in turn, affects the social practices and cultures of these relationships. In addition, though, it is recognized that these processes are not unidirectional, rather that they operate dialectically. This idea forms the crux of the argument in this chapter. However, to provide a theoretical background to these arguments, it is appropriate to introduce, first, the way in which this chapter concerning *retailer*–manufacturer relations fits into the wider debates concerning inter-firm organization, second, the general concept of the embeddedness of inter-firm relationships in social relations and the relationship of such embeddedness to notions of organizational culture, and third, the notion that food retailers and manufacturers are competing, as well as cooperating, functions of capital. To do this, the basic ideas of business strategy are discussed and placed within a political-economic perspective.

Situating food retailer–manufacturer relations within debates on inter-firm organization

The range of literature which has tackled the issues surrounding business organization and inter-firm relations is wide and spans the disciplines of economic geography, industrial economics, economic sociology and political science (Yeung, 1994). Many studies have focused on the adoption and execution of Japanese-style, trust-based forms of inter-firm organization, which Best (1990) argues characterize the 'new competition', while common industrial sectors to receive attention have been the automobile and high-technology industries (Florida and Kenney, 1990; 1991; 1992; Kenney and Florida, 1993; McMillan, 1990; J Morris and Imrie, 1992; Sayer, 1989; Turnbull *et al*, 1992). The economic geography literature, in particular, has addressed questions concerning modes of inter-firm organization associated with flexible specialization within industrial districts (see, for example, Scott,

1988a; Storper and Walker, 1989). Other economic geographers have argued that the process of centralization and the importance of the large corporation still remain fundamental elements of inter-firm organizational networks in the global economy (Amin and Robins, 1990; Florida and Kenney, 1991; Harvey, 1989c; Sayer, 1986). These examples from the literature all engage in analyses and theorization of inter-firm relationships, albeit with different empirical subjects, modes of inquiry, political slants and views of culture. In some sense, then, this chapter should contribute towards this body of literature, but what should become clear, as the text systematically deals with the capitalist processes surrounding the new forms of retailer–manufacturer relations, is the way in which the unique functioning of retail capital influences the business cultures of these particular relations.

The social embeddedness of food retailer–manufacturer relations and the role of organizational culture

Food retailer–manufacturer relationships are an important part of the wider competitive, strategic process that operates within the food production–consumption chain. In this respect, these relationships form a part of the retailers' and manufacturers' competitive strategies to accumulate capital. These competitive strategies, as Schoenberger (1994b) suggests, involve the role of human agency whereby individuals within companies are deeply involved in decision-making which ties in with the strategic aims of the companies, but which does not always follow what could be considered as being an economically 'rational' path of action. In this respect, the inter-firm relations are viewed as being embedded within social relations (as suggested by Block, 1990; Granovetter, 1985; T K Hopkins, 1957; Polanyi, 1944; 1957a; 1957b; Sayer and Walker, 1992; Zukin and Dimaggio, 1990).

This chapter considers the role of human agency in crafting the character of food retailer–manufacturer relations. However, it is recognized that individuals operating within the supply relationships do not have the autonomy to act according to their own personal needs and desires. Rather, they are operating collectively in accordance with shared values and beliefs which are created both within and between firms. It is therefore appropriate to conceptualize the organization of human agency within supply relationships in terms of the production of 'cultures'. As Van Maanen and Barley (1985) argue,

> the notion that organizations have cultures is an attractive heuristic proposition, especially when explanations derived from individual-based psychology or structural sociology prove limiting. Culture implies that human behaviour is partially prescribed by a collectively created and sustained way of life that cannot be personality based because it is shared by diverse individuals. . . . Culture points to an analysis mediating between

deterministic and volunteeristic models of behaviour in organizations. (Van Maanen and Barley, 1985: 31–2)

Such organizational culture is seen to develop both within firms (through the production of corporate culture) and between firms (through the development of inter-firm relationships). These two 'levels' of organizational culture are inextricably linked, though the former receives attention here only in so far as it influences the latter. 'Corporate identity' (Diefenbach, 1987) is fostered within a firm through a complex system of 'signs', including the company's brands, slogans, uniforms, building layout, strategic direction, stated corporate philosophy, etc, which are all arguably elements of a signification process (Barley, 1992) which constructs images and identities in the minds of employees. Directors, buyers, national account managers and technical staff therefore form their identities through interpretations of these 'signs'. These interpretations are transferred on to, and indeed reformulated through, the social organization of the inter-firm relationships at the level of the individual actors to form the cultures of supply relations.

As geographers begin to expand the concept of the 'economic' into the 'cultural', the focus of attention has tended to be placed upon the area of consumption. However, an equally important task remains in recognizing the role played by culture in the spheres of capitalist production and exchange. As such, the idea of organizational culture is critical to an understanding of the process of commodity exchange, which takes place within the social organization of supply relationships. To move away from the static notions of culture previously used in economic geography and towards a more dynamic view, as suggested by Gertler (1995), defies the articulation here of a rigid definition of culture. However, for the purposes of this chapter, certain ideas about what the incorporation of culture might mean within food retailer–manufacturer relations can be outlined. Organizational culture in these relations concerns the way in which particular aspects of commodity exchange are shaped by social practices which involve the conformity of individuals' behaviour to collective corporate and competitive identities. It is the way in which supply relationships are initiated, the forms of communication used by buyers and sellers, the use of meeting places, the tactics utilized in resolving conflict in relationships, the development of personal relationships between buyers and sellers and the organization of jointly developed business ideas. The list goes on. All of these aspects are, in part, socially constructed through action based upon business culture, which is continually reproduced through behaviour which relates to corporate and competitive identity. But in what fundamental way does the logic of capital influence the production of such collective, competitive identities which form the relationship cultures?

The competitive logic of food retailer–manufacturer relations

The arguments made throughout the chapter aim to construct a critical theorization of the emerging new cultures of retailer–manufacturer relations which looks more deeply into co-operative relationships in order to uncover the strands of adversarialism which result from the way in which the retailers and manufacturers are, at the same time, locked in mutual competition. Such co-operation and adversarialism are argued to coexist within the new forms of retailer–manufacturer relationships as a reflection of the underlying capitalist logic which fuels their economic, social and cultural dynamism. The relationship of food retailers and manufacturers to capitalist logic can, initially, best be understood using ideas from business strategy, particularly those of Porter (1980; 1985).

Porter views every industry as being situated within the perpetual motion of five broadly defined competitive forces, namely the threat of new entrants to the industry, the bargaining power of suppliers, the bargaining power of buyers, the threat from substitute products or services and rivalry among existing competitors. Following Porter's suggestions, corporate strategists should seek to 'find a position in the industry where the company can best defend itself against these competitive forces or can influence them in its favour' (Porter, 1980: 4). In this sense, 'customers, suppliers, substitutes and potential entrants are all "competitors" to firms in each industry' (1980: 6). Porter terms this 'extended rivalry'. From the standpoint of a political-economic approach, however, the situation is better viewed as being 'each form of

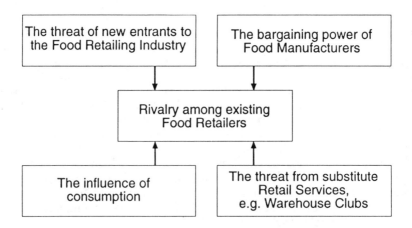

Figure 5.1   The competitive forces operating on food retailers (*Source*: adapted from Porter, 1980)

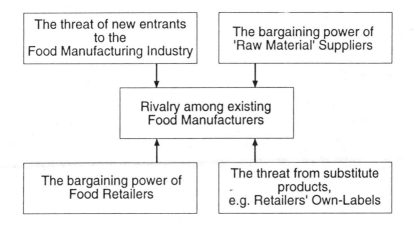

Figure 5.2 The competitive forces operating on food manufacturers (*Source*: adapted from Porter, 1980)

capital seek[ing], as part of its internal logic, to retain the largest share possible of the surplus value created in production' (Ducatel and Blomley, 1990: 214).

Figures 5.1 and 5.2 illustrate the application of the notion of competitive forces to the food retailing and food manufacturing industries respectively. What these ideas generally suggest is that, while it is in the interests and indeed a part of competitive logic for retailers and manufacturers to co-operate with each other in their relationships in order to achieve their aims, they are simultaneously using these relationships in order to compete both with each other and other fractions of capital in the race to extract surplus value. In this sense, the logic driving food retailers is different from that driving the food manufacturers. The dialectical relationship between these two logics is therefore mediated through the retailer–manufacturer relations. While food manufacturers are primarily a function of productive capital, food retailers aim to capitalize on their position as 'managers' of distribution and the final exchange of commodities by exercising some control over the relationship between production and consumption. This is not to argue, however, that retailing constitutes an analytically separate form of capital at a high level of abstraction, as argued by Ducatel and Blomley (1990). Rather, food retailing is seen to draw from the logic of commercial capital and, to some extent, productive capital. For example, two specific ways in which food retailers draw upon the logic of commercial capital concern their attempts to reduce costs in their operations of purchasing food commodities from manufacturers and in their drive to decrease the turnover time of these commodities (Ducatel and Blomley, 1990; Fine and Leopold, 1993b). Such strategies, which undoubtedly emanate from this capitalist logic, will inevitably cause adversarialism in supply relationships. Food retailers are also, in some cases, able to enter into the sphere of productive capital when they produce their own-labels, which adds a further dimension to their competitive logic. This is discussed in later sections.

This chapter proposes that power relations in an economy, which are influenced by state regulation, play a critical role in shaping the intersection of capital logic within retailing. It is argued that a lenient state enables retail capital to become concentrated within an economy. This in turn allows retail capital to assume a hegemonic position in relation to other fractions of capital, which further enables retailers to enter into other areas of the accumulation process (e.g. productive capital, through the development of own-labels). In this sense, then, power relations between food retailers and manufacturers, which are conditioned by their macro-regulatory context, determine the competitive logic used by food retailers. It will be shown that this logic moulds the competitive positioning of retailers and manufacturers, which in turn defines the strategies and cultures of the firms and hence the way in which they form relationships with one another. So, it is argued that competitive logic, developed in a macro-regulatory context, conditions the social practices which, returning to Gertler's argument, produce and reproduce industrial culture. It is against this theoretical backdrop that this chapter aims to examine critically the emerging cultures of food retailer–manufacturer relations in the geographical contexts of the UK and USA. The arguments are supported using empirical material taken from the author's interviews with food retailers, manufacturers, buying co-operatives, brokers and analysts in both the UK and USA.[1]

The role of restructuring, regulation and economic power in shaping the new cultures of food retailer–manufacturer relations

The new emerging cultures of food retailer–manufacturer relations can best be understood within the differing political-economic contexts of the UK and USA. These contexts are examined here in so far as they influence, and are influenced by, food retailer–manufacturer relations. Consideration is given to ways in which industrial restructuring, regulation and economic power shape the new cultures of retailer–manufacturer relations.

The UK

Consolidation in UK food retailing has dramatically increased since the 1970s (see Wrigley, 1987; 1988b), partly due to a favourable, *laissez-faire* regulatory environment in which mergers and acquisitions and oligopolistic practice in the sector have rarely been challenged by the state (Wrigley, 1992a). This has enabled some retailing companies to become big-capital organizations through processes of acquisition (e.g. Argyll), while others have grown organically (e.g. Sainsbury). While centralization, afforded by the first example, and concentration of capital, afforded by the second, are two different processes, they are inextricably linked (Bukharin, 1966; Marx, 1976). Together they have occurred in the UK food industry such that the top five UK food retailers constituted over 50 per cent of the total grocery market in 1992 (see Table 5.1), with the leading companies generating net profit margins of between 7 and 9 per cent (Wrigley, 1994). This has had the effect of creating a concentrated retailing industry which is able to exert oligopsonistic[2] buying power over concentrated food manufacturing industries (Doel, this volume, Chapter 3; Grant, 1987) which have long been dominated by only a handful of large corporations. So, beginning with the abandonment of Resale Price Maintenance in 1964 (Burns *et al*, 1983; Doel, this volume, Chapter 3; Grant, 1987), the balance of power has shifted from the food manufacturers to the food retailers in the UK.

Table 5.1 Leading UK food retailers and their shares (by value) of the UK grocery market,[a] 1992

Supermarket chain	Market share (%)
Sainsbury[b]	15.4
Tesco	13.0
Argyll[c]	9.3
Asda[d]	8.1
Gateway[e]	5.4
Kwik Save	4.9
Marks & Spencer (UK food)	4.0

(*Source*: Institute of Grocery Distribution, Press Information, 6 April 1994)
[a] Grocery market here constitutes a restructured IGD definition of the market using CSO data. This includes all food retailers (and specialist retailers like butchers and bakers), plus Marks & Spencer food sales. Grocery retailers' petrol sales are excluded.
[b] Includes J Sainsbury and Savacentre.
[c] Includes Safeway, Lo-Cost and Presto.
[d] Includes Asda and Dales.
[e] Includes Gateway, Somerfield, Food Giant and Solo.

The domination of UK food retailing by so few companies means that retailers tend to operate within clearly defined segments of the competitive retailing market. Each retailer then develops the growth of this segment according to its overall competitive strategy and its associated corporate philosophy and culture. For example, Sainsbury leads the quality-based competition, followed by Safeway and Tesco. Asda has refocused its offering to meet price-based competition. Kwik Save leads the deep discounters, while at the opposite end of the spectrum Marks & Spencer and Waitrose occupy specialist niches. This implies that individual retail buyers are operating within very tightly defined corporate cultures which pave the way for particular forms of relationships with suppliers (as will be illustrated in the following section).

Since the 1970s, the profits achieved by the 'big capital' retailers have enabled them to invest heavily in information technology and centralized warehousing systems (Lynch, 1990; McKinnon, 1985; D L G Smith and Sparks, 1993; Sparks, 1986b; Wrigley, 1988b). These have played an important role in the formulation of retailer behaviour and demands within supply relationships. Without oligopoly such systems would have been unlikely to develop so quickly within food retailing. At the same time, the use of these systems and the co-operation of the suppliers to fit in with them further fuel the accumulation of capital within the retailing sector. The use of information technology and centralized distribution systems allow the retailers to more effectively perform their competitive function of reducing the turnover time of commodities. The way in which this particular aspect of commercial capital logic is organized within supply relationships is discussed later.

In addition to this oligopolistic power, since the 1980s food retailers have also been handed the responsibility, by the state, to 'police' the food system in the style of neo-conservative private interest (Marsden and Wrigley, this volume, Chapter 2). Such 're-regulation' gives further opportunities for the major retailers to exercise control over their suppliers and any less powerful entrants into UK food retailing, such as the European limited line discounters (see Burt and Sparks, 1994; Gascoigne, 1992; Wrigley, 1993a; 1993b). This supports the view of Christopherson (1993) that the nation-state plays a major role in shaping the 'rules' of competition and capital accumulation within economies. As retailer power has become stronger, particularly in its relationship to manufacturing, each retailing company has taken a greater control of the functions of distribution and the final exchange of commodities. In so doing, retailers have been able to exercise more force in drawing upon the logic of commercial capital in order to compete with food manufacturers for a larger proportion of the surplus value generated in the act of production. This, to some extent, explains the deep-rooted economic foundations for competitive friction infiltrating the new cultures of food retailer–manufacturer relations. This friction coexists with the co-operative dependency which centres on the need for manufacturers to sell their products through the major retailers in order to reach the consumers, and the desire of the retailers to have the major nationally advertised brands on their shelves. But what of some of the other sources of co-operation which may infuse these relationships, particularly those between retailers and their own-label suppliers?

The growth of UK retailers' power and their use of sophisticated logistics systems paved the way for the development of strong own-label strategies. These strategies began as early as the 1960s in some cases, but started to represent a very real competitive force by the 1980s, pioneered by Sainsbury (*The Grocer*, 8 May 1993, 45). By 1992, the share taken by own-labels of the UK Fast Moving Consumer Goods market (by value)[3] was 37.1 per cent (Oxford Institute of Retail Management, published in *The Grocer*, 7 May 1994, 78). The entry of retailers into own-label trading as a competitive strategy appears to be a logical one. It allows the retailers to erode manufacturers' share of the market by influencing patterns of consumption in their favour and by using their bargaining power to lock manufacturers into retailer-led supply situations. They are thereby able to increase their overall profits, particularly if own-labels are in high-margin categories (Doel, this volume, Chapter 3). And, if the strategy is effective, the retailers are able to extract a larger slice of the surplus value created in the act of production. Such own-label strategies, then, represent an opportunity for retailers to compete both with each other and with food manufacturers of national brands, but to do so they must become involved, indirectly, in the production of food commodities. While the retailers' own-labels compete with the manufacturers in the fight for shelf space and market share within product categories, to produce the own-label products the retailers depend upon some manufacturers to become the producers and suppliers of these products. This latter point is fundamental to a comprehension of the nature of co-operation within own-label retailer–manufacturer relations.

The dialectical relationship between the competitive logic driving the food retailers and the competitive logic driving the food manufacturers implies that, while UK retailers have tried to enforce rather despotic logistics and pricing demands on manufacturers in their relationships and competed against their brands with own-labels, they also rely on the competitive position of some of these manufacturers to provide means for the growth of their own-label supply chains. In the UK, only the leading food manufacturers with clear branding strategies and high advertising investment, like Kellogg's, Heinz, Birdseye Wall's and Coca-Cola, are able to 'leap-frog' the power of retail capital (G Davies, 1990) and thus refuse to manufacture own-labels. This exemplifies the power of a particular form of cultural identity, in the form of the manufacturer's brand, to influence power and its execution within supply relationships. The branding strategies of food manufacturing firms are influential in conditioning the decision-making of the companies' directors and account managers with regard to the production of retailers' own-labels. The power of the decision-makers and the way in which this power infuses relationships with retailers results from the strength of the food products' brands. Manufacturers of weak secondary and tertiary brands, which have been pushed off the shelves by own-labels (K Davies *et al*, 1985; 1986), have been forced to produce these own-labels instead.

The Food Safety Act 1990, part of the re-regulation of food retailing, renders food retailers liable for the safety of their own-label products and therefore makes it legally necessary for the retailers to closely monitor the production process of their own-labels. However, in addition, as the suppliers are producing products for a retailer label, they are essentially involved in the manufacture of not only a potential retailer-owned commodity, but also a part of the retailer's *identity* which is internalized by consumers as a part of the retailer's overall service. It is therefore in the interests of the retailer, particularly in the area of innovative premium products, to play as active a part as possible in helping the manufacturers to create a product and packaging which ties in with and accentuates the retailers' overall 'consumer offering'. Since UK food retailers all have very well-defined corporate cultures which occupy clearly defined segments of the competitive retailing market, issues of image and identity are particularly important. For example, the specialist, high-quality image of Marks & Spencer and the contrasting, more price-based 'value for money' socio-economic identity of Tesco. It follows from this that collaboration is logically best fostered through close, personal relationships and multi-contact, though for price-based, low-quality own-labels, questions of economic efficiency will invariably be more important.

The way in which the own-label supply relationships are organized is very much a function of relationship culture. Representatives from retailing companies will be acting upon their need to foster innovation which ties in with their overall corporate identity, and the selection of suitable suppliers will invariably be made based upon the requirement of a manufacturing firm whose culture will allow representatives to co-operate with those of the retailer. As such, the hegemonic position of food retailers in relation to food manufacturers in the UK has led the way for the entry of retail capital into productive capital. To some extent then, the competitive logic of food retailing is appropriately reformulated and grounded in the new cultures of particular forms of own-label supply relationship, discussed in the next section. The 'big capital' retailers often use equally 'big capital' manufacturers to produce their own-labels, but in many cases, particularly where innovative, premium products are concerned, small-scale producers are used. However, in both cases the power of centralized retail capital is evident, supporting the argument that large corporations still maintain advantages over small companies, at least in this situation (Harvey, 1989c).

Overall, what this overview of the UK political-economic context demonstrates is the way in which the concentration of retail capital has led to both the development of well-defined corporate cultures for retailing companies and a shift in the balance of power away from food manufacturers and towards the food retailers. This paves the way for the execution of retailer power in supply relationships which undoubtedly conditions the power and identity of individual actors involved in these relationships. As such, the retailer–manufacturer relationship cultures, centring around modes of their social organization, are shaped by their political-economic context.

The USA

Table 5.2 illustrates the contrast in the consolidation of food retailing in the USA. The top five US chains constituted only just over 20 per cent of the total US grocery market in 1992. This is largely due to the strict enforcement of anti-trust legislation, in particular the Clayton Act 1914, the Robinson-Patman Act 1936 and the Celler-Kefauver Act 1950 (see

Wrigley, 1992a), which effectively stalled the centralization, and thus concentration, of food retail capital. This has meant that some US retail chains which were growing on a national scale during the 1930s, were restricted from further expansion (Wrigley, 1992a). The regional character of US food retailing which emerged, relates in part then to the role played by the nation-state, and stands in contrast to the powerful, *nationally* concentrated US food manufacturing industries which were privileged by the nation-state (in so far as they were not stalled in their path towards consolidation). Much of the divergence from the UK situation concerning cultures of food retailer–manufacturer relations in the USA can be, at least in part, explained by this striking difference in power relations between the food retailers and manufacturers which has been affected so strongly by the US regulatory state.

Table 5.2 Leading US food retailers and their shares (by value) of the US grocery market, 1992

Supermarket chain	Market share (%)
Kroger Company	5.8
American Stores Company	5.0
Safeway Inc.	4.0
Great Atlantic and Pacific Tea	
Company (A & P)	2.7
Winn-Dixie Stores Inc.	2.7
Albertson's Inc.	2.7
Food Lion, Inc.	1.9
Publix Supermarkets, Inc.	1.7
Vons Companies Inc.	1.5
Pathmark Stores, Inc.	
(previously Supermarkets General)	1.1

Source: adapted from *Progressive Grocer* (1994)

The proliferation of competing retailing companies at the national level in the USA makes it difficult to distinguish each one from the others along the lines of clearly defined strategy. Indeed, unlike their UK counterparts, US food retailers do not have strong 'brand images'. Their identities are marked only on a regional level. At the national scale, overall retailing strategies fall into two categories: the traditional 'hi-lo' pricing strategy with its emphasis on promotions and discounting, and the 'Every Day Low Price' (EDLP) strategy which focuses on more consistent low prices (NatWest Securities, 1993). These almost homogenized retailing strategies tend to favour the development of similarly homogenized business relationships between the retailers and their manufacturing suppliers. For example, buyers representing the 'hi-lo' retailers will always want to negotiate promotional deals in meetings with suppliers. This leads to the establishment of certain set routines within these meetings.

There has been a period of de-regulation in the USA since the 1980s which has involved a relaxation of the enforcement of anti-merger policy (NatWest Securities, 1993; Wrigley, 1992a; 1995). However, the legacy since the mid-1940s and the effects of the leveraged buyouts of the late 1980s, which left many leading retailers with massive debt burdens, have kept US food retailing fragmented and regional in form. The leveraged buyouts (LBOs) are an important phenomenon which has affected the cultures of US food retailers at the national level. These buyouts had the effect of focusing the food retailers' businesses on short-termist financial gain to satisfy their shareholders and pay off their debts (see Wrigley, 1995). This undoubtedly reshaped the cultures of the relationships which these LBO retailers had with manufacturers, as the emphasis was shifted away from the long term. Individual employees acting within these relationships have inevitably been forced to comply with these short-termist strategies.

The use of brokers, which are commonly utilized as extra-firm salesforces on the part of many US food manufacturers (discussed within the next section), can be attributed to the enormity of the USA in terms of its geographic size, which makes it difficult for manufacturing companies to facilitate regular face-to-face meetings with buyers at the headquarters of all the major US food retailers using their own salesforces. It is far easier for them to utilize local brokers for each region of the USA, despite the resulting lack of close inter-firm bonds between themselves and the retailers. However, while the issue is primarily a spatial one, it seems more plausibly explained as a geographical outcome of a relative power imbalance which has been influenced by regulation. Had the retailers been allowed by the state to centralize and consolidate, then regardless of the size of the USA, there would have been fewer headquarters in fewer locations for the manufacturers' salespeople to visit in order to get their products on the shelves of the same proportion of US supermarket outlets. Under such circumstances, it is questionable whether brokerages would have been as heavily used as they are within current retailer–manufacturer relations.

Owing to the highly competitive nature of US retailing, net profit margins are much lower than those generated by UK food retailers. In the mid 1980s US retailers struggled to achieve margins of 1 per cent (Litwak, 1987, cited in Wrigley, 1992a). Partly as a result of this, investment in information technology and centralized warehousing systems by retailers has been much slower in the USA than in the UK. In short, all of this has stalled US food retailers in their ability to take effective control of the functions of distribution and the final exchange of commodities, implying that the configuration of the forms of capitalist logic informing US retailing practice differ from those driving UK retailing. US retailers have been less successful than their UK counterparts, in the past, in locking manufacturing suppliers into their own logistics systems, though all this is beginning to change. But added to this, the enforcement of the Robinson-Patman Act 1996 has favoured the manufacturers still further (Hamm, 1982; Wrigley, 1992a), not only as a piece of anti-trust legislation, but also through its capacity to prevent large retailers from receiving discriminatory discounts from manufacturers. Despite the decline in the enforcement of this piece of legislation since the 1950s, it is yet another example of the impact of regulation on the shaping of retailer–manufacturer relationship cultures, in this case within the sphere of financial exchange. Overall, less aggression on the part of the US retailers in US supply relations can largely be attributed to a slower shift in the balance of power away from the manufacturers and towards the retailers compared to the UK (though the situation appears to be increasingly moving in the retailers' favour).

Hitherto, own-label strategic action in the USA has been at quantitatively lower and qualitatively contrasting levels than in the UK. Indeed, the share (of value) taken by retailers' own-labels in the US grocery market of 1992 was only 13.7 per cent (IRI figures, published in C Walker, 1991: 54).[4] It is also important to recognize the very low level of product innovation emanating from retailers' own-labels in the USA; own-labels are almost all copy-cats of manufacturers' brands. While this is the case for some UK own-labels, there are many dynamic areas of innovation in the UK, for example, within the field of sub-branding and the category of chilled ready meals (Doel, this volume, Chapter 3). This is largely absent from the USA, which appears to affect the emerging cultures of retailer–manufacturer relations in that there is less collaboration concerning product development and less interaction between the technical departments of the two parties. In addition, the fact that the corporate cultures of food retailers in the USA are not as clearly defined as they are in the UK implies that the issue of carving out a strategic identity through the own-labels produced by the manufacturing suppliers is arguably less important in the USA than it is in the UK. This perhaps eliminates the need for close, personal relationships concerning research and development which can be attributed to the weakness of own-labels in the USA compared to the UK situation. Individual representatives from both the retailing and the supplying firms expect to conduct arm's-length relationships. Again, this is not resultant from individuals' autonomous decisions, but is instead a function of relationship *culture* which has been shaped by economic power relations. The lack of power on the part of the US food retailers has prevented them from becoming as involved in productive capital as their counterparts in the UK.

Finally, because of the weaker threat posed by own-labels in the USA, there are many more US food manufacturers who are able to refuse to supply retailers with own-label products than in the UK. In this sense, then, the dialectical relationship concerning the two competitive logics of food retailing and manufacturing, as discussed earlier in the case of the UK, has not yet been as dynamically activated as it has in the UK. However, the strength of the manufacturers is becoming increasingly precarious, as it is now difficult for food manufacturers to advertise their products nationally due to the growing power of *regional* cable television networks and the burgeoning costs of advertising (Fox, 1994). This, coupled with a rise in retailer power due to de-regulation and more efficient use of logistics systems, could signal the onset of a demise in manufacturer power and fundamental changes to the presently emerging cultures of food retailer–manufacturer relations in the USA.

The emerging new cultures of food retailer–manufacturer relations

This section examines the emerging new cultures of food retailer–manufacturer relations in the UK and USA more closely through an appreciation of the way in which aspects of production, exchange and distribution are socially organized. Such social organization is recognized to form, and continually reshape, the business cultures of the retailer–manufacturer relations through processes of collaboration, co-operation and negotiation. The discussion uses empirical material obtained through in-depth interviews with the actors involved in the relations. As such, the arguments within the text rest heavily on performative notions of organizational culture (Czarniawska-Joerges, 1992) which suggest that it is the individual actors within the companies (through their collectively created 'thought worlds') who continually define and redefine the new cultures of retailer–manufacturer relations. Contrasts are drawn between UK and US business cultures surrounding the organization of these relations and, in addition, the fundamental differences between the relationship cultures centring on manufacturers' brands and retailers' own-labels are highlighted. What should become clear, though, is the way in which competitive logic and the power relations discussed in the previous sections infuse the organization of these relationship cultures.

The UK

Setting up relationships

Most food manufacturers of national brands in the UK have established relationships with the major retailers, despite the ongoing changes and developments within the industry. However, a new form of relationship normally has to be forged whenever the manufacturer markets a new product. This is achieved through an initial sales call made by the 'national account manager' of the manufacturing company which involves the marketing of the new product to the retailers. Personal relationships often develop between the account managers and the retail buyers, since these sales calls and subsequent meetings involve regular contact between these individuals. However, the individuals are not operating independently of any competitive strategy. Rather, their interpersonal tactics are a part of their companies' competitive strategies. Account managers and buyers operate within these strategies according to their own interpretations of overall 'corporate identity' (as discussed earlier).

What is clear in the UK is the existence of strong corporate identities and strategies on the part of both food retailers and manufacturers. As a result of this, when a new product is marketed, national account managers must be aware of both their own corporate strategies and those of the retailers. Some account managers tend to use marketing guides which explicitly lay out how to 'do business' with particular retailing companies. At the director level, many UK manufacturers are in a position whereby they have to actively mould their strategies so that they gel more smoothly with those of the major retailers. The overall situation in the UK is such that only manufacturers with strong brand identities, well-defined corporate strategies and established consumer franchises are able to successfully market their products to the major food retailers. This means that sales calls and marketing presentations have to be confidently managed by account managers who are duty-bound to accurately represent the clear branding strategies of their companies. In view of this increasing pressure on food manufacturers since the mid-1980s, the personal relationships which develop within the marketing and sales processes are being tightened up and kept on a 'professional' level which now excludes rounds of golf and too many informal social meetings. Some retailing companies have also tried to maintain their competitive edge by regularly reshuffling their buyers between departments in order to prevent the development of relationships with suppliers from becoming too close. This situation is very much bound up in the increase of retailer power since the mid-1980s. What this implies for retailer–manufacturer relationship culture is the denial of individual buyers and sellers to stamp their own individual authority on the nature of relationships with each other. The increase in retailer power has intensified these relations and established new emerging cultures of food retailer–manufacturer competition which shape the social action of these individuals.

Setting up relationships for the supply of retailers' own-labels is a very different story. Doel (this volume, Chapter 3) proposes the existence of two polar modes of supply chain initiation for UK retailers' own-labels. These are the utilization of the excess capacity of the food manufacturers of weak, national brands, and the proactive selection of appropriate manufacturers to develop new own-label products. Empirical findings for the product categories of canned soup, ice cream and pasta sauce in the UK support this notion and suggest that some of the most interesting social processes through which own-label supply chains are initiated occur within the second type of initiation mode, which encompasses the more innovative own-label products. Within this mode, important consideration is given to issues of corporate culture and personal relationships which are deemed to facilitate a harmonious retailer–supplier relationship. Very often, large food retailers who require new, innovative own-label products actively seek out suppliers whose corporate philosophy it is to tie in with retailer demands and who are prepared to hold regular face-to-face meetings with retailing representatives. In contrast, within the first type of initiation mode it is questions of economic efficiency which assume far greater importance. However, what is common to both types of processes is the power of retailers to dictate the conditions under which the relationships are set up.

Discussion of product development

Very little close collaboration concerning ideas for product development exists within UK food retailer–manufacturer relations which are built upon the exchange of manufacturers' brands. However, retailers do make some suggestions with regard to product changes, while manufacturers may share their ideas and innovations. Paradoxically, though, a predominant element of adversarialism emanates from the very source of such co-operation itself. This concerns the fear, on the part of the manufacturers, that the retailers may replicate their ideas in the form of copy-cat own-label products. Only the manufacturers of products with very strong brand identities are able to evade such a fear. This is very much tied in with the increasing strength of retailers' own-labels, discussed in the previous section. Account managers are therefore expected not to divulge their companies' product strategies, which once again puts a strain on interpersonal business relations which used to thrive within regular, friendly rounds of golf and informal meetings in wine bars and restaurants.

Within own-label supply relationships, particularly those centring on premium products like pasta sauce and dairy ice cream, the retailer–manufacturer relations tend to be closer, more collaborative and long term. Product development is fostered through interactive communication between both parties at all levels of the companies. Indeed, in one particular case, representatives from the retailing company and the manufacturing supplier (from technical staff to directors) go out to restaurants together in order to sample products which may inspire ideas for new own-labels. In so doing, the occupational hierarchy is collapsed, the 'market' relationship destroyed and innovation is encouraged through the act of the retailer and manufacturer together 'becoming consumers'. Here, particular social relationships are closer and emanate from the need to collaborate in the area of product innovation. This need arises out of the centrality of innovation to the growth in the profits of both companies. As such, the social relations are resultant, in this case, from the co-operative dependency of productive and commercial capital, though in this situation regarding own-labels the hegemony of retail capital is very much the driving force behind the *raison d'être* of the supply relationship. In contrast, though, product development within basic own-label product categories, like canned soup and standard ice cream, lacks innovation and collaboration within supply relationships. Instead, the benchmark is set by copying manufacturers' brands, and retailers dictate product specifications to the suppliers. The issue standing out in both cases, though, is the way in which the organization of product development is very much retailer-led.

Negotiation of payment terms

Within all types of UK food retailer–manufacturer relationships, payment by the retailers for the manufacturers' products must be negotiated by both parties. Whether the retailers pay a net price for the products or whether they demand an 'overrider' is dependent upon their corporate policy; the manufacturers invariably find themselves in a position whereby they have to comply with these policies.[5] Prices for goods are always negotiable, but many manufacturers are forced to offer lower prices and flexible margins in order to remain competitive. Aspects of organizational culture which centre around payment terms within exchange are again dictated by corporate policy and economic power relations.

The sensitivity of the subject of payment terms is undisputed among the actors involved. One sales director of a manufacturing corporation explained that payment terms are always best tackled 'up front', since a misunderstanding could damage a relationship. In view of this sentiment, both parties expect to verbally set specific time limits within which payment should be made by the retailers to the manufacturers. These limits range from 12 to 60 days. However, there is a clear conflict of economic interests at work here. As the manufacturers attempt to enforce rules of prompt payment, the retailers increasingly adopt a tactic whereby they sell their stock well before they pay for it. As such, the retailers are supplied on credit and can therefore take advantage of operating on negative working capital cycles (Wrigley, 1992a). What this competitive logic imposes on the cultures of the supply relationships, then, is a tendency for retailers to abuse the co-operation of the manufacturers by constantly stretching out their time limits for payment. This is easily achieved in view of the absence of written contracts within retailer–manufacturer relationships. It is the relative power between the two parties which is likely to determine how lenient the manufacturer will be towards such retailer action. Many interviewees, while talking about regular co-operative meetings and business lunches with representatives from supplying firms, also recalled occasions on which they actively abused the personal trust of these suppliers by avoiding a discussion of payments and thereby actively refusing to pay on time.

Organization of distribution

In view of the development and increasing use of information technology and centralized distribution systems by UK retailers, manufacturers of both national brands and retailers' own-labels have been expected to tie in with these systems by adopting 'just in time' (JIT) delivery techniques. This has allowed the retailers to pass back the costs of inventory holding to the manufacturers (Wrigley, 1992a). Within their relationships and negotiations, then, the retailers are constantly requesting that the manufacturers should fit in with these sophisticated logistics systems by aiming to reduce the time it takes for them to respond to retailer orders. The everyday retailer–manufacturer interface concerning logistics management is very much technology-driven, but the negotiation of overall lead times and the degree to which the manufacturer is prepared to focus the efforts of its resources on tying in with these systems is bound up within the centralized, verbal inter-firm discussion. Once again, then, a conflict of economic interests is resolved under the guise of a socially co-operative relationship.

Strategies of retailing to consumers

Since the abandonment of Resale Price Maintenance in 1964 (Burns *et al*, 1983; Doel, this volume, Chapter 3; Grant, 1987), manufacturers have had very little influence over the retail prices of their products in the major UK supermarkets, even though suggestions are made within some relationships. This situation, with respect to pricing, sets the scene for the entire picture concerning the ability of UK food manufacturers to influence the way in which their products, be they brands or own-labels, reach their final consumers.

From the mid-1980s to the early 1990s, the leading food retailers embarked upon massive store expansion programmes (Wrigley, 1991, 1994). This has effectively created large, out-of-town sites of symbolic capital which locate the final exchange of commodities in new forms of retailer-controlled spaces of consumption. In this way the foundations for an intense 'fight for shelf space' (K Davies *et al*, 1986) have been laid, which pitch the manufacturers' brands directly against the retailers' own-labels (Leahy, 1987; Roberts and Smith, 1983). Representatives from companies producing national brands not only channel their efforts into persuading the retailers to buy their products, but also make suggestions regarding the positioning of their products within the retail stores. Such suggestions are founded upon computerized store planograms formulated by the manufacturers' technical staff. However, interviewees explained that their suggestions, while listened to within the negotiations, are very rarely taken up by the retailers. This is largely because food retailers are primarily interested in promoting their own brand identity which is actively accentuated by the use and careful positioning of their own-label products within their stores. As such, their entry into the realm of productive capital also takes on a semiotic form in so far as they bind their own brand images and identities into their products which form a part of the identity of their overall retailing service which is experienced and 'decoded' by the final consumers.

The USA

Setting up relationships

As in the UK, food retailer–manufacturer relations built upon the exchange of manufacturers' brands are well established and ongoing in the USA, with fundamental changes to their qualitative characters being attributable to the introduction of new manufacturers' products to the retailers' stocks. In contrast to the UK, the marketing of new products, and also subsequent sales meetings, are often carried out by brokers on behalf of the manufacturers.[6] In this sense, the broker is an intermediary working as an extra-firm sales arm for food manufacturers who do not have the salesforces and resources to facilitate relationships with the many regional US retailers themselves. As brokers operate regionally, they are able to build up a sound local knowledge of retailing and therefore form close bonds with representatives of the retailing companies. Many retailing interviewees talked about how they formed long-standing friendships with brokers with whom they had been dealing for years. While this can be an advantage in some respects, it does prevent a close, strategic linkage from developing between the food manufacturers and the food retailers. Because of this, the very largest food manufacturing giants, such as the Campbell Soup Company, refuse to use brokers in order that they may forge closer relationships with their retailing customers. This latter strategy allows the meeting of corporate cultures, as discussed in the context of the UK, to be direct, avoiding the more common arm's-length relationship which appears to be predominant in the USA due to the wide use of brokers.

Another contrast to the UK situation rests upon the greater strength of manufacturers' brands in the USA. This implies that US manufacturers are less likely to find themselves in a position whereby they have to mould their corporate strategies to fit those of the retailers in order to successfully market their new products. However, this situation is changing as the food retailers and their own-labels gain in strategic strength.

Regarding the initiation of supply relationships for retailers' own-labels, the US story is very different from that of the UK. While utilization of manufacturers' excess capacity and retailers' active selection of suppliers does occur, there are some additional 'modes of own-label supply' and processes through which supply chains are initiated. In the case of the soup industry, for example, there is one major own-label supplier who has been powerful enough to proactively initiate relationships with the food retailers. Another marked divergence from UK practice concerns the role of mediating organizations between many medium-sized US retailers and their own-label suppliers. The Chicago-based buying co-operative, Topco Associates, for example, works on behalf of these retailers to initiate supply relationships with manufacturers for their own-label goods. Suppliers are selected by Topco on the grounds of economic efficiency and production facilities, with corporate culture and personal relationships being very marginal considerations in the process of decision-making.

Overall, regarding the setting up of all types of food retailer–manufacturer relationships in the USA, the processes are far less retailer-led than they are in the UK and the corporate cultures of food retailers appear to be generally less well-defined and influential in supply chain initiation than they are in the UK. In addition, a specific example of the effect of the leveraged buyouts upon the organization of supply relationships is afforded by the story of one representative from a major US LBO food retailing corporation. He explained that one of their prevalent corporate philosophies has been to develop a 'culture of thrift', which the chief executive officer has requested should be filtered through to all aspects of the company's business, including supply relations. This illustrates not only the effect of leveraged buyouts on relationship cultures, but also the influence of heads of corporations in forging corporate organizational cultures, as proposed by Schein (1992).

Discussion of product development

Discussion of ideas between retailers and manufacturers with respect to the development of manufacturers' brands is almost absent in the USA. Sometimes the retailers make suggestions to the manufacturers, but there is no evidence to suggest that manufacturers discuss their product innovation with their buyers. As such, there is no real interface between the two parties concerning production. The picture is slightly different for retailers' own-labels, though there appears to be no collaboration and interface with technical departments on the scale operating in the UK.[7] Retailers' own-label soup products are exclusively developed and produced by one national supplier, with very little contribution made by its retailing customers. In other cases, where a buying co-operative is used by the retailer, this intermediary may help the suppliers to devise recipes for own-label products, but the retailers are generally absent from such discussion. Overall, the extent of US retailer involvement in the area of product development and the production process in general is less than it is in the UK. This is largely due to a lower level of own-label trading on the part of food retailers in the USA. Again, the establishment of arm's-length relationships as the 'norm' within supply relations is resultant from a lack of power in the USA, which in turn has been conditioned by national regulatory context.

Negotiation of payment terms

Unlike the UK, there appears to be a universally used payment term within all US food retailer–manufacturer relationships. This is the '2 per cent 10, net 30 days' agreement. This means that the absolute time limit for retailer payment is within 30 days, but the retailer can receive a 2 per cent discount if payment is made within 10 days. This indicates that there is some element of US buyer–supplier business culture which pervades practice within the food industry. This contrasts with the UK system. However, the way in which companies so often stray from these specified terms parallels behaviour in the UK. For the same competitive reasons, US food retailers actively stretch out these time limits in order to earn interest on their credit for as long as possible. So again, retailers take advantage of their co-operative suppliers, as the logic driving their business dictates and, as in the UK, the absence of written supply contracts enables retailers to achieve this more effectively.

Organization of distribution

Most of the leading US food retail chains now operate their own centralized warehousing and distribution systems, but these have developed, in general, at a slower rate than the equivalent systems in the UK. However, the retailers now increasingly make tough demands for suppliers to reduce their lead times within both their centralized logistics control systems and the 'Direct Store Delivery' mode of distribution (which is used for some product categories, e.g. ice cream). As in the UK, these demands are made in the first instance through the centralized meetings among white-collar staff; the same meetings which are said to take on the character of a 'partnership culture' in view of the interdependence of the two parties. When discussing the retailers' requests to reduce delivery times, one interviewee from a manufacturing corporation commented that this could hardly be perceived as 'partnering', as the retailers more or less dictate conditions of delivery to them. This friction in the relationship, as in the UK, stems from the clashing, competing logics informing manufacturing and retailing, with the latter becoming increasingly powerful in relation to the former in view of its advancement into the sphere of sophisticated logistics control. This is an example of the way in which the movement of US retail restructuring and retailer–manufacturer power relations towards the system operating in the UK is mirrored by a set of emerging retailer–manufacturer relationship cultures which are becoming increasingly similar to those predominating in the UK.

Strategies of retailing to consumers
Although the timing of US retailers' out-of-town store development programmes and the development of their own-label ranges are different from those of their UK counterparts, the concept of the retailers as controllers of the spaces of consumption is appropriate in both geographical contexts. The 'fight for shelf space' in the USA is growing in intensity with the increasing pressure being placed on manufacturers' brands by the retailers' own-labels (Sansolo, 1994; C Walker, 1991). While some manufacturers still dominate the store shelves simply through their monopoly within certain product categories (e.g. the Campbell Soup Company), others are becoming frustrated by a lack of retailer interest in their suggestions regarding the allocation of shelf space to their products. So, despite the idea of 'partnership' relations, there appears to be a general lack of productive two-way discussion as far as the area of the retailing function is concerned. This largely emanates from the increasing interests of the retailers to configure their shelf space in a way which favours the sale of their own-labels above the brands (as in the UK).

Critical reflections on the new cultures of food retailer–manufacturer relations

What is clear from a reading of the previous sections is the complexity of emerging cultures of food retailer–manufacturer relations in the UK and USA, which vary along the axes of their social organization, business culture and economic functioning. Overall, it seems that the cultures of retailer–manufacturer relations range from the close, collaborative, long-term relationships of UK own-label supply relationships to the arm's-length, adversarial character of some US supply relationships which incorporate the use of brokers as a third-party organizational element. The caricature of the former type fits perfectly Best's (1990) notion of the co-ordinated, non-market-based inter-firm organization associated with the 'new competition' (often used to describe Japanese-style supply relationships), while the latter conforms more to the hierarchically organized, market-based relationships of what Best terms the 'old competition' (often used to describe Fordist-style relationships). This in itself confirms an uneven development of certain, supposedly more progressive, modes of organization across space, product sectors and individual firms (Gertler, 1992). In other words, the interpenetration of economic, cultural, social and political factors engender a heterogeneous range of food retailer–manufacturer competitive cultures.

The dynamism with regard to the way in which the relationships are organized and re-organized by the individual actors, which is apparent through a consideration of 'performative' concepts of organizational culture, denies the establishment of one, all-encompassing notion of 'relationship culture'. This falls in line with Gertler's (1995) view that business cultures are constantly produced rather than inherited. It is proposed that cultures of retailer–manufacturer relations are constantly produced and reproduced through the social organization of the relations, based upon the ways in which individuals interpret their role and position within the competitive process. This is to argue further, then, that cultures of relations are forged through human agency, but that this human agency is itself situated within a wider competitive process which is also riven with cultural forces. As it was proposed at the beginning of the chapter then, the use of the concept of 'cultures' to problematize the role of human agency within commodity exchange relationships has been appropriate in view of its promotion of conditioned, collective social action as opposed to the autonomy of individuals. In addition, it has permitted a theorization of food retailer–manufacturer relationships which has shed light upon the way in which the social organization of retailer–manufacturer relations is shaped by economic power and capitalist logic.

The UK–USA comparison running through this chapter has aided a critical theorization of food retailer–manufacturer relations in its capacity to explicitly demonstrate the historical and geographical specificity of the relationship forms and cultures. The influence of nationally constituted regulation has received particular attention, though this does not deny the power of global or local influences. Indeed, many companies operating within both national economies are parts of global corporations. At the other end of the spectrum the part played by small, local suppliers within the food production–consumption chain should not be ignored. Yet, as has been discussed, national regulation plays a crucial role in constructing particular environments for the cultures of food retailer–manufacturer relations to develop. This appears to support the view held by Gertler (1995) regarding the importance of the nation-state in forming 'enabling' environments in which industrial cultures can emerge.

In particular, the role of the nation-state has been highlighted in its capacity to shape economic power relations which themselves form a part of the historical and geographical process of embedding (Dicken and Thrift, 1992). The centralization of capital and the playing out of power relations have been critical to the reproduction of new cultures of food retailer–manufacturer relations. They have shaped both the nature of co-operation and conflict which have dynamically accentuated the contrasts in cultures between the UK and USA. However, a movement of the balance of power relations in the retailers' favour in the USA is resulting in the emergence of some forms of business relationships which are becoming similar to the cultures of those operating in the UK.

Generally, the balance of power has been shifting towards the retailers and away from the manufacturers at a faster rate in the UK than in the USA. As such, it appears to have been the food retailers who have, especially in the UK, called the shots in shaping supply relationship cultures in order to accumulate capital. In so doing, they have, in a sense, helped to 'creatively destroy' the power of the food manufacturers, the effects of which are visible in terms of the demise of national brands and the way in which manufacturers must tie in with retailer-led supply chain management. The new cultures, therefore, seem to be an important element in the process of 'creative destruction'. Viewing the new forms of retailer–manufacturer relationships in this way takes on a style of Schumpeterian economic thinking, which carries with it the idea of entrepreneurial innovation. While the entrepreneurialism taking place in the forging of new cultures of retailer–manufacturer relations (and the products being developed within them) is very different from the entrepreneurialism of which Schumpeter wrote in the 1940s, his theories could still be applied in this context, particularly in the light of the performative notions of organizational culture. But, a shadow looms over this theoretical application which is well illustrated by Catephores' (1994) argument that Schumpeter overplayed the power of the entrepreneur to facilitate economic development within capitalism. In agreement with this view then, and continuing the line of argument developed throughout the chapter, it is argued that the collective innovative capacity of the social actors within companies, which forges the cultures of supply relationships, is driven very much by capital's logic.

The notion of food retailing and food manufacturing as interdependent, but also competing, fractions of capital has been proposed throughout the chapter. What appears to have been confirmed is that, as Fine and Leopold (1993b: 295) explain, 'retail capital has to be formed, not simply to have a form'. In this sense, then, the power relations in national economies, shaped by regulation, have actively formed the development of retail capital, so that the intersection of capital logics within UK food retailing contrasts with that which informs US retailers. For example, the extent to which UK retailers have become involved in the area of innovative productive capital is greater than (or rather, different from) their US counterparts. While this functional specificity of retail capital informs and drives individuals in their continual creation and re-creation of cultures of supply relationships, the cultures of the relationships also play an active role in further redefining the development of retailing and its power to draw upon different capital logics in order to accumulate capital.

The most difficult theoretical challenge, however, remains in carrying this argument still further. The specificity of retail capital is, in part, characterized by its relationship with the process of consumption; the *way* in which it locates the final exchange of commodities in a retailer-controlled service space of symbolic capital. Such spaces, as Clarke (this volume, Chapter 16) recognizes, can be viewed as being elements of postmodern hyperspace which ground the 'uncontrollable cultural energies' of capitalism (D B Clarke and Purvis, 1994: 1099) in new ways. Hence, there are forces of the new cultures of retailer–manufacturer relations which play a role in shaping such space. For example, the production through collaborative inter-firm organization of innovative own-labels which help to construct a retailer's image and identity through a 'branding' process.

The power of the multiple logics of capital in conditioning social practices in the form of business culture and in grounding the functions of capital has been stressed throughout. However, without the emerging new business cultures, these multiple logics of capital have no meaning in the contemporary processes of capital accumulation taking place within food retailing and manufacturing. The symbiotic links between cultures of retailer–manufacturer relations, which are shaped by macro-regulatory forces, and the logics of capital is critical in advancing notions of a 'new retail geography'. It is clear that Clarke and Purvis (1994) are right to recognize the cultural energies of capitalism. This chapter has shown that such cultural energies are not confined to branding, advertising and consumption; they also dynamically infuse the processes of commodity exchange.

Notes

1   This fieldwork was based upon an inquiry into food retailer–manufacturer power relations in three product categories: canned soup, ice cream and pasta sauce. However, where appropriate, empirical information from other product group appearing in trade journals and press reports is also used.

2   Collusive, often anti-competitive buying power associated with oligopoly.

3   From the Nielsen definition of Fast Moving Consumer Goods which is based upon three categories of groceries: (i) personal care, (ii) household goods and (iii) food and beverages.

4   This figure is taken from an IRI Infoscan scan of 202 general product categories sold through grocery retailing outlets.

5   An 'overrider' is a payment made by the manufacturer to the retailer if the retailer achieves a certain amount of cash turnover. This implies that retailers using such a policy build their margins up out of several cash funds.
6   Brokers are generally used in the UK only by very small food manufacturing firms producing own-labels for food retailers.
7   One exception to such retailer exclusion from the sphere of product development occurs in the cases where some leading US retailers are vertically integrated into the manufacturing of several own-label products (including ice cream). However, there is still very little innovation, even within this organizational arrangement, on a level which is comparable to that occurring in UK own-label development.

CHAPTER 6

Sunk costs and corporate restructuring: British food retailing and the property crisis

Neil Wrigley

After a decade in which the major British food retailers enjoyed unrivalled growth and profitability, the early 1990s witnessed a significant shift in competitive conditions. By the autumn of 1993, leaders of the industry were publicly endorsing the view that 'the halcyon days in the industry in terms of increasing profitability are over' (Archie Norman, Chief Executive, Asda, *Daily Telegraph*, 3 July 1993), the capital markets had experienced a collapse in confidence in the food retailers, and the press was filled with stories proclaiming the 'End of the Supermarket Era' (*Sunday Times*, 7 November 1993).

There were three major influences on this shift in sentiment:

1   The rise of the discounters, led by the market entry of the low-margin, low-capital intensity European limited-range discounters Aldi, Netto, Ed, etc, and forecast to capture 15.5 per cent of the UK market by the mid-1990s (see Burt and Sparks, 1994; Wrigley, 1993a; 1994).
2   Growing worries over the marked disparity which emerged in the early 1990s between the general UK property market and the food retail property market, about the rates of return on capital employed on new store development programmes, about the 'sunk costs' of UK food retailers, and about the costs of exit.
3   Growing public unease about the excesses of retailer dominance which had resulted from the late 1980s 'golden age' of increasing concentration and profitability (see Marsden and Wrigley, this volume, Chapter 2; Wrigley, 1993b).

In this chapter I shall consider the second of these influences on the chronicle of retail restructuring in the UK. It is a story of how what were previously viewed as assets came to be viewed as sunk costs, and why announcements such as those by Argyll (the operators of Safeway) in December 1993 that it was to start depreciating its store values, and by Tesco and Sainsbury in January 1994 that they were to follow Argyll's lead over depreciation and, in addition, to make major write-downs on land and buildings, proved to be of considerable cumulative importance. Moreover, it is a story which has important theoretical linkages to an emerging area of debate in economic geography – namely the significance of sunk costs and market exit strategies on industrial restructuring.

Although case studies of the patterns and consequences of corporate restructuring have formed a highly significant part of economic geography since the late 1970s, and although much of that work has concerned itself with issues relating to the specificity and durability of the inherited configuration of production and to notions of spatial fixity and persistence, surprisingly little has been written in geography about the role of sunk costs in corporate decision-making and corporate restructuring – where sunk costs are defined as those costs of a firm 'which are irrevocably committed to a particular use, and therefore are not recoverable in case of exit' (Mata, 1991: 52). Yet issues of non-recoverable investment and market exit pervade analysis of the economic landscape – be it the £7 billion total abandonment costs estimated for the decommissioning of the ageing North Sea oil production platforms which currently hang as a major liability over the oil companies (*The Times*, 27 January, 1995: 25), the significant losses sustained by British building societies as they were forced to bail out of their expensively created estate agency chains in the early 1990s (Beaverstock *et al*, 1992), or the huge losses sustained by Volkswagen (VW) when it was forced to cease production in the USA in 1988 and close down its Westmoreland (Pennsylvania) assembly plant. Recently, however, that neglect has begun to be redressed (see G L Clark, 1994; G L Clark and Wrigley, 1995a). A framework for research on corporate strategy and restructuring in economic geography which focuses explicitly upon the role of sunk costs has been suggested, and attempts have been made to interrelate types of sunk costs ('set-up', 'accumulated' or 'exit' sunk costs), characteristics of sunk costs ('recoverability', 'transferability', 'longevity', and 'recurrent financial need'), and the management of sunk costs, in contrasting market structures or 'domains of competition'. It has been argued that the logic of sunk costs not only offers a valuable analytical framework for understanding the spatial patterns of restructuring, but also serves as a vitally important bridging concept, linking firm-specific case studies with more abstract notions of spatial fixity and plasticity (G L Clark and Wrigley, 1995a). Moreover, it has been argued that the management of sunk costs provides an important key to a firm's long-term viability and growth, and to competitive success in a volatile world of global competition.

An examination of the concerns which surfaced in the early 1990s about retail property overvaluation, non-recoverable initial investment, market exit, and the general sunk costs of UK food retailers provides, therefore, an opportunity to link an analysis of a specific moment in the transformation of British retail capital to emerging theoretical issues in economic geography. I shall argue that to understand the true nature of the competitive impact of the UK property crisis on food retailing requires an appreciation of the interaction of sunk costs, strategies of corporate restructuring and market structures. In addition, I shall argue the management of sunk costs appears set to become an increasingly vital component in any explanation of the future patterns of corporate restructuring in UK food retailing.

The UK property crisis and the food retailers

Overvaluation, depreciation and capitalization of interest

The deep recession which afflicted the UK economy from 1989/90 to 1993 had very different characteristics from that which ushered in the first Thatcher administration a decade earlier. It was a service-led and property-led recession whose urban and regional pattern of impact was almost the mirror image of that of 1979–82. As such, it was the boom areas and sectors of Thatcher's Britain, the south and east, the financial sector, property, niche-market retailing, and so on which felt the greatest impact, which experienced the largest relative rises in unemployment, and falls in exchange values. After more than 25 years in which the UK property market had provided a seemingly low-risk escalator to the accumulation of household and corporate wealth, commercial and domestic property values fell precipitously in real terms. By late 1992 and early 1993 average domestic property values in southern England (from East Anglia across to the South-West) had fallen by 30 per cent from the peaks which they had reached in the fourth quarter of 1988. The consequence was a dramatic rise in housing repossessions by the banks and building societies and the trapping, on Bank of England estimates (*Sunday Telegraph*, 4 April 1993: 2), of 1.7 million households into a position of 'negative equity' (i.e. mortgage debt higher than the value of their houses). Similarly, in the commercial property market, the early 1990s were marked by spectacular failures – the problems of Canary Wharf and the failure of Olympia and York providing the most potent icon.

Curiously, during these years, the UK food-retail property market seemed to have managed to isolate itself from the malaise affecting the rest of the property market. Perversely, because the late 1980s had become an era of 'store wars' in which strategic capital investment and an ability to ground that capital via new store development programmes had become the engine of corporate growth (Wrigley, 1991; 1993a; 1994), the major UK food retailers continued to bid up the prices paid for superstore development sites. As a result, freehold site costs were driven up by around 30 per cent in the three years to spring 1992, with the average site capital costs of a new Tesco superstore rising from £15 million to £22 million. Not surprisingly, by the spring of 1992, after a year in which capital expenditure on new store development by the 'big three' food retailers (Sainsbury, Tesco and Argyll) had reached £2 billion per annum, during which they had raised £1.4 billion of new capital via rights issues to fund continued expansion (Wrigley, 1991), increasing concern began to be voiced about the incredible disparity that had emerged between the trajectories of the general UK property market and the food-retail property market. In particular, the views of Tony Shiret (then of Credit Lyonnais Laing) came to have particular prominence (Shiret, 1991; 1992a; 1992b; 1992c).

Essentially there were three facets to Shiret's arguments.

1   The asset portfolios (superstores and superstore development sites) of the major UK food retailers had become significantly overvalued, and their policy of non-depreciation of freehold (and long-leasehold) land and buildings could no longer be justified in the face of the much reduced 'residual value' assumptions which flowed from the UK property crisis.
2   The accountancy practices of the major UK food retailers – specifically the *capitalization of interest* paid on the finance used to fund the development of new superstores – appeared to have exacerbated the overvaluation of the superstores constructed since the mid-1980s.
3   Correction of (1) and (2) by depreciation and discontinuation of the 'capitalization of interest', was likely to reduce significantly the pre-tax profits and earnings per share of the major food retailers.

The policy of non-depreciation of land and buildings (that is carrying property assets at 'cost') operated by the major UK food retailers dated from a period in which moderate to high levels of property inflation could be assumed to offset any diminution in the underlying value of the assets. In fact, sizeable surpluses were usually realized by the retailers on disposal (or sale and leaseback) of their property. However, in the period of much lower general inflation and massive deflation in the property sector which characterized the early 1990s, these assumptions became no longer justifiable – particularly in the case of property assets acquired since the peak of the general UK market. Unfortunately for the 'big three' food retailers, a large proportion of their property fell into just this category, having opened in the late 1980s and early 1990s, reflecting the hugely increased new-store investment programmes which had defined their competitive strategy during this period. Indeed, Shiret (1992a) suggested that, in spring 1992, between 70 and 80 per cent of the property asset values of the 'big three' represented capital investment made since 1987. Moreover, as Figure 6.1 shows very clearly, the new store openings of Tesco in particular were heavily concentrated during the early 1990s in the very areas of the country which were experiencing the most dramatic falls in property values.

In this environment, there was considerable dispute over just what the appropriate property valuations of the major food retailers should be. Tesco, for example, published a sample 'open market valuation' by Healey and Baker of 82 of its stores which purported to show a surplus over cost of 22 per cent. However, the limited evidence from the sale and leaseback market was far more pessimistic and revealed a pattern of falling surpluses which contradicted the external valuation evidence

(Shiret, 1992b). Moreover, even those sale and leaseback deals which were successfully completed appeared to rest on over-optimistic assumptions concerning long-term committed rentals and, significantly, included very few of the most problematic stores – those built after the peak of the general property market in 1988 on the most expensive ('overvalued') sites. On the basis of this evidence, plus a continued absence of traditional institutional investors, such as pension funds,

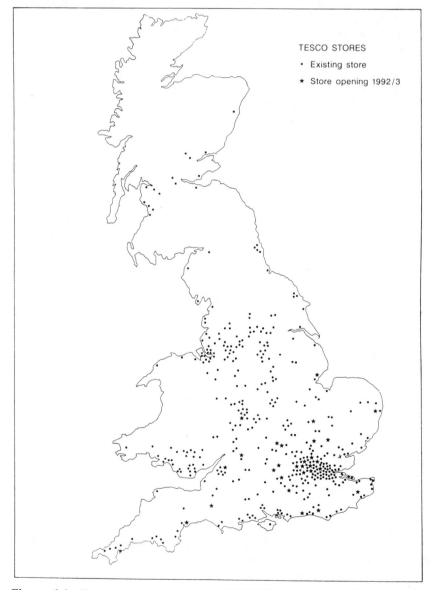

Figure 6.1 Tesco's new store opening, 1992/3 (*Source*: adapted from company annual report)

from the market, Shiret (1992a: 3) suggested that 'currently opening sites are about 20–30 percent overvalued and that disposal (via leaseback) for any site opened after 1986/7 would probably give rise to a capital loss'. As a result, he argued that superstores opened between 1986 and 1989 should have land and buildings depreciated at 1 per cent per annum, and that superstores opened since 1989 should be depreciated by between 2 and 3 per cent per annum.

The second strand of Shiret's argument – 'capitalization of interest' – relates to how the cost of providing the finance used to fund the development of new superstores was being treated in company accounts. Beginning in the early 1980s, the major UK food retailers had come to adopt the practice of treating the interest paid on the finance used to fund the development of a new superstore as part of the cost of acquiring the asset. As a result the interest paid was *capitalized* (added to the capital cost of the asset) rather than being 'written off' (that is to say, charged against the operating revenue of the retailer during the period over which the interest was payable). The result was that the annual pre-tax profits, declared by the major food retailers, were higher than they would otherwise have been if a 'writing off' policy had been adopted.

Accounting practice in the UK (and International Accountancy Standard 23) permits capitalization of interest in this manner and in the early to mid-1980s it constituted a relatively minor element in the pre-tax profits of the major food retailers (Rutherford and Waring, 1987: 26–34). However, such was the pace of the new store expansion programmes during the late 1980s and early 1990s that capitalized interest rapidly became a much more significant item in the composition of the pre-tax profits of the major food retailers. In the case of Tesco, for example, capitalized interest amounted to £88 million or 16 per cent of pre-tax profits in 1991/92. Shiret argued that capitalization of interest on this scale had encouraged some dangerous tendencies in the corporate strategies of the 'big three' food retailers. By protecting their annual pre-tax profits from the interest payments on the finance used to fund the massive expansion in their new-store programmes, it had facilitated continual growth in pre-tax profits and earnings per share. Successful performance on these latter indicators, and a certain blindness to the issue of capitalization of interest, had then fuelled the belief both of the capital markets and of the companies themselves in the wisdom of escalating store expansion programmes, facilitated the raising of new capital (via the 1991 rights issues – see Wrigley, 1991), and had encouraged both the overvaluation of retail property and property investment of debatable quality since the peak of the general UK market in 1988. In addition, it had allowed Tesco in particular to carry disproportionately large amounts of unproductive assets (in the form of a 'land bank' which included £100 million worth of sites without planning permission) without incurring any apparent penalty in its year-end results (Shiret, 1991: 21).

Shiret's view was that capitalization of interest should be discontinued until food-retail property costs/valuations moved back into line with the rest of the UK property market. In the mean time, he argued that the major food retailers should revert to the 'writing off' method of dealing with the interest paid on borrowings. Taking this together with the depreciation charges which he suggested should be applied to all superstores opened since 1986 (up to 3 per cent per annum for those opened since 1989) to reflect the realities of the property crisis, he calculated (Shiret, 1992a: 4) that the 1992 pre-tax profits of Tesco, Sainsbury and Argyll should be adjusted downwards by 22, 14 and 18 per cent, respectively, and the expected 1993 pre-tax profits by 21, 15 and 11 per cent respectively.

The response of the food retailers

At first, the response of the major food retailers to the concerns voiced by Shiret and others was extremely muted. They appeared locked into common corporate trajectories (chosen paths of accumulation) based upon the raising of entry barriers by hugely increased investment and differential access to capital. Those trajectories were threatening to become, at the very least, treadmills. At worst, they were potentially serious burdens to the major retailers' ability to face the threat of a new type of market entrant, and a risk to their long-term corporate viability. The only firm which moved immediately towards adopting Shiret's suggestions was Wm Morrison, one of the largest regional chains. In late 1992, Morrison, which almost uniquely in UK food retailing, already depreciated freehold (and long-leasehold) buildings, announced that it would also begin to depreciate freehold (and long-leasehold) land at the rate of 1 per cent per annum.

Far more significant than the announcement of Morrison, however, was the acknowledgement by the fourth ranking UK food retailer, Asda, that it was to write off £280 million on property values. The majority of this write-off related to a downward valuation of the 61 superstores which Asda had acquired for almost £700 million in 1989 from Gateway, at the time of the leveraged buyout (LBO) of Gateway by the Isoceles consortium. Seeking to keep pace with the 'big three', and to compensate for problems in the pace of its store expansion programme in the late 1980s, Asda had sought to gain market share in critical regions of the UK by the purchase of the Gateway superstores. Unfortunately these stores, bought at the peak of the market, were significantly overvalued. Moreover, they left Asda with a burden of debt which became increasingly difficult to service as recession began to bite. The result was that Asda's capital expenditure programme had to be dramatically curtailed, net profits began to decline, its share price fell dramatically, and in June 1991 its chief executive left the company. From a position of being one of the UK's 'big three' food retailers in the mid-1980s, Asda found itself by 1992 in an extremely difficult competitive position. It was caught in the middle ground between the new 'big three' (Sainsbury, Tesco and Argyll) with their seemingly ever-increasing capital investment programmes at one end of the spectrum and, at the other end of the spectrum, a rapidly expanding low capital-intensity, low-margin deep discount sector dynamized by the entry of the European discounters Aldi and Netto, who were targeting the 'value-sensitive' urban/industrial regions (e.g. the north-west and West Yorkshire) which had traditionally formed Asda's heartland.

Clearly, a major reformulation of corporate strategy was required at Asda. In 1992, under a new chief executive (Archie Norman) bought in from Kingfisher, and with £357 million of vital refinancing from a rescue rights issue in September 1991, it became clear that three elements of that reformulation were to be: a write-off of the overvaluation of the ex-Gateway superstores, a clear acknowledgement of the threat posed by the deep discounters, and a re-evaluation of the implications of sunk costs (in the form of largely unrecoverable property investment) for corporate strategy. As a result, corporate strategy was refocused on price-competitiveness and the threat of the deep discounters. In addition, certain Asda stores which were at the point of obsolescence, underperforming, and/or facing locally intense competitive pressure from the deep discounters, were 'repositioned' into a discount superstore format under the label 'Dales'. In other words, rather than face the sunk cost implications of exit from these sites, the decision was taken to convert them, at relatively limited cost, into a low-price, low-margin, format. This allowed Asda to develop a more flexible competitive response to the market entry of the European deep discounters and, by facilitating a leverage of low-cost assets, provided a strategy for managing sunk costs.

A similar strategy, albeit driven by somewhat different corporate imperatives, was also adopted by Gateway (another second tier, highly debt-encumbered, food retailer as a result of its LBO in 1989) and by the Co-op. The result was that by 1993, in response to the progressive expansion of Aldi and Netto (Figures 6.2 and 6.3), the market entry or anticipated entry of other European discounters (Ed, Lidl, etc), and the expansion of the native UK 'deep' discounter, Shoprite, a network of extended-range discount superstores – Food Giant (Gateway), Dales (Asda) and Pioneer (Co-op) – was beginning to take shape (Figure 6.4). In general terms, this network can be viewed as part of a wider attempt to develop a competitive response to the expansion of the deep discounters via the management of sunk costs.

It is clear, therefore, that the burden of debt which afflicted the second-tier food retailers and their difficult competitive position prompted a re-evaluation of competitive strategy and, by default, both a medium-term curtailment of property investment, and long-term reappraisal of the nature of store expansion policies. In contrast, the impact of rapidly changing competitive conditions in UK food retailing, and the concerns of Shiret and others regarding the overvaluation of property portfolios, had little obvious effect on the 'big three' food retailers during 1992 and the early months of 1993. The argument was mounted that the wider price-competition spillover effects feared at the time of Aldi and Netto's entry into the UK market had been overstated, and that the discounters had entered a sub-sector of the market which

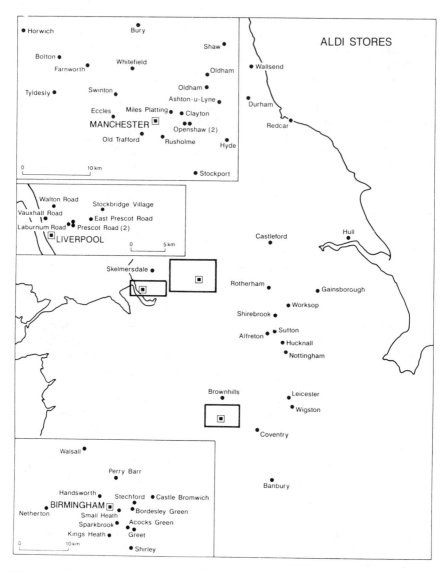

Figure 6.2 Aldi's UK store network in early 1993 (*Source*: company listings, press announcements, compiled by R Gascoigne)

to a large extent was totally separated from that occupied by the 'big three'. The image was painted of an era of mutual coexistence, with direct price-competition effects being unlikely to cross the market segment boundaries, and in which the corporate trajectories of the 'big three', rooted in strategic capital investment via ever-accelerating new store expansion programmes, could remain essentially unchanged. However, by the autumn of 1993 it was becoming clearer by the day that this image was incorrect, that the 'big three' were being seriously affected by the wider chain reaction (involving Asda, Gateway, etc) to

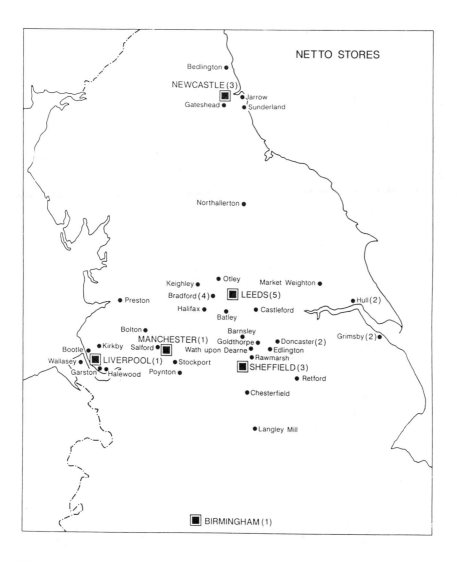

Figure 6.3 Netto's UK store network in mid-1993 (*Source*: company listings, press announcements, compiled by R Gasgoigne)

the entry of the deep discounters, and that they could no longer attempt to sustain a position aloof from the realities of rapidly changing competitive conditions and untouched by growing worries concerning property valuations, sunk costs and 'exit'.

In September 1993 Tesco reported, to capital markets which were becoming increasingly alarmed about the prospects of the 'big three' food retailers, that its gross profit margin had declined for the first time since the early 1980s as a result of attempts to become more competitive on price to meet the growing threats of the discounters and the re-

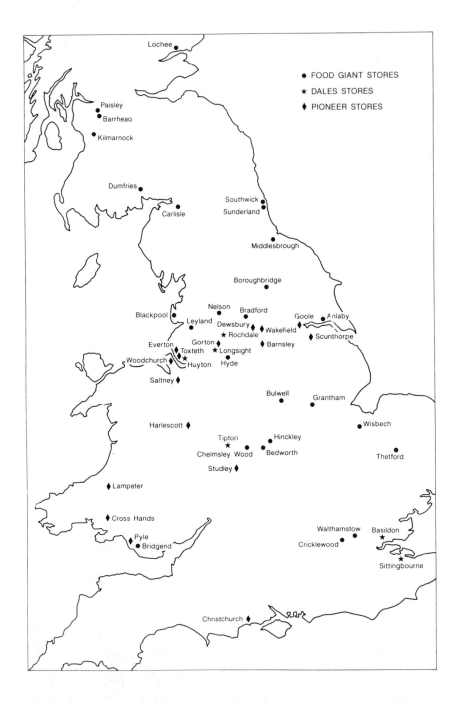

Figure 6.4 The emerging network of discount superstores in mid-1993 (*Source*: company listings, press announcments, compiled by R Gascoigne)

configured second-tier chains. It also acknowledged that it faced significant erosion of the local spatial monopolies, so vital to the profitability of its superstores in the late 1980s, as the discounters sought 'parasitic' locations adjacent to its stores. (The chairman of Tesco ruefully noted that, 'whoever you are, you now have the Aldis, Nettos and Eds sitting on your car park', Sir Ian MacLaurin, Chairman, Tesco, *Financial Times*, 22 September 1993.) In October, the 'big three' were then seen to fail conspicuously in their joint High Court action to block the opening by Costco of Britain's first American-style discount 'warehouse club', prompting major press coverage of the likelihood of price wars and speculation about a scenario of 'mutually assured destruction'. Finally, in early November, Sainsbury acknowledged the threat to competitive conditions posed by the discounters and announced a major and long-term downward repositioning on price. The Sainsbury announcement, coming from the market leader previously unwilling to debate such issues, shocked the capital markets and the share prices of the major food retailers fell dramatically.

Acknowledgement by the 'big three' of the threat of the discounters and the changing nature of competition in UK food retailing, was then followed by their belated acceptance of the validity of Shiret's arguments on property overvaluation and depreciation. In December 1993, Argyll became the first of the major food retailers to announce that it was to start depreciating its store values and cutting back its new store development programme. The decision was taken to depreciate buildings and land over a 40 year period, with the result that Argyll's pre-tax profits were to be subject to a recurring reduction of £40 million per annum. In addition, its capital spend programme (largely on new store development) was cut back by £100 million per annum.

The view of most retail analysts was that Argyll's decision made similar announcements by Tesco and Sainsbury inevitable. As a result, it came as no surprise when, in January 1994, Tesco announced that it was to begin depreciating its buildings over a 40 year period at a cost of £36 million per annum. In addition, Tesco had decided to depreciate the value of its land and to accept that it had paid in the late 1980s and early 1990s a 'premium' for much of the land on which its superstores were built which was well in excess of any conceivable 'alternative use value' which might be realized on exit from those sites. By deciding to amortize those 'premiums' over 25 years, at a cost of £32 million per annum, the total depreciation charge accepted by Tesco was a recurring £68 million per annum, or approximately 12 per cent of its pre-tax profits. In addition, Tesco announced that it was to cut back its store expansion programme dramatically – from a capital spend of £1 billion per annum in 1991/92 to just £450 million per annum by 1996/97. As a result, Tesco accepted that it must make a one-off write-down of a further £85 million in 1993/94 to take account of the surplus land in its 'land bank'; that is to say land purchased during the frantic store-building boom of the 1980s which would no longer be required for building superstores and which, surplus to requirements, would need to be sold.

Clearly, therefore, Tesco's decisions were even more significant than those of Argyll. The cut-back in the capital expenditure programme implied that floor space expansion would fall from 1.2 million square feet of new floor space in 1991/92 to just 450 000 square feet by 1996/97. In addition, the average cost of a new Tesco store was projected to shrink from £22 million to £16 million, reflecting a shift away from the construction of very large out-of-town superstores and towards the construction of smaller (20 000 sq. ft.) stores, aimed at smaller (market) towns and city suburbs, and of small (10 000 sq. ft) 'Metro' stores in city centres. Not only had the impact of the property crisis turned what had previously been viewed as assets into sunk costs, but also the realization of the potentially catastrophic impact of such sunk costs on corporate performance (annual profits, the ability to meet new forms of competition, etc) had resulted in a fundamental reappraisal of corporate strategy.

The spotlight then shifted to Sainsbury, the member of the 'big three' that had publicly resisted the implications of the property crisis and the need to depreciate its buildings and land most vociferously. In late January 1994, Sainsbury was forced to retract those views and announce that it was to follow Argyll and Tesco in terms of depreciating its freehold and long leasehold buildings, thus incurring an annual depreciation charge of £40 million. Unlike Tesco, however, Sainsbury took the view that the fall in the value of the land (superstore sites) it had purchased in the 1980s and early 1990s should be reflected not via an annual amortization but via a major one-off write-down of £365 million. In addition, as in the case of Argyll and Tesco, the new store expansion programme was to be scaled back, though by only £100 million per annum, reflecting the opportunities for new store investment elsewhere in Sainsbury's more diversified group structure (e.g. in its Shaws food retailing operation in the USA, and its Homebase home improvement and garden centre chain). Nevertheless, the result of Sainsbury's volte-face (particularly the major write-down it had accepted in the value of its land) was that its shares suffered their largest ever one-day fall, wiping £850 million off the market valuation of the company in a single day.

Less than two years, therefore, after the concerns about property valuations had first been raised and to a large extent dismissed by the major UK food retailers, all had been forced, by the nature of changing competitive conditions, to accept the validity of the arguments.

The management of what had come, in the intervening period, to be seen very clearly as sunk costs had become critical to the reformulation of corporate strategy. The only questions remaining in early 1994 were whether or not the property write-downs and new policies on depreciation went far enough. Some analysts were beginning to take that view that awakening from the 'superstore dream' which had driven the corporate trajectories of the major UK food retailers in the 'golden age' of the late 1980s and early 1990s might be even more difficult and painful than first thought. What was clear, however, was that the potential costs of 'exit', the management of sunk costs, and the future pattern of profit margins in the industry were as likely to be as intimately interconnected during a period of scaling back of new store development programmes as the costs of entry and profit margins had been in the period of frenetic superstore development during the 1980s and early 1990s. Indeed, the *Financial Times* captured the essence of this interlinkage as early as September 1993 when it noted that:

> The horrendous costs of quitting and high fixed overheads of superstores force the grocers to run them for cash. That effectively means that there is almost no limit to the margin erosion which could occur if the grocers descended into a game of competitive devaluation.

Sunk costs and corporate strategies: exploring the linkages

By invoking a general definition of sunk costs as that proportion of a firm's investment which cannot be recovered should the firm change its strategy of accumulation, we have seen in broad terms how the management of sunk costs (specifically, in the retailers' case, non-recoverable initial investment in land and buildings) became an increasingly vital issue in the corporate restructuring of British food retailing in the mid-1990s. Underpinning our analysis is a definition of corporate restructuring as the 'deliberate process of *re*making the inherited configuration of production with respect to a possible and more desirable path of accumulation' (G L Clark, 1994: 9; Webber *et al*, 1991). Given, therefore, that for the food retailers the inherited configuration of 'production' is to a large extent represented by their property portfolios (store networks), the linkage between sunk costs and corporate reconfiguration in response to changed competitive conditions is unsurprising. Nevertheless, several facets of that linkage require theorizing. In this section and the next an attempt will be made to do that, drawing upon some of the basic propositions about the economic and spatial logic of sunk costs outlined in the work of G L Clark and Wrigley (1995a; 1995b).

Assets into sunk costs: the functional value of capital

A central feature in the story of the property crisis of the UK food retailers was the way in which what were previously regarded as assets came increasingly to be regarded as potential or actual sunk costs. G L Clark and Wrigley (1995b) have considered in more general terms this process whereby as asset starts out as an exchangeable commodity and over time becomes an entirely specific non-tradable liability (sunk cost). Figure 6.5 attempts to summarize, in a simple form, some aspects of that argument by decomposing into a number of elements the functional value of a capital asset to a firm over the life cycle of the asset.

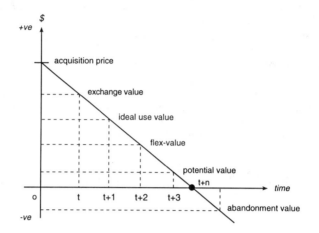

Figure 6.5 The functional value of a capital asset to a firm over the life cycle of the asset (*Source*: adapted from G L Clark and Wrigley, 1995b)

Beginning at time t_0 in Figure 6.5 with an acquisition price (in the case of a new superstore, the total cost – land/buildings/fitting out, etc – of developing the store) the asset is conceived as being worth, over the period t_0 to t, its acquisition price less depreciation. As the value of the asset continues to decline over time, it is then viewed as retaining its *exchange value* (saleability to other firms) through to t+1, its *ideal use value* through to time t+2, its so-called *flex-value* (recognizing that the asset can be used in a variety of less than ideal ways) through to time t+3, and its so-called *potential value* – its value in an idle state (recognizing that even in an idle state it will have value in deterring new competitors from entering the market) – through to time t+n. In the end, however, once all these 'values' have been exhausted, it is important to note that the abandonment value of the asset is likely to be negative. For example, it is likely to cost the firm money to disassemble or reconfigure the 'asset', and rehabilitate the space it occupied.

Although Figure 6.5 is to be understood as nothing more than a simple heuristic device (e.g. in reality some form of exchange value is likely to be retained throughout the various 'use value' stages), the diagram is valuable in two distinct ways. First, in representing the process of increasing specificity whereby, as an asset ages and loses exchange value, the range and flexibility of options which it provides to the firm progressively narrows. That is to say, in representing how an exchangeable asset becomes, over time, an entirely specific non-tradable liability. Second, the diagram is valuable in representing the notion that the valuation of a capital asset is more than just an accounting issue. It is also a strategic issue involving considerations related to the competitive strategy of the firm and the likely actions of its competitors. Paradoxically, as a capital asset ages, it may retain considerable competitive value or even, in some circumstances, become *more* valuable to a firm in terms of competitive strategy within the industry than when the asset was at the peak of its exchange value. The case of an asset in an idle state retaining competitive value in terms of deterring new competitors from entering the market (i.e. the threat that spare capacity in the hands of a determined incumbent might be used to so drive-down market price that potential competitors judge the cost of entry to be too high) is a obvious example which has already been noted. More generally, however, we have the notion of there being potential competitive value in the increased specificity (non-replicable local-level knowledge, accumulated and related investments in infrastructure and work practices, etc) of an asset, and of that specificity becoming a potential strategic competitive variable. In turn, this can be used to explain why it is often the case that firms can be highly competitive even without capital assets of the most recent vintage (e.g. with deliberately retained second-best capital equipment).

Residual value, alternative uses and repositioning

Debate on the property crisis of the UK food retailers and corporate restructuring in the industry has touched implicitly upon several of these broader concepts relating to the functional value of a capital asset. Attempts have been made, for example, to estimate 'residual value' at the point of obsolescence for a food superstore (i.e. at point t+2 in Figure 6.5 when its 'ideal use' value has been exhausted). Residual value has been estimated (Guy, 1995a; Shiret, 1992a: 19–22; 1992c: 5) on the basis of 'alternative use' assumptions – for example, for non-food retailing, warehousing, leisure use, commercial office space, residential land use, etc. That is to say, attempts have been made in the terminology of Figure 6.5 to estimate the so-called 'flex-value' of a food superstore (and, more rarely, its 'potential value' in an idle state). However, the exercise has proved extremely difficult to conduct for the obvious reason that there is simply little experience, as yet, in the UK of what can be done with a 35 000 sq. ft. out-of-town superstore of the type that were built during the 'store wars' of the 1980s (Wrigley, 1994), if changing competitive conditions were to result in any very drastic 'remaking of the inherited configuration of production with respect to a . . . more desirable path of accumulation'. Whereas in the era of smaller 'in town' supermarkets a degree of interchangeability between food-retail and alternative uses existed, and a considerable amount of 'open market' disposal and rental evidence built up, 'the move out of town has left the alternative use value far behind, throwing into doubt the long-term rental prospects for the property' (Shiret, 1992c: 6).

What is clear, however, from the alternative use value exercises that have been conducted, is that industrial or warehouse uses, and even residential property uses, are likely to produce very low values in most of the UK in comparison to the prices paid (particularly during the era of the 'store wars') for food superstore sites. In addition, the location characteristics which made those food superstore sites so attractive during that era, namely 'limited competition from stores of similar size and vintage' (Moir, 1990: 108), that is to say local spatial monopoly/ dominance, may not be characteristics which are attractive to non-food retail uses. Such uses will often require *groupings* of compatible retailers whose joint attractiveness to consumers is greater (as a result of multipurpose trip economies) then the sum of their individual drawing powers. As a result, if non-food-retailing is the assumed alternative use, food retailers are likely to achieve reasonable residual values from such sites only if they are prepared, and can obtain planning consent, to develop them as more broadly based retail parks. More generally, whatever the alternative use configuration envisaged, it is likely that the food retailers will obtain the most reasonable residual values only if they are prepared to 'take on the role of developer and take the development margin' (Shiret, 1992c: 22). The implications of this, of course, is that they must be prepared to allow management of sunk costs (avoidance of the risk of assets becoming sunk costs) to impact very significantly indeed upon the nature of their corporate strategies.

However, as we have seen in the case of the debt-encumbered second-tier UK food retailers, there is a more likely intermediate scenario to such fully blown 'alternative use' positions. Conventional food superstores of older vintage and with little remaining 'ideal use' value or exchange value can often be effectively repositioned within the food retailing spectrum; for example, into the Food Giant/Dales–type of extended-range discount superstore format discussed above. Again little is known about the long-term trading record of such stores in the UK, but the shorter-term trading record appears to be very successful and the wider competitive impact of these repositioned superstores has been considerable. Repositioning can therefore be seen as facilitating a leveraging of capital assets with little remaining conventional exchange value. But, very significantly, that much reduced value of itself and the significant costs of exit (given the type of alternative use considerations discussed above) which competitors are aware would otherwise have to be borne, combine to make the repositioning a credible threat to both other market incumbents and to potential market entrants. This neatly illustrates the argument of how a capital asset, as it ages, can sometimes become more valuable to a firm in terms of competitive strategy within the industry, than when it was at the peak of its exchange value.

Repositioning of older vintage superstores into 'second label' discount food operations of the 'Dales' type may not, however, be an option open to all the UK food retailers. The 'big three' are locked into very focused corporate strategies in which a high capital-intensity store format and 'quality' image are central, mutually reinforcing, elements. To adopt a 'second label' discount format for older vintage superstores would involve fundamental risks to a laboriously built positionality in the market and would, in any event, pose very considerable problems of managing low capital-intensity and high capital-intensity operations in tandem.

As a result, although Sainsbury has conducted a very limited experiment with a bulk-purchase discounter store in Essex to meet the local competition of the first Costco 'warehouse club' in the UK, it has not, at the time of writing, expanded out that experiment. In addition, Argyll (the only member of the 'big three' to operate a discount-label format in the late 1980s and early 1990s via its Lo-Cost stores) has chosen to sell those stores and to adopt a 'core-focus' strategy.

In the absence of a realistic 'repositioning' option for their older vintage superstores, the 'big three' are now attempting to manage sunk costs via a hybrid combination of property write-downs, depreciation, sale and leaseback deals where possible, store remodelling (i.e. refurbishment in situ), refocusing of the 'offer' within the stores (e.g. the introduction of secondary own-labels – such as the Tesco 'Value' lines – to meet intensifying price competition), and via strategic diversification of the entire business to reduce long-term dependence on UK food retailing. The latter involves both internationalization and sectoral diversification. Internationalization is represented by Sainsbury's rapidly expanding food retailing business in the USA – via its Shaw's chain in New England (Shackleton, this volume, Chapter 7; Wrigley, 1993a) and its more recent purchase of a significant share of the Giant chain in the Washington DC/Baltimore area – and by Tesco's food retailing business in France (via its Catteau chain in northern France). Diversification into other sectors of retailing is represented by Sainsbury's Homebase DIY operation, and by its purchase of the Texas DIY chain from Ladbroke in early 1995 for £290 million to lever Homebase into second position in terms of market share in that section of UK retailing.

Conclusion: grounding retail capital and managing sunk costs

At the heart of the accumulation process in retailing is the constant need to 'ground' retail capital. However, that fixing in place (however short-term) brings associated vulnerabilities. It is the manner in which these tensions and contradictions are played out which forms a central component of the corporate strategies of major retailers. Yet, surprisingly, and in marked contrast to investigations of tensions at the interface between retail capital and productive capital (see Doel; Foord, Bowlby and Tillsley; Hughes, this volume, Chapters 3, 4 and 5), little has been written in the fields of retail geography and planning about these issues. Indeed, Guy (1994: 114) has observed that despite the fact that 'the property development, investment and disposal activities of the major retailers in Britain [have] major implications for the profitability of retailers themselves, as well as for the built environment' they remain a remarkably 'under-researched topic'.

This neglect is all the more curious given the fact that during the 'store wars' of the 1980s the major UK food retailers became locked into corporate strategies of accumulation in which strategic capital investment and an ability to ground that capital via new store development programmes became the all-consuming engine of corporate growth. In turn, that resulted in what Guy (1995b) has described as 'one of the largest construction programmes ever to have taken place in western Europe'. One interpretation of that massive level of investment was that it was an attempt to raise barriers to market entry to such an extent that potential entrants would be faced, if their entry were to fail as a result of retaliatory strategic or tactical responses by the incumbents, with a level of non-recoverable sunk costs which would be quite unacceptable. (See G L Clark and Wrigley, 1995a, for further discussion of sunk costs as barriers to market entry.) To the extent that the 'big three' UK food retailers still appear unchallengeable in terms of their own strictly defined market position, that investment in the raising of entry barriers was to a large degree successful. However, it is also well known that excessive entry-discouraging investment involves considerable risks for incumbent firms, and that it may increase the probability of ruinous loss by increasing the *fixity of costs* and by lowering the average salvage value of the firms' assets (G L Clark and Wrigley, 1995a). Faced, therefore, with a new form of competition (the deep discounters) who chose not (or were not able) to accept the sunk cost risks of challenging the incumbent major food retailers on their own terms, but whose impact on the competitive structure of UK food retailing was gradually transmitted via a chain reaction involving the debt-encumbered second-tier food retailers, and faced also by a re-evaluation of the role of store expansion programmes within the context of rapidly changing competitive conditions and the belated impact of the UK property crisis, the major food retailers were seen to have locked into local paths of capital accumulation that became dangerously self-reinforcing and narrow. The questions which must be asked therefore are:

1   Why did the major food retailers persist with such competitive strategies in the early 1990s when it was becoming increasingly obvious to commentators outside the industry that a change in the strategy of accumulation that had characterized the era of the store wars was becoming necessary?
2   What was the role of sunk costs in this corporate lock-in?
3   How can firms characterized by potentially significant sunk costs manage those costs to ensure their long-term viability and growth?

The first (and tangentially the second) of these questions is increasingly being posed and answered more generally within economic geography. Schoenberger (1994a), for example, has attempted to understand why it is that there are so many well-documented examples of firms that become locked into inappropriate corporate strategies, delaying essential corporate restructuring, even though those firms realize the need for transformation and often know quite a lot about the dimensions of the transformation required. She has also posed the question of 'why firms flinch in the face of high sunk costs yet simultaneously invest gigantic sums in disastrously misguided initiatives' (1994a: 438). Her answers to these questions centre on the way that top managers of these firms seek to defend their own social asset structures, as a result foreclosing certain kinds of corporate strategies however appropriate and vital. Schoenberger's view is that economic geographers must focus on how 'the need to transform the firm in order to remain competitive may encounter its most serious obstacle in the social being, position, and perceptions of the people that run it' (1994a: 448), and on 'the ways in which corporate identity and corporate culture frame the kinds of knowledge that can be produced and utilized by the firm in the creation and implementation of competitive strategies' (1994a: 449).

G L Clark and Wrigley (1995b) address similar themes in an attempt to answer the third of these questions. They argue that the management of sunk costs is a profoundly social process in which there will inevitably be 'principal–agent' type problems in firms characterized by the separation of ownership and control, and contested bilateral relationships between managers and the firms internal stakeholders (such as workers) which must be taken into consideration. The management of sunk costs within the firm (more specifically the retail manager's capacity to exploit the strategic/competitive options implicit in a portfolio of stores differentiated by age and exchange/use value) is embedded within the more general underlying problem addressed by Schoenberger – namely how do managers achieve their goals and defend their social asset structures relative to the goals and interests of the firms shareholders and stakeholders. G L Clark and Wrigley (1995b) outline, in the context of manufacturing firms, a range of possible institutional options for stabilizing conflict between management and stakeholders and resolving problems of information flow, co-operation and commitment in firms characterized by significant sunk costs. What emerges from that analysis is that, in order to manage its sunk costs, a firm may have to differentiate spatially its institutional structure and differentiate (between production sites) its contracts with local stakeholders. It is of interest to ask, therefore, questions such as: to what extent are attempts to manage sunk costs in British food retailing leading to spatially differentiated labour contracts and work practices *within* firms, e.g. between the repositioned and non-repositioned store types/labels within a single firm?

More generally, G L Clark and Wrigley (1995b) suggest that how sunk costs are managed in relation to competitors and in relation to the interests of corporate managers and their stakeholders is a vital determinant of a firm's long-term growth. The sudden and dramatic problems of property overvaluation, non-recoverable initial investment, and the implications of sunk costs for corporate strategy, which engulfed the UK food retailers in late 1993 and early 1994 confirm this and serve to highlight the fact that many aspects of the 'grounding' of retail capital have remained surprisingly unproblematized in retail geography. Clearly there is a great deal yet to be written about the realization of value in firms characterized by significant sunk costs but, given the centrality and potential vulnerabilities that follow from the constant need to 'ground' retail capital, it is a task which cannot be ignored.

CHAPTER 7

Retailer internationalization: a culturally constructed phenomenon

Ruth Shackleton

In the mid-1990s there has been an increased interest within economic geography in the power of corporate culture to control and dictate business strategies and economic change. Indeed, Schoenberger (1994a; 1994b) has argued that notions of corporate culture and corporate strategy have become 'central to a number of discourses within economic geography' (1994b: 1010). Gertler (1995), meanwhile, has called for economic geographers to move away from their 'surprisingly uncritical, super organic, static conception of culture' and concentrate upon the 'process by which industrial cultures are themselves produced and reproduced by social practices' (1995: 2). As geographers begin to recognize that 'corporations are run by real people' (Schoenberger, 1994a: 448) and that corporate strategists' social positions shape their interpretation of the world and their ability to formulate corporate strategy, case studies of the way that corporate culture 'produces strategy' while 'at the same time it is being shaped by the strategic trajectory of the firm' (Schoenberger, 1994a: 449) are becoming a fundamental component of the research agenda of economic geography.

The objective of this chapter is to augment the evolving debate by demonstrating that corporate culture is a particularly useful lens through which to view contemporary changes within retailing. Three main points are considered. First, the chapter demonstrates the power and influence of corporate culture to direct and control industrial restructuring. In addition, it argues that the entrenched nature of corporate culture directs the strategic decisions that executives make.

Second, the chapter highlights an inadequacy of the existing corporate strategy and economic restructuring literatures. It demonstrates that traditional accounts of corporate strategy and economic restructuring, while thorough in their descriptions of how markets operate, are overly mechanistic. In particular they fail to consider that corporate strategy and economic change are 'socially and culturally inflicted process[es]' (Schoenberger, 1994b: 1011). This is shown to be a fundamental flaw as corporate strategy is clearly contingent upon corporate culture.

Third, the chapter demonstrates the need for economic geographers to rethink fundamentally notions of corporate culture and business strategy. Geographers must recognize that social and economic systems are inextricably bound up with each other (Gertler, 1995). More recognition must also be given to the power of corporate culture to dictate and control economic change. The way forward therefore, in constructing the new retail geography, is for economic geographers to discard traditional assumptions which considered corporate culture to be a soft, marginal, phenomenon which has little, if any, direct impact upon the economic restructuring process. The new retail geography must interrogate the complex dynamics associated with corporate culture in order to fully understand processes of retail restructuring.

Defining corporate culture

The obscurity surrounding the term 'corporate culture' is a major obstacle when using the term to explain contemporary changes within retailing. The term is frequently misunderstood and consequently has often been categorized as a 'soft' variable that has little direct impact on the fate of an organization. This is clearly untrue. Defining corporate culture should serve to clarify the meaning of the term and eradicate any obscurity surrounding it.

The anthropologist Kluckhohn (1962) defined culture as 'the traditional set of habitual and traditional ways of thinking, feeling and reacting that are characteristic of the ways that a particular society meets its problems at a particular point in time'. This static definition of culture has subsequently been widely adopted within the management literature (e.g. Hampden-Turner, 1992; Kotter and Heskett, 1990). Corporate culture is seen, therefore, as the underlying beliefs and principles of an organization that serve as foundation for a set of practices and behaviours that employ and re-enforce these principles. These underlying beliefs and values then produce situational norms that powerfully shape the behaviour of all individuals in the organization (Schwartz and Davis, 1981). More recently, it has been argued that this conceptualization of corporate culture is far too narrow and that it considers custom and tradition as the principle barriers to cultural change (Schoenberger, 1994a: 449). Moreover, it is a view of corporate culture that is extremely static and unresponsive to the complex processes inherent within the contemporary business environment.

A new, more responsive, definition of corporate culture is therefore required. Schoenberger (1994a: 449) suggests an alternative view which 'sees culture inherently and deeply implicated in how and what we know about the world and ourselves'. This definition recognizes that corporate culture is 'being produced (and contested) and cannot be reduced to a set of stable attributes' (1994a: 449). Corporate culture is seen as a dynamic phenomenon that is subject to internal and external influences which cause it to adapt and change over time. Internal change, it is argued, comes from the executives' perceptions of the world and how they adapt their values and perceptions as their vision of the world changes. Consequently, when that vision of the world is transferred to their business interests, corporate cultures change accordingly. In addition, it is argued that corporate culture is heavily influenced by the external 'broader dynamics of the system'. Gertler (1995: 3) elaborates this concept by arguing that corporate culture is heavily influenced by the structure of the macro-regulatory environment in which it functions.

Corporate culture and the internationalization of retail capital

This chapter interrogates the above arguments by examining, in general terms and via a specific case study, the internationalization of retail capital. The international diversification process, particularly where that process involves acquisition, is shown to be heavily influenced by corporate culture and as such represents a good example through which to examine the power of corporate culture to influence economic change. It is argued that corporate culture is particularly influential during the post-acquisition period when two divergent corporate cultures collide. The post-acquisition period is shown to be characterized by a series of power struggles as the corporate cultures contend for supremacy.

The case study examined is that of the market entry of British food retail capital into the USA. More specifically it concerns the leading UK food retailer, Sainsbury, who in 1987 acquired the US food retailing chain Shaw's Supermarkets as a first stage in a long-term strategy of reducing dependency on the UK market. Sainsbury has a distinctly British corporate culture and a highly focused corporate strategy which it has subsequently attempted to transfer to the USA. The acquired company, Shaw's, despite having some superficial similarities, had in practice operated with a very different strategic and cultural dynamic. As a result, the acquisition was followed by a period of considerable turmoil and readjustment.

Preliminary evidence (Shackleton, 1994, 1995) suggests that Sainsbury's corporate culture and strategies are impinging upon Shaw's whole supply chain. The chapter examines the impact that the changes to Shaw's corporate culture have had upon one particular group within this chain, Shaw's employees. The chapter also discusses the extent to which the changes seen are the result of the transfer of Sainsbury's values and ideas or whether they are merely associated with the fact that the 'retailing sector is shedding employment rapidly as a consequence of the consolidation of sector, cost cutting strategies and the success of applying just-in-time strategies which began in the 1980s' (see Chapter 8).

The Sainsbury case study is particularly important as it demonstrates the inherent power struggle and tensions that inevitably follow when 'big' corporate capital is injected into a 'small', less capital-intensive company. It also raises many issues related to the corporate cultures associated with these very different forms of corporate capital. Research concerning international diversification needs to recognize that a spectrum of corporate culture exists, and that the type of power struggle which occurs when two corporate cultures collide will be determined by the position of the corporate cultures within that spectrum.

Corporate culture: asset or liability?

Corporate culture has both postive and negative effects. The direction of the influence is dependent upon the prevailing competitive environment. A strong, 'appropriate' corporate culture is clearly a beneficial asset for a firm to have: the entrenched underlying beliefs, known to all, motivate employees to strive for a common goal. Executives are therefore more able to control the thinking and behaviour of employees without having to rely upon stiff, formal bureaucratic channels. In addition, company executives can gauge in an instinctive way how their employees are likely to react in an unpredictable environment. Corporate culture clearly has strong integrative properties which, in the right situation, can prove extremely beneficial (for more details see Hampden-Turner, 1992; Kotter and Heskett, 1992; J Martin, 1992; Ray, 1986).

However, there are a variety of problems with the assumption that a strong corporate culture equals automatic success. It is clear from a variety of studies that strong corporate cultures include dysfunctional elements as well as vigorous functional ones (Denison 1984; 1990; Kotter and Heskett, 1992; Schoenberger, 1994a; 1994b). In particular they can encourage 'lock in' and misguided strategic decision-making. This situation is extremely problematic as it prevents managers from reacting to changing competitive conditions and can lead to the demise of the firm. The 'extraordinary power of people's (management's) commitments to the way things are despite the danger those commitments pose to the very people who hold them' (Schoenberger, 1994a: 448) has been neglected within economic geography. This is a fundamental omission as the power of corporate culture to blind managers to the need for strategic adaptation clearly explains why firms fail to react appropriately to new competitive conditions. This situation is particularly perilous during periods of economic turbulence as companies can quickly become locked into a debilitating downward spiral. The more entrenched the culture becomes then the more difficult it is for the organization to release itself from its cultural trap. Release is usually only associated with the accession of a new management team. Clearly, corporate culture is a powerful phenomenon that determines the fate of an organization. Moreover, economic success is only likely with contextually and strategically appropriate corporate cultures.

Corporate culture is clearly, therefore, a vital element which dictates the long-term performance of firms (for more discussion see Denison,

1990; Gertler, 1995; Schoenberger, 1994a; 1994b). The entrenched management inertia associated with corporate culture can be both an invaluable asset and a hindrance within the business environment. It is clear that in order to understand the restructuring process it is necessary then to examine the power and influence of corporate culture to dictate and control strategic decision-making. The following sections will concentrate on one specific area of restructuring, the process of retailer international diversification. They demonstrate that corporate culture offers an important theoretical tool with which to examine the complex processes involved within retail restructuring.

Retailer internationalization: a cultural affair

Academic interest in the international diversification strategies of retailers has grown since the mid-1980s (see e.g. Treadgold and Davies, 1988). However, existing studies have, arguably, been theoretically weak and lacking in empirical rigour. These studies, while worthwhile in the fact that they brought the subject to the attention of geographers, concentrated specifically upon why and where companies invested abroad and ignored the crucial, post-entry phase of the process. More importantly, they failed to acknowledge the power and influence of corporate culture in dictating the outcome of international diversification strategies. This chapter attempts to demonstrate that these omissions were extremely significant by arguing that corporate culture is particularly influential during the post-entry and consolidation phases of international diversification when the firms involved are attempting to assimilate their corporate cultures.

In addition, it is argued that the transfer of corporate culture during the overseas diversification process can stimulate industry-wide restructuring. For example, the entry of a culturally divergent competitor can incite significant periods of dislocation and restructuring among the incumbent firms. Given the power of corporate culture to blind management to the need for cultural and strategic change, companies pursuing international diversification strategies can create competitive advantage by acquiring a 'locked-in' incumbent firm relatively cheaply and by transferring a less inertia-ridden corporate culture to the acquired firm. This move, if coupled with a large amount of capital available for investment, allows the firm entering the market to redefine the competitive arena. The result of this process will often be industry-wide restructuring and strategic reassessment as the incumbent firms attempt to counter the competitive advantage of the entering firm.

The process of international diversification is, clearly, highly influenced by corporate culture, and to that extent previous studies concerning retailer internationalization have been fundamentally flawed. The way forward when constructing the new retail geography is to abandon traditional explanations of retailer international diversification. A new, more appropriate theoretical approach is required. Examining retailer international diversification through the lens of corporate culture provides the means whereby a fuller understanding of the complex processes involved can be gained.

Contrasting interpretations of the role of corporate culture in international diversification

Substantial literature exists concerning the impact of corporate culture on the international diversification process (e.g. Kotter and Heskett, 1992; Prichett, 1987). This section examines this existing literature to determine its applicability for the new retail geography and, in particular, contrasts the two, counterposed views on the subject which exist in that literature. The first of the views is that found in the organizational management literature. Here a static interpretation of culture is adopted and the successful transfer of corporate culture abroad is viewed as being contingent upon several, limited factors. The second is that currently being developed within economic geography (e.g. Gertler, 1995; Schoenberger, 1994a; 1994b). Here a more dynamic, flexible view of culture is adopted. In this section these views are contrasted and their implications for the post-entry phase of the international diversification process are considered. While both views agree that corporate culture greatly influences international diversification they fundamentally disagree upon the direction of the influence.

Despite their fundamentally different interpretations of the direction of corporate culture's power and influence, both views agree about the importance of the post-entry phase of the international diversification process. Indeed, both demonstrate that the success of the international diversification process depends upon the corporate cultures of the incoming and incumbent firm assimilating and operating as one. What they disagree upon is which corporate culture is likely to be assimilated. The 'static' organizational management view suggests that diversifying companies do not have the power to enter and change prevailing corporate cultures. The 'dynamic', counter-view suggests that companies can undertake successful, international diversification strategies within markets with divergent corporate cultures and that they do have the power to subsume the existing corporate cultures.

In more detail, the viewpoint of organizational management literature (e.g. Denison, 1990; Hampden-Turner, 1992; Kotter and Heskett, 1992; Kransdorf, 1993; Prichett, 1987) on the impact of corporate culture on the international diversification process suggests that corporate culture is a critical determinant of the success of the process. In particular, the literature suggests that the biggest obstacle to the successful implementation of international diversification strategies is 'the ethereal culture *clash*' between the corporate cultures of incoming and incumbent firms with the principal reason why the majority of company acquisitions fail being assigned to the lack of understanding among the staff of the acquired company of their new employer's corporate culture (Kransdorf, 1993). The literature argues that the corporate culture of the incumbent company is often more compatible with its competitive environment than that of the acquiring company; the reason for this being due to the fact that all corporate cultures act out themes and patterns of a wider culture. Indeed, the organizational management literature suggests that all corporate cultures are partly the result of negotiations with the larger, macro-cultures in which they are located (Hampden-Turner, 1992). Consequently, all US corporations will have corporate cultures that display particular versions of the North American theme, while the success of Japanese companies is attributed to aspects of 'Asian' culture (Ouchi, 1981). As a result the organizational management literature assumes that the corporate culture of the incumbent company is likely to be more reactive to the subtleties of the market than that of the acquiring company and that the success of international diversification depends ultimately upon companies diversifying into countries with similar macro-cultures and acquiring companies with similar corporate cultures. It also suggests that the entrenched power of corporate culture is such that it acts as a barrier to keep potential entrants out. The organizational management literature supports its arguments by high- lighting the high number of casualties among companies pursuing international diversification strategies.

However, there is evidence which suggests that the organizational management literature fails to tell the whole story and that it finds difficulty in accounting for firms that have *successfully* diversified into culturally dissimilar companies and markets. The burgeoning 'dynamic' interpretation of corporate culture (Gertler, 1995; Schoenberger, 1994a; 1994b) suggests that this is an important flaw. It argues that acquiring companies may have more 'appropriate' corporate cultures and business strategies than those of incumbent firms. The evidence to support this argument relates to the power of corporate culture to control and direct economic change. Indeed, as suggested in the previous section, the market entry of culturally dissimilar firms is often a 'Trojan horse' which can stimulate significant industrial restructuring (Yip, 1982). Success, the 'dynamic' view argues, does not depend upon companies investing in and assimilating with culturally compatible firms.

In this view market entrants recognize the competitive weakness of incumbent firms and successfully export their corporate cultures abroad. This, in turn, leads to a wider restructuring of traditional methods of business practice. The best example to support this counter-argument is the expansion of the Japanese into the European and North American automobile industries. This has clearly been extremely successful yet the success of the Japanese cannot be attributed to the fact that they adhered to the corporate cultures and practices of their host markets. Indeed, rather than adapting their corporate culture to match that of their host nation, they located in markets where they believed the existing corporate culture to be ineffective. They then exploited these markets. The result of their strategy was the reverse of that suggested by the organizational management literature. Instead of adapting their culture to conform to their host nation they succeeded in converting the incumbent firms into adopting radically different corporate cultures and business practices.

This section has highlighted, therefore, two divergent views concerning the power and influence of corporate culture upon the international diversification process. Both views consider international diversification to be an extremely destabilizing event. The two counter-views, however, fundamentally disagree about the source of the instability. The 'dynamic' view considers the direction of the power of corporate culture to be very different from that portrayed in the organizational management literature. It argues that corporate culture is a powerful phenomenon that can, through market entry, induce significant periods of industrial restructuring. Any threat to the entry process, it is argued, lies with the corporate culture of the acquiring company rather than the corporate culture of the incumbent firm. The organizational management literature fundamentally disagrees and argues that the power of corporate culture can act as a barrier to entry.

This chapter suggests that the dynamic view is more appropriate for constructing the new retail geography. The traditional, organizational management view and its static definition of corporate culture is simply too inflexible and limiting in terms of explaining the complex processes involved within the international diversification process. The dynamic view adopts a more vigorous definition of corporate culture which captures the power and influence of corporate culture to influence economic change. As such, it offers retail geographers greater understanding of the significance of corporate culture during the international diversification process.

These propositions will now be examined in the context of a case study of the international diversification strategy of the UK's leading food retailer. Sainsbury, it will be seen, did not adopt the cultures of the market and company it acquired. Indeed, it transplanted its strong, British corporate culture in its entirety and subsumed the existing corporate culture of the acquired firm (Shaw's). The repercussions of the collision of the two divergent cultures were felt by all parties involved. This chapter concentrates in particular upon one group affected by the collision of corporate cultures, Shaw's employees. As such, the case study provides a small exploration into the large area of the power and influence of corporate culture to control economic change.

UK food retailing investment in the USA

The UK food retailing industry has been subjected to many competitive changes since the mid-1970s. Changing competitive conditions have meant that the traditional methods of income generation have become increasingly unreliable (see Wrigley, 1993a; 1994). The major UK food retailers (Sainsbury, Tesco and Argyll) have therefore been forced to strategically reassess their accumulation strategies in order to counteract the declining opportunities within their domestic markets, and to consider international diversification. Indeed, international diversification now plays a significant and growing role within the corporate strategies of the major UK food retailers.

Sainsbury, the leading UK food retailer, was the first to initiate the strategy of international diversification. It recognized the need for diversification in the early 1980s and began establishing 'a learning curve which would mean that it would have developed an efficient Sainsburyized organization by the time new sources of income generation were required'.[1] Sainsbury's internationalization began in 1982 with a partial stake in Shaw's Supermarkets in New England. It then gradually increased its interest in Shaw's, taking full control in July 1987 via a $261 million purchase.

Several questions can be raised concerning Sainsbury's international diversification strategy. The first addressed here is why was Sainsbury the first UK food retailer to adopt this strategy? The second relates to the reasons why Shaw's was chosen for that initial international foray. It was no surprise to industry commentators that Sainsbury was the first UK food retailing company to recognize the need for international diversification and then implement it. The reason for Sainsbury's foresight is undoubtedly related to the strength of its forward-thinking corporate culture. Sainsbury has long been the industry leader and it has achieved this role by being one step ahead of its competitors; in particular, it has always been the first to initiate new strategies and innovations (e.g. in the area of own-label goods), while the remainder of the industry has to a large extent played a continual game of catch-up. As a result, Sainsbury's corporate culture has been described as 'offensive'. Consequently, while its rivals were still assessing their domestic strategy, Sainsbury had the opportunity and the financial capability to initiate international diversification. In contrast, Tesco's initiation of a similar strategy in the early 1990s was arguably far more of a 'defensive' reaction to rapidly changing market conditions.[2]

Sainsbury's reasons for acquiring Shaw's were numerous. Many of them related to the overall attraction of investing in the USA, and US food retailing in particular (Wrigley, 1989; 1993a). In addition, Shaw's was perceived as having many superficial similarities to Sainsbury. Shaw's focused on offering customers good value and quality products with high standards of service. Shaw's was also seen as an innovator in supermarket technology. All these factors would have made Shaw's an attractive acquisition to Sainsbury. However, the fact that Shaw's was a company that Sainsbury considered 'underweight' (*The Times*, 20 June 1987) and ripe for investment probably was the deciding factor. In particular, Shaw's employed the traditional business strategies associated with 'small' capital and had a corporate culture rooted in those origins. This meant that Sainsbury would be in a position to transplant its UK 'big capital' corporate culture and business strategies in their entirety as Shaw's offered great scope for Sainsburyization.

Sainsbury's strategy in the post-acquisition period has been exactly that. Accordingly, since 1987, Sainsbury has been investing heavily in Shaw's. The main emphasis has been on store development (see Figure 7.1), gaining increasing control over the supply chain, and managing labour costs.

Table 7.1 shows the rate of Shaw's store expansion programme from its acquisition in 1987. The result of Sainsbury's investment has been a dramatic transformation of Shaw's with the company more than doubling in size between 1987 and 1995.[3] Shaw's internal structure and its methods of business practice have also radically altered. These changes have impinged heavily upon Shaw's existing relationships with

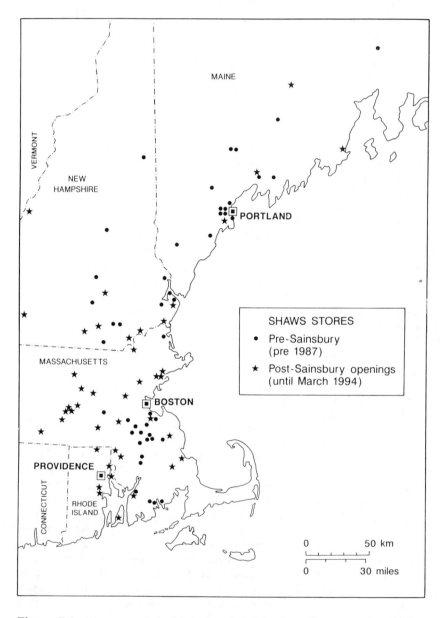

Figure 7.1 The expansion of Sainsbury's US food retailing operations (*Source*: Wrigley, 1994)

employees and suppliers. Indeed, these relationships have been fundamentally restructured so that they are compatible with Sainsbury's UK model. The following sections examine in more detail the impact that the import of such business practices and the consequent changes to Shaw's corporate culture have had on one particular group within that chain, Shaw's employees.

Table 7.1 Shaw's store expansion programme 1987/88 to 1994/95

Year[a]	1988	1989	1990	1991	1992	1993	1994	1995(est)
Sales area (000 ft^2)	1 592	1 693	1 928	2 107	2 229	2 448	2 775	2 903
Increase on previous year (%)	–	6	14	9	6	10	13	5
Stores	60[b]	61	66	70	73	79	87	91
New store openings in year	–	6	8	6	3	7	9	3

Sources: Adapted from Wrigley (1994) plus Sainsbury's *Annual Reports*
[a]   Trading year to March of stated year
[b]   Includes acquisition (October 1987) of ten Iandoli stores

The acculturation process

It is clear that the full potency of organizational culture can be seen during an acquisition when two divergent cultures are forced to become one (Ogbonna and Wilkinson, 1988). Sainsbury's acquisition of Shaw's demonstrates clearly the cultural conflicts involved during the acquisition process. Shaw's managers and employees were embedded in their own culture, which had its own distinct values and beliefs on how best to manage their company. For example a US union official suggested that 'It was more family oriented [i.e. prior to acquisition] . . . In fact it was family owned. And the owner at the time, Stanton Davis, felt that the people that worked for him had made the company what it is. As long as they continued to do a good job, well basically you take care of them, through good times and bad.'[4] The loss of a family atmosphere is clearly only one facet associated with the transfer of Sainsbury's culture into the Shaw's organization. All changes to Shaw's corporate culture and philosophy must be seen in the context of the spectrum of corporate cultures described in the previous section. The implementation of Sainsbury's 'big' capital ethos induced fundamental restructuring as strategies were initiated that were at variance with the previous 'small' capital corporate culture of Shaw's.

Sainsbury had a clear vision of how it wanted Shaw's to be organized and the role that all Shaw's employees were to play. This can be seen clearly in terms of the labour force strategies that Shaw's now employs which mirror those employed by Sainsbury within the UK. The reasons Sainsbury initiated these restructuring strategies are clearly twofold. First, Sainsbury hoped that, as in the UK, these strategies would result in productivity growth and drive Shaw's profits up. Second, labour force restructuring is an important mechanism by which companies establish their beliefs and attitudes. Sainsbury clearly viewed this as a necessary prerequisite to its 'Sainsburyization' programme. The following discussion will demonstrate the extent of the labour force restructuring that has occurred to date, and will demonstrate how these changes have altered the cultural values previously espoused by Shaw's. Shaw's is now seen as 'less caring about the employee and more bottom line conscious'.[5]

Sainsbury has implemented changes throughout the whole of Shaw's labour force. It clearly recognized that the internalization of the norms and values of its corporate philosophy depended on compelling persuasion, convincing communication and 'credible threat'. Consequently, in order to implant the required corporate culture and beliefs, and to facilitate the implementation of new strategies, change began at the top.

Shaw's senior management has undergone a radical transformation and executives who retained the beliefs of the old culture have been replaced. Indeed, it has been suggested by a US union official that 'senior management who were seen to be associated with the old regime appear to have been pushed to one side and demoted'.[6] Another commentator stated that 'it seems like they're trying to do away with the people that have been involved with the company long-term, it's because they felt that they were too close to the employees to get the job done effectively'.[7] As a result, a new aggressive management team has been installed which Sainsbury clearly hopes will facilitate the internalization of its beliefs and values. The remaining management from the old Shaw's organization have been retrained so that they are better able to focus on what Sainsbury believes are the critical factors that ensure competitive success.

Figures 7.2 and 7.3 illustrate this phenomenon. They clearly illustrate, as one ex-employee stated, that 'the scenery's changed drastically'.[8] Figures 7.2 and 7.3 demonstrate that the management team in 1993/94 was rather different from that which Sainsbury inherited in 1987 and that the management structure itself had undergone a transformation. New positions had been created that better represent the functional/operational areas that Sainsbury uses in its UK operation. In addition, Sainsbury regularly seconded key UK Directors, such as David Quarmby, Joint Managing Director, in 1991, Ian Coull, Director of Property Development in 1992, and Dino Adriano in 1993, to help instill new business practices. For example, Ian Coull was instrumental in changing the nature of Shaw's store development process from a reactive, property-developer led, strategy to a proactive UK-type model in which Shaw's took control of the entire process.

The changes that Sainsbury has introduced indicate that it felt that Shaw's management was too constrained by the existing corporate culture to allow the successful assimilation of the norms and values of the Sainsbury corporate philosophy. Indeed, the existing management's 'sense of self' meant that managers felt that Sainsbury's directives contravened the existing corporate culture. Sainsbury clearly made the mistake of allowing Shaw's management too much autonomy in the early post-acquisition stage. Analyst C felt that

[Sainsbury] should have had someone significant from Sainsbury on the ground out there. They didn't do that. They hired a guy to be President and CEO, who came from a wholesale background, and he just did not perform. He basically made the mistake of not responding to directives from Blackfriars and even when Sainsbury people went over he didn't deliver the goods that were requested at meetings.[9]

Sainsbury clearly recognized its mistake. The CEO was removed and replaced.

It is clear that significant changes occurred only when David Sainsbury took control of the Sainsbury Group on the retirement of Lord Sainsbury in November 1992. His 'positionality' is clearly critical and it has been suggested that his sense of self is very different from his predecessor. He recognized the need for centralized control of the US operations and his accession to chairmanship of Shaw's has been followed by extensive changes to the top executive positions. These changes have allowed Sainsbury to weave its beliefs and aims into the entire Shaw's organization. Shaw's is now centrally controlled from London with a president and chief executive (CEO) who rigidly ensures that Sainsbury's directives are implemented.

Structural change: a questionable morality

The lower echelons of Shaw's workforce have also been subjected to significant periods of restructuring. Three major structural changes are evident: a change in the types of jobs offered, a change in the type of people who fill these jobs, and a redistribution of the work time that Shaw's employees are allocated. These restructuring strategies are an attempt by Sainsbury to casualize Shaw's workforce and increase its flexibility so it effectively responds to the ebb and flow of its consumer demand.

The methods Sainsbury utilized mirror the methods being used within the retailing more generally in the UK and the USA (for USA see Christopherson, 1989; this volume, Chapter 8). The casualization of the UK food-retailing workforce has continued unabated since the mid-1980s with part-time workers far outnumbering full-time employees. However, in the USA Christopherson (this volume, Chapter 8) has shown that during the late 1980s the number of full-time workers increased at the expense of part-time workers. It is suggested, therefore, that the post-acquisition policies that Sainsbury employed may have been counter to the prevailing US trend. This is, as yet, only an assumption in the absence of readily available data for the US retailing sector from 1990 onwards. Recessionary factors (not captured in Christopherson's figures) may well have reversed the overall trend within US retailing. What is clear, however, is the significance of the flexibilization programme adopted. Sainsbury had a clear plan to restructure Shaw's workforce in order to make it responsive to contemporary business needs. This has involved several periods of

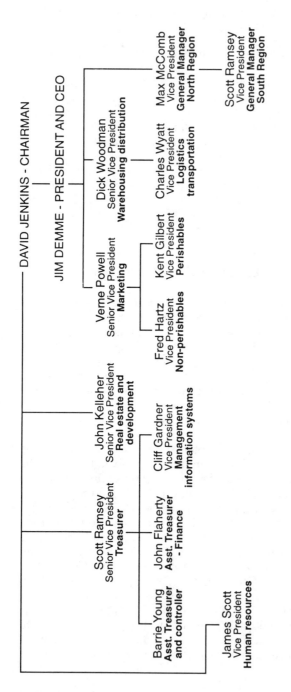

Figure 7.2 The management team at Shaw's 1989 (*Source*: press announcements)

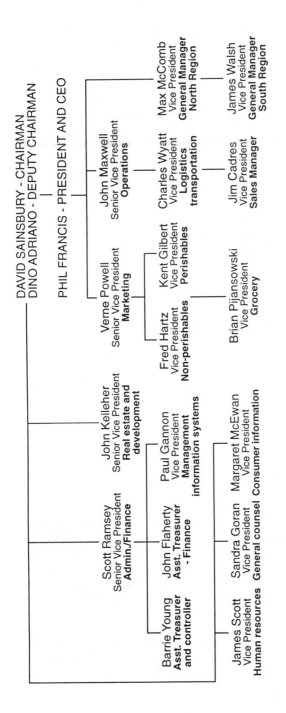

Figure 7.3 The management team at Shaw's 1993/4 (*Source*: press announcements)

significant rationalization with a large proportion of Shaw's employees being affected.

The first major period of structural change occurred in October 1991. Sainsbury initiated a period of labour force restructuring within Shaw's when it 'laid off' 218 full-time employees. This move was particularly significant as it occurred despite reassurances from Shaw's that 'the word lay-off was not in its [i.e. Shaw's] vocabulary'.[10] This move also signified that Sainsbury held little regard for the powers of the United Food and Commercial Workers Union (UFCW) which represents a large number of Shaw's employees. Shaw's and the UFCW had ratified their agreement on 8 August 1991 after an acrimonious period of negotiation that had almost ended in industrial action. Despite this 'the ink wasn't even dry on the contract' when Sainsbury began to instigate its rationalization programme.[11]

More importantly, this move signalled Sainsbury's intention to casualize Shaw's workforce and replace full-time staff with contingent, part-time workers. Table 7.2 demonstrates the significance of this period of restructuring on the structure of Shaw's workforce. During the period 1989–94 the number of full-time staff employed by Shaw's fell by 5.8 per cent. In the same period the number of part-time staff increased by over 25.4 per cent.

Table 7.2 Changes in the number of full and part-time workers at Shaw's 1989–94

Year	Full-time	% Annual change	Part-time	% Annual change
1989	4 511	*	9 499	*
1990	4 844	7.3	10 068	5.9
1991	4 659	-3.8	10 704	6.3
1992	3 972	–14.7	11 812	10.4
1993	4 061	2.2	11 867	0.5
1994	4 248	4.6	11 913	0.4
Total % change 1989–94		-5.8		+25.4

Source: Sainsbury's Annual Reports
* data unavailable

A new period of labour force restructuring was initiated within Shaw's during February 1994. This time it was the actual number of hours that people worked that was rationalized. Shaw's instigated a scheme whereby it cut the number of hours available to existing part-time staff while at the same time it hired new part-time staff. This strategy allowed Shaw's to further increase the flexibility of its workforce, and to reduce its hourly wage bill.

More specifically, the introduction of this new strategy has had serious implications for Shaw's 'career' or 'retention' part-timers.[12] These are the people who have worked part-time for Shaw's for a significant period of time, i.e. over ten years. Contractually, these workers are guaranteed only 15 hours of work per week. However in the past they have actually been working 25, 30 or even 35 hours per week. Consequently, these workers have become accustomed to a particular standard of living. One US union official expressed his concern at the recent move: 'we have some single mums that are the sole supporter of their household, and all of a sudden they are in severe financial difficulties because Shaw's want to lower the average hourly wage'.[13]

The third and final change to affect Shaw's labour force relates to the type of people that Shaw's employs to fulfil its labour requirements. It is increasingly evident that Shaw's now relies less on voluntary, career part-timers and prefers to employ secondary, involuntary part-timers to fill its positions. Shaw's obviously feels that these kinds of employees offer further opportunities to reduce costs as they are less likely to qualify for any form of benefits. Shaw's has encountered few problems in recruiting such employees in part because the New England area has suffered from a period of severe recession. Indeed, it was not until late 1993 that the region began to emerge from the bottom of one of its worst recessions ever, made particularly harsh by the fact that the region had previously been enjoying the spoils of the 'Massachusetts miracle' during the 1980s. As one commentator stated: 'the employment situation in this area of the country isn't the best right now, I don't think the figures show it, but the unemployment's high, people are either unemployed or under employed, people are grabbing jobs in the stores because they've lost their job and they're just trying to supplement their income'.[14] The most intense periods of restructuring at Shaw's occurred therefore during the deepest part of the New England recession and Sainsbury had no problems in driving through its labour force restructuring programmes.

As a result of that restructuring, the composition of Shaw's labour force and the hours that individuals work have changed dramatically. These changes have allowed Shaw's to make significant savings and when coupled with the introduction of information technology systems have facilitated a notable increase in productivity. This increase in productivity is beginning to show through in operating profit. Indeed, during 1993–94 (i.e. with the easing of the New England recession) Shaw's profits increased dramatically by 66.7 per cent.

The increase in operating profit has arguably been made at the expense of certain elements of the Shaw's workforce and the changes being introduced have become a matter of increasing concern for the UFCW. One US union official suggested that 'morale is very low within Shaw's at present, people are at best apprehensive . . . they are worried about job security'.[15] Moreover, as the message of the new corporate culture is being transmitted throughout the company, with it is being passed a new uneasiness. As the UFCW official noted, 'it's filtering downhill. The store management are at best walking on egg shells. They're on edge so they are treating the employees not in the way they have been treating them in the past.' In an attempt to reassure both management and workers, the new president and CEO at Shaw's

(Phil Francis) issued a statement addressing the uncertainty being felt within Shaw's. This statement is particularly significant as it represents an attempt by Shaw's CEO to internalize the message associated with the change in corporate culture. It provides, therefore, an example of both compelling persuasion and the 'credible threat' highlighted in the previous section.

In simple terms, Francis (1994) argued that the uncertainty felt within Shaw's was the result of a mismatch between the 'psychological contract' that Shaw's traditionally maintained with its employees and the new corporate philosophy. Francis characterized the old psychological contract as: 'If I work hard and well, and I am loyal to the company, I will always have a job and the Company will always take care of me.' He saw that as 'assigning the employer the role of parent and the associate (employee) the role of the dependent child' and he argued that this was no longer appropriate for the business environment in which Shaw's now found itself. As a result, Francis suggested that a new psychological contract must be adopted, whereby 'the child must grow up, and the parent must acknowledge that the child is an adult'. In other words a vision of 'a partnership of shared responsibilities' which involves 'you, the employees, better utilising our talents and increasing your ownership of the company's results'. The methods adopted to encourage the development of the new contract were to include methods used by Sainsbury in the UK and transplanted to the USA, for example, a much increased emphasis on training. Francis's address was clearly an attempt to internalize and clarify the beliefs and values of Shaw's new corporate culture and to instil Sainsbury's general corporate philosophy but implicit within it was the 'credible threat'.

Sainsbury has clearly driven through a significant labour force restructuring programme at Shaw's. Most importantly, the changes instigated suggest that Sainsbury has made a determined effort to transplant its corporate culture and beliefs into the Shaw's organization. The replacement of parts of the management team, and the fact that the majority of employees are new to the company, has aided this assimilation. The introduction of 'big capital' culture to Shaw's has meant a concern with the bottom line and a replacement of the previous 'family firm' culture. In this respect, the post-acquisition period has been characterized by a power struggle between the corporate cultures of 'big' and 'small' capital with the values and beliefs associated with 'small' capital being replaced by the norms and values of Sainsbury's 'big capital' corporate philosophy.

Conclusions

This chapter has interrogated the value of corporate culture as a useful lens through which to view contemporary changes within retailing. In addition, the chapter has highlighted the inadequacies of the traditional organizational management literature's views concerning the impact of corporate culture on the international diversification process. The more 'dynamic' view of culture now being adopted by economic geographers suggests that there is no reason why companies cannot successfully transfer corporate cultures into culturally dissimilar markets. It also suggests that debate should move away from previous 'surprisingly uncritical super organic, static conception[s] of culture' (Gertler, 1995: 2). This chapter suggests that this approach has considerable potential in terms of demystifying some of the complex processes inherent within retail restructuring.

More specifically, the chapter has highlighted the powerful influence of corporate culture on the international diversification strategies of retailers. The Shaw's case study demonstrates that corporate culture impacts upon the process of retailer internationalization in a variety of ways. Not only does it help explain which companies undertake the process, but also it controls the crucial post-acquisition period. The transfer of corporate culture is clearly an extremely destabilizing event which, as the Shaw's case study highlights, can cause severe dislocation for all parties involved. This case study serves, therefore, to highlight the power of corporate culture in the process of corporate restructuring and its importance as a lens through which to examine critical dimensions of contemporary change within retailing.

Notes

1　Analyst B interview in the City of London, September 1993.
2　Tesco acquired Catteau, a chain in northern France, in December 1993. It has subsequently acquired an interest in a chain in Hungary, although the extent of investment is nowhere as large as that invested by Sainsbury in the USA.
3　Sainsbury has subsequently (in October 1994) obtained a 16 per cent stake (and more importantly 50 per cent of the voting stock) in another US food retailing Giant. This move clearly confirms that Sainsbury's accumulation strategy is driven by the realization that expansion and improved earnings within the UK are limited. Giant is the leading food retailer within the Washington DC and Baltimore areas, which, like New England, are among the richest areas in the USA, and also have huge expansion opportunities. Sainsbury is now the eleventh largest supermarket retailer in the USA.
4　Meeting at UFCW headquarters, March 1993.
5　UFCW official, meeting at UFCW headquarters, March 1994.
6　Interview at UFCW headquarters, March 1994.
7　Present at meeting at UFCW headquarters, March 1994.
8　Present at meeting at UFCW headquarters, March 1994.
9　Interview in the City of London, September 1993.
10　Meeting with UFCW official, March 1994.
11　Meeting with UFCW official, March 1994.
12　Retention part-timers is a concept developed by Tilly (1991). This refers to valued employees whose life circumstances prevent them from working full-time, e.g. women with small children. They are the people who have traditionally made up the part-time division of the labour market, consequently they are likely to be highly productive and display company loyalty and as such have low turn-over rates.

13   Interview at UFCW headquarters, March 1994.
14   Interview at Federal Reserve Bank of Boston, March 1993.
15   Interview at UFCW headquarters, March 1994.

Part 3

Retail employment relations

CHAPTER 8

The production of consumption: retail restructuring and labour demand in the USA

Susan Christopherson

While the culture of consumption received increasing attention during the 1980s, consumption workplaces and production methods were relatively neglected.[1] One reason for this neglect is that the retail sector was considered peripheral to processes of industrial restructuring. It was one of the places where displaced manufacturing workers (or more likely their wives and children) were destined to land but, as a static sector, had little intrinsic interest. That this neglect was unwarranted is evident from only a cursory look at what has been possibly the most dynamic process of sectoral change in the USA and UK in the 1980s and 1990s. The organization of consumption work, in fact, has changed dramatically in the USA, affecting approximately 19 million people whose livelihoods depend on selling things and on (as we shall see) how they are sold. Some of these new patterns of distributing and selling goods contradict depictions of contemporary work as characterized by a deepening division of labour and 'the fine parceling of tasks in the workplace' (Sayer and Walker, 1992: 10). In the retail sector, many of the tasks involved in selling commodities have been redesigned and combined so as to decrease labour inputs or direct them to serving the most profitable market segments. Other jobs such as those in the intermediary occupations which link manufacturers and retailers, are being eliminated as 'just-in-time' retailing becomes more prevalent.

The restructuring of the retail work process is an aspect of a broader process of capital accumulation, a 'new mercantilism', in which buyer-driven commodity chains play a major role. Buyer-driven commodity chains link products and services together in a sequence of value-adding activities. These activities have a spatial dimension – dispersed production and concentrated distribution in selected markets – and require sophisticated co-ordination and managerial flexibility. Core companies in buyer-driven commodity chains, including mechandisers, such as Nike, and retail chains, such as Wal-mart, derive their profits from design, marketing, sales, and financial services (Gereffi, 1993). Technological advances in such areas as networking, inventory control, and 'article surveillance' enable the core firm to control a vast complex of production, marketing, and sales activities. The core company's domination of the entire commodity chain, from production to consumption, extends its influence on the work process throughout the chain. Its labour demands result in the elimination of some jobs, such as manufacturers' representatives, and the creation of others – for example, in computer-controlled inventory management.

State regulatory policies intersect with buyer-driven commodity chains at both the production and consumption ends of the chain (Marsden and Wrigley, 1995; this volume, Chapter 2). At the production end, state policies generate the infrastructure for export processing zones, including the transportation and communications infrastructure which effectively links the suppliers to their buyers (Gereffi, 1993). At the consumption end, state policies play complex and contradictory roles, regulating product quality and the degree of competition as well as shaping sourcing practices through quotas and tariffs (which are bypassed by clever management of sourcing by the core firms). State policies directly affect expectations of core firm profits, openness to foreign direct investment, and labour practices (Christopherson, 1993). Indirectly they influence firm behaviour with respect to suppliers and within national markets.

In the USA, openness to foreign investment, pressure for high short-term returns, and considerable latitude with respect to labour deployment (i.e. flexibility) continue to revolutionize the work process at the market end of the buyer-driven commodity chain. The changes from the 1980s into the 1990s in the retail sector dramatically illustrate the consequences of a *laissez faire* investment regime – volatility, instability, and the pursuit of short-term speculative profits (Bienefeld, 1989). In this chapter I examine the consequences of these investment patterns for production organization in the consumption sector, and for patterns of labour deployment.

Investment patterns in the retail sector

Investment across firms

Since the emergence of the department store and mass merchandising at the turn of the century, an increasing portion of sales and employment in the US retail sector has been controlled by large corporations. Although smaller corporations and independent retailers still make up the majority of firms and establishments (workplaces or stores), the largest firms have surpassed the smallest in their portion of retail employment.

The continuing prevalence of small businesses in retail may be attributed to the ease of entry into this industry. In 1986, the ten most frequent business starts for the entire economy included nine retail sub-sectors, all small-business dominated. As the Small Business Administration report states, 'Small businesses in industries like these are among the first to experiment with new products, new locations, and new methods of service. Business formations and closings are a means by which consumer tastes and preferences are relayed to suppliers and manufacturers' (US Small Business Administration, 1987: 8). However, while small businesses play an important role in the retail sector, large firms provide an increasing portion of total jobs and of stable jobs.

An analysis of trends in firm distribution by sales class (Table 8.1) indicates that the firms in the top sales class grew throughout the 1970s and 1980s but comprised only 0.12 per cent of all firms by 1992 (the year for which the most recent complete information is available). The percentage of establishments or actual workplaces accounted for in the top sales class was 20 per cent of total establishments in 1992 (Table 8.2). The concentration of establishments reflects two phases of retail restructuring. The first phase occurred in the 1960s and 1970s as large retailers, particularly department stores, replaced independent retailers (Bluestone *et al*, 1981). In the second phase, in the 1980s and into the 1990s, department store and general merchandiser chains were dismantled and replaced by discount retailers and specialty chains.

Table 8.1 % Distribution of retail firms* by sales class

Sales class ($1000)	1972	1977	1982	1987	1992
$100000+	0.01	0.02	0.04	0.09	0.12
$50,000 to $99999	0.01	0.02	0.04	0.12	0.15
$25000 to $49999	0.02	0.05	0.10	0.36	0.43
$10000 to $24999	0.10	0.25	0.47	1.21	1.3
$5000 to $9999	0.26	0.51	0.81	1.63	1.78
$1000 to $4999	2.34	4.01	6.72	13.05	15.38
$500 to $999	3.12	5.41	8.43	15.38	17.14
<$500	94.14	89.73	83.39	68.17	63.62

Source: US Department of Commerce (1972, 1977, 1982, 1987, 1992)
*Firms operating all year.

Table 8.2 % Distribution of retail establishments* by sales class

Sales class ($1000)	1972	1977	1982	1987	1992
$25000+	6.58	8.84	12.63	14.24	20.00
$10000 to $24999	1.06	1.48	1.96	2.94	3.02
$5000 to $9999	1.02	1.45	1.92	2.00	3.23
$1000 to $4999	4.09	5.89	8.21	13.14	14.26
$500 to $999	3.69	5.58	7.69	11.67	13.80
<$500	83.56	76.77	67.59	47.05	44.0

Source: US Department of Commerce (1972, 1977, 1982, 1987, 1992)
*Establishments operating all year

The pattern of concentration was reflected in employment in the mid-1980s. Between 1984 and 1986, employment in retail firms with 500 or more employees increased 16 per cent compared to an increase of only 2 per cent in retail firms with fewer than 100 employees. This trend was especially strong in high-growth sub-sectors such as building supply stores and home furnishing stores and reflects the transformation of the sector away from general merchandise stores and small firms and toward specialty chains (Federal Reserve Bank of Chicago, 1989). During this growth period, shopping malls with anchor stores and specialty shops replaced independent 'main street' stores.

Beginning in the late 1980s, the retail sector was profoundly affected by a wave of mergers and acquisitions. In 1988, 80 companies were acquired, many by foreign investors (Hallsworth, 1990; Wrigley, 1989). Among the effects of these acquisitions, mergers, and hostile takeovers were high levels of acquisition-related debt, store closures, and bankruptcies (Harrison and Hill, 1989).

Retailers also consolidated divisions under a single corporate identity.[2] Consolidation enabled firms to penetrate new markets without new construction, increased the velocity of asset transfer and increased the holdings of the largest national and regional chains. Retail corporations pursued strategies which allowed them to reduce the risks associated with any one location by centralized control of geographically dispersed stores. Chain organization enables the firms to control labour and merchandising in myriad remote stores, to take advantage of economies of scale, and to circulate capital around a geographically dispersed system. Finally, as will be shown below, chain organization in a labour-intensive industry, such as retail, provides capital and organizational capacity for the development of managerial strategies and technologies to achieve long-term savings on labour costs. An example of the patterns in the sector is that of Montgomery Ward, a low-end-of-the-market general retailer which was the object of a leveraged buyout in the late 1980s. Montgomery Ward subsequently sold a division, Jefferson Ward; closed its $1.2 billion catalogue business; closed stores in less profitable markets; and reduced its workforce by 17 000 people (Brennan, 1991).

Sears, another low-end general merchandise chain, with over 800 stores and approximately 350 000 employees in the USA, has undergone continuous reorganization since 1990. In 1991 and 1992, the chain reduced its workforce by 39 900 (14 000 full-time and 25 900 part-time) saving $750 million a year via payroll cuts. In 1993, they announced plans to eliminate 50 000 jobs (16 000 full-time), close 113 stores and discontinue their catalogue mail order sales (Bureau of National Affairs, 1993).

Macy's, which has 200 stores, grew massively in the 1980s through acquisition of specialty goods chains and other major general merchandise chains (Bullocks and I Magnin). It is the biggest US retailer to file for bankruptcy protection with $5.3 billion in debts and $4.95 billion in assets. Macy's, too, is responding to debt pressure through closure of the acquired specialty goods chains and selected general merchandise department stores.

These stories of restructuring suggest some of the general pressures reshaping retail trade and firm employment in the 1990s – sectoral concentration, debt, and competition to produce high short-term returns for stock-holders. The concentration that occurred in the 1980s, though, also made it possible for retailers to respond to these new competitive pressures by changing investment patterns within the firm. Their responses are focused in three major areas – managerial innovations, technological innovations, and new labour deployment strategies.

Investment within the firm

Although corporate goals in the retail sector emphasize cost reduction, capital budgets are at record highs (*Standard and Poor's Industry Surveys*, 1987). Retail managers are investing heavily in improved inventory and information systems, and in streamlining and remodelling the firm and the establishment. One important area of investment is in systems to eliminate 'pipe line leakages' which produce losses of an estimated $25 billion a year.[3] The largest share of leakages is due to stock-outs and mark-downs, the first due to shortages of inventory, the latter to excess inventory. Stimulated by the declines in sales growth and the possibilities offered by computerized management systems, large retail firms are making substantial investments in 'quick response' inventory control systems in order to control losses. These quick response systems combine bar coding and electronic data interchange (EDI) but the key to the success of this 'just-in-time' system is bargaining power with suppliers. In this respect large firms are at a significant advantage and their advantage has increased with concentration in the sector. Retailers who buy in mass quantitites may choose from a number of suppliers and may set the terms of the transaction. So, for example, Wal-Mart, the most successful discount retail firm in the United States, refuses to deal with marketing agents or intermediaries between the manufacturer and the retailer, preferring instead to use its own marketing information and to use suppliers only to supply products (Preston, 1992). In some cases, shorter lead times favour domestic over foreign suppliers, especially if the domestic supplier is willing to invest in compatible product movement information technologies.[4]

Inventory control is taking many forms. At the high-technology extreme, satellite technologies link product movement information at every point in the pipeline, and materials handling systems in the warehouse actually move the products in and out.[5] Other retailers are sub-contracting storage and delivery services (*Chain Store Age Executive*, 1988), or building massive strategically located warehouses. In the case of Macy's, inventory control reduced the number of warehousing employees by 90 per cent in the 1980s (Noyelle, 1987).

The restructuring of production in retail is also reflected in consumption spaces. Rapid physical expansion in the 1960s and 1970s led to a crisis driven by excess selling space.[6] In the 1980s, discount department stores and general merchandisers were faced with a steadily declining number of homes per store. New options for physical growth became fewer but, in some respects, more diverse. According to *Chain Store Age Executive*, traditional shopping centre construction slowed throughout the 1980s as market saturation levels were reached and real estate costs rose. Developer diversification strategies include smaller shopping centres, remodelling the old large centres, mixed-use development or remodelling, and in some cases direct ownership of retail tenants (*Standard and Poor's Industry Surveys*, 1987), all with implications for the retailer shopping for selling space.

Within existing shopping areas and centres, patterns of spatial allocation have shifted. The 're-tenanting' of US shopping centres is being fuelled by the same processes of concentration and redistribution of investment that are shaping the sector as a whole. Spatial reallocation reflects in a quite visible way the market repositioning that is central to contemporary management strategies. As supermarkets have been transformed into hypermarkets, for example, they have vacated small shopping centres. Developers searching for new anchors have turned increasingly to 'super' specialty stores dealing in merchandise lines once sold by department stores. This trend reflects a symbiotic relationship between the strategies of mature and less developed retail sub-sectors in a geographically saturated market. This symbiotic relationship and the technological and organizational innovations being implemented across the industry are homogenizing production practices and employment practices. This is occurring in an industry with historically quite distinct sub-sectoral employment patterns. To see how and why this homogenization is occurring we can look briefly at some evidence from important sub-sectors within the retail sector.

Department stores

By definition department stores employ more than 25 people, and have specific merchandise lines and distributional requirements.[7] Discount department stores are included in this category. Firm distribution figures show that by 1972 a majority of firms were in the largest sales category (US Department of Commerce, 1972) and that the smallest class of department stores had disappeared.

The Filene Brothers of Boston pioneered national department store ownership, with the organization of many specialty stores under one roof. In 1916 they founded the Retail Research Association to study problems of merchandising and store operations, establish a uniform system of record keeping, and a collaborative programme for buying, recruiting, and training, and to improve advertising (Bluestone *et al*, 1981). Most department stores were organized into chains by 1967 (Friedman, 1988).

The structure of the contemporary department store industry is markedly different from that of other retail sub-sectors. The differences between department stores and other sub-sectors provide evidence for the department store's unique position of maturity and concentration. At the same time, similarities among the top sales classes of sub-sectors suggest converging growth strategies. While other sub-sectors are enlarging stores and workforces, department stores are getting smaller and reducing their workforces. Since the early 1980s department stores have reduced their dependence on labour: employees per establishment have decreased consistently. Having failed to compete as combined specialty and discount retailers, the traditional department stores (as opposed to the discount retailers) are turning more and more to specialty retailing. Specifically, department stores are concentrating on the high-end apparel, soft goods, and home furnishings market. Pared-down stores are also adopting specialty formats for individual departments. High margin exclusive labels and higher levels of service are replacing mark-downs and discount departments. Many traditional lines of merchandise have been relinquished to competing specialty stores: furniture, consumer electronics, major appliances, toys, photographic supplies, and sewing supplies (*Standard and Poor's Industry Surveys*, 1987). With department store firms relinquishing lines of merchandise to specialty stores and investing in specialty formats, the traditional department store is disintegrating into separate departments.

The current strategies of department stores affect their relations with suppliers and thus extend the impact of changing retail distribution into the realm of product manufacturing. For example, the use of exclusive private labels combined with mass-buying practices puts retailers in a stronger negotiating position relative to suppliers. Many manufacturers are finding themselves with fewer retail outlet options for their products. In response, some manufacturers, particularly apparel-makers, are diversifying forward into retail sales, or burying their own labels and shifting production to private retail labels. This shift may signify a tendency for suppliers to depend on 'captured' production for retailers, with independence gained only through penetration of the retail sector itself (*Wall Street Journal*, 3 August 1988).

The specialty format and its associated higher margins per sale are associated with competition through provision of personal customer service. This is encouraging some firms (led by Nordstrom Department Store) to train and deploy labour in different ways, such as buying or alterations services. These services require training and some are less effectively carried out by part-time personnel. At the same time that up-scale department stores are increasing personal service, the down-market stores are eliminating it. Sears decided in the early 1990s to close its customer service department in order to achieve labour cost reductions. Selling is a self-service process in the discount store, with a small number of cashiers at central islands conducting transactions and virtually no sales staff on the floor.

These emerging labour deployment strategies have implications for the continuing debate over whether labour is being de-skilled or up-skilled by changing methods of production and distribution. Both processes appear to be occurring. On the one hand, much routine sales work is being eliminated. In the 1970s, Bluestone documented increases in advertising expenditures which accompanied the expansion of part-time employment, suggesting that advertising eliminates the need for 'selling skills'. This trend has accelerated with the use of in-store videos, promotions and other devices to lure the customer without a personal sales pitch. Marketing at the store level has lessened demands for information from salespeople. These marketing tools are also used to create the 'perception of service', again reducing dependence on human sellers. At the same time, increased competition and higher turnover has increased demands for faster, more efficient sales transactions. These still require human sales clerks. The information demanded of them is considerably different than it was in the 1960s, however, because there are more sources of product information available from television, specialized buying services, and other customer information services. Sales information is less related to the character of the product and more related to its availability (delivery time, colour and size availability, next shipment date, etc).

The current reorganization of work in department stores has emerged out of the 'two ladder' employment structure in department stores described by Noyelle (1987). Reorganization in the early 1960s separated merchandising from store management, creating two distinct sets of career opportunities. New information technologies 'up-skilled' many occupations, and redefined others, allowing sharper divisions among functions and a homogenization of skills across sectors. Decreased time spent on the 'drudgery' associated with administrative functions has allowed employees in some occupations to focus on increasingly diverse marketing functions. A smaller number of part-timers, on the other hand, may focus their attention on processing customers through the store.

Food stores

The grocery store sub-sector is the largest food store retail sub-sector. It includes grocery stores from supermarkets to convenience stores. The remainder of the food store sub-sectors are made up of specialty food retailers: bakeries, butchers, seafood markets, fruit and vegetable markets, confectioneries, and dairy stores. Since the *Census of Retail Trade* data are incomplete for food store sub-sectors, the data presented here are for all food stores. Specific figures are given for grocery stores when available.

Firm distribution for all food stores shows that firms in the top sales class represent a very small proportion, although larger than the industry average. Employment distribution figures indicate that as of 1972, employment share in the top class already exceeded that of the smallest class. By 1982, 25 per cent of grocery stores employed more than half of all grocery store employees. Employees per store increased for the top sales class by 1982, despite self-service and universal product codes (UPC) or bar codes. Larger stores (in terms of square feet, employees, and merchandise lines) are attributable to a number of factors, including the nature of competition and a particular tradition of food merchandising in the United States.

Food products have low profit margins and supermarkets originated to compensate for low margins with sales quantity. In response to decreasing food expenditure relative to disposable income and increasing expenditure on pre-prepared food, stores have become ever larger and provide a broader array of convenience food items (Therrien, 1988).

In the 1980s the number of 'superstores' steadily increased in the US. The superstore or 'hypermarket' format evolved from conventional supermarkets, which upgraded to offer an expanded selection of non-foods, and extensive service and perishables departments. By carrying higher margin general merchandise and convenience food items, food retailers have increased sales per customer and per square foot.

Joint ventures with discount department stores in hypermarkets have allowed food retailers to experiment with larger formats without directly assuming the risks of expanding merchandise lines. The purpose of these large format stores is to enable food retailers to regain their dollar share. At the same time, general merchandisers benefit from the regular clientele brought in by perishables and edibles.

Another advantage of large-scale retailing in this sub-sector as in the others is leverage over suppliers. Retailers are now routinely demanding and receiving up-front cash payments for stocking new products, in addition to regular promotion programmes and allowances.

Apparel and accessory stores

The dominant mode of retail distribution in nineteenth-century USA re-emerged in the 1970s. From 1972 to 1982 apparel specialty stores underwent marked changes towards chain organization, and in the 1980s, these chains benefitted from the fragmentation of the market, the disintegration of the department store, and the re-tenanting of the country's shopping centres.

Firm distribution figures indicate that apparel stores are still overwhelmingly small firms, with 98 per cent of firms in the smallest three size classes. Employment growth and establishments per firm increases were largest for the largest sales class from 1977 to 1982. The decline in employees per establishment for this class indicates that these enterprises did not hire employees at the previous rate as their operations expanded.

During the 1980s specialty retailing continued to benefit from ongoing changes in the marketplace. However, large specialty apparel chains show signs of reaching maturity. Although most studies indicate (based on various trade performance measures) that specialty retailers consistently outperform department stores (*Standard and Poor's Industry Surveys*, 1987), the narrowness of product lines poses a problem for specialty chain growth. Some specialty apparel retailers are building 'mini' department stores featuring new lines of merchandise including children's wear, fragrances, luggage, and home furnishings. One model for this multiple line specialty store is Next in the UK.

In the traditionally service-oriented work environment of specialty apparel stores the effort to reduce labour costs is notable. Some of the largest and most influential specialty apparel retailers, such as The Gap, have constructed their retail strategy around 'just-in-time' delivery systems linked to store level product tracking.

The converging merchandising strategies of specialty apparel chains and department store chains imply a homogenization of staffing and compensation structures in these firms, and increased competition for similar and possibly smaller labour segments. This is particularly true for youth-oriented chains which employ young people (many part-time) as a marketing strategy.

Furniture, home furnishings and equipment stores

The ageing of the US population has produced changes in consumption patterns with an increasing demand for furniture, home decoration merchandise, and consumer electronics (Schlosberg, 1988). While this specialty store sub-sector stands to benefit from the ongoing marketplace changes described for apparel stores, it is developing somewhat differently, with chain organization emerging only recently. The complexity of inventory control in these stores made them less profitable investments for chains until inventory control technology was sufficiently developed and could be applied to this sector.

Firm distribution figures indicate that FHF&E stores remained small-business dominated through the mid-1980s. However, since the late 1980s, there has been a consistent development toward large retail chains (US Department of Commerce, 1987; 1988).

In the 1980s, employment growth in this sub-sector (which at that time remained dominated by small firms) was sluggish and heavily weighted by lower or negative rates in the smallest classes. Data on establishments per firm indicated decreases over the decade, except for small increases by firms in the second largest and smallest size classes. The large number of establishments per firm in this sub-sector was attributable to the radio, television and music store sub-sector. Employment per establishment showed total declines from 1972 to 1982, suggesting some attempt to reduce labour costs.

During the 1990s, furniture, home furnishings, and equipment store chains have become highly visible parts of the retail configuration. In addition to representing a new trend in chain organization, they are selling 'big-ticket' items in new ways, corresponding to new customer buying patterns. All types of stores in this category generally carry large inventory stocks available for immediate customer pick-up. As a result, consumer electronics and home furnishings stores have grown larger, while furniture stores, always large, are changing their image. The Swedish retailer IKEA, for example, caters to customers who wish to buy single items rather than sets, and are willing to transport and assemble pieces themselves for a cost advantage.

In the USA, this sub-sector is amongst the most innovative, changing buying patterns and affecting a new category of supplier-manufacturer.

Non-store retailing

Non-store retailing includes mail order houses, vending operations, and direct sales but excludes catalogue operations by department stores. Growth in this sub-sector reflects a significant change in purchasing habits. In 1992, US consumers purchased $42 billion of merchandise from home by check or credit card, an increase (after inflation) of 30 per cent over 1988. Visa credit card purchases at home doubled between 1988 and 1992 to $17.8 billion (Morgenson, 1993). There are a number of reasons for these altered buying patterns. The restructuring of the retail sector has made shopping in malls more difficult. Regional shopping centres may be an hour or more from customers' homes and local retailing has been eliminated by the competition in the 1970s and 1980s. At the same time, product information is more readily distributed at home through buying services and consumer product guides available by mail, phone, computer, or on television. According to Morgenson's (1993) study of US retail, 'stores are becoming places where people kick the tires, lift the lid on a washing machine or listen to the sound of a stereo speaker – and then go home and call an 800 number to order the same item at a 40 per cent discount'.

Non-store retailers have changed dramatically from the mid-1980s to the 1990s. One of the most successful, CUC International, offers consumers discounted prices on 250 000 name brand products. Its revenues in 1992 were $644 million – up 44 per cent from 1988. These firms have significant advantages over their store competitors – no sales staff, inventory, customer service, or parking lot, and less insurance. Ease of entry into non-store retailing due to lower (or non-existent) real estate costs ensures that new small firms will continue to enter the market.

Employment distribution for the non-store sub-sector differs from that in all other retail sub-sectors. Almost half the employment in the sector was controlled by the largest firms in 1972, and although there was some increase to 1977, the class actually lost employment share by 1982. During the 1980s the largest and smallest firms lost employment share to firms in the middle. Employment growth during the decade and into the late 1980s was almost flat despite dramatic growth in the sector.

Establishments per firm also show idiosyncratic changes. For all non-store retailers, establishments per firm decreased, or remained the same, for all size classes. The number of establishments in the top sales class of mail order houses decreased faster than the sectoral average between 1982 and 1987 indicating trends toward concentration of operations.

Employment per establishment figures show a decrease over the decade of the 1980s for all size classes, except the smallest. Employment in mail-order or direct selling involves many warehousing duties, such as picking, packing, order taking, and direct marketing by mail or telephone. In every case materials handling and information technologies directly benefit the non-store retailer's efforts to reduce dependency on labour.

The implications of retail restructuring for labour demand

Retail has always been a labour-intensive economic activity, with any growth in sales accompanied by a parallel growth in the number of employees. In the 1980s, and especially in the 1990s, however, the application of information technologies and managerial innovations is allowing retail firms to redefine the working environment and occupational requirements. The same strategies are decreasing variation in employment conditions across sub-sectors, homogenizing skill requirements.

Corporate retail has come to control a plurality of employment and, in some cases, a majority, although the large corporations still make up only a small proportion of firms. The growing role of chains as employers is homogenizing workplaces and labour utilization strategies across sub-sectors, within parameters unique to those sub-sectors. Employment growth figures for retail from 1972 to 1992 (Table 8.3) show the vulnerability of smaller businesses to economic downturns – particularly evidenced by the sharp employment declines in the 1977–92 period, followed by recovery in the boom period of the mid-1980s and repeated in the decline in the early 1990s.

Table 8.3 % Change in retail employment growth by firm

Sales class (millions)	1972–77	1977–82	1982–87	1987–92
<1.0	−12.0	−19.8	−20.0	−12.9
1.0 – 4.99	11.6	18.5	1.6	−4.2
5.0 – 9.99	12.1	14.9	4.5	−6.7
10.0 – 24.99	26.6	12.6	19.2	−3.8
25.0 – 49.99	−5.7	33.9	26.6	2.0
50.0 – 99.99	2.0	0.0	8.5	18.8
100+	10.4	11.3	12.0	11.2

Source: US Department of Commerce (1972, 1977, 1982, 1987, 1992)

Table 8.4 % Retail employment distribution

Sales class (millions)	1972	1977	1982	1987	1992
<1.0	46.84	41.06	32.89	26.31	22.91
1.0 – 4.99	13.35	14.90	17.66	17.95	17.19
5.0 – 9.99	4.11	4.61	5.30	5.54	5.17
10.0 – 24.99	3.87	4.90	5.52	6.58	6.33
25.0 – 49.99	2.44	2.30	3.08	3.90	3.98
50.0 – 99.99	2.89	2.95	2.95	3.20	3.80
100+	26.51	29.28	32.59	36.53	40.63

Source: US Department of Commerce (1972, 1977, 1982, 1987, 1992)

Employment distribution by sales size class (Table 8.4) shows that as of 1987, firms in the top class controlled a plurality of jobs in retail. Retail remains a small establishment dominated industry but the data indicate that the largest firms employ the greatest number and proportion of employees.

One consequence of corporate restructuring and consolidation in retail in the late 1980s and into the 1990s is a reorientation of employment growth away from management and towards marketing and information management. In department stores, the most concentrated sub-sector, non-supervisory employment grew at an average annual rate of 1.8 per cent between 1967 and 1986 while supervisory employment declined at an average annual rate of 0.6 per cent (Friedman, 1988). Changes in the relationship between suppliers and retailers and in the production process in retail are also having an effect on labour demand in the industry. According to the Department of Labor, three occupations associated with product movement are expected to decline in the 1990s: order fillers, stocking clerks, and wholesale and retail buyers (US Department of Labor, 1988, Appendix D-1). Although it is difficult to predict the total amount of job loss, it is clear that the skills required for the remaining jobs will certainly change, involving computerized monitoring rather than manual work.

Evidence developing in the early 1990s indicates that the retail sector is shedding employment rapidly as a consequence of the consolidation of the sector, cost-cutting strategies, and success in applying just-in-time retail strategies begun in the 1980s. The Displaced Worker Survey, a supplement to the Current Population Survey, shows 'a clear shift in the composition of displacements from manufacturing to service and retail industries over the decade' (Podgursky, 1992). Steep declines in retail employment began to register in the first half of 1991 with a loss of 285,000 jobs. Employment plummeted throughout 1991, especially in general merchandise stores which were hit hardest by the financial restructuring described earlier (Meisenheimer *et al*, 1992).

Changes in the structure of the sector are further reflected in the allocation of work hours and employment security. The restructuring of the retail sector has a strong effect on contingent labour patterns in the workforce as a whole because the sector has historically been the largest employer of contingent workers.

Contingent work in the emerging retail sector

The retail sector has been the major employer of contingent workers, the vast majority of whom are voluntary part-time workers. Retail has also historically employed a disproportionate share of self-employed and unpaid family workers (Haugen, 1986). The self-employed portion of employment in this sector declined from 10 per cent to 8 per cent between 1973 and 1985 and unpaid family member employment registered less than 1 per cent of the retail workforce by 1985. Both of these figures support the trend toward decline of small independent businesses.

The increasing 'flexibility' of the retail workforce over the 1980s is demonstrated in changing patterns of work hours. Over the time period 1972 to 1987 the average weekly hours of non-supervisory workers in retail declined from 33.3 hours to 28.8 hours. The averages for all private industry also show a decline, but in 1972 average hours for all private industry exceeded average retail hours by 3.5 hours per week, and in 1987 by 5.8 hours per week. This decline in hours is attributable to an increase in the proportion of part-time workers in the industry (Table 8.5). In 1957, 20 per cent of the workers in retail trade held part-time jobs; in 1987, 35.8 per cent of the workers were part-timers. It is also attributable to a decline in the number of hours per worker. In 1982 employees in all of retail sub-sectors averaged less than 35 hours per week.

Flexibility is also a function of labour turnover. Employment turnover in retail was 60 per cent in 1986 (Friedman, 1988). High rates of turnover for part-timers are attributed to the 'high proclivity' of young and female workers towards shorter hours and 'stop gap' earnings. On the one hand this creates extra training costs and decreases labour productivity. On the other hand, because this proclivity is generalized to the entire contingent retail workforce, retailers can take advantage of the staffing flexibility it allows.

Table 8.5 Distribution of part-time and full-time workers in the US retail sector, 1972–89

	Total (000s)	Part-time	Full-time [a]	Full-time < =40 hours/week	>40 hours/week
1989	17 243	34.7	65.3	40.3	25.0
1988	16 815	35.7	64.3	39.4	24.9
1987	16 477	35.8	64.2	40.0	24.1
1986	16 128	36.3	63.7	39.2	24.5
1985	15 670	36.2	63.8	39.9	23.9
1984	15 372	37.2	62.8	40.5	22.3
1983	14 439	38.6	61.4	40.5	20.9
1982	14 221	38.6	61.4	40.9	20.6
1981[b]	14 107	37.7	62.3	41.0	21.3
1981[c]	13 780	37.9	62.1	40.9	21.3
1980	13 513	37.0	63.0	40.8	22.2
1979	13 520	35.4	64.6	40.7	23.9
1978	13 300	35.2	64.8	41.1	23.8
1977	12 777	35.3	64.7	40.3	24.3
1976	12 283	35.1	64.9	40.5	24.3
1975	11 836	34.8	65.2	40.4	24.7
1974	11 655	33.6	66.4	40.5	25.9
1973	11 386	32.9	67.1	40.2	26.9
1972	11 124	32.5	67.5	40.5	27.0

Source: US Department of Labor, Bureau of Labor Statistics, Current Population Survey, unpublished statistics
[a] In 1989, includes persons who are usually full-time and working 1–34 hours per week, for non-economic reasons.
[b] Benchmarked on the 1980 census.
[c] Benchmarked on the 1970 census.

Although the retail sector is conventionally depicted as dominated by part-time workers, employment trends emerging in the late 1980s and into the 1990s signal a shift away from part-time work in the sector. The concentration of retail activity in regional centres and away from local residential areas has affected labour supply conditions. The traditional part-time retail worker – the married woman and teenager – is no longer available in sufficient numbers to allow for a strategy emphasizing numerical flexibility. The majority of US women work full-time and are unavailable for part-time work. In addition, because of a low birth rate in the 1970s, there are many fewer teenagers available for part-time work in the 1990s than there were in the 1960s and 1970s.

In response to these supply trends and intense pressures to reduce labour costs, employers have begun to shift away from numerical flexibility in the sector and towards functional flexibility, using one full-time worker to do multiple tasks – cashiering, shelf-stocking, etc. By the end of the 1980s, hours per worker had begun to rise from the low of the early 1980s and many more part-time workers were employed part-time involuntarily.

Labour segmentation

Women and young people have consistently made up a disproportiona.e share of retail employees. In the 1980s, women in retail exceeded their representation in the population and 40 per cent of all retail employees were less than 25 years old (Haugen, 1986).

Women accounted for two-thirds of employment growth in retail in the 1970s and 1980s. The proportion of women employed throughout the sector has increased except in restaurants and department stores, both of which had relatively high proportions of women in 1972. Although the difference between the proportions of women employed by the sectors with the largest and smallest percentages of women employees has not decreased (41 per cent), the range has shifted upward.

Differences among sub-sectors employing either predominantly men or predominantly women are reflected in high variations of weekly earnings relative to the retail average which in turn reflect relative variations in weekly hours and hourly wages. The sub-sectors offering the lowest hourly wages, shortest weekly hours, and lowest weekly earnings have also consistently employed a greater number of women than men. Apparel specialty stores, for example, consistently paid weekly wages lower than the sectoral average from 1972 to 1987 and the wage differential increased during this period.

Slow growth in wages is associated with increased competition between independent apparel stores and the 'chains' which have enormous scale advantages. Independent apparel stores have been fighting to control labour costs while holding on to market share. The chain operated portion of the sector was expanding quickly in the 1980s and to attract enough workers, wages had to rise more quickly in these firms. To maintain their labour cost advantage, the chains hired more part-time workers at fewer hours, decreasing non-wage benefit costs.

Department stores, another female dominant sector, were plagued by overscaled operations throughout the late 1970s and 1980s. Having cut labour costs in the 1970s and 1980s by reaching out to labour pools willing to work part-time, women and young people, they are now faced with the problem of continuing to decrease labour cost while offering more service. Investment in labour saving technology is one answer to this problem. Another is an increase in 'pay-for-perfomance' schemes. In some stores, employees' working hours are being scheduled on the basis of productivity rather than seniority (Gupta, 1991). This trend has exacerbated bifurcation in total earnings in the sector, especially since many more retail workers earn commissions on sales than was the case in the 1970s. In the contemporary labour market efforts to reduce labour costs are confounded by the need to pay relatively higher wages to attract enough suitable employees.

The retail sub-sectors employing a majority of men are also among the highest paying. All have increased the proportion of women employed, which has not in and of itself depressed wages. The two male strongholds, in home furnishings and equipment, improved their positions relative to the retail average in the 1970s and 1980s.

Food retailing, a sub-sector with historically high proportions of male employment, is also the most unionized sub-sector in retailing, possibly because of its association with crafts such as meat cutting. In the late 1980s, management began seeking, and getting, lower labour costs and more flexibility with respect to work rules. Coincidentally, the decline of union power is accompanied by a growing number of women employees in supermarkets. By 1987 women made up almost half of the grocery store labour force in the US.

Weekly earnings in grocery stores were the highest among all retail sub-sectors by 1982. While remaining above average in the late 1980s, relative earnings declined sharply. Unlike the patterns in other sectors, wages did not increase more slowly, but actually declined. Food retailing management is pursuing a classic 'union busting' strategy, reaching out to new labour pools willing to start at a lower wage, diluting union ranks. At the same time negotiated agreements have decreased wages in return for longer hours and tenure benefits for that portion of the workforce in the bargaining unit.

Of the sub-sectors analysed, radio and television stores, currently referred to as consumer electronics stores, employ the lowest proportion of women. Gender stereotypes regarding mechanical aptitudes and interests have historically affected hiring practices in this sub-sector. However, as is true across the economy, fewer women in a sector means higher pay for those who are employed. Women in consumer electronics have benefited from consistently higher weekly earnings than in other sub-sectors. Weekly hours have also decreased more slowly than the sectoral average since the 1970s.

The male dominant sectors may be making an unwilling transition to conditions of the new labour market and cost-cutting measures associated with larger firms. Where the proportion of women changed little, slow employment growth and slowly declining hours would suggest a sector making do with their existing labour force and controlling costs by depressing the rate of wage growth. The extent of participation by women and part-timers, on the other hand, reflects decreased resistance possibly associated with the involvement of larger firms. Relatively large wage increases during the 1980s may reflect some combination of expansion in a tight labour market and continued commitment to their traditional labour force.

Conclusions

An analysis of sectoral change in the retail sector suggests the extent to which our markets, our consumption 'choices', are created and constructed by the rules that govern firm profitability. It also suggests the contradictions of market segmentation in a global economy. Market segmentation theoretically makes it possible for small firms to reach specialized markets. And, there is evidence of this phenomenon alongside concentrated retailing (Crewe and Forster, 1993a). The advantages in the US and UK retail market appear to lie with the large firm, however, because of their ability to apply new technological solutions, and bargain with suppliers. They also have the resources to allow market positioning, away from the saturated local market toward national or global 'simultaneous segments' (Pickholz, 1988: 42). Computer technologies allow large firms to approximate small business proximity and as one market consultant said, 'squeeze every last dollar' from targeted population niches (Edmondson, 1988: 26).

Retailers surviving the 'shake-out' of the late 1980s and early 1990s have redefined what selling means and how it takes place. Marketing technologies determine how the shelves are stocked, and retailers have begun to pare down merchandise lines, design store layouts based on customer traffic patterns, and provide product information directly to the customer. All combined create the 'perception of service' (Gebhardt, 1988: 100), allowing retailers more flexibility in staffing.

Across sub-sectors, the shopping 'environment' has been changed. On the up-market side the goal has been to increase service without increasing labour costs. On the down-market side, the goal has been to move to self-service. Not only do the remaining retail employees work in smaller workplaces than in the previous retail era, but also the size of those workplaces is declining, most notably in the top sales class of firms.

The transformation of the retail sector and of consumption work represents the second wave of restructuring. The computer-driven technologies that have transformed manufacturing work are now being applied (albeit in different forms) to the consumption sphere and consumption work. These applications can be expected to increase productivity in what traditionally has been considered a static sector. One consequence will be a decline in the labour absorptive capacity of the sector.

Notes

1   *Sociology* 24, (1 February, 1990).
2   'Of the eight companies that constituted the S&P department store index at the beginning of 1986, three [were] acquired or taken private [during 1986], while a fourth [was planning] a major restructuring that would split the firm into two separate, publicly traded companies' (*Standard and Poor's Industry Surveys*, 1987: R79). In addition, food retailing mergers hit a record high in 1986. Fending off hostile takeover attempts by the Dart Group, both Safeway and Supermarkets General went private in leverage buyouts.
3   A study by Kurt Salmon Associates (*Discount Merchandiser* 1988) describes a 66 week pipeline from raw material producer to retailer: 55 of those weeks are spent in inventory.
4   The trade-offs for domestic suppliers and retailers include: retailers save expensive quota prices, and boost profit margins due to fewer mark-downs, smaller inventory, and faster turnover associated with shorter lead times (Weiner *et al*, 1988: 117), and suppliers not only receive more business, but also prompt payment once reserved only for overseas suppliers (Barrier 1988: 18). Also see Gereffi (1993).

5   'Quick response' strategies have been pioneered by Wal-mart in conjunction with suppliers such as Milliken Apparel (Barrier, 1988: 18).

6   'According to Shopping Centre World, the total number of shopping centres in the US surged 93% between 1972 and 1984, sharply outpacing population growth, while shopping space square footage grew by more than 200%' (*Standard and Poor's Industry Surveys*, 1987: R81).

7   'Sales of apparel and softgoods combined amounting to 20 percent or more of total sales, and selling each of the following lines of merchandies: furniture, home furnishings, appliances, and radio and TV sets; a general line of family apparel; and household linens and dry goods. To qualify as a department store, sales of each of lines listed above must be less than 80 percent of total sales. An establishment with total sales of $10 million or more is classified as a department store even if sales of one of the merchandise lines listed above exceed the maximum percent of total sales, provided that the combined sales of the other two groups are $1 million or more. Relatively few stores are included in this classification as a result of this special rule and most of those which are would otherwise have been classified in the apparel group' (US Department of Commerce, 1977: A–7).

CHAPTER 9

Understanding retail employment relations

Paul Freathy and Leigh Sparks

The job of a checkout assistant working at a cash desk is reminiscent of mass production in manufacturing and has the same negative repercussions on health. (*Supermarketing*, 12 April 1985: 3)

The unique element in department store labour policy (as opposed to factory practice) was the encouragement of skilled selling: the use of trained sales clerks to increase the size and number of sales transactions through merchandise information and sales psychology. (Benson, 1986: 125)

The retail sector, when combined with wholesaling, accounts for almost 16 per cent of all employees in employment in Britain. Distribution employs approximately 3.4 million people of whom 2.14 million are employed within retail distribution, 0.9 million in wholesaling and the remainder in dealing, commission agency and repairs. To these figures can be added the self-employed in retailing, estimated at approximately 408 000. Within these massive totals are obvious polarities (Sparks, 1987) such as spatial (no retail employment at all in a locality opposed to a shopping centre employing many thousands), numerical (an owner-only operated store compared to a flagship department store such as Harrods), temporal (workers employed for a few hours a week or a few days a year contrasted with a manager working 60+ hours a week every week of the year) and financial (from a multi-million pound a year chief executive to a family employee paid nothing). How can we therefore understand employment relations in retailing? What are people doing and why? What factors are structuring this labour force? The scale, breadth and diversity of the sector makes answering such questions complicated. However, the central or pivotal role of retailing in reflecting and linking production and consumption (Bowlby *et al*, 1992; Gibbs, 1992; Hallsworth, 1992) and the scale of the sector (Lowe and Crewe, 1991) makes understanding retail employment relations vital. Achieving this understanding is the focus of this chapter.

To achieve answers to the questions above, the chapter is divided into five main sections. First, the changing nature of the retail sector is examined, focusing particularly on employment implications. Second, a section on conceptualizing retail employment is presented. Third, contemporary developments within the retail labour market are analysed in the context of the conceptualization. Fourth, key aspects to the analysis are discussed in more detail. Finally, conclusions are drawn.

The changing nature of the retail sector

Retailing has a history of change, conflict and competition (D Davis, 1966; Jeffreys, 1954; Mui and Mui, 1989). Since the Second World War, major retail changes in the UK can be identified including the development of self-service, the rise of corporate chains and the development of new locational and format alternatives. The 1980s saw the full development of many of these changes. While the retail transformation has been a long time in the making (Mathias, 1967), the consumer-based boom of the 1980s, driven by credit expansion and savings reduction, brought retailing change to the forefront of attention (Gardner and Sheppard, 1989). As du Gay (1992: 1) notes 'retailing can be seen to have promoted "enterprise" through its role in encouraging the progressive penetration of the "market" into all areas of social and cultural life'. The factors that have prompted these changes (Dawson and Sparks, 1985) are reviewed here to develop understanding of employment relationships.

Changes in business organization

Changes in business organization include alterations to the control and ownership of retail businesses, the increasing size of retail companies, competitive effects among organizational types and the development of management methods and corporate strategy.

An examination of the food sector provides examples of these changes. Over the 1980s and 1990s (and before) multiple chains gained market share and profitability at the expense of independent and co-operative retailers particularly. The 1961 Census of Distribution results suggests that independent retailers accounted for 54 per cent of retail sales with co-operative societies at approximately 10.5 per cent (see Moir and Dawson, 1992). Comparable data are not available, but the Retailing Inquiry series (SDA 25) shows that by 1980 the market shares of independents, multiples and co-operatives were 32.2 per cent, 61.4 per cent and 6.3 per cent respectively (Moir and Dawson, 1992). By 1990 the equivalent figures were 27.2 per cent, 69.0 per cent, and 3.8 per cent. Within the figure for multiples, the proportion accounted for by large (as opposed to small) multiple retailers had risen from 79 per cent to 84 per cent over this period. This rising multiple market share was gained initially through price competition generated by economies of scale and operation. In the 1980s particularly, the share increase was obtained by better meeting customer needs and by a vigorous search for operating efficiencies. In order to continue their expansionary paths, finance was raised and this altered the control and to an extent, the ownership of many companies. Those that were successful grew even larger, taking over smaller companies in the process (Akehurst, 1983). At the same time the direction of such companies became clearer and more focused with a much more strategic outlook. A comparison of the 'big three' in food retailing – Sainsbury, Tesco and Argyll (Safeway) – in 1993 and in 1980 reveals a world of difference. The imperatives may be the same, but the way in which they are met has altered fundamentally (Hallsworth, 1992; Sparks, 1993; Wrigley, 1987; 1991; 1993a). Their mode of retail and distribution operations has been transformed in terms of their outlets (location, size, range, service, design, etc) and their policies (service, non-price competition, site acquisition, employment, etc). The position of these companies within retailing and within the economy is now far stronger (Akehurst, 1984; Hallsworth, 1992; Sparks, 1993; Wrigley, 1987; 1991; 1993a).

From an employment perspective the changes in business organization have focused on the search for efficiencies at store and head office levels. This has occurred at the same time as the development of high-profile retail leaders such as Terence Conran, Alistair Grant, George Davies, Anita Roddick, Ralph Halpern, Richard Greenbury, Alec Monk, Geoff Mulcahy, Gerald Ratner and Ian MacLaurin among others. The price of failure is high as evidenced by some of the names on the above list and the changes in the less successful chains. For example, during the period May 1990 to January 1993 there were 13 director level departures from Gateway (Isosceles) as the company attempted to come to terms with its difficulties. It is estimated that the compensation to these directors on departure totalled at least £3.7 million (*Daily Mail*, 26 January 1993: 35). At regional and store levels, the corporate mergers have brought store and labour rationalization (e.g. Currys/Dixons, Tesco/Hillards) and competitive effects themselves have forced businesses to become more efficient (i.e. reduce costs) or to lose business and even close.

Changes in retail operations

The changes in business organization are interlinked with changes in retail operations. The search for operating efficiencies and improved methods of meeting customer needs have transformed the operations of leading corporate retailers. There have been changes to the number and size of stores, as well as their locations (intra-urban and inter-regional). Computerization has become widespread and the supply of products and services has been transformed. Labour use has been refined within many companies both to reduce costs and provide better service. Technology investment and labour rationalization have produced massive productivity gains. In short, corporate retailers have looked for ways to make their operations both more efficient and more effective. Many of these (though not all) are retailer responses to the consumer marketplace. Changes in consumption have become critically important in structuring and restructuring retailing, as retailers have sought to better match their offer to rising consumer affluence and changing consumer desires. Market segmentation and polarization at the demand side have been matched by supply side changes (Gibbs, 1992; Sparks, 1993).

Again it is possible to examine these changes by reference to the food retailing sector. Stores have become fewer in number as corporate retailers have expanded. The formats have polarized in size with a major emphasis on superstore development off-centre (B K Davies and Sparks, 1989; Thorpe, 1991a). Companies have replaced stock with information and modernized their supply chain and supplier base (D L G Smith and Sparks, 1993). The movement up-market of many leading chains has been coupled with a vigorous attack on labour costs throughout the company's operation.

Operationally, retailing has placed a major emphasis on cost reduction. Large stores bring economies of scale (S Shaw *et al*, 1989) and savings of labour have also arisen through the introduction of technology (Dawson *et al*, 1987b; S Smith, 1988; Whitmore, 1990). Changes in supply chains have also reduced the need for store staff. In short, the attention to the detail of retail operations that is now required has focused attention on the total labour used and its composition.

The driving force of these changes to business organization and retail operations has been the requirement to maintain business momentum as indicated by measures such as market capitalization, which is itself dependent on issues such as market share and profitability as well as potential returns to shareholders. These requirements have proved too much for some retailers – in food notably Gateway – while others have struggled to meet expectations – such as Asda. The very success of the 'big three' in food retailing has itself drawn in new competition most notably from abroad (Wrigley, 1993a), although indigenous discounters such as Kwik Save (Sparks, 1990) have developed steadily, focused on their own segments and operational efficiencies (Davis and Kay, 1990).

Whatever the format and competitive situation, labour is critical to retail operations and business development. It is critical because of the need for people to serve (or process) customers and to manage stores and direct businesses, but it is also critical for another reason: labour is the single biggest expense a retailer has after the purchase of goods. Efficiencies in the area of labour are therefore of tremendous importance. It is to the conceptualization of, and then the contemporary developments in, retail labour that attention is now turned.

Conceptualizing retail employment: a theoretical framework

There are a number of ways of looking at retail employment. The dichotomy between cost and service provides the notion of an ambivalent relationship. Retailers want service as service is felt to improve sales by encouraging customers and can be used to obtain higher margins. However, the provision of added service is a real cost to the retailer and one that in many cases is seen as being too expensive. Retailers are often unconvinced that the extra costs are offset by extra sales or believe that once sales have been gained, service can be reduced without damaging the sales pattern (Sparks, 1992b). Labour therefore tends to be seen by most retailers as a cost that is to be minimized and reduced so as to provide a better margin or to realize a higher proportion of surplus-value. Employee relations or human resources management can then be used to mediate this relationship (Marchington and Harrison, 1991). Ducatel and Blomley (1990) place labour in the context of a reduction of circulation costs and argue that retailers will seek to reduce these as far as possible because 'retail labour does not create value. This means that there is no imminent limit to the reduction of labour costs within retailing' (1990: 222). The introduction of self-service and the undertaking by consumers of more of the shopping effort aids this process, as does the structuring of retail space in store or shopping centre layouts. Fundamentally, however, Ducatel and Blomley (1990) propose that costs have been reduced by 'a steady dismantling of a relatively skilled, male-dominated labour force, and its subsequent replacement by a low-skilled, lowly paid, feminized workforce, complete with the increasing use of part-time and juvenile labour' (1990: 222).

While this basic description of the process is undeniable and has been described before (Sparks, 1986a; 1987; Bluestone *et al*, 1981), we argue here that the situation is more complicated than that described by Ducatel and Blomley (1990). The processes they claim have occurred and the rationale for cost reductions can be accepted readily. However, we would argue that a more detailed examination of the retail labour market identifies some of the nuances behind these general tendencies. We suggest that it is possible for some retail workers to add value and that the simple cost reduction approach is mediated by the need to manage more complex retail and corporate situations and to deliver an acceptable service level. In some situations as well, the labour cost argument is bypassed by the power relationship arguments in the supply chain. Finally it is possible to suggest that the current retail labour issue may not be one of shop-floor staff, but is rather one of managerial concerns. This is a topic that has not received as much attention as it deserves (Freathy and Sparks, 1995a).

One way of beginning this re-examination of retail employment is by providing a theoretical conceptualization of the labour market (see Freathy, 1993, for a longer review).

Much academic debate has focused upon the segmented nature of labour markets (Ashton and Snug, 1992; Ashton *et al*, 1982; Atkinson, 1985; Peck; 1989b; Rubery, 1988). It has been argued that labour markets are both hierarchical and segmented and can be divided broadly into primary and secondary forms of employment. Primary employment conditions are characterized by having secure terms of employment, high wages and good working conditions. According to Piore (1975) the primary sector could be further divided between the upper and lower primary sectors. What distinguishes each element is the control exercised over the job. The upper primary tier comprises professional and managerial positions where individuals have control and autonomy over their working environment. In contrast, the lower primary tier comprises jobs where individuals have little control over their working environment.

The secondary sector is characterized by jobs with little security, poor wages and high turnover. As with the primary sector, the secondary sector is also structured into tiers. Employment is both hierarchical and segmented, with jobs differing in both quality and quantity. A degree of differentiation therefore exists within the secondary sector. Rubery (1988) notes that certain elements of the secondary workforce have both responsibility and job specific skills. The terms and conditions attached to the job will be dependent upon a variety of internal and external influences including the availability of labour, the strength of the overall economy and the nature of the organization itself. What is of importance in this context is the dynamic nature within which labour markets operate. The terms and conditions that surround employment categories are not fixed and change as market conditions change. Thus in periods of labour shortage employers may increase the attractiveness of the package they offer to employees (Peck, 1989a).

Michon (1987) maintains that the existence of a secondary labour market provides employers with a series of material benefits. Its main advantage is in allowing managers to respond flexibly to changing economic circumstances. Employees in the secondary sector may be hired by the hour, day, week or month. A variety of different employment contracts exist to provide the employer with the maximum level of flexibility. For example, in the retail sector part-time employees have been used successfully to cover trading peaks. Paid by the hour, they undertake part-time shifts to cover periods of peak customer flow.

In addition to providing a degree of flexibility, secondary sector employment can provide significant savings on labour costs. In many instances secondary employment is part-time. Because of the lack of hours worked, part-time employees are often ineligible for sickness, maternity or holiday benefits. Their attractiveness as a low-cost flexible labour force is reinforced with their easy substitution. While economic conditions may regulate the overall demand for labour, the low level of skills typically required for secondary employment allows their easy replacement.

For many sales assistants on the shop-floor, working part-time, the terms and conditions applying to their job could loosely be classed as secondary. An illustration of the secondary condition is the statement by Couch (1992: 192) that 'one major food retail company estimated that over 70 per cent of its full-time staff employed in stores were in receipt of state family income support'. The secondary nature of elements of this workforce are reinforced by their hours of work, labour turnover rates and pay. Pay in retailing is relatively low for many shop-floor workers, a fact reinforced by the removal of Wages Council protection and the decline of collective bargaining (M P Jackson *et al*, 1993). On a broader front the unwillingness of the British government to sign the Social Chapter of the Maastricht Agreement is symptomatic of their views about labour costs and employee relations. This stance is acceptable to many retailers as it keeps costs down, particularly of part-time workers.

We have therefore argued that the retail sector divides broadly into primary and secondary forms of employment. While the nature of this relationship may change, a distinction has been drawn between the different terms and conditions applying to each. An integral element to understanding the nature of the retail labour market is the concept of the internal labour market. Based upon the work of Slichter (1950), Lester (1952) and Kerr (1954) internal labour markets were seen as methods of sheltering specific groups of workers from the open market. Entry into the internal market is defined by the organization and once achieved the pricing and allocation of labour is not affected by the market but is governed through a series of institutional rules and procedures. The internal market is distinguished from the external when labour is no longer controlled by economic variables (Doeringer and Piore, 1971).

Access into an internal labour market is through a 'port of entry'. Entry at a specific port provides access to higher positions through an internal promotion system. Piore (1975) argued that the existence of a defined career structure for individuals provides benefits for both employer and employee. Internal labour markets provide employers with greater flexibility. Employees are provided with a range of specific company skills which makes it difficult for them to transfer to comparable positions elsewhere. Once a worker has begun to move up the career ladder switching to another firm can become less attractive as they may be relegated to a lower port of entry. The internal labour market helps place a voluntary tie upon the individual by making it unattractive to leave the firm. The practice of restricting entry in this way also allows firms to use their internal markets as screening devices against opportunistic labour. Those workers who were hired in error can either be dismissed or the firm can minimize its losses by halting the progression of an individual on the career ladder (Wachter, 1974; O Williamson, 1975).

The boundaries between the primary and secondary are not fixed and may be redrawn as employers respond to product market conditions or labour market changes (Rubery, 1988). Atkinson (1985) argues that employers will seek to reduce the size of their core workforce during periods of economic uncertainty. The use of sub-contractors, temporary workers and part-timers provide firms with an increased numerical flexibility. While having some support, Atkinson's (1985) hypothesis underestimates the importance of external factors in producing labour market changes (Rubery, 1988).

The supply of labour within the labour market is also segmented by factors such as gender, age, race and residential location (Ashton and Snug, 1992; Ashton et al, 1982; Peck 1989b; Rubery, 1988). Particular forms of labour are considered to occupy particular market segments or niches (Crompton et al, 1990), in which their allocation is a function of both external pressures and internal, organizational decisions. The inequitable treatment of different groups within the labour market allows wide pay differentials for workers of comparable jobs. Identifying broad trends therefore obfuscates the highly complex nature of labour market allocation. For example, some have suggested that women as a whole represent a secondary labour force (Barron and Norris, 1976). This, we maintain, ignores sectoral, locational and organizational differences in the interaction between labour and capital.

In terms of the earlier discussion of the role of labour in realizing surplus-value and the overriding aim to reduce costs of labour, the primary market is seen as a somewhat ill-fitting conception. The secondary market can be broadly understood as the market where skills and rewards are low and costs are readily minimized. The internal market concept, or protected worker concept, suggests a value to the retail business above that of simply cost reduction (although there is an element of this in reduced switching or recruitment costs). The employment of such workers is a necessary cost on the business and may become a barrier to entry to the sector. This is examined later in the chapter.

Contemporary developments within the retail labour market

The size and diversity of the retail sector, and its employment relations have already been alluded to in the introduction. Figure 9.1 provides a disaggregation of retail employment by Standard Industrial Classification (SIC) code and gender and hours worked. The importance of the food sector can be noted. Equally numerically important is the 'other' category which covers businesses such as variety and mixed goods retailers. The prevalence of part-time work in retailing is marked in Figure 9.1, and whilst predominantly female in nature, there is a substantial male component. There are some gender specificities by SIC code, but as a generality retailing is a female and part-time sector.

The total number of people employed in retailing has remained relatively static since the late 1970s (Figure 9.2), although with variations depending on general economic performance. This, however, masks a number of labour market changes that have occurred within retailing.

Structurally, in employment terms, it is believed that the labour force is becoming more polarized. Many retail outlets (and not just food supermarkets or large retail warehouses) contain a core of full-time staff with part-time and (to a lesser extent) casual staff brought in and out of the labour force as required. While it remains very difficult to quantify accurately, the effect of this is to further reduce the Full Time Equivalent (FTE) input into retailing. The larger firms recruit and reward well the full-time managerial staff and use part-time staff to match the vagaries (or certainties) of trading demand.

Retailers have therefore to reconcile supply and demand issues and cost and service balances in their employment of labour. An illustration

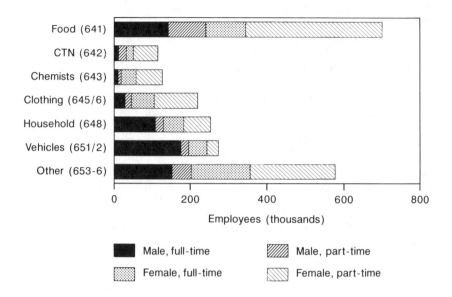

Figure 9.1   Retail employment by sector, June 1994

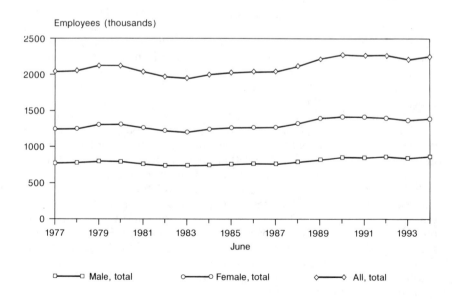

Figure 9.2   Retail employment by gender, 1977–94

of this is the demand for an increasingly professional management structure. The marked increase in the number of graduates, and graduate management training schemes bear testimony to this. Emphasis is placed increasingly upon the development of the individual manager through structured off and on the job training. Post experience and more formal academic courses such as MBAs (Master of Business Administration) have become available to both store-based and head office personnel. Investment in people in this way can also be considered as a part of the internal labour market process with the aim of increasing switching costs and investment protection (Broadbridge and Davies, 1993).

Within large retail stores it remains possible to identify those employees (store managers) who are full-time, have a relatively secure degree of employment and conditions approaching that identified as primary employment. This management structure may be further sub-divided between senior and junior management teams. While the exact comparison of such groups will vary, the senior team in a superstore typically comprises store and deputy manager, operations, personnel and administration. Department heads and deputies are considered outside of this. At a level below department managers are supervisory grades. As with managerial positions the conditions of employment are relatively secure and full-time. Supervisors are primarily in charge of the sales floor and check-out areas. The work is often repetitive and concentrates upon co-ordinating check-out areas and acting as first line of complaint from the customer. Such jobs could be classed as comprising lower primary tier employment.

There is a gender dimension to retail management reinforcing Rubery's (1988) observations on segmentation. Evidence suggests that a disproportionate number of retail managers are male (Dawson *et al*, 1987a; Sparks 1983; 1991b). Within superstores Sparks (1991b) and Freathy (1993) for example identify a management structure that is biased towards male store and deputy store managers. Only the personnel function has a more balanced gender breakdown.

The desire to control costs, however, has resulted in a decline in the number of full-time positions. While aggregate numbers have remained relatively stable, there has been a marked increase in the number of part-time workers employed within retailing. Over 45 per cent of all jobs in retailing are part-time. While this growth has not been confined to any single area of retailing, its occurrence has been most notable within the large, food multiples and at store rather than head office level. For the retailer the use of part-time labour provides both cost and service benefits. Part-time employees are often cheaper to employ than full-time workers and may not obtain the same employee-related benefits such as pensions and sickness pay. Part-time workers also enable the varying demands of trading to be covered, for example the daily, weekly and seasonal peaks and troughs.

Employment relations at the store level illustrate this movement towards part-time working. The greater responsiveness to customer needs and the increasingly competitive nature of the sector has led to a much closer monitoring of workers and day-to-day operations. Technology now allows employees to be tracked from till to till and their performance monitored throughout their working period. Sales information available through Electronic Point of Sale (EPOS) is used to assist in deliberations over store operations and the tasks to be undertaken, e.g. check-out openings, product replenishment and staff scheduling. Individuals may therefore find themselves deployed flexibly across a wide range of separate store functions. Technology provides a better understanding of consumer demands on the store and also allows better control of staff as they are matched to this demand (Whitmore, 1990). Staff are therefore brought in and out of the workforce as demand dictates and used where appropriate in the store. At its extreme this has resulted in the so-called 'flexible contracts' or 'annual contracts' where the hours to be worked are left open and the staff brought in as required.

Among part-time workers a gender dimension is again in evidence. Women have since the Second World War comprised a large proportion of retail employees. The 1980s witnessed a small increase in their total numbers, and a major switch to part-time employment as the dominant form of contract. As Figures 9.2 and 9.3 illustrate, women account for approximately 63% of all persons employed within the retail sector, and approximately 83% of all part-time workers. Conversely, as Figure 9.4 shows, male workers outnumber female workers in the full-time category. The utilization of women to fill part-time vacancies has provided supply side as well as demand side benefits. Married women

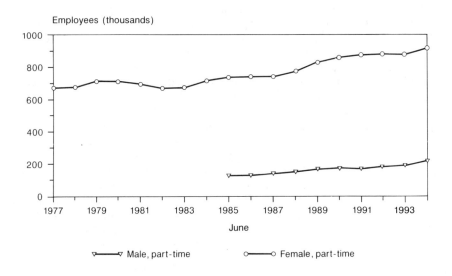

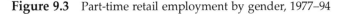

Figure 9.3 Part-time retail employment by gender, 1977–94

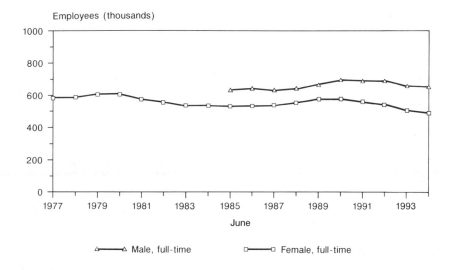

Figure 9.4   Full-time retail employment by gender, 1977–94

especially have used the opportunity to work short part-time shifts of three to five hours, finding such work compatible with other demands in the domestic division of labour. Women's earnings in retailing remain below those of men (Broadbridge, 1993).

For many retailers the recruitment of female part-timers has enabled them to reconcile other changes within the labour market. The late 1980s and early 1990s saw a decline in the number of young people leaving school and entering the retail sector. The current recession has enabled retailers to avoid some, though not all, of the problems the decline in the youth labour market was going to bring. The potential demographic timebomb, combined with the high turnover rates and the threat of equal pay legislation in Europe led to substantial pay increases for some key groups of workers in the late 1980s. For example Tesco in 1990 gave junior workers rises of 13.5–20.2 per cent, which in turn followed on a 22 per cent increase in 1989. In contrast adult rates were increased by 10 and 8 per cent respectively in 1990 and 1989. J Sainsbury, W H Smith and Marks & Spencer have consolidated all rates for 16 and 17 year olds into an under-18 rate which in W H Smith is now equivalent to 80 per cent of the adult rate. J Sainsbury, Tesco and Safeway changed their pay structures after job evaluation concerning equal value, a move which resulted in double-figure percentage increases for many check-out operators. Retailers were also prompted to source alternative supplies of labour. For example B&Q undertook a recruitment drive towards older people (Hogarth and Barth, 1991). The onset of recession and consequent high unemployment has modified such changes in the early 1990s and defused the timebomb.

189

The suggestion above is that the retail sector has polarized in employment terms. On the one hand are the bulk of shop-floor workers who are overwhelmingly female, part-time and lowly paid. On the other hand, there is a cadre of management which is male, full-time and rewarded extensively. Table 9.1 provides a comparison of the reward and remuneration packages of typical examples of each category (see also Broadbridge, 1993). While much attention has been focused on the ability of shop-floor workers to provide retailers with operational flexibility and thus to enhance perceived service levels, managerial concerns have had less attention. The assumption has been that the reward packages at this level are such as to ameliorate any problems or dissension. This assumption can be challenged, as illustrated by the debate over Sunday working.

Freathy and Sparks (1993) obtained questionnaire data from over 5000 Sunday workers in food and DIY superstores operated by nine multiple retailers across Britain. The contrasts between the responses by shop-floor and managerial staff shed light on changing attitudes and potential problems.

Of those working on a Sunday, the survey work shows that managers were more likely to identify disadvantages to Sunday working. Of the 363 store managers who responded, 69 per cent identified disadvantages; corresponding percentages for departmental managers (334 respondents) and supervisors/controllers (457 respondents) were 63 per cent and 55 per cent. The sales/general/check-out category on the other hand showed that of the 3026 respondents, only 40 per cent identified disadvantages, with the majority identifying no disadvantages at all. These differences are due to the job contract and life stage of groups of respondents. Many shop-floor workers worked part-time or Sunday only, so viewed Sunday working as integral to the job. Income (essential and extra) was the main reason for Sunday working in both managerial and shop-floor groups but while overall numbers were low, managers felt more pressurized to work on a Sunday or were required to work on a Sunday. Their dissatisfaction levels were therefore much higher.

While there are many interrelationships in this data set which are beyond the scope of this chapter, it is worth noting that the level of satisfaction among women workers was substantially higher than among male workers. Women workers of course are numerically concentrated in the sales/general/check-out categories. Approximately 60 per cent of all women workers (who were themselves 60 per cent of the respondents) saw no disadvantages at all to Sunday working, compared with 45 per cent of males. While this is interrelated with job level and hours of work, it does suggest that Sunday working meets supply-side issues for a proportion of the female population. Other results also show that women particularly value the financial independence that Sunday working gives to them (Freathy and Sparks, 1995b).

Table 9.1 Reward and remuneration – examples from a food retailer, 1992

	General manager
Category 8	(Band from £39 000–£49 000, performance rated)
Salary	£45 000 per annum consolidated (no premiums)
Overtime	Double time for Sundays
	Fixed payment of £100 for bank holidays
Benefits	Employee profit sharing – average 6% per annum*
	Executive share options
	Annual bonus of up to 30% of annual salary*
	Private medical insurance
	Annual medical (Harley Street)
	Company car, ranges from BMW 520-Audi Coupe,
	Volvo 960–Senator, includes all costs including petrol
	Staff discount card – 10% off over £3.00
	29 days' paid holiday per annum
	26 weeks' company sick pay
	PEPs schemes
	Company pension scheme (including life assurance)
	Subsidized staff restaurant
	5% discount at Hogg Robinson Travel Agents

* Dependent on company profit performance

	Shop-floor staff salary package
General assistant at age 18+	£7 374.54 per annum
Cashier at age 18+	£7 743.21 per annum
Benefits	10% staff discount
	Full-time and part-time pension scheme
	Save As You Earn scheme
	Profit sharing
	Subsidized staff restaurant
	5% discount at Hogg Robinson Travel Agents
	4 weeks' and 2 days' paid holiday as soon as joining
	company
	Full uniform provided
	Staff social club

Discussion of key aspects

The description of retail employment in the previous section draws heavily on the work of Sparks (1983; 1991b) and Freathy (1993) on superstores. While it is true that superstores are at the leading edge of employee restructuring, it is believed that similar employee relations can be seen in other store categories such as variety stores, department stores and (albeit in a limited way) small shops.

It is therefore possible to broadly categorize employment relations in the retail sector by Piore's (1975) and Doeringer and Piore's (1971) conception of the labour market. However while not denying the applicability or usefulness of this theoretical framework its weakness lies in its focus upon the individual firms without reference to the wider structural issues operative within the labour market. What remains difficult to gauge is the relative change in autonomy and responsibility of individuals and the factors behind such change.

As discussed, the retail sector has become increasingly competitive, with market pressures forcing retail firms to monitor costs tightly. Technological developments have assisted in this process. Increasingly the emphasis has been upon responding flexibly to the needs of the individual consumer. The decline of the mass market has led to a growth of lifestyle products and niche and micro-marketing techniques.

In employment terms these changes have led to a removal of many of the areas of responsibility away from the store and their replacement by decision-making at head office. The control that senior management has at store level over areas such as space allocation, pricing, promotion and staffing is limited. The autonomy and control, prevalent in Piore's (1975) upper primary tiers, have been reduced over time due to competitive pressures and operational efficiencies. While this may seem to be an attempt to de-skill management to a lower primary position, a contradiction exists in the increased remuneration package offered and the tying in of senior store management to structured career paths. This is a particularly British rather than European approach (Burt, 1989), but does reflect the need for good quality implementation staff rather than strategic decision-making staff at store level.

The trend to increased employment flexibility has been highlighted by Doogan (1992) and particularly Atkinson and Meager (1986) who suggest that it involves numerical flexibility, distancing (i.e. contract labour) functional flexibility and pay flexibility. The discussion above recognizes that retailers, particularly in the large stores, have moved towards a flexible labour force by introducing in particular numerical and functional flexibility. Some jobs have been let to sub-contractors, and there is evidence of pay flexibility, particularly at management level. What is important, however, is to recognize the driving forces behind flexibility.

The growth of more flexible retailing is based on consumer knowledge and the ability to use this knowledge (Fuller and Smith, 1991). By understanding consumer demand more closely, the retail offer can be reconstructed to meet these demands as in the scheduling of labour, the timing of deliveries, the type of labour used, etc. The emphasis upon external pressures structuring employment relations reinforces Rubery's (1988) conclusions that labour market changes are associated more with sectoral changes than with autonomous changes in employer strategy. Consumption therefore is an integral element to understanding the structure of retailer employment strategies. Changing and restructuring retailing structures are therefore crucial through their reflection of consumption to the general move towards a service-oriented society. In turn, the employment practices of retailing and those supplying retailers have to become more flexible in order to meet the cost/service balances imposed by changing consumption requirements.

The complexity of retail employment relations should therefore be apparent. While it is true that for many retailers cost reduction is a major driving force, it is not possible to say with certainty that no retail employee adds value. There is a limit to the cost reduction of labour that can be undertaken. Some labour is required in most retail stores. The ultimate nightmare of a card-operated retail booth with electronic lighting and heating and orders, selected form a laser disk, transmitted electronically is not one that can be realistically followed for all retailing. While for many retailers it is true that staff do not add value in a direct sense and are minimized, some retailers do pride themselves and their staff on the service provision. Without such staff, the sales would not be so great. While self-service has de-skilled much retail work, not all retail work is totally de-skilled and adds nothing. Nor can it really be argued that all retail work is focused on least cost surplus-value realization alone.

While cost reduction can often be pursued at shop-floor level, many retailers have realized that store management levels are required to organize and manage what cannot be controlled centrally. While there is evidence for de-skilling at this level in the UK, there remains a need for their presence. It is true however that a de-layering of management is taking place in British retailing, reflecting some concerns about organizational and operational issues at store and head office levels. This may be a periodic restructuring consequent on recession and technology investment. There is a limit to this however, as store management does provide a valued-added function.

These issues are interrelated with service levels. The limits to the cost-reduction strategies of retailers are determined by the service level that the market agrees among itself or is deemed acceptable by the consumers. In Britain a low level of customer service is tolerated enabling retailers to reduce their costs considerably. When segments demand more service and respond positively to those that supply it, then retailers generally have to react. Conversely, when the service/price balance for consumers moves towards the latter then the service/cost (labour) balance for retailers also tends to tilt.

The emergence of market segmentation as a strategy has combined with the extension of labour segmentation particularly in the staffing of stores and the priorities accorded to costs and service. While stores have always been staffed according to the market (see the history of department stores, for example, Benson, 1986), the practice is much more common and attainable now. This can be seen in the staffing of stores to reflect customer types (Lowe, 1991) both in terms of shared beliefs and lifestyle as well as attributes.

A wider perspective can also be taken. British retailers have been very successful in their restructuring of operations and labour relations to become more efficient and effective. Internationalization forces them to encounter and adapt to new situations and legal requirements. Wrigley (1993a) points to the restructuring of the Shaw's labour force in the USA that J Sainsbury have undertaken, mainly by increasing the proportion of part-time working. However, legal requirements in France raise the costs of employment, a disparity that will become increasingly important (A Gregory, 1991).

Conclusions

This chapter aimed to provide a broad overview of the major developments in retail employment and to conceptualize these events within the context of retail and labour market changes. The changes that have taken place in employment relationships in the 1970s and 1980s cannot be divorced from wider structural developments occurring in the sector as a whole. The concentration of market power, the increasing level of competition among multiple retailers and developments in technology have all directly affected the structure of the retail labour market, by increasing retailers' power and freedom to change. British retailers and particularly the top food retailers have developed highly sophisticated solutions balancing the costs and requirements of labour.

Within stores (particularly superstores), it remains possible to identify a broad division between different forms of employment. A core of well-paid management with relative job security is responsible for the running of many stores. In contrast there exists a much larger group of less well-paid individuals, who experience high levels of turnover and have little job security, although within this there are some categories for whom the job is an acceptable compromise with domestic arrangements and who therefore have low turnover. Retailers have attempted to recruit these categories at the expense of more volatile categories in order to reduce recruitment and retention costs overall and potentially improve service provision. This patchwork of employment requirements and employees is far more than a simple cost reduction strategy.

An understanding of the dynamics of these relationships is of crucial importance. Retailing reflects its customers and as consumers change retailers seek to reflect that change in the nature of their offer. The growth of more discerning customers demanding greater choice and value, has led retailers to respond flexibly to their needs. This has changed the employment relationships in many stores. At a managerial level the autonomy of the senior managers has declined as many elements of the decision making process have become centralized. Some companies believe that this process has gone too far. The notion of distinguishable primary tiers therefore becomes confused as elements of both the upper and lower primary tier combine. The secondary sector also reveals elements contradictory to traditional labour market theory. Most notable are the opportunities for access from the secondary to the primary sector. While such opportunities are becoming increasingly limited, the 'hands on' nature of the retail sector does allow the transition from secondary sector employment to primary. However, for the future the key in retailing is flexibility in its widest sense. Consumption patterns are reflected by the retailers in their employment relations, and as a consequence these relations are being reassessed and changed as consumption and society changes.

While it can be accepted that retailers are restructuring retail employment relations to reduce costs and if possible improve service, it is necessary to draw limits to this. For the future, the major additional concerns will be the increasing pressure on managers and their ability and willingness to cope and the restructuring that longer trading days and weeks will bring. The position can only become more fragmented with research opportunities on the spatial dimensions of these developments. Longer term, perhaps a future British government will agree to a more level playing field by accepting the Social Contract part of Maastricht and thus increasing the true costs of part-time working!

CHAPTER 10

Shop work: image, customer care and the restructuring of retail employment

Michelle Lowe and Louise Crewe

Service looks set to be to the 1990s what designer interiors were to the 1980s. . . . In a progressively competitive high street, the quality of service retailers offer will further determine the industry's winners and losers. (Gardner and Sheppard, 1989: 185–203)

On the high street everybody has forgotten the customer. . . . We have to remember the customer or we're sunk. (Sally Grayson, managing director of Long Tall Sally, quoted in *DR The Fashion Business*, 5 September 1992)

A glance at the shop windows in the High Street during the run up to the Christmas retail 'boom' period points to a fascinating phenomenon. No longer interested purely and simply in available sales assistants many retailers in the mid-1990s are keen to appoint sales advisers or consultants who are variously 'enthusiastic' and 'committed', possessing 'imagination', 'flair', 'talent', 'confidence' and 'energy'. The Disney Store, for example, often seen as a 'brand leader' in this respect, asks that potential applicants are 'Full of fun and young at heart. Flexible and Hard Working. [with] A Commitment to Good Service', while BHS on advertising boards outside its stores enquires 'Do you have a lively personality and a sense of fun? Could you keep smiling through the Christmas rush? Would you like to work in a team atmosphere? Come and join the festive spirit at BHS'. Meanwhile Habitat asks for 'enthusiastic sales consultants' who must be 'stylish and confident with a lively personality and a belief in good service'. In many senses, of course, this apparent 'up-skilling' of the retail sales workforce is to be welcomed. The recognition that selling skills are an important asset to the High Street retailer has the potential to allow the retail salesforce leverage in their negotiations regarding pay and conditions. Dixons, for example, are reputedly keen to 'recruit better quality staff' and correspondingly 'pay them better, train them better and support them with better systems' (Cowe, 1991). However, we are rather more sceptical of these trends and suggest that the current struggle on the

High Street to differentiate on the grounds of 'customer care' is merely the latest technique being utilized by many retailers in their drive to achieve competitive advantage. Nevertheless, we accept that it may have important and far-reaching implications for the restructuring of retail employment. In the course of this chapter then, attention will be paid to qualitative elements of the transformation of 'consumption work' which are often ignored in more traditional empirical surveys of retail employment (although see Christopherson, this volume, Chapter 8; Lowe and Crewe, 1991). This chapter will focus on the 'critical role of customer service' (Doogan, 1992: 23) and 'quality of staff' issues (Sparks, 1992a: 11) as key determinants in contemporary strategies of retail competition. We shall begin by outlining the way in which we see 'customer care' and 'image' as important facets in the current round of retail restructuring. We shall then focus on The Gap, Inc. a 'retail pioneer' with regard to its employment practices. Finally we shall look at the trade union response to these new issues. Via an evaluation of the forces shaping retail change in the 1990s it is hoped that some conclusions can be reached concerning retail employment in the future.

As Christopherson suggests, the 'restructuring of the retail work process is an aspect of a broader process of capital accumulation in which "buyer driven commodity chains" play a major role' (Christopherson, this volume, Chapter 8). As a result, there is, we suggest, a clear association between the rise of 'customer service' as an important facet of the retail business and the competitive edge which can be gained as a result of that service by the retailer (Gardner and Sheppard, 1989: 185). In other words, we would argue that the 'caring 1990s' in the retail trade must be viewed as much more than a humanistic reaction to the 'competitive 1980s'. Rather, the caring 1990s means exactly that – caring for your most prized asset, your clientele (Marshall, 1992). Retailers are generally convinced then that customer service is the coming management programme that will bring success in the 1990s (Sparks, 1992b). Hence these new trends can be seen as part and parcel of the way in which retail spaces are significant sites in the circulation of commodities (Dowling, 1993; M Morris, 1988). Shopping centres are engaged in 'producing a sense of place for economic "come hither" reasons (M Morris, 1988). In this sense we are attempting to move beyond much recent work on the geography of retail activities which has tended to examine these as 'cultural' phenomena (e.g. by focusing attention on the 'subject position of shopper' – see e.g. Glennie and Thrift, this volume, Chapter 12; Jackson, 1994) rather than through the lens of political economy. And it is this latter approach which we suggest has the potential to view retailing (and more specifically the retail labour process) in a more critical light. Despite attempts to redress this imbalance, for example by Jackson (1994) who is concerned to analyse 'consumption and identity' through an examination of the *process* of consumption – and to move away from semiotic analyses (Jackson, 1994) – the focus is still ethnographic work on the 'shopper' (her/his skills, shopping as a negotiated and gendered activity, shopping as work rather than leisure or lifestyle (Jackson, 1994)) and employees serving these individuals have been forgotten. We are concerned here then to illuminate the 'social relations of consumption work'. Nevertheless, we have tried to recognize the fact that social representations accompany, adapt to, and even formulate the nature of changes and trends in the capitalist economy (P Smith, 1988). In so doing we have attempted to follow Sayer and Walker (1992) in their suggestion that the division of labour has shifted more towards work done in support of the immense *social* process of selling (Sayer and Walker, 1992: 85). Part of this move has been concerned 'to entice customers with a feeling of personal service' such that 'Retailers are less and less merely offering shelf space for goods, and more and more actively mediating the producer-consumer relation' (Sayer and Walker, 1992: 90–1).

From retail concentration to customer care

During the so-called 'retail revolution' of the 1980s in the UK the struggle for capital accumulation and differentiation in retailing was met through a variety of strategies including: the imposition of the oligopsonistic buying power of retailers on manufacturers/suppliers (Wrigley, 1992a); the spatial switching of retail capital – in particular via the rise to prominence of the out-of-town and edge-of-town shopping centre (Hudson *et al*, 1992; Sheffield City Council, 1987; Sparks, 1992a; Wrigley 1993a); the reorganization of selling space – what Ducatel and Blomley (1990) describe as the 'premeditated configuration of retail space in an attempt to induce consumption', technological change – including massive investment in computer-based IT systems (Christopherson, this volume, Chapter 8; Gardner and Sheppard, 1989; Wrigley, 1993a); transformation of the supply chain (D L G Smith and Sparks, 1993); the shift from full-time to part-time employment (Christopherson, 1989; this volume, Chapter 8; Wrigley, 1993a); property investment/development (Guy, 1994; Wrigley, this volume, Chapter 6); and differential access to capital (Wrigley, 1991). In general it has been suggested that such restructuring strategies in the retail industry (Doogan, 1992: 11) can be seen to have been broadly based around *concentration*. By contrast, the latest round of retail restructuring we suggest is centred on *customer care* (including the provision of higher levels of 'personal service' (Christopherson, this volume, Chapter 8; Hudson *et al*, 1992: 23) such that 'the ability to communicate, be polite and smile and have a neat appearance' (Hudson *et al*, 1992: 25) is now of central importance to the retail sales assistant. What is ironic here, perhaps, is the fact that, in many senses of course, retail concentration in the 1980s can be seen to have been a major factor in the deterioration of customer service into the 1990s. Increased efficiency for the retailer has often meant declining standards of service to the customer (Gardner and Sheppard, 1989: 203) and this imbalance must be redressed. But it is also the case that, faced with recession in the early 1990s, High Street retailers had clear vested interests in maintaining their customer base.

Hence the (post)modern retailer does more than simply 'sell goods' but also 'sells' the retail company as well. In 'selling' the company the store operator sells the label, the facilities and the service, and in the process 'sells the staff' (Doogan, 1992: 22). All of this has considerable implications for the restructuring of retail employment.

Let us, at this stage, go back a step and note that during the late 1980s much of this differentiation via image was achieved by the utilization of 'design interiors' to retail stores. As Fitch and Knobel (1990) observed, 'with so much competition, with constant change in merchandise and with the importance of image above all, design can play a key role in differentiating one retailer from another'. In the 1990s, however, concerns regarding image and presentation have been transferred to the retail workforce. Hence, many retailers currently attempt to inculcate a strong sense of company culture and corporate identity in the workforce (Doogan, 1992: 26, 38). Recruits have to have the right personality, the ability to mix with the right people and also to identify with the product image (Johnson and Rahtz, 1992). At The Body Shop, for example, issues of image, design, style and creativity are of paramount importance. As Anita Roddick herself has suggested:

> The closest we came to conventional training for the retail trade was a course on customer care. . . . On our customer care course we encouraged staff to treat customers as potential friends, to say hello, smile, make eye contact and to offer advice if it was wanted, to thank them, and always to invite them back. (Roddick, 1991: 144)

The Body Shop reinforced this via a training video on customer care entitled *Smile, Dammit, Smile*, while Laura Ashley introduced the Jim Maxim Award for Outstanding Customer Service which rewarded the winning sales assistant with a trip on Concorde to visit a flagship store. The chief executive of Laura Ashley saw this 'new management strategy' as the key to better sales: 'You don't stimulate sales by discounting or with high levels of promotion. We believe in empowering our staff to improve results' (Warkentin, 1992). As a result, the company began to be viewed as one of the most innovative in terms of staff training (Carr, 1993).

None of this, of course, is new. Companies like Marks and Spencer have for a long time employed 'customer relations' techniques in order to enhance their market position (Tse, 1985) – most often stressing 'a smile and eye contact' (Garner, 1992) – while fast food outlets such as McDonalds have been long keen to increase their profit margins via 'suggestive selling' (where another item on the menu is suggested, e.g. 'fries with your burger') or 'up-selling' (would you like a large [coke]?). Indeed, Burger King view 'customer service' as a premium in their staff recruitment and advertising: 'You've got it? We want it!' their shop window advertisements suggest. Dowling (1993) even notes that 'place making' (including the creation of store image) was an important aspect of retailers' attempts to attract customers in 1950s Vancouver. Such strategies, as these examples indicate, are perhaps more commonplace

...ie USA (see Sparks, 1992b) where the serial incantation of 'Have a ...e Day!' and 'Enjoy!' are well known. Saks Fifth Avenue, for example, even train their staff to

> send thank you notes to customers for shopping in the store, carry out follow up phone calls, endeavour to respond to customers requests on the same day, and even go so far as to walk customers to their car with their goods or call a cab for them. The staff even shop on behalf of the customer. (Pipe, 1993:23)

However, we would suggest that the latest retail trends towards 'customer care' involving, centrally, *selling* rather than *serving* are demonstrable examples of the ways in which such strategies are now being deployed as central features of the retail competition process in the UK – alongside moves towards part-time and flexible working, out-of-town retail employment, and so on.

> Retailers now realise that good salesmanship means more than using that well worn phrase 'Can I help you?' (a line used to initiate 80–85% of all sales pitches). Creating a strong image for the store, giving the public a reason to walk in the door and good service are all essential. . . . Keeping the customer happy has never been this tricky. (Warkentin, 1992:18)

Indeed such trends are considered so essential that a wealth of consultants are springing up in order to educate retailers in the nuances of the new hard sell. At Peter Flemming Associates, for example, managing director Peter Flemming, who lectures on selling for the British Shops and Stores Association, says arm folding, nose scratching and slouching posture are all vital body language signs now being quashed – partly because the recession of the early 1990s highlighted the need for more emphasis on customer care (see Table 10.1).

Significantly, however, not all retailers are choosing this route as a means to stay ahead of the competition. At the same time that up-market stores are increasing personal service the down-market discounters are eliminating it (simultaneously eliminating design interiors in the process – ugly stores, great prices!). Indeed, it can be argued that both de-skilling and up-skilling are occurring in tandem, that is the retail labour process is reflecting identifiable trends to retail polarization. This, we suggest, has clear and significant implications for the polarization of the retail workforce. Set in the context of fragmentation and differentiation on the High Street, the renewed emphasis on 'customer care' particularly (although not exclusively) employed by speciality retail chains can be viewed as part and parcel of the reaction to mass production on the High Street (Crewe and Davenport, 1992) and adds further potential fuel to the separating out of 'consumption centres'. More specifically, customer service has become part of the individualized responsive package available to customers in upmarket (niche) retailers or in speciality retail centres (Crewe and Lowe, 1995).

Table 10.1 Body matters

DO

smile

establish eye contact but not a constant stare

keep an open stance – no folded arms

pay full attention to customers – don't do two things at once

convince yourself you want to meet and sell to every customer

remain calm in the face of adversity – like complaining customers

use body language to your advantage – sit down a complaining customer and remain standing to achieve dominance

mirror friendly body language but avoid reflecting aggressive postures

watch customers body language – try to assess if they will welcome an approach

DON'T

fidget or stand on one leg – even behind a counter

cross arms or legs when talking – both give out the wrong messages

look bored yawn, or lean – for obvious reasons

imitate body language – humans tend to copy those close to them

scratch your nose or pull earlobes – these are classic signs of uncertainty

make your own bad day into everyone else's – project confidence and it will boost your ego

---

Source: Adapted from Garner (1992)

Such issues also have clear ramifications for the *types* of people employed to distribute the new 'customer care'. At Sainsbury, for example, the employment of older workers is considered beneficial since 'more mature employees have a good sense of the service ethic' (Gardner and Sheppard, 1989: 206). Some of this of course reflects sheer demographics – the food retailers in particular panicked about the availability of young sales assistant recruits in the late 1980s. But image is central here too. 'Smart appearance' is often no longer enough to guarantee employment in retailing. Rather, style and image are increasingly important factors in a highly competitive retail sector. A glance at the types of 'sales assistants' in certain stores is testimony to this effect. For example, the employment of young people (many part-time) can be seen as a clear marketing strategy (Christopherson, this volume, Chapter 8), while at Susan Woolf (formerly Episode) staff training programmes are offered by the style consultants *Color Me Beautiful* who focus on the staff's image and aid them in their selection of flattering cuts, fabrics and colours.

Arguably, of course, the new customer care strategies outlined above are even more significant in the large out-of-town shopping and leisure complexes which are reliant for their success on customers intention to do more than simply purchase commodities they need. Centres such as Metrocentre in Gateshead, Merry Hill in the West Midlands, Lakeside in Thurrock and Meadowhall in Sheffield 'try to promote an up market image with the emphasis on leisure, quality and customer service' (Johnson and Rahtz, 1992: 2). At Meadowhall, for example, the developers and managers of the centre decided that the 'new shopping experience' would include high quality customer service pioneered by a special training initiative (The Meadowhall Academy) which focused strongly on attitude and commitment (The Meadowhall Magic) (Johnson and Rahtz, 1992) and featured instruction in selling skills, motivation and interpersonal communication. What must be stressed, however, is that the emphasis on corporate culture, increasing flexibility, individual labour markets, investments in training, appraisal systems and individualization of rewards (Johnson and Rahtz, 1992) were all considered to be necessary aspects of the new centre aimed specifically at 'setting Meadowhall apart' through the service it provides to its customers (Denise Williams, Head of Human Resources, The Meadowhall Academy, 1991).

Having demonstrated therefore that 'customer care' programmes are important competitive strategies for the contemporary retailer, and outlined briefly the various ways in which such strategies gained prevalence in the late 1980s and into the 1990s, we next intend to add weight to our argument via a focus on The Gap, Inc. – a 'retail pioneer' with regard to its employment practices. As we shall see, The Gap (a US company which moved into Britain during the late 1980s) prides itself on customer care and sees this as a key attribute in its continuing competitive success. The Gap encourages its staff to conform to its corporate doctrine by being helpful, upbeat and keen (Pipe, 1993), and its retail employment practices are having important spillover effects across the entire UK retail spectrum.

The Gap, Inc. – a case study in customer care

Vision, imagination and leadership make a successful business – but above all it's a team effort. (Donald G Fisher, Founder, Chairman of the Board, quoted in *A Brief History of The Gap, Inc.*, 1991)

Running our business successfully means really just one thing – satisfying the customer. To ensure that we offer merchandise of good style and good taste with good value in an environment that is friendly, we have assembled a knowledgeable passionate staff. They keep us focused on our primary task. (The Gap, Inc. 1991)

The Gap is a company that connects with consumers the way only a few other giant brands such as *Coca Cola* or *McDonalds* manage to do. . . . Already firmly ensconced in 700 of the country's 1500 biggest malls it is taking advantage of recessionary blues by locking up sweet lease deals moving into downtowns and urban neighbourhoods and opening up on the main streets of midsize American cities. (Mitchell, 1992)

The Gap, Inc. is the largest apparel retailer in the USA (Kahn, 1992) – a speciality retailer which operates stores selling casual and active wear for men, women and children under four brand names: Gap, GapKids, babyGap and Banana Republic. At the end of fiscal 1991 The Gap operated a total of 1216 stores: 844 Gap, 223 GapKids and 149 Banana Republic stores. Of the Gap and GapKids stores, 33 were located in the UK, and 34 were located in Canada. Stores in the United States were located in 44 states (including all of the 50 largest metropolitan statistical areas) as well as in Puerto Rico. The stores were generally leased with no stores being franchised or operated by others.

The Gap is considered to be one of the most successful speciality chains in retail history – 'the Japan of retailing' (Kahn, 1992). Indeed, by the early 1990s The Gap's Gap label clothes had become the second largest selling brand name in the United States (after Levi Strauss). In the fight to achieve the objective of increased market share, customer service is considered to be one of The Gap's strongest competitive advantages. Knowledgeable, helpful 'sales associates' are one of the company's signature attributes. The company recognizes that 'it is our dedicated dynamic staff that makes real our most ambitious plans' (The Gap, Inc., 1991). It stresses that:

> As a company we are measured by sales and profit and earnings per share but these measurements are simple extrapolations from how good we are at satisfying the customer. Every day in our 1200+ stores our sales staff make hundreds of thousands of impressions. Each one of these represents the future of the company. Friendly, helpful service has become one of the quality features which markedly distinguishes our company from other retailers. We spend a great deal of time and effort ensuring that all our store employees understand the crucial role they play. Our customers want to be treated exactly as we do when we are shopping. To always meet and hopefully to exceed their expectations is our constant daily plan. (The Gap, Inc., 1991).

Interestingly at The Gap the utilization of EPOS is viewed as allowing retail 'sales assistants' (staffers) the opportunity to concentrate on serving customers effectively. 'Through bar codes and optical scanners sales information is entered into the company's database and used to manage inventory levels at each location. These systems free up sales staff to focus on serving the customer' (The Gap, Inc., 1991). Significantly then, technological change (a critical focus of retail restructuring in the 1980s) which has taken away decisions regarding merchandise range, pricing, space allocation from the level of the store has allowed 'customer care' at a local level to become the critical frontier of competitive advantage. At The Gap 'you are not in the store for 30 seconds before the good natured young salesperson asks "Do you like our new colors?" Another minute "Are you finding your size?" Either they are Stepford children or we are so used to young people who are so surly that this behaviour seems weird' (Kahn, 1992). It must certainly seem weird for those employed at The Gap. 'Sales staff at *The Gap* receive no commissions, but James V O'Donnell *The Gap's* Chief Operating Officer pumps up workers with constant contests. Bring the most multiple purchases to the register for instance and win a Gap-logo watch' (Kahn, 1992).

The so-called Gap Lexicon (Table 10.2) is used to instruct 'staffers' how to operate while in the store. However, the regimentation does not appeal to all. For example, Jami Hiyakumoto, 21, a San Diego State University junior who quit her job at a Gap store in San Diego after only one day stated

> They had all these policies, all this little lingo. You were supposed to be really pushy. And you had to fold the jeans in a certain way so the crotch was tucked in. After stacking up a wall of jeans – and I'm trying to be as anal as possible – the manager says 'not bad for a first try'. (Kahn, 1992: section 9)

Table 10.2 The Gap Lexicon

Gappers People who work at the Gap

Gap Act How a Gapper is supposed to deal with a customer. Each letter stands for an action:

Greet the customer in the first 30 seconds in the store.

Approach and ask if there's anything you can find.

Product information. Know the merchandise.

Add-ons. Suggest a great top to complete the outfit.

Close the sale. If something looks terrible, don't lie.

Thank the customer.

Super sales Sales of more than $200 to one customer gets your name in the company paper, The Gap Rap.

L.Y. Stands for Last Year. Refers to the same-store sales on the same day last year. The aim is to top the L.Y.

Goal The total sales amount that the store expects to make on a given day.

Secret Shoppers and Mystery Callers Anonymous testers from headquarters.

Five in, two out Gappers should encourage the customer to take five items into the dressing room and to come out with two to purchase.

Color blocking Laying out the tables so that the colors are pleasing to the eye.

U.P.T.s Units per transaction, or the number of items one customer buys. The Gapper with the most U.P.T.s in a day per store can win a Gap T-shirt.

Source: Adapted from Kahn (1992)

Implications for the restructuring o ' retail employment

While it would clearly be incorrect to imply that all High Street retailers are intent on following the example of The Gap, questions regarding customer care and image in employment have clear and considerable implications for the restructuring of retail work practices and should be considered alongside other critical issues likely to impact on 'shop work' in the future. Many of the strategies outlined above are general shifts from numerical to functional flexibility of employment which have been discussed in detail elsewhere (Christopherson, this volume, Chapter 8) and which need critical evaluation. Having said this, it is possible to argue that the renewed focus on 'customer service' in the 1990s may have the potential to improve retail employment conditions. In particular it has been suggested that the new focus may force a change in the traditional view of part-time work, namely as a cut-price substitute for full-time employment (Atkinson, quoted in Gardner and Sheppard, 1989: 205). However, we remain somewhat sceptical of such arguments. In general we would agree with Christopherson's suggestion that the ultimate goal of the strategies outlined above 'has been to increase service without increasing labour costs' (Christopherson, this volume, Chapter 8). As a result we believe that it is vital to analyse the trade union response to such issues.

The Union of Shop, Distributive and Allied Workers (USDAW) has identified the general question of 'customer care' schemes for priority attention. As the union's 1990 ADM Executive Council Statement *Retailing in the 1990s* states:

> In principle we are absolutely committed in USDAW to caring for customers through a highly skilled, highly motivated and properly rewarded workforce. The way forward for the retail sector undoubtedly lies in the development of quality service and investment in a properly trained workforce with the opportunity and the skills to deliver that service. (USDAW, 1990: 9)

The priority of the union, however, is to ensure that 'customer care schemes' are not exploitative of the retail workforce. In particular, shopworkers

(a) Need the time and the opportunity to deal professionally with consumers and their needs. It is difficult to provide a decent service and deal with customers properly if staffing levels are too low and shopworkers are rushed off their feet and under stress.

(b) Want to be able to give real practical help to consumers and make their own jobs more interesting by knowing more about the goods they sell, what they are for, how they work, how to use them etc. They need the opportunity to develop product knowledge and give informed helpful advice to consumers about the goods and services they sell. Consumers often complain about lack of information and advice in shops but shopworkers cannot provide it unless they have the necessary information in the first place, regularly updated and added to as necessary.

(c) Want to be encouraged and supported in exercising their own initiative to deal with customer enquiries and even complaints in a helpful and resourceful way. But they can't do that unless they are clear about how their stores are run and organised, who does what and how each individual worker fits in. And they need the opportunity to feed back and share their experiences at the point of sale so that they can improve their skills, work better as a team and provide a better service for consumers.

(d) To be sure that they are valued and respected by employers who have a clear investment in them as valuable contributors to the success of the company or society. Real customer care depends on the motivation and commitment of shopworkers. That means decent pay and conditions and a comfortable working environment. (USDAW, 1990: 9–10)

In short, if workers are rushed off their feet due to staffing shortages or denied any genuine skills training to assist customers then they do not have the time or the opportunity to offer a genuine service. Moreover, when standards of dress are required the union is keen to ensure that the costs of such 'images' are not unfairly borne by their members. Notwithstanding this, however, USDAW believes that some of the skills and attributes which 'customer care' schemes attempt to promote can benefit both shopworkers and consumers providing they form part of a proper training package to equip shopworkers with skills and knowledge in key areas. To provide genuine customer care, though, shopworkers need

(a) *A high degree of product knowledge.* In the non-food sector, for example, shopworkers need to know about the range of goods being sold, their technical specifications, what they are for, how to use them, what after-sales service is available, etc. In the food sector, similarly, shopworkers need to know, for example, about nutritional information, proper and safe storage and handling, cooking and preparation requirements, etc. This kind of knowledge not only helps shopworkers to respond to detailed enquiries effectively, it can also increase turnover as consumers respond to advice and quality service with additional purchases and return visits.

(b) *A detailed understanding of how their store and their company is organised.* Shopworkers need to know where particular goods are stocked, where they themselves fit into the operation of the store, what services are available and how to arrange them. Consumers understandably expect shopworkers to know about where goods are stocked and how a store operates. A knowledgeable workforce means less confusion for consumers, less stress for shopworkers and potentially higher turnover as consumers are able to shop more efficiently.

(c) *A range of interpersonal skills.* The time and ability to listen to customers' enquiries, respond helpfully and make them feel welcome are all important. So too are the confidence and initiative which come from having these skills. Shopworkers then cannot only respond to enquiries but also handle complaints effectively and deal firmly with difficult or abusive customers. That means having appropriate support and back-up and knowing when to call on others and work together as a team.

(d) *A working understanding of consumer rights and fair trading regulations.*
No-one expects shopworkers to have a detailed understanding of the
law but it is important to know what rights consumers have and how
complaints and difficulties can best be settled quickly. That means
knowing not only where consumers stand technically, but also what
policies and procedures the organisation has for dealing with complaints
as they arise. Consumers have a right to a prompt and fair response
when they have a complaint and it only adds to their annoyance and to
the potentially stressful position of shopworkers if there is no clear
understanding of how to proceed. (USDAW, 1990: 11–12)

We have quoted at length here from USDAW's policy documents. The
very fact that the trade union gives detailed consideration to 'customer
care' programmes is we believe evidence of the growing significance of
such schemes in the UK in the 1990s. We would, of course, like to
believe that campaigns around such issues will be successful. We
remain, however, somewhat pessimistic as to the likely success of
USDAW's strategy. As we have demonstrated here, a major threat to
potential resistance to 'customer care' in the UK are the North American
retailers which have gained competitive advantage in the UK via their
'customer is king' ethos. The alternative 'corporate culture' of
companies like The Gap has transformed the British High Street and
importantly the British shop assistant beyond all recognition such that
what advances the trade union can make are likely to only be at the
margin (see also Shackleton, this volume, Chapter 7). In general then we
can conclude that until retailers 'link customer care with adequate staff
care . . . the retailers intentions are at best flawed and at worst
suspicious' (Gardner and Sheppard, 1989: 207). In the mean time the
retail stores wage rates remain some of the lowest in the UK (Pipe, 1992)
and importantly, although perhaps unsurprisingly, our 'consumption
choices continue to be constructed by the rules that govern firm
profitability' (Christopherson, this volume, Chapter 8).

CHAPTER 11

Geographical dimensions of UK retailing employment change

Alan Townsend, David Sadler and Ray Hudson

Changes in forms and levels of retailing employment must be understood as one element in a restructuring of the overall production process. While production (in the narrow sense) has become increasingly internationalized, consumption has remained much more focused on national – or sub-national – markets, so that the changing relationships between production and consumption, mediated via the retailing sector, have been complicated ones. This is the case within Britain, as it is in other advanced capitalist states. Retail employment in Britain in the early 1990s (at around 2.2 million) was some 10 per cent higher than it had been twenty years earlier. This represented a smaller rate of increase than in many other industrialized countries, and in other service sector activities. Despite a rapid expansion in numbers of new (frequently out-of-town) superstore outlets, in other words (see B K Davies and Sparks, 1989), restructuring in retailing had not resulted in a substantial net increase of jobs. However, intense competition among leading companies had led to greater labour productivity, partly achieved through new standards of numerical flexibility in the sector's employment patterns, particularly with the expanded use of part-time workers. This chapter therefore offers a description of the changing structure of employment in the retail industry in Britain.

The context of employment change was very much conditioned by superstore growth and the demise of smaller shops, in turn associated with a centralization of capital in retailing. During the 1980s major retail firms grew in size – by new store development and through acquisition of competitors – to rival the biggest companies in most other sectors of the economy (see Wrigley, 1993a). In part too this was associated with internationalization, both by groups based in Britain (moving into the European Union and North America) and with expansion into Britain from these areas. On the whole, however, strategies of British retail chain groups remained mainly focused on their domestic market. Hence while changes in retailing in Britain need to be seen as part of a broader picture of employment restructuring, there is a very real sense in which certain clearly identifiable corporate strategies refashioned the geography of retailing employment there.

New store building formed a significant component of retail expansion programmes, fuelled by the climate of institutional investment in property-led speculation during the mid to late 1980s government-induced boom. Retail development peaked in the years 1986 to 1989, when there was a 60 per cent increase in total financial return on retail investment (Investment Property Databank, 1991). While the early 1990s recession led to some concern over how the major chains could continue to generate sufficient funds for their new store opening programmes (or alternatively scale back expansion without losing market share; see Wrigley, 1994a, this volume, Chapter 6), it also served once again to focus attention on employment issues, particularly through changes such as Sunday trading (which enabled more efficient utilization of capital investment and smoother scheduling of deliveries, but also affected employment requirements quite markedly). Despite high levels of capital investment associated with the use of electronic scanning equipment at check-outs, and the use of electronic data interchange to link stores with suppliers, labour remained a significant component of retail industry costs.

The expansion of leading retail store groups was also closely related to changing patterns of consumption in British society. Out-of-town developments owed much to increased car ownership, but related changes in public transport provision helped to generate a new geography of inequality, which disadvantaged those without access to a car (see Bromley and Thomas, 1993). Phenomena such as the rise of self-service outlets, the growth of mail order and warehouse shopping, and the expansion of retail sectors such as home improvement, all reflected diverse aspects of changing social and economic relationships, including greater home ownership and more diversified household income profiles. While there was partly a regional pattern to this, there were also substantial differences at smaller spatial scales, both between and within urban and rural areas. At the most basic level, population shifts and changing disposable incomes associated with differing rates of unemployment and wages for those in paid employment also had an impact on the distribution of retail jobs.

We therefore explore below how these consumption patterns, and various corporate strategies for containing costs, were reflected in changing patterns of employment within the retail sector. This chapter identifies the key elements of change in aggregate national and regional statistics. We would not suggest, however, that it is possible to infer explanation of processes from such evidence without further empirical research and fuller consideration of a range of conceptual issues than is possible here. In order for instance to separate out consumption-led shifts from corporate responses to inter-firm competition, and to account for regionally differentiated combinations of these factors, it would be necessary to explore other sources (see for instance Freathy and Sparks, this volume, Chapter 9). We are able, though, to point to some significant questions for more detailed investigation.

Changes in labour force structure: numerical flexibility

The enhanced power of multiple chains, in connection with increases in the average size of store and the widespread use of self-service sales, has radically altered the nature of employment. Supermarket retailing led to a profound process of de-skilling as it reduced the specialization previously required of a shop assistant (who was expected to give personal service and to have a detailed knowledge of goods), and changed the bulk of tasks in major stores to shelf-filling and till operation (Sparks, 1983). Intensive competition, particularly in food retailing, created a strong requirement to match workforce levels over the day and during the week to fluctuations in consumer demand. This had important implications for the organization of the labour process in both production and retailing. In retailing, the greater use of part-timers started as a convenient way of meeting peak daytime pressures but, with the additional spur of longer opening hours in the evening and at weekends, became essential to the competitive running of a large outlet. Thus, retailing was one of the industries studied in Atkinson and Meager's (1986) influential study on changing working patterns. Retailing became characterized by widespread use of numerical flexibility, the capacity rapidly to adjust the number of workers or hours worked to variations in the level and incidence of demand (Penn and Worth, 1993).

This led to cost savings for companies in the sector in other ways, too. Available evidence suggests that although paid at the same basic rate, part-timers' hourly earnings are less than those of their equivalent full-time colleagues. In 1987, for example, there was an 11 per cent differential between the gross hourly earnings of women part-timers in retailing compared with those of full-time women employees in the sector. In turn, women part-timers in retailing earned 40 per cent less than the hourly earnings of male full-time retail workers (see NEDO, 1988: 15). Seen from the companies' point of view, such savings came from part-timers' exclusion from pension schemes, sick pay and other benefits, and by avoiding exceeding threshold levels that might trigger national insurance contributions and employment protection rights. These were basic factors which underpinned Britain's greater use of part-timers in retailing than all other European Union countries except Denmark (Economist Intelligence Unit, 1993).

Many strains and pressures remained to be absorbed from these changes. There were, however, differences of view over the advantages of part-time contracts to employers. Before its abolition, the Distributive Trades Economic Development Committee of the National Economic Development Office was so concerned about some aspects of part-time employment as to mount a study at establishment level (see NEDO, 1988). It saw major long-term problems in part-timers' training and promotion prospects. In general, the study found that training was not available to part-time workers beyond the statutory minimum, partly because of difficulties associated with the timing of different shifts. This fed in turn into reduced prospects for promotion. While many part-time workers claimed to be well satisfied (especially married women, for whom this was often one way of reconciling the competing demands of waged and unwaged domestic labour), many were working well below their potential, and their scope for promotion was severely restricted or non-existent.

There were some differences between firms by size in these findings, with longer service and better benefits being prevalent in small firms. Penn and Worth (1993) also emphasized how many variations there were even between just five main stores in the Lancaster area. All firms saw some disadvantages in employing part-timers, to be offset against the advantage of flexibility. Yet a shared set of perceptions (or perhaps more accurately prejudices) existed, for instance over attitudes to the employment of married women workers. Further complexity was added by the issue of Sunday trading (see Watson, 1993). Poorer public transport provision on Sunday might well reinforce existing inequalities in the retail workforce between those with access to a car and those without (see Kirby, 1993). While part-time employment is an answer to retail capital's search for flexibility and cost reduction in the short to medium term, however, it rests upon conditions such as high national unemployment and workforce acquiescence in sharply divided terms and conditions of work (between full-time and part-time, within the part-timers, and between men and women). In other words, the prevalence of part-time work is predicated upon the existence of deeply and multiply segmented labour markets. Whether this solution is tenable in the longer term is another matter, to which we shall return in our concluding comments.

National employment trends

Including part-time workers in the number of employees, there was remarkable stability in total retailing employment from the early 1970s to the early 1990s, with a cyclical response which was surprisingly moderate (Table 11.1). There was slightly greater expansion if measured from one trough of the economic cycle to another, 1983 to 1993. Expressed as a proportion of total employees in employment, the retail sector grew from 9.6 per cent of the British workforce in 1981 to 10.7 per cent in 1993. As described above, however, the biggest changes concerned the expanded use of part-time workers, mainly women, entailing some recomposition of the retailing workforce. The proportion of retailing employees working part-time increased from 35 per cent in 1971 to 40 per cent in 1981, 46 per cent in 1991 and 48 per cent in 1993 (Table 11.2). In this respect retailing more than matched national trends: part-time as a proportion of total employment in all sectors of the British economy grew from 21 per cent in 1981 to 26 per cent in 1991 and 28 per cent in 1993. Retailing was, therefore, one of those sectors that typified the labour market strategies of Thatcherism, centred around the growth of poorly paid, part-time jobs with little skill content.

Table 11.1 Time series for employees in employment in distribution*

	Retail distribution	Wholesale distribution and repairs
1971	1 954	972
1973	2 066	1 030
1975	2 050	1 032
1977	2 052	1 042
1979	2 135	1 111
1981	2 051	1 112
1983	1 964	1 124
1985	2 038	1 148
1987	2 057	1 138
1989	2 234	1 206
1990	2 301	1 198
1991	2 294	1 131
1992	2 287	1 087
1993 (est)	2 221	1 062

Source: Adapted from *Employment Gazette*, incl. Historical Supplement 3 (1992)
* Great Britain, 1971–93, in thousands (June)

Virtually the whole of the net gain of retailing jobs from 1981 to 1993 was accounted for by women. There was a slight growth in the proportion of men working part-time, but there was still considerable discrepancy between genders, with 63 per cent of women and just 24 per cent of men working part-time in 1993. Female full-time employment did grow absolutely, by 40 000, from 1987 to 1989 – indicative of the boom conditions of those years and roughly the same gain as took place over that period in female part-time employment. This was in contrast to trends earlier in the decade. Female full-time employment fell again decisively, however, in the recession after 1990. The early 1990s probably saw some substitution of jobs and re-designation of workers from full-time to part-time.

The application of the more finely disaggregated Standard Industrial Classification of 1980 to the Census of Employment allows for a more precise view of retail employment trends by sub-sector during the 1980s (Table 11.3). Mixed businesses, filling stations, and confectioners and off-licences declined substantially, perhaps reflecting the demise of the 'corner shop'. Food retailing demonstrated the largest increase in numbers (up by 150 000, or 28 per cent, from 1981 to 1991), although strong percentage gains were also recorded in clothing, household textiles and household goods, along with the category 'other retailing'.

Regional variations

Previous analyses (Reynolds, 1983) found a general relationship between changes in retail employment and population shifts over the period 1971 to 1981, but with marked departures in a minority of

Table 11.2 Employment structure in all industries and in the distributive trades*

	Male			Female			All	
	Full-time	Part-time	As % of all males	Full-time	Part-time	As % of all females		% of part-time employees
September 1981								
All industries and services	11 506	718	5.8	5 304	3 781	41.6	21 309	21.1
Retailing	639	131	17.0	582	697	54.4	2 049	40.4
Wholesaling	569	25	4.2	190	91	32.3	875	13.2
September 1984								
All industries and services	10 928	771	6.5	5 289	3 858	42.1	20 846	22.2
Retailing	642	117	15.4	544	722	57.0	2 025	41.4
Wholesaling	585	25	4.0	197	86	30.3	893	12.4
September 1987								
All industries and services	10 815	881	7.5	5 475	4 244	43.6	21 416	23.9
Retailing	623	143	18.6	529	786	59.7	2 080	44.6
Wholesaling	604	14	2.2	208	91	30.5	917	11.4
September 1989								
All industries and services	10 877	921	7.8	5 962	4 474	42.9	22 234	24.3
Retailing	674	168	19.9	572	829	59.2	2 242	44.4
Wholesaling	612	26	4.1	222	89	28.6	948	9.4
September 1991								
All industries and services	10 188	981	8.8	5 767	4 632	44.5	21 569	26.0
Retailing	687	184	21.1	559	881	61.2	2 311	46.1
Wholesaling	568	26	4.7	202	83	29.1	879	12.4
June 1993 (est)								
All industries and services	9 439	1 143	10.8	5 497	4 716	46.2	20 795	28.2
Retailing	645	199	23.6	506	872	63.3	2 221	48.2
Wholesaling	531	38	6.7	185	80	30.4	834	14.2

Source: Adapted from *Employment Gazette*, incl. Historical Supplement (1992)
* Great Britain, 1981–93, in thousands

Table 11.3 Employees in retailing by 'activity heading'*

	1981	1991	Change 1981–91 (nos.)	(%)	1993 (est)
Food retailing	564.0	720.1	+156.1	+27.7	685.2
Confectioners, off-licences	158.7	110.2	−48.5	−30.6	114.6
Chemists	125.0	125.9	+0.9	+0.8	122.7
Clothing	148.9	175.7	+26.8	+18.1	238.1
Leather goods	58.6	68.3	+9.7	+16.5	
Household textiles	22.1	30.9	+8.8	+39.9	260.3
Household goods	175.3	239.6	+64.3	+36.7	
Books, stationery	68.4	70.7	+2.4	+3.5	
Other retail	106.5	204.7	+98.2	+92.9	538.0
Mixed businesses	350.2	292.5	−57.6	−16.5	
Motor vehicles and parts	192.6	211.2	+18.7	+9.7	262.3
Filling stations	79.0	61.3	−17.7	−22.4	
Total, Retail	2 049.3	2 311.3	+262.0	+12.8	2 221.2

Source: National Online Manpower Information System, *Employment Gazette*
* Great Britain, 1981–91, in thousands (September)

regions. These were attributed to 'delays' in the restructuring of the industry in certain areas, to rapid income growth in the East Midlands (resulting in higher retail employment gains) and to the role of retired people (with lower spending needs per head) in the population growth occurring without corresponding retail employment growth in the South West.

The overall regional pattern of retailing employment for the years 1981 to 1991 again showed some correspondence with population change (Table 11.4). The three regions which had net increases in population (the South West, East Anglia and the East Midlands) showed high rates of increases in full-time and part-time retail employment. There were some differences from the previous decade, with the South West now clearly ahead in its growth of retail employees and the East Midlands expanding substantially less than it had in the 1980s. This meant that by 1991 the South West had the second highest location quotient, giving it more retailing employment than would be expected on the basis of its share of national population (behind the rest of the South East outside London) while the East Midlands had the third lowest (just ahead of London and the West Midlands). The new anomaly was represented by Wales, with a 27 per cent increase of jobs, compared with no net population change (although in effect this only took its location quotient close to the national average). The 'excess' employment growth was spread across a number of types of retailing, although concentrated particularly in food. In general, however, these patterns reaffirmed a relationship established in Townsend (1986) between the distribution of increase in part-time jobs in general and that of resident population across the regions of Britain as a whole, although they were suggestive of new relationships between population and income growth associated with the short-lived property boom of the mid to late 1980s.

Table 11.4 Employees in retailing by region*

| | 1981 | 1991 | Change 1981–91 % | | | Location quotient 1991 |
			All	Part-time	Total population	
London	318.1	320.3	+0.7	+6.2		0.92
Rest of South East	404.5	477.4	+18.0	+27.0		1.12
South East, total	722.5	797.7	+10.4	+18.8	–0.1	1.03
South West	161.4	199.6	+38.2	+48.9	+5.5	1.09
East Anglia	69.6	85.5	+22.8	+49.4	+7.7	1.01
East Midlands	129.1	154.3	+19.5	+33.0	+2.5	0.94
West Midlands	173.7	196.6	+13.2	+29.8	–1.4	0.90
Yorkshire and						
Humberside	173.8	197.9	+13.8	+29.9	–1.8	1.00
North West	234.5	260.4	+11.0	+29.2	–4.3	1.03
North	112.6	114.9	+2.1	+17.3	–3.0	0.98
Wales	79.5	101.0	+27.1	+57.6	–0.0	0.98
Scotland	192.3	203.3	+5.7	+27.1	–3.4	0.95
Total GB	2 049.3	2 311.3	+12.8	+28.4		1.00

Source : National Onpower Manpower Information System, *Employment Gazette*
* Great Britain, 1981–91, in thousands (September)
Note: quarterly estimates by region since 1991 are available only for distribution, hotels and catering together. The overall trend of total employment of –3.7% from September 1991 to June 1993 is led by East Anglia, the South East and West Midlands. There was no reduction in the East Midlands or Scotland.

Among total retailing employees, part-timers represented the largest proportion of the 1981 total in the Northern Region and the South East excluding London, and the lowest by far in London. From 1981 to 1991 the largest gain in the part-time share of total employment occurred in Wales and East Anglia. Coupled with differential rates of change in other regions, this means that in 1991 Wales, Scotland and the South West had the greatest dependence on part-timers, while London still had the lowest. Thus, the phenomenon of part-time retail employment also varied unevenly both spatially and temporally between regions.

The marked contrast between London and other, more rural regions was symptomatic of a finer-grained and more systematic gradation between urban and rural areas as a whole. It is possible to elaborate this view by organizing Census of Employment data according to an urban–rural classification of local authority districts (Table 11.5). While the spatial building block of this system might not reflect the reality of retail catchment areas, it is significant in land-use planning terms. Many superstores have been placed outside built-up areas. Thus, the classification may be well suited to pick up retail displacement across planning authority boundaries from more urban to less urban areas.

Table 11.5 Employees in retailing by type of area*

	1981	1991	Change 1981–91 (%)	Location quotient 1991
Inner London	152.8	142.8	−6.6	0.73
Principal cities	193.4	183.0	−5.4	0.88
Outer London	165.2	177.7	+7.6	1.16
Other Metropolitan Boroughs	287.3	312.3	+8.7	1.00
Other cities	292.4	308.5	+5.5	1.01
Industrial districts	227.0	275.2	+21.2	0.97
Ports and resorts	131.3	147.9	+12.6	1.18
Districts with new towns	97.7	133.7	+36.8	1.08
Mixed urban/rural	329.3	413.9	+25.7	1.07
Outer rural	175.9	220.3	+25.3	1.00
Total	2 049.3	2 311.3	+12.8	1.00

Source: National Online Manpower Information System, *Employment Gazette*
* Great Britain, 1981–91, in thousands (September)

In general, there is a wider range of values for percentage change than in the regional mesh of Table 11.4. Inner London was the main area of decline, confirming its position with the lowest location quotient in 1991 by a sizeable margin. The importance of the capital's high order shops failed to prevent a net decentralization of employment to the suburban centres of outer London. The principal cities – Birmingham, Liverpool, Manchester, Sheffield, Leeds, Newcastle upon Tyne and Glasgow – also saw a reduction in their aggregate number of retail employees. Their loss, however, was more than offset by the gain of surrounding metropolitan boroughs, including for instance Dudley (with the Merry Hill development: see Lowe, 1991, 1993) and Gateshead (with the Metro Centre, which impacted adversely on retail employment in the city centre of Newcastle upon Tyne: see BDP Planning and Oxford Institute of Retail Management, 1992). 'Other cities' – places such as Bristol or Stoke-on-Trent – saw only modest retail employment gains, whereas the 'industrial districts', including wide areas of South Wales, the East Midlands, Staffordshire, North East England and Central Scotland, experienced double the average rate of expansion. New towns also saw major gains. So too did mixed urban/rural and outer rural areas, although in 1991 the highest location quotients were to be found in outer London and ports and resorts. In general terms, then, there was a decline or below average increase in retail employment – partly linked to population shifts – in urban areas, and above average increases in rural areas.

Similar trends were evident at a sub-regional scale, as shown in Table 11.6 which lists the ten highest and ten lowest counties (or regions in Scotland) ranked by retail employment growth from 1981 to 1991 on the basis of a chi-squared test (carried out to minimize the impact of counties with a very low population). The greatest gains of retail jobs were mostly shown by 'mixed urban/rural' counties. Some, such as Berkshire, Buckinghamshire and Essex, adjoin Greater London, while others (including Wiltshire, Leicestershire and Suffolk) reflected the dispersal of population and wealth to the South West, East Midlands and East Anglia respectively. The growth of retail employment in Cheshire and Lancashire possibly attested to the presence of parallel forces in the shape of decentralization within the North West, from Greater Manchester and Merseyside. Correspondingly, the conurbations of the north accounted for most of the worst ten performances, in the form of only tiny increases – or even reductions – in retail employment. Stagnation in Greater London was accompanied by similar or worse trends in northern areas of high unemployment and depopulation, such as Tyne and Wear, Strathclyde, Merseyside and Cleveland. The loss of retail jobs in East Sussex, however, was one indication of the emergent employment problems of some resort towns, part of a more complex pattern of change.

Table 11.6 Employees in retailing by county (and regions of Scotland)*

	1981	1991	Change 1981–91 (%)	Location quotient 1991
Cheshire	32.6	44.3	+35.6	1.08
Berkshire	34.0	45.8	+34.7	1.28
Clwyd	11.2	16.7	+49.6	1.10
Buckinghamshire	20.8	29.0	+39.7	1.05
Suffolk	20.2	27.0	+33.7	1.02
Leicestershire	30.0	38.8	+29.4	1.00
Wiltshire	18.9	25.2	+33.4	1.04
Essex	49.9	62.1	+24.6	1.18
Lancashire	45.2	56.6	+25.2	1.02
Avon	35.0	44.2	+26.4	1.02
Fife	11.9	12.1	+1.9	1.01
Tayside	17.2	17.6	+1.9	1.11
Cleveland	20.0	19.9	–0.6	0.92
Merseyside	53.9	55.7	+3.4	1.09
East Sussex	28.2	27.6	–1.9	1.15
West Midlands	92.6	96.4	+4.1	0.83
Greater Manchester	102.8	103.8	+1.0	0.97
Strathclyde	85.4	85.2	–0.2	0.93
Tyne and Wear	51.7	47.4	–0.3	1.04
Greater London	318.1	320.5	+0.8	0.92
Total	2 049.3	2 311.3	+12.8	1.00

Source : National Online Manpower Information System, *Employment Gazette*
* Great Britain, 1981–91, in thousands (September); change ranked by chi-square test

Concluding comments and further questions

Retail employment changes have partly reflected the spatial pattern of population in Britain, and the shifting distribution of the country's incomes and wealth. At the same time radical changes to customers' time–space paths (due to rising female activity rates and increased car ownership) have meshed with corporate pressures to reduce labour costs, resulting in transformed shop opening hours. In turn, this has reinforced the attractions to retailers of a workforce half of which is part-time. There have also been other important changes in the character of retail employment, which are not evident from official statistics. In particular, the de-skilling of much retail employment, associated with trends towards self-service and the growth in electronic sales technologies, has had profound implications. While in general terms it is an over-simplification to regard de-skilling – as opposed to re-skilling – as the only secular tendency within employment, the dominant trend in retailing (for most but not all employees) has been, and is, one of de-skilling. This is linked to new managerial strategies encompassing less employee discretion over the labour process, and the increased routinization of tasks for the new 'shop-floor' employees. It represents a reworking of capital–labour relationships, and is also part of a broader restructuring of relationships between companies within the overall production filiere. Such changes cannot be understood in isolation from the circulation of capital in the forms of property investment and consumer credit. Increasingly, the retail sector involves new forms of linkage between global production and local consumption.

Changes in retailing employment in Britain since the mid-1970s – as with so many other aspects of economic and social change – cannot be divorced from the abandonment of an inclusive 'One Nation' politics and its replacement by a divisive 'Two Nations' project, exemplified most sharply in the political economy of Thatcherism. Part of this neo-liberal strategy involved moves towards a much more deeply segmented labour market, with retailing employees occupying some of the most exploited, poorly paid part-time jobs (many of which were taken by women in reinforcement of existing gendered inequalities of opportunity). Whether this pattern of employment is sustainable into the twenty-first century depends in part, therefore, on the feasibility of the 'Two Nations' project. There is some evidence to suggest that it will not prove stable in the long term, and this would have distinctive (if indeterminate) implications for retailing and retailers. None the less, the restructuring of the retailing sector partly predates that project and it seems likely that for the immediate future retailing will remain heavily reliant upon a low-paid and largely part-time workforce.

Part 4

Consumption and capital

CHAPTER 12

Consumption, shopping and gender

Paul Glennie and Nigel Thrift

The 1980s witnessed a striking upsurge across several disciplines in work on economic and cultural dimensions of retailing. Much of this work related fairly directly to striking changes in the nature of retailing itself, and in the wider economic context of the retailing sector. By the end of the 1980s retailing had (re)emerged as an important and dynamic economic sector in many developed nations. In the process, it had spawned and spread new urban shopping environments.

What are the connections between changing retail spaces, and changes in consumption cultures and practices? Significant remodellings of retailing environments, from large shopping malls to smaller 'village-style' developments, are clearly attempts to shape particular retail cultures among consumers. But remodelled retailing environments are also seen by the controllers of retail capital as having been a response: a response to changing social practices in respect both of consumption in general, and of shopping in particular. On their own accounts, and that of analysts of store strategy and advertising, controllers of retail capital have recognized (if only imperfectly understood) shifts in consumption practices as more than a passive response to selling and advertising environments (Gardner and Sheppard, 1989).

However, social scientists have been far from unanimous on what has happened to consumption practices. There are probably two main interpretations. One of these arises out of a dystopic notion of postmodern economies and societies. In this interpretation, the increased speed of circulation of objects and images empties out both subjects and objects of meanings. The abstraction, meaninglessness and challenges to history and tradition, all issuing out of modernism done to the extreme, result in a long list of real-cum-imagined ills, including homogenization (even as differentiation of commodities becomes greater and greater), the flattening effects of the society of the spectacle, disposability, the death of the subject and a generalized sense of anomie (Baudrillard, 1988a; Harvey, 1989c; Jameson, 1984). As a result, a chaotic process of *cultural fragmentation* has been occurring, in which previously stable social markers, such as class, have dissolved to a considerable extent, at least in so far as they connect with the structuring of consumer behaviour. Associated with this is the disappearance of place-specificity as part of everyday life (Meyrowitz, 1985).

But there is another possible interpretation of postmodern economies and societies, one in which supposedly dystopic processes are bound up in a process of *reflexive modernization*, which opens up the possibility of another – more positive – landscape that is interwoven with the darker dystopic one (Beck, 1992a; 1992b; Giddens, 1991; 1992; Lash and Urry, 1993). This second landscape is one in which there are still possibilities to recast the meanings of work, leisure and consumption; to redefine and reconstitute community; to reconstitute subjectivity; and to recognize and reorganize space and everyday life. In particular, in this reworking much attention has been paid to the ways in which human subjects and senses of self are not necessarily being emptied out or flattened, but may in fact be being deepened, opening up many positive as well as negative possibilities for social relations, ranging from pure intimate relationships (Giddens, 1992), through friendship, to work relations, leisure and, not least, consumption, all of which are increasingly worked on, and all of which show growing promise of liberation because of that work. Exponents of this view see a cultural *segmentation* of consumers occurring, rather than fragmentation: the creation of myriad sub-groups of consumers in place of earlier and larger class-centred constellations (Willis *et al*, 1990).

This is an impassioned debate (see Featherstone, 1991). Compare, for example, the optimistic view that

> patriarchal capitalism has failed to homogenize the thinking and the culture of its subjects, despite nearly two centuries of economic domination (and much longer in the domains of gender and race). Our societies are intransigently diverse . . . [beyond] capitalism's requirements for controlled diversity. (Fiske, 1989b: 29)

with the pessimism of Susan Willis when she writes that to think of identity in terms of consumption, especially among professional and managerial social groups is to encourage

> falsely construed notions of control over the social reproduction of daily life. . . . The impression that consumption has come to replace one's relationship to the means of production in the determination of class actually upholds the domination of production. (Willis, 1991: 177)

This chapter lies broadly within the more positive of the two interpretations outlined above. Our central focus is on what consumers do in urban retailing environments, in particular, consumers' interaction within 'the throng' as an influence on their behaviour. Naturally, there are corresponding exclusions: we shall concentrate on practices of consumption and shopping rather than shops *per se*; and we shall concentrate on retailing in central urban spaces rather than retailing through other channels.

In line with the promise made in Glennie and Thrift (1992), at several points we try to consider the gendering of consumption practices, although our considerations remain preliminary. We strongly agree with Catherine Hall's comment that 'the complexities of the relation between class and culture have received much attention. It is time for gender and culture to be subjected to more critical scrutiny ' (Hall, 1992a: 99).

This chapter consists of three sections. We first outline some features of the dominant genealogy of modern shopping and consumption cultures. We identify two lacunae within many analyses of consumption, whose persistence we attribute to the viewing of consumption mainly in terms of buying, and to a neglect of consumption practices in favour of analyses of selling and advertising. The lacunae concern the social nature of shopping and consumption practices (including the class specificity of gender divisions in shopping) and the capacity of consumers to engage in self-reflection. The following two sections discuss these topics through recent theoretical and empirical work. The second section outlines notions of *sociality*, which are used to discuss consumption and shopping practices from the late seventeenth to the twentieth centuries. We then turn to another key area of theorizing: the theorizing of notions of *reflexivity*, which we use to discuss consumption practices since the late 1960s.

Inevitably, there is a provisional or speculative tone to parts of this chapter, simply because there are several areas in which appropriate empirical material is lacking. It is not that there is a complete absence of empirical work on either the historical or the contemporary topics that we address, but most of this work has not been done in a way which maps directly on to our current concerns. We therefore point to some of our argument's implications for empirical research at the close of the chapter.

Alongside this explicit focus there is also an 'other agenda' to this chapter. Our emphasis on consumption practices is an attempt to move away from semiotic approaches to consumption, especially the analysis of advertisements. This is not to suggest that we are not interested in aesthetic issues. We are (as will become clear later). However, we derive this interest from the belief that aesthetic issues are increasingly central to *practices* of shopping and consumption, rather than from the semiotic interest in advertising images as the hub of consumer knowledges (Glennie and Thrift, 1992, 1993).

Genealogies of modern shopping: creating the modern consumer

In the history of retailing, analysts have placed great emphasis on the development of the department store, especially in relation to female consumers. In turn this reflects an appreciation of the power of bourgeois discourses of the social world as consisting of 'separate spheres': a public/political sphere which is essentially the preserve of men; and a domestic/private sphere in which women are more prominent (although the home was also very much a sphere of masculine power). Public–private dichotomies embraced consumption. Men's consumption was important, noteworthy, skilled and rational, while women's consumption was trivial, routine, unskilled and unreflective or irrational or both. Consumption was just one area of life among many in which separate spheres concepts shaped contemporary discourses (e.g. Cohen, 1992; Hall, 1992a; Kaplan, 1992).

Although separate spheres arguments were not new, the eighteenth and nineteenth centuries saw a decisive acceleration in their spread through and beyond the bourgeois middle classes, influenced by political economy and Christianity (Crawford, 1992; Hall, 1992b; Snell, 1985). Indeed, an emphasis on the extreme contrast of masculine and feminine was one of the central components in emerging middle-class identity.

While labouring and working-class society did not adopt middle-class family values wholesale, their notions of masculinity and femininity were much influenced by them. Both conformist and radical working-class cultures also positioned women as wives, as mothers and as daughters (despite the demographic and other obstacles to many women being all or any of these); also developed images of the home as a nest for its male breadwinner head; and also saw women and men as governed by very different rules of deportment (Kasson, 1990). Once established, these gender discourses strongly reinforced highly gendered social relations, and everyday time–space paths.

What is particularly relevant as regards consumption is that the price of women's domestic respectability was a denial of women's competence in negotiating public space. Just as much of women's work in nursing, welfare, training and childrearing was 'only vestigially defined as work' yet was 'fundamental to the maintenance of social well-being' (M Roberts, 1985: 154), so much of women's activity in buying was only vestigially defined as consumption, yet was fundamental to the continued functioning of households, and to the maintenance of social standing. Denials of women's competence in public space posed problems for the retailers whose numbers were increasing with the accelerating commodification of everyday life. It is in this context that the department store has received so much attention.

Department stores are widely seen as having been sensitive to the gendering of consumption, as well as making selling much more efficient and a more controllable process for the retailer (M B Miller, 1981; R Williams, 1982). Like the promenade (Scobey, 1992), the department store brought order to chaos, making part of 'the public' safe for women. In a safe public arena, the department store taught women to be consumers; and made encounters with consumer goods a norm of everyday life (R Bowlby, 1985). This was achieved through the design and control of gendered spaces, the advertising and display of commodities as spectacle (Richards, 1991), and the use of demonstrations and specialist shop staff (Laermans, 1993; M B Miller, 1981). Shopping became a skilled, knowledge-based activity, with consumers' knowledge controlled by retailers and advertisers. This is a striking inversion of earlier notions of female consumption as unskilled. But in the literature, shoppers' skills are presented as solitary and observational, like those of the *flâneur*, rather than as social and participatory.

This narrative contains certain gaps and problem areas which are more than empirical concerns, because they affect the *meanings* that we ascribe to consumption and shopping practices, and their interpretation and theorizing (Vickery, 1993). Accounts of consumption skills and practices prior to the department store are particularly sketchy, and rest more on contemporary social commentary than on substantive studies, (but see Brewer and Porter, 1993; Weatherill, 1986). In particular, we wish to point to a neglect of three topics: first, the social nature of shopping and consumption practices; second, the class specificity of gender divisions in shopping; and third, the capacity of consumers to engage in self-reflection.

We trace these problems with the portrayal of consumption practices to the public–private dichotomy of separate spheres arguments. Many social spaces were intermediate between the public sphere (especially when this is conceived of as an arena of politically competent actors) and the home. How may these intermediate social spaces, and the geographical spaces associated with them, be theorized? We have previously argued for the historical significance of what we termed 'the throng' in consumers' knowledges (Glennie and Thrift, 1992). Here, we develop that discussion through the concept of sociality.

Sociality and consumption practices

Concepts of sociality

We define sociality as the basic everyday ways in which people relate to one another and maintain an atmosphere of normality, even in the midst of antagonisms based on gender, race, class or other social fractures: what Shields calls 'the connecting tissues of everyday interaction and co-operation' (1992b: 106). It is not, therefore, to be understood as a strong 'contractual' form of community, like *gemeinschaft* (Tonnies, 1957), rather it consists of a 'contact' or tactile community built up from the solidarity and reciprocity of everyday life.

A sense of the significance of everyday direct human contact has been a central feature of definitions of sociality, at least since the work of Simmel (1908). Co-present interaction remains, just as Simmel long ago observed, the fundamental mode of human intercourse and socialization, the primordial site for sociability. For Boden and Molotch (1994), there are three facets of co-present sociality which are significant because they cannot be fully reproduced by other means of communication. First, co-presence is 'thick' with information: body language and other cues deliver the detailed contexts within which words derive their meanings. Second, the density of verbal and gestural exchange in groups means that fine nuances and ambivalences can be communicated very effectively. This is particularly important in exchanges which involve processes of exploration, or of negotiation – what Boden terms 'working out a view' in conditions of uncertainty (such as reacting to new experiences). Last, but by no means least, there is the centrality of social interaction to the creation and maintenance of a social self, including the values attached to co-presence as a pleasure in itself.

We think that sociality is worth examining at the present time because of important differences between early and current formulations of the concept, which in themselves are revealing. Early formulations of sociality, such as those of Simmel (1908; 1950) and Goffman (1959), were more rigid than those being discussed in the 1990s. Older approaches emphasize the self-presentation of social actors in social roles, as with Goffman's discussions of 'front-region' behaviour in public arenas, and 'back-region' behaviour in private or family settings (Giddens, 1987: ch 5; T G Miller, 1986; Weatherill, 1988). In contrast, current formulations (Maffesoli, 1991; Shields, 1992a) emphasize the flexibility of much co-present social interaction. Their questions about how people behave and identify or differentiate themselves from others stress mutable *relationships* rather than fixed *roles*.

Thus sociality is currently being analysed as a relatively weak, relatively fluid form of social relation. But, suggests Shields, it is not unimportant because it is weak: rather the reverse, because sociality involves – we might almost say revolves around – flexibility of social interaction and identity. People 'change among a veritable dramatis personae of [identifications] . . . in a given social group scene' (Shields 1992b: 107).

Since practices of sociality are many and varied, they do not produce a homogenous throng or mass. Neither does sociality produce hard and fast social groups which demand definition through appropriately clearly defined social roles. Rather, sociality produces a series of loosely bonded and temporary social groups crystallized out of the mass: what Maffesoli terms *tribes*. Temporarily, the status of the individual is eroded in favour of a transient group – the tribe – as individual identifications are aligned with, or differentiated from, such transient group norms. The metaphor of tribes is intended to convey a sense of these groups as 'marked by their orientation and rituals of inclusion and exclusion, membership and rites of passage, rather than legalistic codes of conduct and membership' (Maffesoli, 1991: 50).

Practices of sociality have close connections with urban space. The identifications that people adopt are conditioned by specific public sites of social centrality around which crowds and constituent groups form. Such public sites have always been important in the formation of sociality because of its tactile constitution through relations of co-presence, and co-present interaction: talking, gesturing, touching, feeling, arguing, debating, expressing, and so on. Moreover, visually rich public sites provide an intensive level of stimuli and imaginative cues. In the past, the street, marketplaces, and public gatherings of all sorts have been important sites. In the twentieth century, spaces of retailing, recreation, leisure, and entertainment have become increasingly significant as settings for group involvement and interaction.

This claim for the importance of sociality does *not* seek to occlude the significance of 'strong' social relations such as gender, class or ethnicity. These social relations, and the time–space routines associated with them, do much to determine patterns of sociality. But it is to assert two things. The first is the continuous production of co-present sociality as a social relation. The second is that the relative importance of sociality and of other social relations varies considerably over time.

An account of changing patterns and arenas of sociality in connection with consumption ought, therefore, to be incorporated within narratives of urban shopping. We illustrate the suggestion that historical consumption practices partially constituted sociality, and were partially shaped by patterns of sociality, with respect to two themes: the nature of intermediate spaces between public and domestic spaces, such as 'the street', and the nature of shopping as an activity.

Intermediate spaces: 'the street' in pre-modern cities

Despite a neglect in historical accounts of spaces intermediate between the private domestic home, and the formally structured public sphere, it is clear that contemporaries did recognize the street as a structured and skilful space. This is apparent both from anecdotal sources, in the proliferation of manuals available from the seventeenth century, and in other literature on city life (Corfield, 1990; Gay, 1716). However, the skills outlined in the many manuals were not the silent, solitary observational expertise of the bourgeois promenader or of the *flâneur*. Rather, they were skills of presentation, interpretation, and improvization as one participated in street-space based activities. These street activities ranged from the most fragmentary of fleeting encounters, to sustained sociality in everyday experiences that might be utterly routine, but that could be completely novel, as in encounters with new commodities.

In other words, the throng itself functioned as a kind of 'classroom', as a means of reflexivity, in which people learned about commodities, styles, and their uses and meanings. The street and other intermediate spaces were places where people deployed their pre-existing (learned) understanding.

It is stating the obvious to observe that involvement with the street and other informal public spaces or semi-public spaces was *class-specific*. Urban streets belonged in large part to their labouring-class people (Willen, 1992). Family economies bridged the distance between public and private to make the streets a sphere of domestic life. For poor men, women, and children, the streets were workplaces and playgrounds. 'Street life, with its panoply of choices, its rich and varied texture, its motley society, played a central role in virtually all aspects of their lives' (Stansell, 1987: 203).

227

The domestic roles, and requisite skills, of labouring-class women were also very different from those of their middle-class equivalents. Middle-class ideologies might stress the moral and managerial aspects of womanhood, but working-class ideals for wives and mothers emphasized practical skills of buying, cooking, cleaning and childrearing.

> For the wife to manage the family finances seems to have been a very widespread pattern in both town and countryside, a distinctive difference from their middle-class counterparts with their exclusion from money matters. The working man was to earn, the working woman was to spend, using her hard-won knowledge of domestic needs and the relative merits of available goods, to eke out what money was coming in. (Hall, 1992a: 97)

Thus 'separate spheres' discourses affected middle-class and labouring-class women differently. The inexperience of middle-class women in intermediate social and geographical spaces was atypical, and it is misleading to treat their experience as paradigmatic. Concepts of sociality provide a framework within which the less-formal social relations of the street may be analysed.

The nature of shopping

It is easy to overlook the extent to which the shop was but one channel among many through which goods might be bought. Very large numbers of purchasers bought goods in open markets and fairs, or directly from artisan producers, or from hawkers and chapmen. Consumers of almost all social strata routinely acquired goods in face-to-face interaction with vendors in public settings, rather than in specialist shops. To focus on shops is also to ignore the very large numbers of poor consumers involved in the huge, informal trade in second hand clothing (Lemire, 1988; 1991; Styles, 1994), and second-hand household, farm and trade items (Cox and Cox, 1985–6; Woodward, 1985).

Thus purchasers did not need to be visitors to shops in order to acquire and develop skills related to buying: skills relating to pricing, value, quality, adulteration, design, imitation. For example, women in early-modern Europe feature prominently as initiators of bread or grain price riots, precisely because they were the most involved with buying these items, and were acutely sensitive to issues of price or adulteration in the context of providing for their household or family.

In the context of the present discussion, the extent of consumers' pre-existing skills qualifies one of the innovative roles ascribed to department stores. That consumers' shopping skills were exercised in social settings, rather than by isolated consumers, makes notions of sociality useful in their explication. This was true not only in the purchasing channels that we have just described, but also in shops, and it is to early-modern shops that we now turn.

One's expectation from much of the literature is that most shopping was done by individuals on their own. This was emphatically not the case. A great deal of shopping, especially by women, was done in pairs or in larger groups, at least on the basis of diary entries, and shopmen's manuals. It is also clear that both urban and rural shops in the eighteenth century were more than mere buying-places, especially 'the small village general stores, with . . . their half doors, stocks of treacle, tea, candles, and remnants of cotton velveret, [were places] where customers largely drawn from among the labouring poor could sit and pass the time of day' (Styles, 1993: 11). Even in big urban drapers' shops, the presence of poor people was not something that automatically set off socially sensitive alarm bells among shop staff or well-to-do customers. Similarly, when shopmen's manuals and novels discuss shoplifting, it is sometimes in terms of individual consumers, and sometimes in respect of groups (Abelson, 1989; Defoe, 1721). The solitary customer was not a dominant figure, except at the top end of the market.

The character of shopping as a social activity weakens analyses grounded in a model of the shopper as solitary, silent and introverted. Sociality was an integral part of 'going shopping'. This was even more the case where the purpose of visiting a shop or other retail outlet was part of a pre-purchase deliberating process rather than the execution of a purchase. Important literatures are beginning to develop on the sheer variety of shops in pre-modern and early-modern times (Mui and Mui, 1989; Shammas, 1990; Styles, 1993), and on the variety among department stores themselves (Benson, 1986; Lawrence, 1992; Reekie, 1992; Strasser, 1989), addressing such topics as the implications for shopping practices of different clienteles, locations, layouts, salesforce organization, and interaction among managers, store workers and customers. This literature promises to change our appreciation of the significance of particular innovations in retail spaces, by more closely specifying exactly what aspects of shopping experiences they changed for which groups of consumers. We also wish to emphasize geographical differences in the ownership and meanings of consumer goods, and in the processes by which consumers acquired commodities (Thrift and Glennie, 1993: 40–2).

Reflexivity and the constitution of consumers' identities

Concepts of relexivity

In this section we summarize a new area of work on the nature of late-modern, high-modern or post-modern societies as it relates to consumption and gender. This is the growing body of work on reflexivity.

Beck, Giddens, and Lash and Urry bring different but complementary slants to their investigations of reflexive modernization. Beck (1992a; 1992b) provides a vision of late-modern societies as increasingly reflexive because of two interlocking processes. The first of these is the sheer quantitative growth in abstract systems of knowledge and the institutions (education, the media, cultural industries) that generate these systems of knowledge. The second is the corresponding growth of individualism founded in the decline of traditional centres of individuation like social class, the nuclear family, and mass industrial production, and in an increased questioning of established systems of thought, like science. The first process is indexed in the growth of educational systems, the media, and numerous other cultural-critical institutions. The second process forces people to use the knowledge supplied by these institutions as they find it increasingly important to take decisions about the course of their lives that they previously did not have to take because they were inexorably positioned in social structures like class and gender.

This kind of general framework is made more explicit in Giddens (1991; 1992). For Giddens, the growth of reflexivity in high modernity is also based on expert systems of social and scientific knowledge, but Giddens is much more explicitly concerned with increasing monitoring of the conduct of the self, and of how abstract systems of social and scientific knowledge are applied to this monitoring, thereby ineradicably altering the nature of the self, which becomes people's fount of reflexivity: 'their project'. In late modernity, these abstract expert systems are increasingly opened to doubt leading to a chronic systematic questionning of them, which can, however, only be answered by appealing to other such systems. Thus reflexivity becomes 'chronic revision of self-identity in the light of new information and knowledge' (Giddens, 1991: 20), undermining older certainties of self-identity established through appeals to stable ideal-characters.

The self becomes a crucial element of high modernity, consisting of a reflexive project based on biographical pluralism, a way of 'sustaining coherent, yet continuously revised, biographical narratives . . . in the context of multiple choice as filtered through abstract systems' (Giddens, 1991: 6). Thus, as also found in Beck, social relationships come to be based less and less on the traditional social anchors of class, the family and mass industrial production, and the established positions that they generate, and become valued for themselves. Thus, in both Beck and Giddens, reflexivity transfers from monitoring the social to monitoring the self, from standard biography to elective biography, and from social identity to personal identity. In other words, there is an increase in individuation. In turn, this results in higher levels of social anxiety which can only be solved by recourse to knowledge systems of one form or another.

Lash (1993) and Lash and Urry (1993) take Beck and Giddens to task for concentrating on *cognitive* reflexivity to the detriment of *aesthetic* reflexivity. Their major criticisms are as follows. First, in both Beck and Giddens, bodies are regarded as things to be monitored by practical consciousness on the model of the ego, rather than as constitutive parts of what is doing the monitoring. In particular, Giddens's presents the self *mastering* the body rather than the self *involving* the body. Second, Beck and Giddens pay too little attention to aesthetic reflexivity. They overemphasize the Cartesian-Enlightenment tradition of self-monitoring at the expense of the mirroring Romantic-aesthetic tradition (with its emphasis on the invention of symbols and symbolic systems, forming a counter to the overwhelming rationality of the other tradition). And they underestimate the fundamentally aesthetic nature of interpretative dimensions of contemporary everyday life, involving a proliferation of images resulting from the expansion of education, the media, leisure, tourism, consumption, and other cultural or culturally attuned systems (including guides about landscapes themselves).

During the 1970s and 1980s aesthetic elements came to concern wider and wider groups of people, and aesthetic cultural capital is now important in the everyday lives of most western people. This social spread has occurred through television, music, places of sociality, cinema, travel, heritage and so on. As Lash and Urry point out, 'it is only in late modernity (or postmodernity) that aesthetic reflexivity comes to pervade social processes' (1993: 44). This spread of aesthetic knowledge must therefore be added to Beck's spread of knowledge of science and the environment, and Giddens's spread of social scientific knowledge and self-therapy.

Reflexivity and gender

The growth of reflexivity, both cognitive and aesthetic, is particularly associated with gender in the analyses of Beck, Giddens, and Lash and Urry. There are two main reasons for the prominence of gender issues. First, because the collapse of the traditional order of the nuclear family is one of the most important reasons for the growth of reflexivity. That the relationship is two-way is evident from the very extensive literature on fertility and the family (Lesthaeghe, 1983; Simons, 1986; Watkins, 1991).

Thus, as Beck (1992a; 1992b) notes, the traditional nuclear family has come under increasing pressures – from demographic 'liberation' (simply the length of time that people now live); from the de-skilling of housework; from new anti-reproductive technologies and especially contraceptive devices; from changes in attitudes and legislation concerning divorce; from higher female participation in education and occupations; and from various social movements that recognize inequality and proselytize against it (including the general feminization of politics). In turn, this has led to the rise of numerous different household structures based on biographical pluralism.

Second, gender is important because of the rise since the nineteenth century of discourses on sexuality which in combination with growing biographical pluralism have led to sex becoming the object of increasing cognitive and aesthetic reflexivity, blurring traditional constitutions of gender. In particular, discourses on sexuality and biographical pluralism have promoted new kinds of identities based on various combinations of sexual difference which are potent sources of identity politics because they are also emotional narratives of the self: 'sexuality functions as a malleable feature of the self, a prime connecting point between body, self-identity, and social norms' (Giddens, 1992: 15). Sexual identity ceases to be anatomical destiny and more and more becomes a lifestyle issue. As Weeks (1986) puts it,

> There no longer appears to be a great continent of normality surrounded by small islands of disorder. Instead we can now witness clusters of islands, great and small. . . . New categories and erratic minorities have emerged. Older orders have experienced a process of sub-division as specialized tastes, specific aptitudes and needs become the basis for proliferating social identities. (Weeks, 1986: 23)

The competence and skill of late-twentieth-century consumers at virtually all levels of the market is much less differentiated by gender, compared with those at any levels of the market in the later nineteenth century. Gender variety has become both a cause and an effect of increasing reflexivity.

Increasing cognitive and aesthetic reflexivity, based on multiple systems of knowledge and biographical pluralism, has in turn fostered a growing *identity politics* of the body and self (e.g. hooks, 1991). Of course, this growth in identity politics has been a constant theme of much social and cultural research since the mid-1970s, as have the links between it and consumption and gender, but the links to reflexivity make it possible to provide a more general and generalized explanation in a way that has previously been lacking.

Reflexivity and risk

In the late-modern, high-modern or post-modern period, as has already been noted, there has been an erosion of traditional social structures like class and the nuclear family. Consequently, the active construction of individual identities has become more important, founded in expanded cognitive and aesthetic reflexivity and serviced by a vast social and cultural apparatus of reflexivity (education, the media, etc).

However, because of the contingent and constantly revised nature of biography/biographical planning, identity has become less fixed and, in a sense, more political. In other words, we now live in an increasingly individualized world, in which

> each person's biography is removed from given determinations and placed in his or her own hands; open and dependent on decisions. The proportion of life opportunities which are fundamentally closed to decision-making is decreasing and the proportion of the biography which is open and must be constituted personally is increasing. Individualization of life situations and processes means that biographies become self-reflective. Socially prescribed biography is transformed into biography that is self-produced and continues to be produced. (Beck, 1992a: 135)

The effect of all this is to throw much more responsibility for decision-making about individuals' conduct on to individuals themselves. Both Beck (1992a) (witness his title *Risk Society*) and Giddens (1991: 109–43) stress that these developments force people to take at least some risks in decision-making about the content and meaning of their identity.

In such an increasingly individuated society, the individual must increasingly learn to think of herself or himself as a node of permanent action whose desires lead to consequences for which only she/he can be blamed. These are 'personal' successes and 'personal' failures, and they must include decisions about what identity is adopted.

> One even has to choose one's social identity and group membership, in this way managing one's own self, changing its image. In the individualized society, risks do not just increase quantitatively. Qualitatively new types of personal risk arise: the risk of the chosen and changed personal identity. And what is an additional burden, new forms of 'guilt ascription' come into being. Sooner or later . . . constraints to a personal and reflexive handling, planning and production of biography will produce new demands on education, advice-giving, therapy and politics. (Beck, 1992a: 136)

Reflexivity and consumption

Thus self-formation, identity politics and risk-taking, come to centre stage in modern societies. This observation is particularly relevant to areas of social action like consumption and gender. These two areas are increasingly linked by the need to fashion a successfully communicated, and communicative, self and a clearly justified biography (of both self and others).

Consumption practices are particularly affected by the spread of aesthetic reflexivity, for three reasons. First, there is an increased choice element to consumption. There are more and more commodities to choose amongst and to build identities from. For example,

> even in traditional societies there existed a plurality of dress styles. But the latter were symbolically distributed by specific social positions. Dress styles in modernity are much more personality specific rather than specific to social positions. They suggest a freedom from the symbolic distribution of the latter by the social. Further, as 'taste', they instantiate not just a set of individual status and class distinctions, but an autonomy from such ascribed distinctions. They thus involve a very important set of identity-choices and identity-risks, especially for young people. (Lash and Urry, 1993: 51).

This choice element spawns opportunities for creativity in the way in which commodities are used, especially in new combinations (MacRobbie, 1989; E Wilson, 1985). Other workers like D Miller (1987; 1990), Cheal (1988) and Silverstone and Hirsch (1992) show how commodities are often consumed in ways which add to or even create new meanings through practices like giving, collecting and so on. Both examples challenge the post-modern thesis in which commodities become increasingly disposable and meaningless.

The second reason why aesthetic reflexivity and consumption are particularly closely related is that consumption increasingly involves travel and mobility. Travel and tourism have become an integral part of modern consumption practices, involving both a commitment to researching and documenting particular places (for example through photography), the better to consume them and the conditions associated with them, and at the same time, an ironic realization of the constitutedness of the whole experience. Third, the upsurge in aesthetic reflexivity produces a vast real economy of retailing outlets, hotels, restaurants, art galleries, theatres, cinemas, rock concerts, heritage events, architects and designers, airports and airlines, and so on (Zukin, 1991). As has already been remarked, these constitute some major sectors of economic growth.

It is through markets for commodities that many choices about self and biography must be made. Consumer goods increasingly become the means by which gender and sexual identities are sought out and fixed, and their use has become increasingly flexible and creative. Witness, for example, accounts of the sophisticated interpretative and discriminatory skills of youthful consumers (Nava, 1992; S Willis, 1991), or of the creative use of second-hand or adapted clothes and other goods to create new identifications (MacRobbie, 1989; P Willis, 1978; P Willis *et al*, 1990: 84–97). Particularly since the mid-1980s there are numerous instances where industrial production and advertising has followed in the wake of youthful tribes within the throng rather than vice versa.

Reflexivity, sociality and urban space

In turn, the reflexive turn, and the rising importance of individuation and identity politics that come with this turn, have produced an increasing emphasis on sociality; on the play of different identifications adapted to particular social settings; and on the sites of social centrality that promote it. Low personal risk is concentrated in places of sociality. This combination of sociability and sites of social centrality allows different forms of the self to be 'tried on'. In other words, it allows the identifications necessary to fashion the self to be made through alignment with, or modification of, one or more of the various transient social groups that inhabit the throng in these sites, but this is an investment which can normally be made without too much in the way of personal commitment or risk. Such an investment can be withdrawn without undue damage to those involved.

This turn to sociality is being responded to and shaped by many of those associated with the marketing of commodities, from those associated with shopping centres and shopping malls to those associated with heritage sites. Thus the managers at shopping malls and shopping centres have moved away from the modernist emphases on convenience and 'rational' shopping towards the promotion of these sites as central because of their carnivalesque atmosphere. There is a significant difference here from the classic department store, in which displays and the like were instructive or educational in intent towards consumers (cf. this volume, Chapter 13). An excellent example of this promotion of the carnivalesque is discussed by Reekie (1992) in her analysis of the transformation of McWhirter's department store in Brisbane into a 'festive market'. Here a highly structured retail environment has been broken up in an attempt to create a focus of sociality for the throng. The department store has, as it were, been turned inside-out to become what we term a 'quasi-street'.

Increasingly shopping environments are public spaces, promoting festivals (like Christmas and Easter, community events, special displays and seasons, and so on), and carefully building up local affinities in order to produce what Maffesoli (1991: 11) calls 'an affective ambience'. They may not be profound or authentic, but this is not the point. They are simply sites of social centrality where people can interact lightly in crowds without too much hinging on the outcome.

But there is a crucial difference between the sociality of the crowd or throng in these kinds of sites and in previous eras, and in this sense the late-modern, high-modern or post-modern crowd can be said to constitute a new mode of people being together. In previous historical times, social identities were generally comparatively fixed. Social identities were displayed as a kind of mirror of the extant social structure: even when these identities transgressed in various forms of carnivalesque behaviour, the unusual nature of their behaviour made it plain that the social structure was only being temporarily disrupted.

But in current circumstances, as a result of the lessening of the influence of traditional institutions, and the massive increases in cognitive and aesthetic reflexivity, this no longer holds. The crowd or throng is performative *and* cognitive *and* aesthetic. It has become a place in which new variants of the self can be tried out in a state of permanent mutation. New or remodelled arenas of sociality provide relatively safe 'proving grounds' for the individualized self (M Morris, 1988).

The crowd takes on significance chiefly because of the information which it provides on the host of imaginary orders that constitute people's self-projects. First, this occurs through low-level sociality itself, a constant engagement with, and checking-out of, others: Maffesoli's 'collective narcissism'. Second, information is generated through the 'tribes' that form and reform.

> Overall within massification, processes of condensation are constantly occurring through which more or less ephemeral tribal groupings are organized which cohere on the basis of their own minor values, and which attract or collide with each other in an endless dance, [placing] themselves into a constellation whose vague boundaries are perfectly fluid. (Maffesoli, 1992: 12)

The individual, then, ends up by being absorbed into a *differentiated crowd* which allows for or limits identity with others, thereby gaining a supplement to her or his identity which may be immediately used, or reflected upon, or discarded, in the longer-term work of producing her or his own biography. This identification will be both cognitive and aesthetic: the value, the taste, the admiration which is held in common cements a sense of the self which is increasingly aesthetic 'because what it involves is a particular style, a particular mode of life, of ideology, of dress, of sexual manners, in short everything pertaining to the collective passion' (Maffesoli, 1991: 16).

So far as gender is concerned, the crowd is, first of all, a place where new gender identities can actually be identified, tried out, explored, especially through the medium of wearing/using appropriate consumer goods in appropriate ways, through dressing up and presenting the body, often as part of 'tribes'. The work of MacRobbie (1989), Mort (1989), and others shows this to be very widely the case among younger men and women, but by no means restricted to younger age groups. Second, the crowd is a place where discourses of gender and sexuality can be negotiated and renegotiated without becoming immediate threats to identity, resulting in crossovers, cross-referencing, and so on.

At this point, it hopefully becomes clear that the throng and its inherent sociality are crucial elements of both consumption and gender in late-modern, high-modern or postmodern times. So far as consumption is concerned, the throng provides an important part of the *raison d'être* of shopping. As Shields (1992b) puts it:

> The latent social functions of retail capital and retail institutions such as the shopping-centre move to the foreground, overwhelming the rational pursuit of commodities. . . . Consumption as commodity exchange hasn't disappeared but it is now less significant in determining the whole 'play' of the scene. . . . It is necessary to recognize that consumption itself is partly determined by the non-rational [*note, not irrational*], cultural, element of sociality. Shopping is not just a functional activity. Consumption has become a communal activity, even a form of social solidarity. (Shields, 1992b: 110)

Conclusions

As we stressed at the outset, this has been a speculative rather than a definitive chapter, so firm conclusions would be inappropriate. What we have sought to do is to begin to gain a purchase on the role of the crowd, or the throng, in constituting consumption practices and gender relations. We find notions of sociality and reflexivity useful in exploring the historical significance of the urban throng, and in pointing to the contemporary significance of much greater fluidity and differentiations within the urban throng than was seen in the modern era, not least in respect of gender. We see the late twentieth century as a particularly flexible period in the development of novel consumption practices, because sociality has become more autonomous of other social relations in the late twentieth century, and because of the expanded scope and scale of reflexivity.

In turn, these thoughts lead us to suggest four pressing areas for further research. The first of these is simply a continuation of work on *consumption and gender relations*. We have started to sketch one of the lines down which such work might go, but there are many others. Daniel Miller's (1990) pioneering work in Trinidad on consumer goods and sexual freedom, work by MacRobbie (1989) and Nava (1992) on fashion and young women, and by Jackson (1991a) and Mort (1989) on masculinities, all show that this is an exciting area of work which still suffers from a relative lack of information. So does work on links between consumption practices and political consciousness (S Willis, 1991). Linked to this first research area is a second, dealing with the *interpretation, use and re-creation of new retailing and other spaces*, as performed by their users (Shields, 1991).

If geographers have been involved in both the research areas just mentioned (see this volume, Chapters 13 and 14), the same cannot be said of a third pressing area of research. This, we suggest, is the economics and culture of *gift giving and buying for others*, especially through the medium of consumption festivals. Festivals such as Christmas, Easter, the sales, weddings, and so on account for a very significant proportion of consumer spending, to which retailers are increasingly attuned. On one estimate, the Christmas period alone accounts for nearly one-fifth of annual expenditure on consumer goods in the United States, and a similar figure in the UK. The great majority of gift purchases are made by women. Yet we know remarkably little about this important crescendo of consumption. The works of Cheal and others make it clear that gifts have important relations of power, affection and mutual-identification associated with them (Burgoyne and Routh, 1991; Cheal, 1988), with which advertisers and retailers attempt to engage (Davidson, 1992). This emphasis on gift-giving is one example of a number of types of consuming behaviour, which also merit greater attention. Another good example is that of *collecting* behaviour, the scale of which seems currently to be increasing, not least because of retailers' success in fostering ideas about collecting, from childhood onwards.

Finally, there is a methodological dimension to all this, which is that geography and sociology will have to pay more attention to work in other fields than has hitherto been the case. In particular, we are thinking of work in the burgeoning field of economic psychology (Cheal, 1988; Lunt and Livingstone, 1992), as well as the more familiar fields of consumer research and anthropology. We suspect that the kinds of consumption and gender practices that we have tried to approach in this chapter can be fully understood only from within the methodological frames that these disciplines are constructing.

CHAPTER 13

'I'd like to dress her all over': masculinity, power and retail space

Nicholas Blomley

In early 1883, Émile Zola completed *Au Bonheur des Dames*, his strange, compelling account of the French department store. While the novel was not a great literary success, it has gone on to trace its own curious biography over the last century, as successive generations reinterpret its meaning for their own ends. In this chapter I want to use *Au Bonheur* (translated as *The Ladies' Paradise*), as a signpost toward a 'new retail geography'. I shall argue that the novel not only offers some telling insights into the geographies of retail capital accumulation, but also speaks of the cultural geographies of retailing, notably the implication of retail spaces in the reproduction of both femininity and, of special interest here, masculinity. A retail geography worthy of its name, I shall claim, must take both its economic and its cultural geographies seriously.

Retail geography

For far too long, retail geography has been oblivious, indifferent and occasionally hostile to changes outside its self-contained 'applied' loop. Ken Ducatel and I sought to challenge this closure, by noting the degree to which the field had been completely bypassed by the insights of the 'new industrial geography' (Ducatel and Blomley, 1990). As a consequence, the dynamics of retail capital accumulation had been woefully under-theorized. We offered one such theorization, drawing upon a Marxist reading of the circuits of capital. The concept of 'separation-in-unity' was advanced, by which retail capital was seen both as a component part of a larger system of production and consumption, yet as having a unique (and sometimes contradictory) institutional logic within that larger system. It is heartening to see a number of excellent studies – most notably those within in the present collection – that have begun to explore such questions as the interface between retail and financial capital, the regulation of capital concentration, and the structure of channel relations. Finally, retail geography has begun to take its economic geographies seriously.

However, another lag can be discerned. If at that time the high-ground in the discipline was held by the industrial geographers, it seems now to have shifted, as a 'critical cultural geography' has begun to coalesce, insisting on an interrogation of the geographies of gender, racism and colonialism. At the same time, many feminists and cultural theorists – usually outside the discipline – have turned their attention to the retail sector, exploring the spaces of consumption in both an historical and contemporary context. Such spaces – rather than passive surfaces – are increasingly being cast as actively produced, represented and contested. Examples might include Janice Williamson's (1992a; 1992b) 'pedestrian feminist reading' of West Edmonton Mall; Susan Buck-Morss's (1989) imaginative interpretation of Benjamin's Arcade project; Rob Shields's (1992a) edited volume on 'lifestyle shopping'; Sharon Zukin's (1991) discussion of the current shift from production spaces to consumption spaces; Robyn Dowling's (1991) analysis of femininity, modernity and the department store in Vancouver; Meaghan Morris's (1988) exploration of the shopping centre, and Elaine Abelson's (1989) treatment of middle-class shopping in the Victorian department store.

However, retail geography still seems to be lagging. While embracing the new economic geographies of retailing, the cultural geographies have been forgotten (although see Lowe and Wrigley, Glennie and Thrift, Domosh, and Clarke, this volume, Chapters 1, 12, 14 and 16). It is this gap that I want to pursue in this chapter, by asking whether a 'new retail geography' can combine an exploration of the economic structures of retail capital with an analysis of the cultural logic of retailing. More specifically, I want to ask about the significance of space in both processes: is there an economic *and* a cultural geography to retailing? Of special interest to me for reasons that I develop below is the implication of masculinity in the geographies of retailing. How do notions of masculine identity and masculine sexuality figure in both retail restructuring and consumption?

'Un poeme de la vie moderne'

Answering these questions is, of course, a difficult task. I don't think that the traditional luminaries of retail geography can help us. To answer an unusual question, then, requires that we look in unusual places. The French writer Émile Zola (1840–1902) is usually seen simply as a novelist. A novelist he is, and a very accomplished one at that, but he is also, I want to argue, a consumate retail geographer, alert to questions of space, capitalism and patriarchy. As expressed most clearly in his novel *Au Bonheur des Dames*, he offers a number of valuable insights that I think could be of central importance to a new retail geography. These include the social construction of masculinity and femininity; the intersection of space and power; sexuality and consumption; and the nature of retailing as a public and private space.[1]

As with any geographer, it is important to set writer and writing in context. *Au Bonheur* is one of twenty novels in Zola's massive *Rougon-Macquart* series, a historically sweeping survey of two families during France's Second Empire that included most of his great works, including *Germinal*, *Nana* and *La Terre*. All were written in the 'naturalist' style that he pioneered, along with contemporaries such as Flaubert, Goncourt and Turgenev. Eschewing romanticism, the naturalists took the modern world, forming around them, seriously. Not only did they seek to make sense of modern life, but also they embraced its vigour, promise and potential. Zola saw the artistic possibilities inherent in modernity and, embracing progress and science, promised a new art form, appropriate to the day. In 1860 he claimed that:

> each society has its own particular poetry, and since our society is not that of 1830 and does not as yet have its own poetry, the man who finds it will be justly famous. . . . The whole problem is to find a new form, to sing worthily of the peoples of the future, to show in a fittingly grandiose manner humanity ascending the steps of the Temple (quoted in P Walker, 1985: 33)

Although he was adept at depicting the rural landscape, he would have embraced Walter Benjamin's characterization of Paris as the capital of the nineteenth century: 'I feel [Paris] rocked by the immense labour of the century', he declaimed, 'I see it about to give birth to a new world, and my proudest wish would be to cast it, all warm and full of its titanic task, into some gigantic work of art' (quoted in P Walker, 1985: 114).

Au Bonheur des Dames, published in 1883, was the eleventh in the Rougon-Macquart series. Set in Paris, it combines many of his recurrent preoccupations. Documenting the rise of one of the quintessentially modern institutions, the great department store, Zola's aim, as he put it, was to craft 'un poeme de la vie moderne'. He enjoined himself to 'go along with the century, express the century, which is a century of action and conquest, of effort in every direction' (in P Walker, 1985: 158). To Walker (1985), the novel is 'first and foremost a hymn to modern business, a lyrical affirmation of the joy of existence, a glorification of the entrepreneurial spirit, a salute to the victors in the struggle for survival, a social Darwinistic tract' (ibid: 158).

The hero of his 'poeme' is one Octave Mouret, an aggressive, unscrupulous and predatory merchant modelled, perhaps, on Aristide Bouccicaut, founder of the Bon Marché. Following the death of his wife, Mouret deploys innovative management techniques to expand his drapery business at the expense of the traditional retail sector. At the close of the novel Au Bonheur is employing over 3000 people, and has taken in a million francs in one day. Denise Baudu, a young woman from the provinces, climbs up the career ladder of the store as it grows until, after an extended resistance, agreeing to marry Mouret.

The novel is much more than this, however. Like many of Zola's works, it resists closure, playing on a series of ambivalences. While it offers a dispassionate accounting of modern commerce, it also provides lush, lyrical and sensuous prose. While lauding the aspirations of Mouret, it also carefully and sympathetically documents the store's annihilation of the traditional retail landscape, especially the neighbouring shop owned by Denise Baudu's uncle. While the novel can be read as an endorsement of certain patriarchal claims, ending as it does with marriage and the triumph of a woman who wins, as Zola notes, 'purely with her femininity', it also carefully documents the manner in which Mouret himself cynically and cold-heartedly manipulates and conquers his women customers: the store, he exclaims, is built upon 'women's flesh and blood' (Zola, 1992: 68).

The history of the novel over the last century reveals these multivalences and ambiguities. The novel was, apparently, the first of Zola's to be translated into English. It has been suggested that this novel was chosen because of the growing notoriety of the author in Britain. With the subtitle 'A realistic novel' it was marketed as a 'racy', even pornographic piece. A more accurate (and hence more explicit) translation was issued in 1886 by a firm specializing in sensational fiction. Henry Viztelly, the publisher, was later imprisoned for three months for publishing Zola's *La Terre*, deemed an 'obscene libel' by the English courts.

As interest in Zola waned, so the novel disappeared from view, such that I had a hard job finding an English translation in 1990. An extensive library search finally unearthed a copy, reissued in 1976. A limited edition of the 1886 translation had been reprinted, curiously enough, by the Ohio-based retail consultancy Management Horizons. They deemed this a 'Service to Retailing', 'assuring the continued prosperity' of the company's clients. Reflecting the spatial preoccupations of retail capital, the book was characterized as primer of store design, or:

> a truly unique and distinctive work on how to create store excitement. The principles and techniques described in Ladies' Paradise are as pertinent today as they were one hundred years ago. Ladies' Paradise, therefore, is a pragmatic guide which can be used in our time to increase the merchandising effectiveness of almost any retail store.

In 1992, the Viztelly translation again resurfaced with a reprinting by the fashionable University of California Press, with an introduction by the equally fashionable Kristin Ross, author of *The Emergence of Social Space; Rimbaud and the Paris Commune*. She notes the relevance of the novel in very different terms:

> with the convergence of a wide variety of theoretical interests – those of Marxists, postmodernists and feminists, cultural theorists and social historians – intent on charting the transition from an economy based on production to one based on consumption, Zola's novel has again come to the forefront as an indispensable document in the history of . . . 'the society of the spectacle.' (Zola, 1992: iii)

So from pornography to pragmatic marketing guide, and on to post-modern road-map, the novel has been positioned in very different ways over time. This seems suggestive: given its subtlety and resistance to closure, the novel can indeed be read in all of these ways. It is precisely for this reason that it lends itself to a reconstructed retail geography. Not only does it offer a detailed economic statement – as Management Horizons realized – but also it provides a cultural account of consumption and sexuality, as perceived by the first and most recent characterizations. What all three miss, however, is the degree to which the novel is richly geographic. I hope to explore its economic and cultural geographies, beginning with the former.

Don't be afraid! Blind them!

The interest of Management Horizons, a staid consultancy, is highly appropriate, given the novel's naturalistic grounding. As in all of his works, Zola spent a considerable amount of time researching his subject, writing three preparatory articles on the psychology and sociology of department store workers, and spending four to five hours a day for a month at Parisian department stores (the Bon Marché and the Louvre), compiling over 380 pages of notes. He consulted with many authorities, inviting his architect friend Frantz Jourdain to construct a plan for his fictional store. Ironically, when Jourdain was later called upon to remodel La Samaritaine, the new store closely resembled Au Bonheur.

As a consequence, many of the economic concerns that he identifies are carefully drawn. Indeed, while we must remember the novel's historical specificity, its contemporary echoes are striking (see Doel, Foord, Bowlby and Tillsley, and Lowe and Crewe, this volume, Chapters 3, 4 and 10). Channel relations between producer and retailer are described, for example, as both struggle over surplus value. With his rapid stockturn and bulk ordering, Mouret is able to negotiate favourable wholesale prices: many manufacturers fear he will be their ruin. Producers are unable to 'lay down the law', however; they are 'obliged to have continual outlets, the quickest and largest possible, so that they are on their knees before the big shops' (Zola, 1992: 171).

The spatial and sexual segmentation of the labour force is also documented (cf Freathy and Sparks, this volume, Chapter 9). Labour flexibility seems a concern: one-third of the workforce is laid off during the slack summer season, for example. The workforce is mostly segmented along gender lines into the multiple departments of the store. Although there is some room for internal promotion, the key management staff are all men. Workers are treated harshly in the store: pitted against each other individually and by department they are reduced to 'wheels, turned around by the immense machine, abdicating their personalities, simply substituting their strength to this commonplace, powerful total' (Zola, 1992: 119). The internal jealousies and rivalries between workers – where advancement is at another's expense – generates 'a loud noise as of jaw-bones working' (ibid: 143). This 'struggle of appetites' of course, contributes to the 'better working of the machine' (ibid: 143) in a similar manner to the inter-departmental rivalry fostered in many contemporary stores.

242

The structure and workings of the store itself are a central concern of Zola's narrative: indeed, the store itself is the central character of the novel. He spends a good deal of time describing the logic of capital accumulation pioneered by the new department stores. On several occasions, Mouret explains the economic logic of the new retailing:

> We don't want a very large working capital; our sole effort is to get rid as quickly as possible of our stock in order to replace it by another, which will give our capital as many times its interest. In this way we can content ourselves with a very small profit . . . but this will finish by bringing in millions when we can operate on considerable quantities of goods incessantly renewed. (Zola, 1992: 67)

This incessant and seemingly unstoppable process (the almost mystical transubstantiation of commodity capital to money capital and back to commodity capital, in Marxist terms) provides the narrative momentum of the book itself. Three great sales, each larger than the other, are evenly spaced through the book (Chapters 4, 9 and 14), interspersed with three inventories. The monotonic logic of retail capital accumulation seems incessant; hence his frequent depiction of the store as an 'overheated machine', a 'furnace' or a 'factory'.

One of the counterpoints of the novel, indeed, is the comparison between this hard-nosed economic logic and the dream-like consumer paradise that Mouret constructs within the store. While making the functional connections between the two clear, Zola depicts the manner in which the process of consumption has been made to appear uncoupled from its capitalist ordering. While characterized as a machine, the store itself is also described as a 'cathedral', 'ship', 'fairyland' and 'lighthouse' – a magical, dream-like world of consumption. This supposed division – between the 'real', masculine world of production, and the ethereal, non-economic, feminine domain of consumption – is of course with us today, and continues to bedevil retail geography.

The material connection, however, is made clear by Zola. This massive machinery requires an equally massive consumption of goods. As Zola describes it, there is no such certainty. Speculation involves increasingly massive outlays of commodity capital which threatens, at every moment, to lie unrealized. Given this constant gamble, in which Mouret constantly risks all, the engendering of consumption, in both senses of the word, is critical. Not only does Mouret seek to cater to an increasingly affluent group of bourgeois women, increasingly pre-occupied with notions of domesticity and beautification, he must also ensure that these customers buy as they have never bought before.

After explaining the expansionary logic of the modern retailing, he is asked how he proposes to 'keep up such a colossal sale' (Zola, 1992: 67). Mouret replies: 'We can sell what we like when we know how to sell!' (ibid: 68). As Management Horizons realized, the book is indeed an explication of 'how to sell'. Central to this strategy, it seems, is the configuration, annihilation and representation of space. To David Bell (1988), 'Mouret's first weapon is that of space' (Bell, 1988: 102). And indeed, the production and configuration of space within the emergent retail economy is a constant concern. Especially significant is Zola's attention not only to the internal spaces of the store itself, but also to the production of a series of interlocking spaces – urban, national and international – at the centre of which sits the store, the relations between which change with the rise of the store.

These geographies unfold throughout the novel. It is quickly made clear that questions of store design and layout are pivotal to Mouret's success. At the beginning of the novel, the reader is introduced to the spatial configuration of the store itself, as we walk through the store with Mouret on his round of inspection. This is quickly followed by a description of the use of display techniques during a sale. Mouret is a genius at layout and display, anticipating many contemporary discussions on strike zones, customer traffic and product exposure. While the traditional retailers foreswear showy advertisement, Mouret crafts an assertive and aggressive visual economy: 'Every one allowed the governor to be the best displayer in Paris, of a regular revolutionary stamp, who had founded the brutal and colossal school in the science of displaying' (Zola, 1992: 45). He has an obsession with colour, for example: the white sale, in which a profusion of white goods are draped everywhere, is characterized as 'vivified, colossal, burning' (ibid: 352). He criticizes one of his salesman who arranges silks to 'please the eyes'. 'Don't be afraid', he insists, 'blind them. Look! red, green, yellow' (ibid: 45). He delights 'in a tumbling of stuffs, as if they had fallen from the crowded shelves by chance, making them glow with the most ardent colours, lighting each other up by the contrast, declaring that the customers ought to have sore eyes on going out of the shop' (ibid: 45).

These brash and intoxicating displays, in which women lose themselves, are, however, insufficient. Mouret's success also rests on the fact that he was 'an unrivalled master . . . in the interior arrangement of the shops' (Zola, 1992: 209). He realizes the dangers of 'dead space', insisting that every corner of the store must be busy. By careful positioning of displays and restrictions on circulation he directs and manages the crowd. Bargains are placed at the entrance to encourage a crush 'so that the people in the street should mistake it for a riot' (ibid: 210) and be tempted in. He is seized with flashes of spatial insight: just before a sale he realizes that the 'orderly' and 'logical' layout of the store and its departments is 'wrong and stupid', and insists that it be repositioned. The problem, as he puts it, is that it would have 'localised the crowd. A woman would have come in, gone straight to the department she wished . . . then retired, without having lost herself for a moment' (ibid: 210). There is a need to disorder space so as to disorder and 'lose' the consumer. As Mouret explains it:

> Firstly, this continual circulation of customers disperses them all over the shop, multiplies them, and makes them lose their heads; secondly, as they must be conducted from one end of the establishment to the other ... these journeys in every direction triple the size of the house in their eyes; thirdly, they are forced to traverse departments where they would never have set foot otherwise, temptations present themselves on their passage, and they succumb. (Zola, 1992: 211)

These consuming geographies, however, are traced not only within the store but also in the face that is offered to the city. The exterior of the store is a dominant concern of the novel. At the very beginning of the book, a fresh and naive Denise Baudu arrives in Paris with her brothers. The first thing they encounter is the store itself, the windows of which offer up unheard of luxuries. 'That', breathes Baudu, '*is* a shop!' (Zola, 1992: 5). The evolution of the store itself can be traced in its extensions and remodellings. For the final sale of the book, Mouret creates a 'monumental facade . . . plate glass, nothing but glass . . . seemed to open up the depths of the halls and galleries to the full light of the day' (ibid: 346). A frieze depicts the names of goods and the arms of French towns, surmounted by an 'allegorical group . . . woman dressed and kissed by a flight of cupids' (ibid: 347).

Mouret's dream, Zola notes, is to have 'the street running through his shop' (Zola, 1992: 210). Increasingly, this becomes a reality. Not only does the shop open itself to the gaze of Paris, becoming a 'living advertisement . . . its windows large enough to display the entire poem of women's clothing' (ibid: 348), but Paris itself comes under the commercial gaze of Mouret himself. The reach of the store increases as people flood through the shop. At the end of the great white sale, the customers, laden down with goods, leave as 'a sort of continual enlargement, a spreading of the customers, carried off to the four corners of the city, emptying the building with the roaring clamour of a sluice' (ibid: 379). Bombarded by advertising, the store's fame begins to spread wide. One of the sixty-two trucks and vans of the store can even be come upon in the outlying countryside, 'throwing into the mysterious peacefulness . . . the loud advertisement of its varnished panels' (ibid: 300). An advertisement depicts the 'colossus' in:

> exaggerated immensity, . . . this lake of glass and zinc shining in the sun. Beyond, stretched forth Paris, but Paris diminished, eaten up by the monster: the houses, of a cottage-like humility in the neighbourhood of the building . . . to the left two dashes for Notre-Dame, to the right a circumflex accent for the Invalides, in the background the Panthéon, ashamed and lost, no larger than a lentil. The horizon crumbled into powder, became no more than a contemptible framework, as far as the heights of Châtillon, out into the open country, the vanishing expanse of which indicated how far reached the state of slavery. (Zola, 1992: 347–8)

As Bell (1988) notes, the development of the consumer space outside the store is bound up in the modernization of Parisian urban space itself. With the final grand extension of the store, the principal entrance is no longer on the Rue Neuve-Saint-Augustin, 'a dark street of old Paris', but moved to the newly carved Rue du Dix-Décembre, 'one of those modern avenues through which passed the busy crowd of the latter part of the nineteenth century' (Zola, 1992: 277). Given Hausmann's sweeping reconfiguration of Paris, this re-orientation has an especial spatial significance, according to Bell:

> Initially, outside the store, space is opaque, obstructed, full of accidents, while within the store itself space is clear, logical. . . . This interior transformation is accompanied by its opposite outside the store, [becoming] clear and susceptible to unhampered circulation as a result of the construction of the new boulevard. (Bell, 1988: 105)[2]

This is all part of Mouret's plan to dominate and subordinate Paris and its region. In fact the geography of the new consumer society becomes increasingly imperial and colonizing. Catalogues are sent abroad, translated into every language, such that the store fast becomes 'a household word all over the world' (Zola, 1992: 209). Store buyers are dispatched all over the globe, their booty being carefully assembled, commodified and packaged by Mouret. Reflecting the developing obsession with the 'Orient', fuelled by the Great Exhibitions of Europe, buyers begin 'ransacking the Far East, . . . pillaging the palaces and the temples' (ibid: 371). The carpet display plays on Orientalist notions of luxury and depravity: 'Turkey, Arabia, and the Indies were all there. They had emptied the palaces, plundered the mosques and bazaars' (ibid: 79). The 'harem-like' display of carpets evoked '[V]isions of the east . . . beneath the luxury of this barbarous art, amid the strong odour which the old wools had retained of the country of vermin and of the rising sun' (ibid: 79). Not only does the store come to annihilate distance, it is able to telescope it, such that the world can increasingly be found within the store. Distant places can be literally consumed; the world becomes known through its commodities.

'The need of blood'

The novel, then, documents the creation of a landscape of consumption. A store that is at once 'factory' and 'palace' comes to produce spaces that are both internal and external to the store. Such is the potency of these retail geographies that the store is able not only to configure space, but also to collapse it, drawing consumers and commodities from increasingly far-afield and managing both to its own ends. The similarities with today's retail geographies are striking. We need only think of the retail atrium or mall as a logical extension of Mouret's spatial imagination (Ferguson, 1992). Similarly, the incessant spatial reconfiguration of in-store space reflects many of the principles so presciently outlined by Zola, as does the production of 'elsewhereness' by retailers (J Hopkins, 1990). The attention given to both the spaces within the store and the larger urban context is also a welcome one. Too frequently, retail geographers seem to regard the internal geographies of the store as beyond their ambit, whereas many cultural historians of shopping focus exclusively on the store, without an attention to its urban situation (Lawrence, 1992).

However, Zola maps another geography. The novel is unstinting in tracking the dark side of the vortex unleashed by retail capitalism. Consumption, as Rosalind Williams (1982) reminds us, has at least two meanings. Not only does it connote a summation (given the Latin root *cum summa*) or an attainment, achieved through the purchase of commodities, but also it implies a 'using up' or a 'wasting away'. Consumption can thus imply death, decay and disease. The resultant ambiguity, in which consumption comes to imply both 'achievement and destruction, . . . submission to entropy and triumph over it' (R Williams, 1982: 7) plays itself out in the book and, I would suggest, in our contemporary landscapes. Zola, fascinated as he was with the pairing of death and rebirth, life and decay, makes full use of the paradox of consumption, inscribing it upon the very bodies and spaces of his novel.

The tension is foreshadowed at the very outset of the novel. Denise Baudu and her brothers, in search of their shopkeeper uncle, turn from their first encounter with Au Bonheur des Dames to find his drapers immediately opposite the department store. The contrast between the two could not be more pronounced. Whereas the department store is 'colourful, 'endless', 'bursting with goods' and 'delicious', the 'Old Elbeuf' is 'ancient', 'flat and unadorned'. Her eyes 'full of the light airy windows at the Ladies' Paradise', Denise Baudu is struck by the shop, 'crushed by the ceiling, surmounted by a very low storey with half-moon windows, of a prison-like appearance'. Two deep windows, black and dusty, barely revealed the 'heaped-up goods' inside (Zola, 1992: 9). The contrast between the outmoded and dark traditional shops and the emergent spaces of the department store is constantly invoked, as are the very different commercial strategies.

Inevitably, of course, the older stores and their petit bourgeois shopkeepers are consumed by the department stores. Their businesses collapse, their families are disrupted and divided, their buildings (in one case) are literally ingested by the expanding Au Bonheur, which threatens to 'cover the neighbourhood with its roof' (Zola, 1992: 194). One failed shopkeeper hurls himself under an omnibus in despair, while an umbrella merchant is driven to monomania and obsession. M. Baudu's daughter Genevieve, literally 'wastes away' as her betrothed moves his affections to an unattainable shopgirl from Au Bonheur: on her death-bed she reveals her body, 'a bride's body used up by waiting' (ibid: 325), to Denise. In a perverse echo of the Commune, her funeral march parades her body 'around the big shops like the first victim fallen in time of revolution' (ibid: 328). It is a revolution, of course, but it is Mouret, not Genevieve, who is the revolutionary to Zola.[3] In a final apocalyptic vision, Denise imagines all the traditional stores 'disappearing beneath an invisible pick, with a brusque, thundering noise, as of a tumbril being emptied' (ibid: 333). She views this with a 'resigned melancholy'; although tragic and painful, it seemed that

> the necessity of the world to fatten on death . . . was right, . . . all this misery was necessary for the health of the Paris of the future . . . it was the need of blood that every revolution exacted from its martyrs, every step forward was made over the bodies of the dead. (Zola, 1992: 333)

Zola offers a powerful and evocative description of the creative and destructive logic of capitalism, whereby capitalism builds itself a landscape appropriate to one point of time, only to have to destroy it as conditions change. This spatial whirlwind appears ineluctable. He also manages to evoke the temporal compression of modern retail restructuring: a retail revolution that, in fact, took several decades is compressed into five short years (1864–9). The unstoppable temporal logic of sales, inventories and extensions generates a frenzied cycle of capitalist accumulation and expansion. The temporal and spatial rhythms of this process, in this present round of retail restructuring, are still very much in evidence (see Wrigley, 1993a).

Masculinities, space and power

But the novel is, as the University of California Press recognizes, much more than a novel about 'commerce'. Zola, in general, and *Au Bonheur des Dames* in particular, have been revisited by a growing number of feminists and cultural historians, deploying his insights in a very different fashion than Management Horizons. It is to the novel that writers have turned to unpack the construction of 'femininity' in the nineteenth-century city, arguing that there are many contemporary echoes. Femininity necessarily implies certain notions of masculinity, however, which I hope to explore, as well as noting the connections to the retail spaces outlined above.

In her preface, Kristin Ross boldly suggests that of the twenty novels that make up the Rougon-Macquart series, only *Nana* can compete with *Au Bonheur des Dames* 'for the attention of contemporary readers' (Zola, 1992: v). Certainly, the latter has been invoked and explored by a range of writers such that mention seems increasingly *de rigueur* in any historical analysis of consumption and gender. For two very different authors – Elizabeth Wilson (1991; 1992) and Richard Sennett (1977) – the rise of stores such as Au Bonheur reveals certain things concerning the formation of the public and private world. For Sennett, it is paradigmatic of the secularization, demystification and passivity of public space. For Wilson, these new spaces are at once oppressive and liberating for women. 'In the department store', she suggests, 'a woman, too, could become a flâneur' (Wilson, 1992: 100). Rosalind Williams (1982) and Rachel Bowlby (1985; 1987) pay greater attention to consumption itself. Williams uses Zola to explore the advent of mass consumption and its attendant ambiguities, linking the department store to the increasingly commodified and 'dream-like' world of cinema and the exhibitions. Bowlby is more expressly concerned with the role of women in this new commercial world, exploring 'the forms of modern consumer subjectivity and the making of willing female consumers' (Bowlby, 1985: 11). The rise of the department store marks off two domains, masculine and feminine: it is to the latter that Bowlby directs her attention, exploring Zola's novel as a documentation of a 'colonization of the mind' (Bowlby, 1985: 70). She describes the desire and fascination, seduction and conquest, fear and longing that the new commodities generate, whereby women are objectified and fragmented. To Bowlby, Zola's novel is about 'Women and money; ideologies of femininity and ideologies of consumption' (Bowlby, 1985: 66).

To say that the novel is about women and money is accurate, but partial. It is also, as Bowlby implies, about *men* and money. Moreover, if it is about men it is also about the geographies of men. Let me be clear: I do not mean that the novel does not concern women. This would be inaccurate at best, and imperialist at worst. To say that the novel concerns masculinity, however, speaks of the necessary relation between masculinity and femininity – such that masculinity does not derive from any intrinsic character of men but, as Segal (1990) notes, from what men are supposedly *not*.

At first glance, masculinity seems far removed from *Au Bonheur*. Department stores have frequently been cast as feminine spaces. To Benson (1986), they were the 'Adamless Eden', in which women appeared omnipresent, even triumphant. Certainly, Au Bonheur, as its name suggests, appears femininized. Not only does Mouret offer endless diversions targeted at women (such as a children's section, writing rooms and other amenities), but also the pleasures of consumption are deemed peculiarly feminine. At the height of the second sale, for example, the women reign supreme, the salesmen becoming their slaves, 'of whom they disposed with a sovereign's tyranny' (Zola, 1992: 236). The women revel in their new bourgeois wealth and the relative independence that it gives them, ignoring the concerns of their husbands. Male consumers appear notable by their absence in the store. If they are present, they are like children in tow, 'buried beneath the overflow of bosoms, casting anxious glances around them' (ibid: 214).

However important is the construction of femininity, it must not be forgotten that the store is also a masculine space. Not only are the majority of the workers men, but also the geographies of the store itself are powerfully masculine. The spatial logic of the store and its spreading reach across Paris and the world is structured not simply according to the imperatives of capital accumulation, but also in relation to specific conceptions of 'manly' sexuality and identity. The economic geographies of the novel, in other words, are innately gendered.

We can see this when we return to the first characterization of the novel; as a racy, almost pornographic pot-boiler. Pornography it is not; but Zola is indeed explicit in his depiction of sexuality.[4] Sexual liaisons, sexed rumour and gossip, sexual metaphors and *double entendres*, and sexed bodies reoccur, often in striking and unusual juxtapositions. As a relation, this sexuality operates largely one-way: it is men talking about, lusting after and depicting women. By way of introduction, we can get a sense of both from Zola's discussion of a sale:

> A fine dust rose from the floor, laden with the odour of woman, the odour of her linen and her bust, of her skirts and her hair, an invading, penetrating odour, which seemed to be the incense of this temple raised for the worship

of her body. . . . Mouret . . . was inhaling this odour, intoxicating himself with it, and repeating: They are quite at home. I know some who spend the whole day here, eating cakes and writing their letters. There's only one thing more to do, and that is, to find them beds'. (Zola, 1922: 225–6)

Masculinity here becomes linked to patriarchy: it operates as a power relation by which women are oppressed through forms of physical, material and discursive marginalization and dominance. Masculinity also implies a power relation *vis-à-vis* other men, of course: it is something made, not found – reproduced in multiple settings. This can certainly entail an oppression of gay men, engaged in suspect, threatening and unmanly behaviour; it can also entail a specific form of oppression for heterosexual men, forced to (and, it should be noted, rewarded for) conformity to a cultural and historical model of self-identity and sociality. In my culture, this entails the valuation of emotional and physical self-control, rationality, sexual 'performance' and 'ladsmanship'. Masculinity then, operates as a form of power *and* of knowledge. It is one, however, that should not be deemed monolithic, static or closed. As has been noted (Cocks, 1989; Jackson, 1991a), it is best to think of *masculinities*, recognizing the plurality of subject positions open (more or less) to men, as well as some of the recent transitions in the male code (Segal, 1990).

And such masculinities are geographic, it seems. Peter Jackson (1991a; 1991b) has begun to explore the 'social geographies' of masculinities, noting the manner in which they are constituted and challenged in specific spatial settings (or 'gender regimes') such as the workplace. Burrell and Hearn (1989: 18) allude to the 'spatial relations' bound up in (phallocentric) sexuality, noting their role as settings within which specific sexual practices are performed, as well as the manner in which space itself (such as a red-light district) can be produced in the process. Jeff Hearn (1992) has also drawn attention to the link between masculinity, the rise of large organizations, public and private, and the mapping of the 'public' domain. Heeding Jackson's call for an exposure of the 'spatial structures that support and maintain [masculinity's] dominant forms' (Jackson, 1991a: 210) remains an urgent and under-theorized task, however.

Retail geography, of course, has begun to grapple with questions of gender, usually linking it to the geography of women. Nevertheless, some intriguing insights have been drawn, recognizing that women have long been cast as consumers and, increasingly, play a role as retail workers. This is to be welcomed: the question of masculinity and retail geography remains, however, unexplored. This is not entirely accurate, of course: one can argue that retail geography's intellectual history unwittingly reveals its constitution as a male discipline, concerned with women. This can operate very visibly: the conventional use of the female pronoun in reference to consumers in the marketing literature is one particularly striking example. The consumer choice literature can, perhaps, be re-read as an extended interrogation of Freud's famous question: 'What is it that women want?' Adopting a rationalistic (and arguably masculine) language, (mostly) male researchers have concerned themselves with the rationalities and subjectivities of (mostly) women consumers. The virgin/whore dualism, so often used to characterize women, perhaps re-emerges within the marketing literature in the frequent depiction of (women) consumers as *either* rational, scheming, savvy shoppers *or* as irrational, flighty and given to 'impulse' purchases. Either way, however, it is assumed that women can be made into consumers: indeed are, *by definition*, consumers (see Firat *et al*, 1987). '[W]e can control the customer', one American design analyst ominously puts it, 'both emotionally and psychologically' (*Chain Store Age Executive*, 1985).

The geographies of masculinity are very much in evidence in the Ladies' Paradise, personified most powerfully in the figure of Mouret who, in contrast to Denise Baudu, is painted in striking and vivid colours. Mouret, as his very name implies, conforms to his self-image of a 'man of love', priding himself on his 'amorous' adventures. We are first introduced to him returning to the store in the early morning, fresh from a night on the town with a friend and two women, 'picked up behind the scenes of a small theatre' (Zola, 1992: 30). He boasts of his night with 'little Héloise, of the Folly. Stupid as a donkey, but so comical!' (ibid: 32). Like others of the male staff, he pursues members of his female subordinate staff, maintaining several mistresses, including the haute Mme Desforges and the declassé shopgirl, Clara. He confesses that there have been 'some women who've bothered me awfully. . . . But when I've got hold of one, I keep her. She doesn't always escape me, and then I take my share, I assure you' (ibid: 61). He begins to pursue Denise Baudu with his normal combination of threat and enticement. Her persistent refusal, however, drives him to obsession, only making her more desirable. Like a commodity, he craves possession, increasing his price with every refusal. 'This was the first one' he complains, 'who did not yield. He only had to stoop and pick up the others, they all awaited his pleasure like submissive slaves. . . . Perhaps he had not offered enough, he thought, and he doubled his offers' (ibid: 265). Still she resists. This 'defeat of the master' incites/excites him further:

> 'And yet if I liked –' said he in an ardent voice, seizing her hands. . . . 'I will! I will!' repeated he, in his passionate excitement. 'I expect you to-night, otherwise I will take measures.' (Zola, 1992: 265–6)

Such masculine sexual strategies, Zola implies, are bound up in Mouret's commercial gambits. He claims to be especially skilled in love-making – he was 'seduction itself'. Although he professes to worship women, he maintains an almost clinical poise. He insists that he understands women, noting that one needs to 'excite', inflame' and 'flatter' them. When talking to women he adopts a different persona, speaking 'in a soft, sweet voice, an actor's voice' (Zola, 1992: 71). He is frequently in the company of women, either as a sexual or a commercial actor. The boundaries between the two, it should be noted, are frequently blurred. On one occasion, indeed, he is depicted as a woman himself, to the extent that he is in possession of 'their secret': that is, their fascination with commodities. In the same breath, however, Zola reminds us that he 'still remained their master' (ibid: 75). Surrounded by women, he maintains a carefully crafted distance from their 'overpowering' sensuality and threatening femininity. He was 'strong enough to play with woman . . . without being overcome by the intoxication which she exhales' (ibid: 72).

This familiar masculine distancing, in which women are deemed fascinating yet threatening, is central to his retail tactics. Again and again we are reminded of the degree to which his fortune is premised on 'women's flesh and blood' (Zola, 1992: 68). If the great machine is premised on the expansion of consumption, it is women who fuel that process. 'Doesn't Paris belong to the women', asks Mouret, 'and don't the women belong to us?' (ibid: 279). It is women who make up the great crowds – appearing irrational, driven and vaguely threatening – who sweep through the halls of the store (Schor, 1978). It is women who are tempted, captured and seduced by the new commodities, artfully displayed.

As implied, this process is depicted in masculine terms. As Mouret seduces his lovers, so he seduces his clientele. His price reductions, advertisements and temptations are cast as 'endless gallantries' (Zola, 1992: 237). At Au Bonheur, Mouret notes, 'we really love our customers' (ibid: 288). His 'fresh love affairs' served, Zola notes, 'as an advertisement for his business. One would have said that he enveloped all the women in the same caress, the better to bewilder them and keep them at his mercy' (ibid: 32). However, in much the same way that masculine 'gallantries' come freighted with a baggage, so Mouret's seductions are oppressive and politicized. The masculine space of the store is at once a cathedral to femininity, and a prison. The seductive act of consumption, then, was like seduction itself: double-edged. The linkage is made clear in the metaphors of prostitution and despoliation that re-occur: 'if woman reigned in their shops like a queen, she was an amorous one, on whom her subjects traffic' (ibid: 69). Mouret himself, professing to merely meet the awakening needs of women, is also cast in masculine terms: 'behind her back, when he had emptied her purse and shattered her nerves, he was as full of the secret scorn of man to whom a woman had just been stupid enough to yield herself' (ibid: 70).

The configuration of the internal spaces of the store reveal the degree to which this ostensibly Adamless Eden is constructed under a sexualized and voyeuristic male gaze. The descriptions of Mouret's commodity displays are lush, tactile. Although women are made to revel in these new commodities, losing themselves in their sensuality, the language is conceived in masculine terms. The commodities offer themselves up to women who, in turn, offer themselves up to an invisible but omnipresent masculine observer. Confronted by commodities, women consumers are depicted as gripped by the 'greatest ardour' (Zola, 1992: 105) and 'sensual joy' (ibid: 98), 'trembling with desire' and 'agitated by passion' (ibid: 98).

at the outfitting counter, there was an indiscreet unpacking, women turned round and viewed on all sides . . . an alcove publicly open, of which the concealed luxury . . . became a sort of sexual depravation, as it developed into costly fantasies. Woman was dressing herself again, the white wave of this fall of linen was returning again to the shivering mystery of the petticoats, the chemise stiffened by the fingers of the workwomen, . . . all this cambric and muslin, dead, scattered over the counters, . . . was going to become living with the life of the flesh, odorous and warm with the odour of love, a white cloud become sacred, bathed in night, and of which the least flutter, the pink of a knee disclosed through the whiteness ravaged the world. (Zola, 1992: 363–4)

As the commodity itself is positioned within Mouret's visual economy, so 'Woman' herself is positioned within a wider visualization gathering pace during the late nineteenth century (via the development of photography, and the explosion in printed media and film). To Hearn (1992), the visual increasingly emerges as 'connective, narrative social form' of masculinity (ibid: 197), whereby direct sensual sex(uality) is increasingly divorced from visual sex(uality). 'Sexuality' he suggests, 'could be the conjunction, or more likely disjunction, of sensual pleasure and distanced, separated looking' (ibid: 198).

Such distanced looking is evident in more immediate terms within the store. The male staff constantly engage in the sexist boasting and badinage so common in the masculine workplace. Sexual boasting, flirting and the appraisal of women – whether fellow workers or customers – is common. Sexual harassment of women workers is common, and is not confined only to Mouret. In one especially telling phrase, several male clerks 'take stock' of Baudu when she first arrives at the store. As rumours fly concerning her relationship with Mouret, she feels herself 'disrobed' (Zola, 1992: 261) by the male workers. The women workers are also 'constantly occupied by their affairs with the men' (ibid: 117); however, in their case this seems to be largely a function of the economic security offered by a male lover.

This sexualization continues outside the store. Modernity and the expanding store are coded as masculine – virile, assertive and expansive. As Mouret possesses the women within Au Bonheur, so he lays claim to all of Paris, dominating the landscape. The women carved into the newly remodelled facade conceal a rapacious appetite, conquering space. It is no accident that one old merchant defends his threatened shop 'as a young girl defends her virtue, for honour's sake' (Zola, 1992: 178). He turns down Mouret's bids for his site, complaining that 'They think I'm going to sell myself like a prostitute' (ibid: 183).

'I'd like to dress her all over'

Zola's retail geography, then, could be said to be an unrelenting one. An aggressive masculinity dominates both through the figure of Mouret, seducer and despoiler of women, through the men staff and the male gaze. The consumption spaces within and beyond the store are far from passive, or merely commercial. If they are femininized, offering a site for female *flânerie*, they are also constructed by men. If the spaces offer a 'new religion' for 'a nation of women', the deity is a phallic one. Mouret's rampant power is cast as intoxicating. While mourning the demise of the traditional retail landscape, Denise Baudu is hypnotized by his spatial potency:

> Mouret had invented this mechanism for crushing the world, and its brutal working shocked her; he had sown ruin all over the neighbourhood, despoiled some, killed others; and yet she loved him for the grandeur of his work, she loved him still more at every excess of his power. (Zola, 1992: 345)

Such an unrelenting reading is, indeed, a provocative one for a new retail geography. However, there is more to Zola's reading – and his potential for a reconstructed retail geography – than that. While he does offer an account of a triumphant masculinity, in which masculine and commercial imperatives dovetail, a closer reading reveals that the masculinity of the novel is, in fact, multiple, fractured and far from certain (cf Jackson, 1991a; Segal, 1990).

One is reminded, for example, of the degree to which masculinity is never guaranteed, but must be constantly reproduced. Many men find it hard to conform to this rigorous coding. They include characters such as Lhomme, the chief cashier. He is cast as emasculated: one-armed, he is subservient to his wife and son, and is carried away not by women but by the effete pleasures of music. 'One would think', one of the female shop workers exclaims, as she espies him hurrying to a music rehearsal, that 'he was running to meet his girl' (Zola, 1992: 125). Another failed patriarch is old Baudu, the shopkeeper. Unable to provide for his family, it shatters and dies. His patriarchy gives way under the onslaught of Mouret's new patriarchy, across the road. The salesclerk Deloche also confesses his masculine anxieties and failures to Denise Baudu: 'When one does not know how to rob other fellows of their mistresses, and when one is too awkward to earn as much as the others, why the best thing is to go into some corner and die' (ibid: 132). Although masculinity works to oppress women, through patriarchy, it can also be oppressive to men.

On several occasions, Zola hints at the implication of these fractured masculinities in the geography of retail capital accumulation. It is especially notable, for example, that Mouret explains his commercial secret only twice, to two very different men. One encounter is with the financier Hartmann. In this case, shared masculine codes become the common currency between the two men. Mouret is easily able to forge a business bond with Hartmann given their shared possession of Mme Desforges. She is mistress to them both: as such, they are assured of 'the amiable connection of a woman, so powerful between men of a gallant nature' (Zola, 1992: 65). As Rachel Bowlby (1985: 79) notes, women are reduced to a mere 'relational instrument' in a discourse of masculine sexuality. Mouret whispers his business secrets as if they were the 'amorous secrets that men sometimes risk among themselves' (Zola,

1992: 69). Hartmann, whose 'eyes twinkle knowingly', is quick to grasp Mouret's 'gallant exploitation' of women. It inflames him, stirring up memories of 'his past life of pleasure' (ibid: 70). Mouret's second exposition, however, is very different. It is to Paul de Vallagnosc, an old acquaintance, who is cast as languid and fatalistic with an 'effeminate voice' (ibid: 286). The encounter between the two, in contrast, is almost adversarial and combative, as the thrusting masculinity of the one is goaded by the suspect passivity of the other. Mouret derides 'the despairing ones, the pessimists, all those weak, sickly members of our budding sciences, who assumed the weeping airs of poets, or the mincing ways of sceptics, amidst the immense activity of the present day' (ibid: 61). The edge to Mouret's indictment, perhaps, betokens the anxiety with which he perceives these other masculine models. Masculinity is constructed less in relation to femininity amongst women, in this case, as amongst men.

But there are other ambiguities in the sexuality outlined by Zola. Masculine sexuality itself is cast as increasingly caught up in and mediated by the world of commodities. Time and again, the metaphors of sex and seduction are used interchangeably in the depiction of consumption. At one especially arresting moment the salesclerk Mignot attempts to sell some gloves to Mme Desforges. While the metaphors are those of seduction, it is the *enclothing* of the woman that occupies Mignot's mind:

> Half lying on the counter, he was holding her hand, taking the fingers one by one, slipping the glove on with a long, renewed, and persistently caressing air, looking at her as if he expected to see in her face the signs of a voluptuous joy. . . . When she had gone away, Mignot turned towards his neighbour and winked, and would have liked him to believe that wonderful things had just taken place.
> 'By Jove! I'd like to dress her all over!' said he, coarsely. (Zola, 1992: 90–1)

The male gaze, in Zola's world, passes through a commodified filter. Even the voyeuristic masculine 'look', present in the descriptions of product display, merges the sensuality of the feminized body with the desirability of the commodity. Although the silk department, for example, is described as like 'a great chamber of love', the language undergoes a transformation as the body itself becomes a commodity: 'All the milky tones of an adored person were there, from the velvet of the hips, to the fine silk of the thighs and the shining satin of the bosom' (ibid: 366).

Although offering an account of both the economic and cultural logic of retailing and consumption, Zola makes it hard for us to read from one to the other. We are left, as a consequence, uncertain. What is it that maintains Mouret's 'giant aspiration'? It is clearly not an androgynous 'capitalist logic', coolly and clinically producing and annihilating space. Nor, however, is it merely an uncomplicated masculine sexuality, in which a singular and ahistorical masculinity positions, produces and seduces women. Mouret can claim at one moment that 'it is not so much the women, for to speak truly, I don't care a hang for them; it's the wish to act, to create, in short' (ibid: 61). Yet he also reveals the implication of his sexuality in his commercial drive, exclaiming to de Vallagnosc that if Denise Baudu escapes him, 'you'll see what a place I shall have built to cure myself. . . . To act, to create . . .!' (ibid: 286).

The problem – and the potential – of Zola's retail geography is that categories such as 'economy' or 'culture' are constantly being shattered. The two seem mutually implicated, with both of them expressed in and mediated by the multiple geographies of retailing.[5] It is precisely because of this that his account offers potential for a reconstructed retail geography.

I have often been struck that retail geography could be – should be – one of the most interesting of sub-disciplines, given the subtlety and importance of retail capital, consumption and space. Unfortunately, it had been made into one of the most boring of fields. Perhaps Zola offers us the means by which we can begin to recover its full potential.

Notes

1   In saying this, I am not seeking to 'colonize' Zola; if I call him a retail geographer this is as much a criticism of the present discipline as it is an attempt to extend the boundaries. I am also using Zola as more than a convenient peg to hang my analysis: I want to argue for his importance in his own right.

2   Bell argues that the significance cuts deeper, establishing a linkage between Mouret as speculator and the figure of Napoleon III. Both, he suggests, are masters at crowd control, Mouret through entrapment, direction and provocation, and Napoleon through his wide, sweeping avenues. It is also no accident, Bell argues, that Mouret's store fronts on the Rue du Dix-Décembre. The street commemorates Napoleon's first great victory; his election to the presidency on 10 December 1848. The Société due Dix-Décembre emerged after the event as a semi-political paramilitary pro-Bonapartist faction. The street also figures in other of Zola's novels, running to the stock exchange, the locus of his *L'Argent*.

3   Appropriately enough, a 1929 Soviet film entitled *New Babylon* draws upon the novel, collapsing the narrative of the department store into that of the Paris Commune; in one especially striking scene, grand pianos are pushed through the store windows to be used as barricades.

4   Although, if we adopt Brittan's (1989) characterization, the novel may well be deemed pornographic, or at least a *documentation* of a pornography. For Brittan, pornography is not simply about 'distorted male sexuality, but about power and transcendence. . . . It always presumes a view of women as an object of male transcendence. Put another way, pornography is an articulation of a privileged male discourse' (1989: 67).

5   The work of writers such as Brittan (1989), Hearn (1992), Knopp (1992) and Connell (1987) is perhaps useful here. They argue that masculinity and sexuality are fundamental components of capitalism, yet the one cannot be reduced to the other. For Brittan, although capitalism and masculinity may appear to have an 'elective affinity', the link is never straightforward. The two may coexist or conflict, depending on historical circumstance.

CHAPTER 14

The feminized retail landscape: gender ideology and consumer culture in nineteenth-century New York City

Mona Domosh

That women constitute the major class of consumers in modern, western society is a fact that appears almost uncontestable in our everyday discourse and that is confirmed by our own personal experiences and observations. Men certainly participate in retailing activity, both as owners and workers in retail shops and department stores, and as consumers of their own goods, but women's involvement in retailing is more complex and meaningful. Consumption has often been seen as a defining characteristic of femininity, and has played a key role in shaping women's social and economic activities. Indeed, the association of consumption with women and femininity is long-lived; research indicates that from the eighteenth century onwards, and perhaps earlier, women in Western societies were often assigned the tasks of material procurement even as they were involved in home production and reproduction (Laermans, 1993; Landes, 1988; Glennie and Thrift, this volume, Chapter 12). Industrialization and the creation of a meaningful consumer culture in the nineteenth century further strengthened and elaborated this association. In addition, the nineteenth century witnessed the development of department stores, arguably the most visible, urban representations of consumer culture and the economics of mass production and selling. And here, in these palaces of consumption, the large numbers of women combined with the incredible array and display of goods, recreated and reinforced the association of women, shopping and the values and qualities that were being used to define nineteenth-century notions of femininity and consumption. The relationship between modern consumer culture, the rise of the department store and traditional notions of femininity and masculinity is currently being explored by a wide range of scholars (Abelson, 1989; Benson, 1986; Dowling, 1993; Reekie, 1993; Blomley, this volume, Chapter 13). This research into historical and contemporary consumer activity has demonstrated that retailing needs to be understood both as a cultural and an economic construct, and that assumptions regarding gender roles and consumption cannot remain unexamined. In this chapter, I shall take this argument further by suggesting that the cultural landscape of retailing, the very spaces in which it operates, is fundamentally shaped by the relationship between gender ideology and the development of modern consumer culture. I argue that the historical construction of linkages between two seemingly disparate categories – femininity and consumption – was neither coincidental nor without due cause, but in fact served a very particular purpose for US nineteenth-century society. These two categories were defined in relation to each other – the designation and definition of what we now refer to as the domestic sphere in the nineteenth century was integral to the development and meaning of the consumptive sphere, and vice versa. In addition, I suggest that this mutual self-definition took place in, and had significant impacts upon, the new consumer landscapes of large US cities in the nineteenth century. These spaces of consumption participated in the definitions and meanings assigned to consumer life, and in the association of consumer activities with the construction of notions of femininity and the domestic sphere. Specifically, I shall examine the development of the new retailing space in mid-nineteenth-century New York City, focusing on the city's major department stores. What I hope to provide is an overview of one of the more important episodes in the cultural history and cultural geography of retailing in the United States.

Women in the city

New Yorker Harriet Richards wrote in her diary in 1885 that she went shopping four times in one nine-day period. Later that year, in May, she mentioned shopping as one of her activities on six out of eight days, usually at Macy's (Abelson, 1989). Clara Pardee, another middle-class New Yorker, wrote in her diary that she went downtown to shop in the morning and in the afternoon, returning home for lunch, both on the second and third of May 1893. She shopped again on the eighth and again on the eleventh (Abelson, 1989). Both women went downtown often, and although shopping was one of their most frequent activities, they also met for church prayer groups, to attend lectures or concerts, to pay bills, to make social calls. For middle-class women in the nineteenth century, home was not the refuge it was for men – it was their workplace and often their battleground. For these women, the city streets offered a form of refuge, an escape from their domestic work. As Elaine Abelson writes: 'Rather than posing a threat to these women or their families, the city streets had become an arena for action' (Abelson, 1989: 20).

This presents an inversion of our understanding of the separate spheres in the nineteenth century: home, we have been led to think, was the women's world, while men inhabited and controlled the public arena of the city streets. But as social historians and others continue to explore the reality of middle-class women's lives (Abelson, 1989; Davidoff and Hall, 1987), it is becoming clear that women were important participants in the reshaping of American downtowns in the nineteenth century, albeit participants in a process over which they had little control. Although some have argued that this urban participation was emancipatory for women (Leach, 1984), it is difficult to suggest that this was its guiding principle. Indeed, it seems likely that women's participation in the new public life of the city helped to maintain the existing social order. As literary historian Ann Douglas argues (1977), the full articulation of separate spheres in the nineteenth century – an articulation that associated women with the culture of consumption and therefore provided women with one form of access to the public areas of the city (the retailing district) – served to legitimize the reigning economic–social order in a set of complex ways. Women served Victorian society not only as the keepers of its sentiments, but also as the repository of its commodities. Women were to be both saints and consumers: both roles helped legitimize the economic processes. As saints, women could represent the values that gave a humane face to an increasingly inhuman world; and as consumers, women could act to keep the assembly lines running while not denying society's cultural commitment to the values of production. Douglas explains:

> the lady's function in a capitalist society was to appropriate and preserve both the values and commodities which her competitive husband, father, and son had little time to honor or enjoy; she was to provide an antidote and a purpose for their labor. (Douglas, 1977: 60)

As the largest class of consumers in the city, women, and the qualities ascribed to them by nineteenth-century society, played significant roles in the shaping of the North American city. Women and the feminine were important agents in the development of the nineteenth-century retailing district in Manhattan, and the landscape they helped to create reveals many of the contradictions and tensions in the social construction of the middle class in the mid-nineteenth century.

Women as consumers

Women were targeted as the new consumers of the mid-nineteenth-century United States. As early as 1846, accounts of the opening of Stewart's department store mentioned women as an established consumer class. The *New York Herald* stated that inside the store, 'we found the ladies, as usual, busy pricing goods and feasting their eyes on the profusion of gorgeous articles for sale' (*New York Herald*, 22 September 1846: 2). The opening of the store prompted another commentator to suggest that much of women's time was spent shopping:

> Half the time of the fashionable ladies of New York, at the lowest calculation, is spent in the dry goods store, in laying out plans for personal decoration. Dress forms a subject of the most grave and serious contemplation. It may be said to be the first thing they think of in the morning, and the last at night – nay, it is not the subject of the dream. (*New York Herald*, 26 September 1846: 2)

According to Elaine Abelson (1989), shopping became almost a daily ritual for middle-class women, taking up a disproportionate share of their time. Shopping, in essence, had become a major form of women's work. This new activity increasingly replaced traditional women's labour in food and clothing production. Throughout the nineteenth century, a new ideology of middle-class life dictated that home production of clothing was no longer socially acceptable (Blumin, 1989). The United States' industrial powers needed new markets and new products to keep their ever-expanding factories running profitably, and commodification of the home provided seemingly endless possibilities. The Civil War fuelled increasing industrial production in the north, and when the war ended, those industries sought different outlets to keep their factories running at capacity (Bernstein, 1990). By the end of the nineteenth century, then, food, shelter, clothing and home furnishing had all become commodities. The work of middle and upper-class women shifted from domestic production to public consumption.

The development of the ready-to-wear clothing industry, and with it, the introduction of the notion of fashion to the middle classes, had sweeping impacts on industrial growth and the retailing trade. Although complete ready-to-wear clothing was not available until the 1870s, merchants had spent years using advertising and other sales techniques to convince women that factory-purchased clothing was better, cheaper, and simply more modern than home-made clothing (Blumin, 1989; Leach, 1984). They appealed to a woman's sense of duty to provide the best up-to-date care for her family, as well as to the status that was associated with the most stylish clothing. Yet this fundamental change in how people led their lives, a change that convinced most middle-class women that ready-to-wear clothes were better than what they made at home, was not sufficient to maintain the constant increase in sales demanded by dry goods manufacturers and merchants. Sales, therefore, were kept high by creating a situation of open-ended demand, in other words, by introducing and making available fashion to middle-class life. The dictates of fashion led to perpetual changes in style, and therefore built-in obsolescence. For wealthy women, this meant that, at a minimum, they needed a new wardrobe each season, and, to be truly fashionable, that wardrobe had to include an outfit appropriate for every distinctive occasion. By the late 1870s, a woman could find ads in such magazines as *Harper's Weekly* and *Harper's Bazar* for clothing appropriate for every occasion: for promenades, carriage rides, and walking; for in the house, receiving guests, and dinner; for going out in the evening; for riding, skating, visiting the seaside, and for travelling and getting married. For children, each age group carried with it appropriate garb. To give some sense of what sort of production this demand fuelled, it is estimated that one elegant evening dress in the 1860s required approximately 1100 yards of fabric (Gardner, 1984). An 1872 guide to New York estimated that it was not unusual for fashionable women to have wardrobes worth over $20 000 (McCabe, 1971/1872). A description of the dress worn by one of these women to a charity ball should set the scene:

There was a rich blue satin skirt, en train. Over this there was looped up a magnificent brocade silk, white, with bouquets of flowers woven in all the natural colors. This overskirt was deeply flounced with costly white lace, caught up with bunches of feathers of bright colors. About her shoulders was thrown a 1500 dollar shawl. She had a head-dress of white ostrich feathers, white lace, gold pendants, and purple velvet. Add to this a fan, a bouquet of rare flowers, a lace handkerchief, and jewelry almost beyond estimate, and you see [her] as she appears when full blown. (McCabe, 1872: 143)

These are certainly extreme examples from the very wealthy of New York, but these elite women set the tone and style for middle-class women to emulate. She might not be able to afford gold jewellery or an overskirt completely done in lace, but a middle-class woman could have touches of lace on her dress, and at least a small token of appropriate jewellery. The point was to maintain vigilance and be aware of all fashion changes. Constant consumption, therefore, was required of the middle-class woman, not only because the appearance of herself and her family acted as important indicators of social status, but also because correct consumption also served as reflections of her role as mother and wife. Shopping had become such an onerous occupation for some women that New Yorker Clara Pardee wrote in her diary in 1893: 'I am so sick of the stores and clothes . . . would rather the clothes grew on like feathers!'(Abelson, 1989: 40).

Department stores played an important role in this new consumerism. In the nineteenth century, the needs of department stores for high-volume sales reinforced the fashion industry: perpetual changes in style required constant consumption. Department stores, therefore, became active participants in the fashion world, as they fuelled demand by displaying fashion alternatives in a setting that imbued those commodities with social meaning. At the same time, department stores, because they sold mass-produced and therefore less expensive items, made available to more women the possibility of being fashionable. This further stimulated production, which led, of course, to new demands for consumption and vice versa. Department store owners did their best to cater to their major consumers, women.

In New York, where social status was, for most people, always subject to negotiation, the culture of consumerism was of critical interest. And for women, fashion was of particular interest, because fashion allows one to display status independent of occupation or position. A man's status could be displayed by his job, or membership of a club, or his relative position in a particular segment of society. A woman's status was dependent on a man's, either as his wife or child or mother. Fashion, however, was a status indicator that was specific to the woman. Her choice of styles, fabrics and colours were indeed her decisions and therefore indicative of her 'good' taste, and hence of her social status.

We can begin to see here the developing association between women, shopping and fashion. The changes in the processes of consumption brought on by industrialization led to shopping as a distinct activity, and the introduction of fashion to the middle classes kept the factories running profitably, and women busy shopping. In addition, the techniques that department store owners used to entice women shoppers to buy, techniques that were often meant to seduce the shopper (Laermans, 1993; Reekie, 1993; Blomley, this volume, Chapter 13) were aimed at preventing women from 'just looking' (R Bowlby, 1985). But I still haven't positioned women and the feminine in this association. In what ways did associating shopping with women serve the emerging bourgeois society?

Feminist historians, among others, have shown the importance of the separation of spheres to the reigning ideology of late-nineteenth-century middle-class life (Davidoff and Hall, 1987; Stallybrass and White, 1986). In addition to the male/female, culture/commerce divide, was the separation of production and consumption. In reality, of course, these two different aspects of industrialization were completely interrelated. Production was completely reliant on consumption, and vice versa. However, ideologically they were meant to be kept separate. The values of production – self-denial, hard work, utilitarianism – were distinct from those of consumption, because successful consumption required self-indulgence, leisure time, and playfulness. How, then, could these two value systems be maintained and encouraged without undermining each other? How could hard work be encouraged at the same time as self-indulgence? Here, women and the domestic sphere proved particularly useful. The values of production could be maintained in the face of a growing need for consumption by aligning production with the world of men, and consumption with women. Women could be self-indulgent, while men worked hard to support them. In addition, since women were thought to embody 'naturally' moral characteristics, they could consume without fear of over-indulgence. Women's moral character would keep their materialism in check, thereby protecting the family's moral status.

In her analysis of Victorian Britain, Sally Shuttleworth (1990) argues that the distinction between consumption and production was symbolically played out in a variety of cultural discourses. In particular, she suggests that in contemporary medical literature, discussions of diseases concerning men's and women's bodies reveal cultural anxieties concerning the separate economic and social spheres. Many 'women's' diseases of the era were thought to be caused by women inhibiting their natural bodily flows, while for men, the problems were thought to be caused by men not controlling their bodies. Thus, cultural anxiety focused around the issues of desire and self-control; women were meant to give in to their natural desires, men to resist them. This anxiety, Shuttleworth argues, was a result of the uncertainties the new bourgeois class was facing – an economic system that required constant and continual consumption to fuel its productive sector, and a social system where unabashed wealth was not enough to ensure social legitimacy. Relegating the sphere of consumption to women eased some of those tensions. Women could be consumers and visible symbols of material wealth without undermining their social standing, because, it was thought, women's moral and cultural status would keep their materialism from contaminating the family's 'higher' aspirations. As long as women's desires did not get out of control, their role as consumers served the needs of bourgeois society and economy. In fact, contemporary commentators attributed the success of the department store to women's consumer desires, and those desires were explicitly addressed by department store owners in their attempts to encourage consumption (Laermans, 1993; Blomley, this volume, Chapter 13). The opening of Stewart's 1846 marble palace elicited the following remark in the *New York Herald*:

> As long as the ladies continue to constitute an important feature in the community, the dry goods business must be in a flourishing condition. . . . In fact, dry goods are a passion with the ladies, and whilst they continue to remain so the business must flourish; for woe to the luckless husband who refuses his wife money for shopping. (*New York Herald*, 26 September 1846: 2).

Women's passion for fashion was good for business and did not present a threat to the established values of productivity. E L Godkin's analysis of the success of the dry goods trade led him to the needs of American women:

> The pre-eminence and attractiveness of the dry-goods trade in this country is due mainly to the great purchasing power and varied requirements of American women. . . . The consequence is that the dry-goods man has a sphere of activity opened to him such as is presented to no other trader – women are his principal customers, and their wants are innumerable, whether for use or ornament, and their fancy is a harp of a thousand strings, on which a skilful salesman may play an endless variety of tunes. (Godkin, 1876: 259)

Thus the gender hierarchy helped maintain the distinction between consumption and production, a distinction necessary in a system that required both indulging one's desires through consumption, and at the same time, controlling desire through self-discipline in order to increase production. Thus, with women as the major class of consumers, the new culture of consumption was not disruptive. Department stores, therefore, not only targeted women as their customers, but also incorporated women and the feminine into their landscape. The domestic was brought into the public arena. What, then, did this new, 'domestic' downtown look like?

The feminized retailing district

In late-nineteenth-century New York, the retailing district centred on Fifth Avenue between Union and Madison Squares, extending west to Sixth Avenue and east to Broadway. It was an area of ornamental architecture and grand boulevards, of restaurants and bars, and of small boutiques and large department stores. It was, above all, an urban landscape designed specifically for consumption. This new retailing area was not only functionally different from its predecessors, in that its land use was dedicated only to retailing, but also architecturally distinct. The new department stores that dominated this area were dramatically larger than earlier dry goods stores, and differed from their predecessors in the degree of ornamentation, the attention to decorative detail and display of goods, the concern with internal organization of departments, and the catering to the personal needs of the shoppers, most of whom were women.

New York's first department store, Stewart's, opened on Broadway in 1846 (see Figure 14.1). Its four storeys, all dedicated to retailing, were unprecedented in the city, as was its white marble façade, a feature that made the building perhaps the most conspicuous in a city constructed almost exclusively of brick or wood. Its Italianate style, and its internal design centring on a dome with accompanying rotunda, were direct references to the public structures of the city, particularly the City Hall, which was located just to the south of the store (Resseguie, 1964). The store's owner, A T Stewart, was acutely aware of the importance of the appearance of his store, since he understood that in the new culture of consumption, the actual place of purchase was as important as the goods consumed, a notion that in the 1990s we take for granted in our image-laden shopping malls (J Hopkins, 1990) and festival settings (Knox, 1991). Yet in the mid-nineteenth century, this was a novel idea. Previously, purchasing goods in a small retail/wholesale shop involved a personal encounter with a shop owner or clerk. Given limited space, goods generally were not displayed, so a customer asked to see a particular good, haggled over the price, and made the purchase. However, with industrialization came the standardization of goods and prices, and with it, the elimination of personal haggling. In the new department stores, the customer dealt with a waged labourer, often a woman, and the activity of purchasing became one of comparing the relative worth of different items. The actual act of purchasing became insignificant compared to the activity of shopping. Standardization of prices and goods also meant that social status accorded on the basis of acquisition was further differentiated by the place and means of acquisition. As goods were increasingly standardized, and the act of consumption became more impersonal, it was as if, 'the stage on which it took place became correspondingly more important' (Chaney, 1983: 27).

Thus, Stewart was intent on designing a building that would provide an appropriate setting for consumption. An appeal to civic notions would provide his store with some cultural legitimacy, at the same time as it would diminish its commercial impact, and therefore would not interfere with gender ideology. It was already clear in 1846 that women would be the store's major patrons, yet, under the reigning ideology, women could be allowed to do so only if they did not become too tainted with commercialism. A commercial enterprise with cultural and civic allusions, therefore, would not be seen as disruptive of established gender categories. If the emerging industrial economy required women to become a class of consumers, that consumption would have to take place in an appropriately feminine environment. The qualities associated with nineteenth-century femininity and the domestic sphere were built into the store: there were symbols of civic and cultural aspirations, well-ordered and arranged displays, services and amenities designed for women, and an environment meant to be safe and protected.

The store's large interior was arranged to maximize the display of goods for comparative shopping, as well as to create an atmosphere considered appropriate for women. The central hall of the store was

Figure 14.1 Stewart's marble-fronted department store on Broadway at Chambers Street. (*Source* : illustration courtesy of New York Historical Society)

decorated with frescoes on the walls and ceilings, an ornate chandelier in the centre, and large mirrors imported from Paris (Weisman, 1954). Just opposite the main entrance in the rotunda was a flight of stairs that led up to a gallery that ran around the rotunda. This gallery, as a commentator described it, 'is for the ladies to promenade upon' (*Evening Post*, 1846; quoted in M A Smith, 1974: 25). The rich interior displays included mahogany countertops, marble shelves, and, an elegant ladies' parlour complete with large mirrors, apparently the first such convenience provided in a commercial structure (Boyer, 1985). It was clear to observers that these amenities were meant to appeal to women:

> New York can now boast of the most splendid dry goods store in the world . . . Mr. Stewart has paid the ladies of this city a high compliment in giving them such a beautiful resort in which to while away their leisure hours of the morning. (*New York Herald*, 18 September 1846:1)

As historian William Leach (1984) suggests, it was women who were identified with small, ornamental items, with 'fancy goods,' and these were enticements of the department store. For a man to set foot in a department store for his own pleasure was seen as a symbolic act of emasculation. The appeal of whiling away 'leisure hours' in an ornamental department store was a decidedly feminine attribute.

Figure 14.2 Stewart's cast iron department store on Broadway at 10th Street. (*Source*: McCabe, 1971)

Stewart's later store, completed in 1862 further uptown on Broadway, continued the idea of the department store as a stage of consumption designed to fit into prevailing gender ideology. Using cast-iron for the façade, Stewart again created a visual sensation (see Figure 14.2). This six-storey iron and glass palazzo became a site not to be missed by visitors to the city. Stewart maintained the civic allusions of his earlier store, centring his new building around a large rotunda and dome, while at the same time magnifying the display aspects. The entire store revolved around a skylight, that provided direct light to the large main floor. The five storeys that rose above were arranged as encircling balconies, thus providing natural light to all floors, and enabling shoppers to observe each other as they strolled through the enormous building (see Figure 14.3). This design contributed to the spectacle atmosphere of the store, with shoppers able to view all the doings at the main gallery, while at the same time seeing across and up and down to the various departments that surrounded them. This presented women with a fairly limitless visual experience, as they watched not only each other, but also the range of wares for consumption.

Yet, with all this commercialism, women's presence ensured that the forces of consumption would not disrupt the values of production. In other words, women as the main class of consumers allowed the new culture of consumption to flourish without seriously disturbing the economic order.

William Leach has shown how religion was mixed into the equation of women and fashion, to make less threatening these palaces of consumption. The association of religion with fashion had already become familiar to most Americans by mid-century; as a commentator noted in 1856, 'real ladies and gentlemen are those who belong both to the Church and to fashion' (Sibyl, 1856; quoted in Leach, 1984: 232). Department store owners built on this association between women, fashion and religion, calling their stores cathedrals, and their goods objects of devotion. A commentator compared Stewart's new store with Grace Church, and spoke of the store as dedicated to the worship of dry goods:

> In walking up Broadway on the west side of that most magnificent of thoroughfares, a person must naturally find two striking objects to contemplate at that point where the street makes a bend. One is the graceful, slender, gray spire of Grace Church, piercing the blue atmosphere; the other is the gigantic mass of iron, painted of a white color, erected by Alexander T. Stewart to the worship of dry-goods, covering two acres of ground, and Theban in its Old World massiveness. (DJK 1869: 43)

Department stores learned to schedule the 'openings' of their collections to coincide with Christmas and Easter, thus further aligning religion and fashion, and institutionalizing the commercialization of religious holidays, a practice that continues today. As Leach suggests, 'The department stores, and the fashion industry that underlay them, penetrated into and contaminated the life of established religion,

Figure 14.3 Interior of Stewart's department store on Broadway at 10th Street. (*Source*: illustration courtesy of New York Historical Society)

creating a paradoxical marriage between commodity capitalism and religious life that has persisted into our own time' (Leach, 1984: 232). Department stores, then, were central to both the commercialization of religion and the association of religion with consumption. And, since religion formed an integral part of the women's sphere, the department store served to reinforce the alignment of the feminine with consumption. With stores as 'cathedrals', and women as the 'worshippers', consumption became a moral act, a religious duty of women. Thus, the feminization of consumption made it acceptable without threatening; shopping in the cathedrals of commerce became a necessary, religious duty.

This new culture of consumption, visibly symbolized in the department store, could be tolerated if it was associated with women and the feminine. It was fine for women to have a passion for the department store; it kept sales high, while not threatening the established economic order. Department stores, therefore, not only targeted women as their customers, but also incorporated women and the feminine into their landscape. The domestic, if you will, was brought into the public arena. As historian Gunther Barth has suggested: 'The department store brought into the bustle of downtown the civility that most men had reserved for those aspects of city life they considered properly the social sphere' (Barth, 1980: 127).

This domestication of the city had profound impacts on its cultural landscape. Department stores, themselves, as we have seen, were designed specifically for women, appointed with elegant lounges and spaces to cater to women's needs. By the end of the century, the domestic was more fully incorporated, and department stores began to function almost as home parlours, with tea rooms, restaurants, art galleries and grand architectural displays. Outside the stores, wide sidewalks enabled those fashionable dresses to stay clean, while paved and increasingly gas and electric-lit streets added to the propriety of the area for women. Rapid transit networks enabled women like Clara Pardee to come downtown to shop, return to their middle-class residential enclaves further uptown for lunch, and be back to shop that afternoon. Stewart, for example, was a strong backer of the West Side Association, an organization of capitalists that planned to build an elevated railroad with their own money (Leach, 1980). When the first elevated railway opened on Sixth Avenue in 1878, crowds of women used it to flock to the new stores. But the shopping experience was not limited to the interiors of the stores; by the 1870s, shopping was brought into the streets. The use of plate glass windows on the first storey of most retail stores allowed women to shop without ever stepping off the sidewalks. And in those windows could be displayed anything from bedroom sets to crystal, from corsets to evening gowns. The private world was put on public display, right in the heart of the city.

Thus, although the rapid and massive expansion of New York's retailing area was due to the city's growing economy, and the links of retailing to be close to the middle and upper class residential areas, the shape of that district, its three-dimensional form, can be understood only in relation to the general social and cultural context of New York's bourgeois class. In order to make the values of consumption acceptable, retailers targeted women as their customers. And, to maintain appropriate gender roles, these spaces of consumption had to be feminized, that is, they had to appear as cultural and civic spaces, not completely tainted by commercialism. At the same time, the presence of women and the domestic in their stores gave visible evidence of the cultural legitimacy sought after by these members of a bourgeois class who were always seeking a means of legitimizing their wealth and power in the city.

The cultural landscape of retailing in nineteenth-century New York, then, reveals a complex relationship between gender ideology, class structure and the origins of consumer culture; a relationship that has undergone modifications over the last century, but whose broad contours have remained relatively constant. Twentieth-century retailing is rooted in transformations that occurred in the eighteenth and nineteenth centuries, and the new retail geography should help us detect and delineate how those transformations of two centuries ago continue to shape contemporary retailing activity and design.

CHAPTER 15

United colours? Globalization and localization tendencies in fashion retailing

Louise Crewe and Michelle Lowe

In this chapter we examine the twin processes of globalization and localization in fashion retailing. The particular problem we address is the apparent paradox that fashion retailing faces whereby two simultaneous and in some ways contradictory processes seem to be at work. On the one hand, the globalization of markets continues to weave complex interdependencies between geographically distant locations and tends towards global interconnection and spatial homogeneity. On the other hand, new patterns of regional specialization are emphasizing the importance of place and reinforcing local uniqueness. In this chapter we explore these countervailing forces and examine the complex mediation between the global and the local, as it is both engineered and experienced by clothing retailers. Finally, attention is paid to the various ways in which these processes impact on landscapes of consumption on the ground. In particular, we address the apparent paradox whereby 'one of the most fascinating aspects of place in recent years is that it has become more homogenous in some ways and more heterogenous in others' (Zukin, 1991: 12).

The empirical material contained in this chapter results from a phased series of in-depth, semi-structured interviews conducted in the UK between 1990 and 1993. In total, interviews were carried out with 21 small independent retailers in Nottingham, a quality regional shopping centre with a distinctive structure of supply relations (see Crewe, 1994; Crewe and Forster, 1993a) and 14 large retail chains throughout the UK between 1990 and 1992. Follow-up interviews were then conducted in 1993 with a selection of pioneering retailers who are operating in particularly innovative ways. In addition, 25 retail postal questionnaires were analysed. The retailers surveyed span the full range of size categories, from single-site small independent retailers to large internationalized groups. Every effort was made to target both leading retailers in terms of market share, employees and turnover, and smaller, more specialized retail concepts. Interviews were conducted with 150 clothing manufacturers in the core geographical areas of West Yorkshire, Nottinghamshire and London. These were then supplemented with 42 manufacturer postal questionnaires and 98 telephone interviews. This allowed the analysis of the buyer–supplier connection and enabled us to trace the geographical tracks of retailer sourcing strategies. The particular 'consumption landscapes' we discuss include specialized, high quality retail districts such as Nottingham's Lace Market, and more conventional seemingly 'placeless' indoor malls which house national and international chain stores. For reasons of commercial confidentiality, a full listing of firms surveyed cannot be reproduced.

The chapter begins with a discussion of the simultaneous tendencies towards both localization and globalization. We argue that together these forces are combining to create a new era in the international organization of clothing retailing. The unfolding of this new global–local stage, the emergent retailer responses to such changing contexts and the tensions inherent in this process form the basis of the following discussion.

The emergent global–local nexus

As Swyngedouw (1992) has argued, one of the most significant world changes since the mid-1980s has been the emergence of

> new configurations in which both the local/regional and transnational/global scales have risen to prominence . . . the global/local interplay of contemporary capitalist restructuring processes should be thought of as a single, combined process with two inherently related, albeit contradictory movements. (Swyngedouw 1992: 40)

Indeed, 'globalization . . . is about the achievement of a new *global-local nexus*, about new and intricate relations between global space and local space' (Robins, 1989: 25).

Such double processes, we suggest, are particularly evident in the fashion sector, which is at one and the same time a truly global industry as well as a potent symbol of personal and spatial identity. In sum, then, two countervailing forces are evident. On the one hand we are seeing the emergence of internationalized retailer strategies and the development of sophisticated ways of tapping global markets without facing all the risks involved in direct overseas production and foreign property acquisition. The result is the emergence of a global marketplace in which consumption patterns are becoming more homogenous. In this way the cultural industries such as fashion and the media are helping to bring about a convergence of lifestyle, culture and behaviour among consumer segments across the world through a process of 'world cultural convergence' (Robins, 1989: 23). It has even been suggested that 'the world's needs and desires have been irrevocably homogenized' (Levitt, 1983: 92). This tendency for the spread of global culture to encourage time––space compression and to weaken local distinctiveness is now well documented (Harvey, 1989c; King, 1990; Robins, 1989; Sack, 1988; Shields, 1992a; Zukin, 1991).

272

On the other hand a variety of factors are suggesting a reworking of the conventional internationalization process, as pressures for flexibility, rapid response and constant attention to quality demand a reordering of retailer–supplier relations. As a result we are witnessing the apparent localization of retailing through the building up of dense networks of buyer–supplier relations and through a reappraisal of the importance of local production complexes. It is this sense in which fashion retailing is becoming at once more internationally ubiquitous and yet at the same time more specialized and differentiated that we address below.

The global marketplace: fashion retailing as global industry

The tendency for the spread of national and increasingly global culture to weaken local distinctiveness is particularly apparent in the case of clothing. The global penetration of fashion concepts such as Chanel, Armani and Benetton has united consumers the world over. Their globalization strategies epitomize the connections between internationalized urban form and consumption practises, and their seemingly insatiable appetite for international expansion has had profound impacts on fashion production and consumption. As Luciano Benetton argues, 'The 60s dream of a global village was realized through Benetton. Young people in particular are helping to create a new global village' (Benetton, 1993). Similarly,

> the internationalization of designer clothes . . . their relative affordability, along with international advertising efforts, have made French, Italian, Japanese and American designer labels, often unpronounceable to the locals of the consuming nations, household names in the entire spectrum of the middle class worldwide. Indeed, the names have even penetrated the consumption horizons of the working class, as there are plenty of fakes that bring the 'names' to within their reach even if they cannot afford the real thing. (Huat Chua, 1992)

Globalization strategies

In the following discussion we shall be exploring the ways in which the global spread of a fashion culture has been enabled through strategies such as franchising, licensing and branding, and also through technological developments in electronic ordering, warehousing and distribution systems, which ensure that the goods arrive at each stage of manufacture, distribution and point of sale at exactly the right time, in an acceptable condition and at an economic price (Millar, 1993).

Through the careful restriction of supply, often using systems of franchising and licensing, contemporary retailers maintain competitive advantage in the global marketplace. Such arrangements, enhanced through sophisticated international marketing and advertising campaigns, ensure the maximum penetration of global fashion markets with the minimum risk. As a result, there is a sense in which 'the whole globe has become saturated with Western images of fashion . . . today, the style is in the label' (E Wilson 1989 : 210–11). This love of a label has ensured the global spread of brand names such as Chanel and Gucci, which 'create the impression of sophistication, of internationalization, of taste' (Huat Chua, 1992: 119).

The globalization of fashion has also been facilitated through technological advances in warehousing, distribution and data exchange systems (see also Marsden and Wrigley, this volume, Chapter 2, for a discussion on the impact of such supply chain innovations on the food sector). In particular, concurrent developments in electronic point of sales (EPOS) and distribution systems are revolutionizing the ordering, stocking and supply of garments both nationally and, most significantly, internationally. In the short term, fashion retailers in the UK are preparing for a major transformation in the way they transport and distribute garments with the launch of a new operation called Fashion Logistics. The launch of this new concept brings together under one company the warehousing, pre-retailing and transport services which were previously offered separately to retailers, and will significantly reduce the friction of distance effect, thereby offering real-time and cost savings (Millar, 1993). In the longer term it is probable that pan-European just-in-time (JIT) distribution systems could be serving retailers by the end of the 1990s. The establishment of such technology-intensive information networks has been instrumental in overcoming the time–space barriers to corporate expansion; such systems are 'fundamental to both the co-ordination of internal corporate activities and functions and to the control of external transactions with suppliers, collaborators or customers . . . what is being created is new electronic cultural space, a "placeless" geography of image' (Robins, 1989: 23).

Laura Ashley is an example of a retailer which has made considerable progress towards quick response systems of ordering and distribution. Taking its lead from the food sector (see Marsden and Wrigley, this volume, Chapter 2), the group is now aiming to restock all of its 540 stores worldwide within 48 hours, and estimates that this will reduce the cost of goods in stock in the supply chain by 50 per cent, which represents a real cost saving of some £30 million per annum. The group is moving towards a paperless system whereby orders are transmitted overnight by an EPOS system and electronic data links to the distribution centre, and are handled at 3am the next morning. Plans are also under way to invest in bar-coding equipment which would allow goods to be tracked during transit, and would also give quicker re-ordering at point of sale.

Benetton, the case of a global retailer

Benetton, Italy's biggest fashion firm, is probably the most (in)famous example of a global retailer which has successfully transcended national boundaries. Benetton has developed a total look that merges product, production methods, a specialized consumption experience and an advertising style. The firm began in 1965 in Treviso in northern Italy. From its modest beginnings the concept evolved rapidly, with total sales increasing from 55 billion lire to 322 billion lire between 1978 and 1981. This growth in sales was largely accounted for by exports, which accounted for 54 per cent of total output by 1983 (F Belussi, 1992: 79). By 1992 the group had more than 7040 shops in over 100 countries, including Cuba and China, and a compound annual growth rate of 17 per cent.

The key to the success of Benetton's globalization strategy lies in their innovative approach to systems of both organizational and technological control. First, their 'non-technological' innovations include sophisticated systems of marketing, advertising, sub-contracting and franchising. Benetton was the first company in Italy, and possibly in the world, to introduce a system of franchising in clothing, thereby enabling comparatively risk-free internationalization via 'concession' stores. Through this system Benetton export the entire selling strategy: not only their products but also the Benetton style, the shop organization and the marketing strategy (Belussi, 1992: 80). It proved to be an extremely successful way of pushing their exports worldwide, such that Benetton were opening approximately 100 shops per year by 1975. The key to their expansion was hence not to get embroiled in the unpredictabilities of the property market, which was a mistake made by many UK retailers such as the Burton Group. Rather, Benetton recognized the advantages of operating a system in which the franchisee shoulders the risks and responsibility for their own store. All of Benetton's shops are owned by an independent person, who is accountable for the lease, sales and so on. Moreover, Benetton neither invests in nor collects franchise fees from Benetton stores, but franchisees must buy their entire inventory from Benetton, who also insist on adherence to company standards for store design and layout. This system has enabled Benetton to export their concept worldwide while spreading risk accordingly. Unlike many British fashion companies which did not have the courage or capability to venture across national boundaries in the 1980s, Benetton, through this ingenious risk-minimization strategy, succeeded in satisfying their seemingly insatiable appetite to conquer and consume new markets. In this sense, then, Benetton was perhaps the first middle-market fashion chain to successfully 'go global'. By keeping the brand image tight, and reinforcing it by powerful (and at times controversial) advertising campaigns, Benetton has become an international High Street name. Their shops are ubiquitous in cities around the world, giving strength to their aggressive strategy of international expansion, and satisfying the corporate ambition to 'be everywhere, like McDonalds . . . we consider ourselves the fast food in fashion' (Benetton, 1993).

Second, and linked to this, the Benetton system owes its success to a variety of process-related technologies, which together allow Benetton to operate a flexible just-in-time system. The group has been at the forefront of new investments in dyeing processes, where colour is a key ingredient in the creation of the Benetton image. From their early use of light 'pastello' colours in 1965, the firm introduced in-house dyeing at the final stage of production in 1972. This involves piece (rather than batch) dyeing of individual items to order, which allows stores to place small orders throughout the season. In this way Benetton can respond almost immediately to popular colour stories, rather than having to order large batches in advance of the season. As a result, stores are left with lower stocks of slow movers.

This system of production to order is further facilitated through new technological investments in EPOS, warehousing and distribution. In particular, real-time planning of production, based directly on shops' orders, brings about significant reductions in the size of inventory holding and in the time an item spends in the warehouse. Sales data from around the world are relayed back to Treviso in real time, and are processed, stored and communicated to 'Big Charlie', the automated warehousing and distribution system at Benetton, which handles some 28 000 boxes of garments daily. As a result of such an information intelligence system, Benetton is able to restock any store in the world within about ten days, and in this way almost interacts directly with its consumers. In this way, the stores are said to be 'the antennae of Benetton's information technology' (Belussi, 1992: 87). Such production to order clearly has an enormous influence on costs, on the ability of the firm to follow market trends and ultimately on its ability to expand internationally. As a result of such quick response systems of production and distribution, Benetton argues that it can reach the market six to eight weeks before its competitors. This position as a technological, organizational and market leader rather than follower must go some of the way towards explaining the phenomenal international success of the Benetton concept.

The changing retail environment

A variety of factors are combining at present to transform the international configuration of clothing production and consumption. First, there has been a fragmentation of the mass market, for reasons which relate to both production and consumption changes. In terms of production, intensifying competition from the newly industrializing countries (NICs) during the 1970s rendered British manufacturers highly vulnerable and in a precarious competitive situation. In a very short space of time the logic of price competition was challenged as the NICs nurtured their comparative labour cost advantage and quickly acquired the skills and technology necessary for low cost, high volume garment production. The result was a shift of emphasis by the more successful retailers away from price-based competition towards more fragmented, higher value markets. This trend necessitated simultaneous and complementary adaptation on the part of clothing producers. At the same time, consumption preferences have shifted away from low cost, standardized garments towards more customized, higher quality and design based clothes. The clothing retail system in the UK, which for so long targeted the youth oriented, throwaway middle-market, has been forced to respond and reorient its product offerings towards higher value-added garments with a higher design awareness or a more identifiable image. Such retailer strategies are likely to be differentiated according to demographics and lifestyle perception. For the younger age cohorts, competition will almost certainly centre around strong promotion of image and brand name, in terms of both product offerings and store and staff image (see Lowe and Crewe, this volume, Chapter 10). For other sections of the market the competitive edge is likely to lie with understated, quality classics. Linked to such consumption shifts, the logic which underpins foreign sourcing by retailers in manufacturing capacity abroad is being undermined by a combination of circumstances, including moves towards smaller batches and shorter runs of garments produced to exacting quality and design standards with minimal lead times. Such new consumption preferences are demanding a production formula which is typified by flexibility, rapid response and the strengthening of more collaborative buyer–supplier linkages. Under such circumstances, the balance of advantage may shift from international sourcing and supply to more adaptable localized production constellations (see below).

Second, labour costs are converging on an international scale, thereby making sourcing from the low labour cost countries less attractive in all but the most standardized, non-fashion sensitive product markets. Retail analysts have identified a trend away from foreign sourcing, a tendency which was confirmed through our survey work. In particular, 'leading UK retailers (including Debenhams, Littlewoods and the Storehouse Group) are reviewing their supplier networks, revealing a marked trend away from Far Eastern manufacturers in favour of sourcing closer to home' (Rawlinson, 1991: 3). Given the rapidity of fashion change, such sourcing reviews are largely a result of quick response buying strategies by retailers who have become cautious about ordering merchandise in bulk at the beginning of a season: 'while European manufacturers can rarely compete with Far Eastern prices, they allow greater flexibility and faster delivery' (Moylan, 1991: 3). Thus, 'while sourcing overseas can have its attractions, if the supplier is not geared up to repeating lines or is inflexible when the buyers hopes are not met and orders need to be scaled back, the benefits can be outweighed in terms of lost profits on markdowns and unfulfilled demand' (Ramshaw, 1993: 13). Given that ordering from India for example has to be done three to six months in advance, and that distribution from the Far East takes on average six weeks, the pressure is clearly on for alternative, more localized and responsive sourcing arrangements.

Third, the high of retailing in the 1980s has given way to a deep and protracted recession, which has resulted in a very different operating environment for fashion retailing, with growth and confidence being replaced by uncertainty and caution. The volume of clothing retail sales in the UK fell by 2 per cent between 1989 and 1991, in marked contrast to the growth of 19 per cent experienced between 1986 and 1988

(Economist Intelligence Unit, 1992c). Rising unemployment and large-scale redundancies are acting as continuing brakes on consumer spending which, when coupled with the depressed property market suggest the continuation of recessionary conditions for the foreseeable future. The retail boom showed signs of bottoming out as early as 1988 as interest rates began to rise. A further factor has been the escalating level of retail rents, which are sustainable in a consumer boom but not with the lower volume throughputs of stock associated with recession. Warning bells were first sounded in the late 1980s, when it was stated by retail property interests that multiples were finding it difficult to make new branch premises at top rents pay (Clive Lewis and Partners, 1988). Moreover, many retailers such as the Burton Group found themselves in serious financial difficulties as a result of disastrous forays into property speculation, both in the UK and abroad. The errors of such property- driven expansionist policies of the 1980s are keenly appreciated by retailers, who are seeking new ways of tapping global markets without shouldering the risks associated with unpredictable international property markets.

Localization strategies

Such transformations in the retailing arena are having profound implications on the organization of buyer–supplier relations. The manipulation of supply chains by retailers has been an important means of responding to new market demands towards quality small batch production supplied in quick response to new market demands. In particular, there is evidence of the emergence of stronger, more permanent and more demanding relationships between manufacturers and retailers (see also Foord, Bowlby and Tillsley, this volume, Chapter 4).

By the late 1980s it was apparent that key mass market retailers, including C&A, Marks & Spencer and Richards were increasingly sourcing in smaller volumes from suppliers, and that newer chains such as Next were also seeking smaller average batch sizes (Crewe and Davenport, 1992). While the range of typical batch sizes varies from one retail chain to another, the majority of surveyed retailers are now sourcing in batches of between 100 and 300 garments. Five of the surveyed retailers are sourcing in batches of 50 garments or less, while two retailers are sourcing as few as 10–20 garments. Rapid response and smaller batches are critical: retailers are now demanding 'faster turnaround', 'reduced lead times' and 'more flexibility, smaller quantities, less lead time' (personal interviews, 1993). Furthermore, retailers are increasingly demanding phased deliveries throughout the season, with the final balance of garments and colour combinations being determined by feedback from electronic point of sales (EPOS) systems, which give up-to-date information on the sales performance of different product lines. This trend towards mid-season purchasing alters the predictable equilibrium which characterized buyer–supplier relationships under the two-fashion season regime. Next, for example, place their orders in 'lumps' throughout the season, while Marks & Spencer operate a 60 per cent initial take-up rule, with no guarantee of uptake of the remaining 40 per cent of the order. Similarly, Principles regularly change styles mid-season and feel that their suppliers are quite adept at coping with this. Clearly, such transformations in retailer sourcing strategies are having profound implications on the supply base. The new demands for small batches and short lead times are fundamentally affected by geography, and while the new regime places serious burdens on manufacturing firms, it nevertheless implies a privileging of domestic suppliers over distant overseas rivals. In particular, the need for close monitoring of suppliers who can make the quality grade and respond extremely quickly to fragmenting and shifting consumption signals is resulting in more localized sourcing chains, with obvious benefits to the local manufacturing base.

The importance of a flexible supply chain has been identified by trade analysts and retailers themselves as a key determinant of success in the 1990s. It has frequently been suggested that 'sourcing will be the main issue . . . Retailers should look for what opportunities they have for sourcing as much as possible from UK suppliers' (Hyman, 1993: 18). In particular 'retailers must be able to capitalize on any glimmer of demand on any specific line or product, which necessitates a supply network close to the base of operations, intelligent systems of technology and a close working relationship with manufacturers' (Ramshaw, 1993: 12). Indeed, the Verdict clothing retailers report argues that firms which source heavily from overseas will be left uncompetitive.

The innovative lingerie retailer Knickerbox are an excellent example of the way in which the restructuring of supply relations is benefiting domestic manufacturing firms. The group now sources 80 per cent of their merchandise from the UK, and have recognized the value of developing long-term, collaborative relations with a small number of trusted supplier firms who can meet their quality and delivery schedules. The group hit problems of minimum order sizes when sourcing from the Far East: 'The Far East is a nightmare in terms of design: constantly sending faxes, trying to get quality assurance, size specifications, letters of credit. It's a nightmare' (personal interview, 1993). As a result, Knickerbox are now seeking more responsive local supplier firms:

> We have a very rapid change of lines. We work to a very tight time scale. Randomly picking up and dropping suppliers is horrendous. We used to work with far too many and chuck them out after one season. Now we have a focused supply base. . . . We now need a loyal, devoted exclusive UK supply base. We have shrunk our supply base and now offer loyalty to supplier and ask for loyalty in return. We offer a lot to suppliers in return for design and quality. (Personal interview, 1993)

In particular, Knickerbox recognize that the trends within the retailing environment are benefiting the UK:

> we are looking more and more towards the UK for make up for a variety of reasons: flexibility, rapid response, 12 week lead time. UK suppliers allow for excitement and innovation. Quick response is the key. The trend at present towards real underwear, which demands traditional corsetry skills such as boning, undermines the advantage of the Far East. All the new trends are benefiting the UK. It is a very positive time. (Personal interview, 1993).

Such strategies are evident across the full spectrum of retail chains, from mass-market retailers such as Littlewoods, through middle-market chains such as Marks & Spencer and the Burton Group, to more specialized, quality retailers such as Next and Laura Ashley. Littlewoods, for example, is restructuring its supply network. The group currently has around 3000 suppliers worldwide but it is likely that this figure will shrink as closer ties are established with the most efficient performers (Guha, 1993: 7). Of course, the implications for manufacturers who are successful in achieving preferred supplier status are mixed, and while the benefits of large orders are welcome, the dependency problems of being locked in to such relationships can be devastating (see Crewe and Davenport, 1992, for a fuller discussion). The customer base of the Etam group is similarly being restructured towards a smaller base of favoured suppliers. Etam argue that speed of delivery and flexibility are the keys to supplier success, and appreciate the ability to source batch sizes of 300 from the UK, as compared with a minimum order size from overseas of 2000 (personal interview, 1993). Finally, both Burtons and the Storehouse group are reviewing sourcing away from the Far East, and are steering away from sourcing on price, towards quality and availability of repeats. The Principles arm of the Burton Group, which sources 80 per cent of its merchandise from the UK, is keenly appreciative of the need for quality domestic suppliers, and is currently pursuing close working relationships with domestic manufacturers through 'operation heartland': 'a good supplier is defined by quality, production on time, consistency of standard, high level of design and a very good, close liaison with buyers' (personal interview, 1993).

Localized constellations: the case of Nottingham's Lace Market

The emergence of such localized sourcing, production and design constellations is particularly evident in the case of the Nottingham Lace Market. The fashion sector here comprises some 108 firms, including designers, manufacturers and retailers. The important feature is that the Lace Market is functionally integrated across the entire production pipeline, from design and fabric supply, through all stages of production, to final sale. Indeed, 85 per cent of firms have sourcing or sales links with other local firms. Such dense local sourcing arrangements are important, and the flexibility offered by integrated supplier–producer–buyer linkages is at the heart of the competitive success of the Lace Market.

The system hinges around the production of high-quality, design-based garments produced in small batches to meet customized consumption preferences. The Lace Market has established a strong image associated with quality and exclusivity, with 68 per cent of firms producing garments with their own brand names attached. The importance of own-branding emphasizes the independent character of the clothing sector in the Lace Market, particularly at the top end of the quality spectrum, where designers such as Paul Smith not only manufacture and retail locally, but also in so doing directly employ 80 people in Nottingham and indirectly employ many more through sub-contracting production out locally. Yet at the same time Smith promotes the name of British fashion abroad through exporting 70 per cent of production. His international expansion strategy has centred on concession stores, of which there are currently some 80, primarily in Japan and the USA, alongside his stand-alone stores in Nottingham, London, Manhattan, Paris, Singapore and Tokyo. His operating slogan is 'think global, act local' which appears to perfectly epitomize one of the keys to success in the 1990s, namely localized production for globalized markets.

In terms of marketing and sales appeal, the small independent retailers in the Hockley area of the Lace Market fit well with the broader shifts in clothing retailing outlined earlier. All are operating at the upper reaches of the market, and are competing on factors other than price. Almost all offer very small batches, or even one-offs, and see this exclusivity as one of the major reasons for their success. Interestingly, when asked about the major threats in terms of competition, none of the independent retailers or designers mentioned price-based competition from the low-cost countries. Rather, all recognized the threat posed by the fashion centres of Paris and Milan, thus refuting the suggestion that the British fashion industry is an uncompetitive anachronism, clinging to the remnants of a price-competitive market.

Yet the importance of the Lace Market as a new retail space relates not only to aesthetics or to market orientation. Such attributes are firmly underpinned by a system of economic organization in which 68 per cent of firms employ fewer than ten people, where 80 per cent of firms have no minimum order size and where 72 per cent of firms have a lead time of less than four weeks (Crewe and Forster, 1993a; 1993b). The advantages offered in terms of small-batch availability, rapid style change and exclusivity of design are obvious. Significantly, 85 per cent of firms have local sourcing or supply chains, with local networks being important to the functioning of the complex (Crewe and Forster, 1993a; 1993b). The result is an intricate web of sourcing and sub-contracting relationships, with more than half of all retail outlets sourcing from local designers and producers, who in turn source trims, fabrics and so on from local manufacturers. Such alliances often operate on an informal basis, with local knowledge being an important resource. Issues such as product marketing become comparatively easy under such circumstances, depending on 'reputation' and 'word of mouth'. Firms recognize the advantages offered by local supply chains: 'our relationship with customers is good, and involves the personal touch'; 'proximity to suppliers is important. Our location in the Lace Market is important to customers, suppliers and sub-contractors' (personal interviews, 1993). It may well be that the alliances being forged across the entire fashion system in the Lace Market may be one way of affording greater autonomy to local manufacturers. They certainly indicate that more balanced relationships between manufacturers and retailers are possible, and even desirable under current competitive conditions.

Landscapes of consumption: geographical outcomes of the interrelations between the global and the local

Our argument in this chapter is that we can begin to understand the international evolution of the fashion industry only by simultaneously considering the trends towards both localization and globalization. By understanding such tendencies in a dialectical fashion, a complex picture emerges. It is on the spatial outcomes of such processes that we now focus. On the one hand, we are seeing the homogenization of consumption practices and spaces through the internationalization strategies of global retailers such as Benetton, whose presence on almost every High Street and in every mall unifies international investment, production and consumption. The result is the serial reproduction of a global fashion culture, epitomized by chains of retail stores filled with mainly imported goods in which 'you could be anywhere' (Goss, 1993: 32) since 'shopping centres are the same everywhere' (Morris M, 1993: 297). The spatial expression of such a globalized fashion culture is thus a placeless nowhere, 'and the landscapes that result from modern processes appear to be pastiches, disorienting, unauthentic and juxtaposed. . . . A flatscape' (Sack, 1988: 642, 660). The modern shopping centre which typically houses the ubiquitous chain stores is thus 'literally a utopia, an idealized nowhere (*ou*=no; *topos*=place)' (Goss, 1993: 32), and 'this sign-saturated place and its constant motion represent the spatial and temporal displacement characteristic of the post-modern world'.

Yet the tensions in the structure of retailing and consumption point to a world that is becoming more homogeneous overall, but which is also striving to maintain some sense of local identity. Alongside these tendencies towards an homogenized global fashion culture, then, we are simultaneously seeing a renewed emphasis on local uniqueness, quality and exclusivity, as places attempt to differentiate themselves as part of the continual process of uneven development. The way in which particular localities are being reconstructed and sold not as centres of production but consumption is particularly important in this respect, as

282

new patterns of regional specialization reflect the selective location of highly valued economic activities (Zukin, 1991). In particular, there is evidence of localities being peddled through particular cultural and historical associations, in part as a reaction against the retail monoculture of the 1980s (Crewe, 1994). In the particular case of clothing retailing, such specialization tendencies are reinforced through the strengthening of localized constellations of buyers and suppliers. Such clusters of interacting economic activities assist in the creation of specialized, place-specific identities (Crewe, 1994; Crewe and Forster, 1993a; 1993b). This re-centring of place within retail provision and the associated marketing of consumption centres through capitalizing on reputations for quality, design and reputation is playing an important role in retail profitability (see Crewe and Lowe, 1995).

It is this sense in which fashion culture and its associated consumption landscapes are becoming at once more similar yet more differentiated that we have attempted to capture in this chapter. Such double movements give rise to very real tensions about the appropriateness of particular planning 'solutions' to regulate retail spaces. The conflicts of interest between investments in spectacular yet placeless mega-malls, and those initiatives which promote localized culturally specific consumption quarters, are particularly intransigent.

Our analysis offers some insights into the determinants of successful retail restructuring. The experience of the Nottingham Lace Market in particular suggests that the answer must lie in the development of localized production constellations for global markets. Such systems capture the benefits of well-managed, local supply chains allowing rapid response production enhanced by sensitive well-resourced, strategic public sector policy frameworks, while at the same time allow access to large, high value added and differentiated global markets. Such systems of production and consumption, we argue, represent the optimum combination of localized production intelligence and internationalized markets and consumption preferences. The strategic choice must be for clothing producers and retailers to make the transition into higher value-added, quality, design-based markets which are driven by non-price competition and offer specialized customized quality products in small batches and with quick response. The added advantages are that not only does this harness domestic design talent and open up new, lucrative world markets, but also it offers the potential for enhanced working conditions. Whether retail capitalists seize such opportunities remains to be seen. In the absence of strategic public policy intervention at the national, regional and local levels, however, the sustainability of such a strategy is questionable.

CHAPTER 16

The limits to retail capital

David B. Clarke

> There is no thinking of *limits* that does not deploy a certain model of space.
> (Wood, 1990: xvi)

There can be little doubt that the pace of theoretical change within human geography has picked up considerably since the mid-1980s. In some ways that change appears to have followed something like an exponential path. From another vantage point, however, the discipline seems not to be following a linear progression at all; rather, it appears that we are either going round in circles or perhaps bifurcating in radically opposed directions. It is within this context that this chapter offers an account of three distinctive approaches to the geography – or more accurately geographies – of retailing. Yet at its base lies a more subversive aim: if the body of the present text begins from the premise that a 'geography of retailing' is a coherent idea, ultimately this idea will have been decentred in a call for a far more expansive geography of the consumer society. The narrative to be presented here will have ended far from its starting-point.

If the (as yet still faintly voiced) idea of a 'cultural turn' in economic geography is borne out (Crang, 1993), it can be anticipated that the final turn of this chapter, from a 'restricted' to a 'general' economy, will be placed under this rubric. To this possibility, however, must be added the caveats that this reading may neither represent authorial intention nor exhaust the meanings of the text. The idea of a cultural turn is, in fact, more generally problematic than many allow. A cultural turn in economic geography is likely to have been but part of a wider deconstructive turn within human geography – a turn that has as its reality-effect a blurring of boundaries within (and perhaps outwith) the discipline. (This statement signals the view of 'culture' at work in these pages, a view most adequately located under the sign of 'poststructuralism'.)

A debt to poststructuralism infuses this text on an epistemological level. Poststructuralism has introduced to human geography the *textuality* of the world (Barnes and Duncan, 1992). The implications of this revelation have not, though, been readily absorbed. Debate remains fixed in accordance with a simulated polarity of difference-as-opposition (positivist and realist science) and difference-as-contradiction (dialectics). The deconstructive difference-as-différance has to be set into play (Doel, 1992). In the (twi)light of this polarized disciplinary context rests an immanent critique of opposing positivist and political-economic retail geographies, the latter a relative newcomer to a geographical field long dominated by neo-classical economic thought.

This critique reveals an unfortunate potential in the 'new political economic geography of retailing', to which this volume contributes, in that it may embroil us within a simulated debate and thereby refuel a restricted economism. The development of an *acceptable* radical critique of orthodox retail geography will have performed the purpose of preserving the orthodoxy. To avoid this we need to raise the stakes and look to an *unacceptable* critique. This requires an adventurous leap; a leap towards an analysis of the spaces of 'capitalism' grounded in an acceptance of the ideas of 'general economy' (Bataille, 1991; Baudrillard 1976; Derrida, 1978). Can we live up to, or continue to live without, such a vertiginous theoretical task? Just a few decades ago, geography made a similar leap, as it began to embrace dialectics (Harvey, 1973; 1982; Olsson, 1980). There can be no justification for such moves, just as there can be no criticism. But let me ironically furnish this with the authority of Foucault's (1977: 33) prediction that, at some time in the near future, *transgression* will 'seem as decisive for our culture, as much a part of its soil, as the experience of contradiction was at an earlier time for dialectical thought'.

Contra Olsson's (1992: 91) suggestion that epistemology 'never left the mirror stage', perhaps we are now finally witnessing an epistemological shift to the upper vector of Lacan's (1977: 315) *graphe complet*, the vector of the drive. A wayward line of thought provides us with the possibility of realizing the character of the final stages of the world (Pefanis, 1991). There can, therefore, be no argument for expanding the (delimited) sub-discipline of retail geography. We must instead de-limit geography. Approaching the limit we discover that the most stolid of classical geometries have transmuted themselves into the most hyperreal simulations and the most revolutionary thoughts remain haunted by a rationalist phantom of production. The option to fiddle and tinker with solid theories and iron laws while the fractal world around implodes is, though, no longer open. The time has come to transgress, to cross limits. By exploring the neo-classical and the Marxian foundations of opposing retail geographies (in an inevitably caricatured, but none the less serious, way) this chapter seeks to exaggerate weaknesses in these traditions of thought – to the point where they express a lack that pushes over on to new terrain. In structuring the chapter in this way I am pegging my hopes on a 'pataphysical' move; seeking an imaginary solution.

On orthodox retail geography

Systems obsessed with their systemacity are fascinating. (Baudrillard, 1979: 128)

In applying the term 'orthodox' to a subset of retail geography I would hope to signal the inclusion of the largely empiricist – or, more fairly, empirically directed – work which describes analytically the changing spatial structure of retailing (examples might include Brown, 1987; R L Davies, 1976; 1984; Dawson, 1980; 1983; Dawson and Broadbridge, 1988; Guy, 1980; Jones and Simmons, 1990) as well as more mathematical positivist retail models (for example, much of the material collected in Wrigley, 1988a). These two strands of work find a common ancestry in the spatial science of the 1960s but have subsequently stressed the empirical and theoretical components of this framework differentially. Given that it is the latter strand of work which most strictly adheres to its underlying assumptions, much of this section will lay its focus there. The obvious critique of positivist retail geography properly belongs to an earlier period of human geography (Gregory, 1978). I forewarn the reader of this much, and to a certain extent circumvent any such *detailed* critique. It is not, though, easy to escape the fact that such geographies continue to exert an immense fascination.

I take it that, in principle, it would not be especially difficult to formulate three related areas of critique with respect to this kind of work: first, much orthodox retail geography is founded on a predictive and instrumentalist epistemology; second, most of its ontological presumptions are linked to the neo-classical economic view of the world (and thereby rest on an impoverished conception of space); and third, its capacity to elucidate other social structures is (therefore) under-mined. Note that none of these criticisms is necessarily particularly damning according to orthodox retail geography's own internal criteria. The various components of orthodox retail geography, in some people's hands, can and do work fairly well (Harvey, 1989a: 212). But arguments can certainly be made that invite an examination of the 'ideological' character of this work. I shall briefly tackle these here but it must again be stressed that I am deliberately shying away from any precise or definitive account.

The first area of critique suggests that orthodox retail geography produces knowledge that is unequally powerful with respect to existing divisions in society. The methodologies of everything from spatial interaction modelling to questionnaire surveys of consumers' or shop workers' attitudes aim but to verify a certain instrumental view of the world and to generate knowledge on the basis of that view. Such knowledge generally proves most useful to those already powerful groups in society. Much predictive work is produced precisely for the direct benefit of retailers – an example is provided by Geographical Modelling and Planning (GMAP), a commercial consultancy company based at the University of Leeds – or to inform the policy and planning decisions of the state. In principle, such methodologies could be used to benefit consumers or workers rather than retaile·s and the state. Some may argue that certain of these benefits are harmonious. But it is not beyond the imagination that the interests of these different groups diverge and one suspects that those already endowed with power gain most from such knowledge. This is to present a rather functionalist caricature of the production of knowledge but it would not prove too difficult to develop a more convincing account that reached the same conclusion.

A second mechanism by which power has become increasingly concentrated within particular components of the retail system is a more concrete one. It concerns changes in retail planning as experienced in the British case (R L Davies, 1986). The shift from 1979 onwards towards less 'restrictive' retail planning effectively meant that the central state withdrew from urban planners the right to regard their paternalistic judgements of equitable retail provision as superior to the outcome of the market. This change has certainly not stemmed the battles between the retailers, planners, residential and other interest groups, but there can be little doubt that since the late 1970s retail planners have had the merest vestiges of their former powers (or, indeed, their ideals). The expertise that retailers bring into play over planning applications, in the form of well-rehearsed strategies (G Shaw, 1987), dubious impact predictions (Whystall, 1981) and alleged shady deals, make it impossible to view the knowledge capable of being generated from a positivist retail geography as neutral and objective (though see Norris (1990) for a more sober judgement of impact assessment). Retailers have long since learned to play the system – and planners, often of local economic necessity, have for quite a while now given way to job-creating or infrastructure-improving retail developments (R L Davies and Howard, 1988). Positivism, with its imperative to record how things are rather than how things should be, seems at worst supportive of, and at best a weak tool to counter the existing imbalance of power/knowledge.

To move to my second area of critique, it is evident that the account of retailing presented in those positivist geographies generating such knowledge is underpinned by a staunchly neo-classical economic framework. This is never far from the surface. For example, much retail geography still adheres, to a greater or lesser extent, to central place theory (Thorpe, 1991b). As 'the most elegant approach developed to explain the relationship between the economy and the urban form' (Urry, 1985: 34), the k=3 or 'marketing' hierarchy has exercised considerable sway on the imagination of retail geographers. That central place theory owes much to neo-classical economic theory is uncontroversial (Berry, 1967; Berry and Parr, 1988). A point that is less well taken, though, is that despite major changes in the urban retailing system (A G Wilson and Oulton, 1983), firm theoretical sense can still be made of the world by recourse to geographical theory based on neo-classical economics. This is important in the light of hopeful statements that the neo-classical economic framework has simply become outmoded by 'real-world' change. Neil Smith, for example, has suggested such a 'moving on', noting that 'instead of trying to identify the optimum site for a new supermarket, many geographers turned to identify the broader processes in which whole landscapes were made and remade' (N. Smith, 1989: 142).

This 'real world' change does not necessarily imply the methodological sea-change that Smith supposes. Structural change in the urban retailing system is demonstrably compatible with geographical theory based on neo-classical economics. This compatibility concerns the (not unproblematic) relations between central place theory and the shopping model (cf A G Wilson, 1978). Although these models may be mathematically incompatible (A G Wilson, 1991), the k=3 central place hierarchy can be thought of as a limit case of the production-constrained spatial interaction model. There is no need to conceive of the market areas of shopping centres as constituting rigid, discrete, contiguous zones. Consumers favour near rather than distant shopping centres but the propensity of visiting the nearest centre is probabilistic not deterministic. Market areas, consequently, have fuzzy boundaries – a situation characteristically represented in the shopping model. The validity of this conception renders the switch that Neil Smith (1989) implies essentially superficial in methodological terms.

This is in evidence in the dynamic modelling of changes in the retail landscape (M Clarke and Wilson, 1985; A G Wilson and Clarke, 1979). Catastrophic change in the urban retail system, emanating from the supply side of the retail system (primarily the influence of growing economies of scale – a 'retail revolution' initiating scale and operational changes akin to the production changes initiated by the industrial revolution); the reduction of the friction of distance over time (Poston and Wilson, 1977); and quantitative and qualitative changes in demand (largely in middle-class consumer behaviour pertaining to car and home-freezer ownership) have altered the structure of the urban retail system beyond belief. But these changes have not altered the ability of models based on neo-classical economic foundations to describe and predict that system. The successful dynamic modelling of structural changes in the retail system suggest that the neo-classical approach is alive and well (A G Wilson, 1988: 174–7).

The politics of the positivist neo-classical framework is, however, an interesting one. The faith placed on modelling the market processes involved in retailing tends formally to marginalize questions which involve (political) judgements. It is simply taken as given that the modelling of retail structure and its spatial dynamics as a *market* process is unproblematic. And it is true that such an approach has seen significant technical and instrumental progress. Whether the supply-side is conceived of as bearing traits of perfect or imperfect competition (A G Wilson, 1985), neo-classical economic assumptions about the nature of the firm are reproduced. Whether the demand-side of the system is conceived of as being characterized by optimization or sub-optimization, consumers are theorized in atomistic behavioural terms. (Alternative consumer behaviour modelling techniques, such as those drawing on random utility theory, are compatible with the meso-scale formulations of consumer behaviour in spatial interaction models (A G Wilson, 1981), though the entropy functions of the latter are not to be confused or conflated (A G Wilson, 1991).) These modifications all aim at predictive or instrumental power. Where they suggest public sector planning solutions, they provide expertise to confirm the paternalistic control of the planner as social engineer. Alternatively they aid directly in private sector planning, with respect to retailers' commercial decisions (Birkin and Foulger, 1992; Penny and Broom, 1988).

It is possible to make one limited form of value judgement with respect to different states of such a market system; that is, in assessing formally the welfare implications of different stable equilibria of the retail system. This theoretical possibility is, though, a political chimera. Although there are explicit formulations of consumer surplus in shopping models (Coelho and Wilson, 1976; Coelho et al, 1978) and although a retailers' producer (sic) surplus can be derived (cf A G Wilson, 1976) to evaluate the aggregate desirabilities of different urban retail structures (H C W L Williams et al, 1990) this kind of exercise has a forced political status. To begin with, conceptual problems are still in evidence – such as the ambiguous conception of consumer surplus in the literature (resulting from a failure to distinguish between the Marshallian and compensated demand curve). Although this kind of problem is solvable, it is ultimately impossible to make valid judgements on the basis of the most refined of concepts. As Little (1950) long ago showed, formal tests on the Pareto or potential Pareto efficiency of different system-states never do remove the necessity of baldly political decisions of equity. Such an exercise is irredeemably condemned to be a purely technical nicety.

The liberal-utilitarian political philosophy behind such a theoretical chimera, however, does serve to debar certain political questions from the agenda. One can note here, for example, the failure of orthodox retail geography to acknowledge the historical specificity of consumer sovereignty (Mohun, 1977) and the sexism of economic man (Barnes, 1988). McDowell (1989), in her overview of feminist developments in geography, offers some further comments on women and shopping models in her tellingly entitled sub-section 'Add Women and Stir'. As Barnes (1988) has indicated, these problems are not unrelated and centre around a particular notion of rationality in economic geography (see also Barnes, 1989; 1992a; 1992b). This is something of a crucial issue in that it signals the cultural specificity of notions of 'rationality', a point necessarily incorporating the gendered nature of rationality. The underlying epistemology of neo-classical economic theory is in clear debt to Cartesian rational ideals. 'Economic man' represents a particular incarnation of the Cartesian knowing subject. The critique of this mode of rationality has been most potently formulated from within the discourses of psychoanalysis and of feminism (see C Williams, forthcoming, for an analysis of the subject from the conjunction of these two discourses).

Rather than continue along these lines of critique, however, I would like to make one or two comments on more recent developments on the nature of positivist retail geography. The 'GIS (Geographical Information System) revolution' has at last enabled spatial interaction models to sit on the desks of retail managers in suitably 'user-friendly' forms. When the mathematical explanation offered by shopping models is safely shielded behind maps of easily interpretable performance indicators (see G P Clarke and Wilson, 1986) the need for explanation is finally overtaken by the consideration of the accuracy of prediction (though this is presently limited by computer power). The demonstrated existence of weird-looking but predictively superior spatial interaction models (Openshaw, 1988), which can be generated computationally, takes the former need for explanation to its logical vanishing point. As Baudrillard (1983b) has suggested, the tendency toward simulation has reordered reality into hyperreality, causality is replaced by genetic code and the requirement for meaning is simultaneously eroded. As data are mercantalized (Lyotard, 1984) spatial science enters a postmodern condition.

On retail capital

> To understand capitalism, we maintain, we need to theorize retailing. (Ducatel and Blomley, 1990: 207)

Neil Smith's (1989: 142) remark about 'real world' retail change and academic trends has already been read as too easily implying a necessary relation between the two. On another reading, however, it proves to be entirely accurate. The growing concentration of capital in the retail sector (Wrigley, 1987) has begun to reveal the fundamental inadequacy of much existing geographical work, whether empirically descriptive or mathematically formulated. Orthodox retail geography has maintained its hegemony within the sub-discipline most clearly in its understanding of retail location. Retailers face intense locational pressures and, as argued above, the orthodox knowledge that retail geography generates is practically useful. Where this work is at its most stultifying, though, is in its inability to link this locational imperative to the underlying capitalist dynamic that acts as its driving force. There is a clear possibility of rewriting the historical geography of retailing in terms informed by such a broader framework.

The political economic retheorization of retail geography that is now under way implies a shift within both retail geography and economic geography (Ducatel and Blomley, 1990: 207). Attempts to elucidate the geographical implications of the changed 'real world' situation have begun to generate work that takes on an entirely different flavour to the retail geography considered thus far. Moreover, the kinds of circumstance outlined in this literature precisely explain the conditions for the increasingly widespread uptake of locational modelling techniques and GIS in retailing. Much of this work has been couched in terms of 'retail restructuring' (Wrigley, 1988b, 1992a, 1993a; and more generally Lovering, 1989).

Ideas of retail restructuring and the concentration of capital in the retail sector have effectively appealed to the twin empirical observations that the size of units of capital involved in retailing has increased, together with their market shares – expressed, for example, in the oligopolistic market structure of British grocery retailing (K Davies *et al*, 1985; Hallsworth, 1990; Wrigley, 1987). The consequences stemming from this changed situation have been characterized in terms of an entirely different competitive situation than that conventionally understood in the retail geographical literature; Wrigley (1991: 1540) likens this new situation to a 'predatory game' (interestingly this analogy is also made by A G Wilson 1981: 150) with reference to the Lotka-Volterra equations).

This new understanding has much to say about space but affords attention not to direct influences on store location but to influences on the strategic behaviour of large retail companies and the spatial consequences of this behaviour. The most important emphasis is that large corporate retailers are increasingly driven by a *capital* logic. Thus, retailers have been increasingly concerned to deploy capital more efficiently (e.g. in terms of return on capital employed). This has meant a more intense use of capital in relation to labour, with increases in labour productivity largely attained by the implementation of information technology throughout the distribution channel (Guy, 1988). Retailing practices are also increasingly tied into the financial capital markets (and, to a lesser extent, speculative property markets). As a result of these factors, the geographical manner in which retailers operate has increased in complexity.

An important dimension of this work is to be found in its ability to relate a number of empirical trends to the heightened capital imperative facing corporate retailers. Certain points raised by the 'new' literature undoubtedly have their antecedents in orthodox work, such as the issue of retail power in the marketing channel (Dawson, 1979; see, more recently, Dawson and Shaw, 1990). In the new literature this has been related to an increasingly efficient use of capital by retailers who, as monopsonistic buyers, are able to attain net positive cash flows (Wrigley, 1987). This situation has implications in terms of the consumer; for example, Wrigley (1991), developing an idea in Moir (1990), provides *prima facie* evidence of the existence of monopoly profits in British grocery retailing. Despite such insights, however, there is a potential danger here in maintaining a focus primarily on the retailer rather than on the commodity channel as a whole. This may continue to provide a restricted view, concentrating on the geography of stores and neglecting the geography of such important trends as the centralization of retail distribution operations (McKinnon, 1985; Sparks, 1986b), the development of the contract market in physical distribution (Fernie, 1989) and increasing levels of trade marketing by manufacturers to retailers (G Davies, 1990).

The most important element of this new work, however, lies in its more adequate understanding of space as a product of social activity rather than merely a given context. It is only silhouetted against this literature that the impoverished view of space in orthodox retail geography becomes fully apparent. Geographical work deriving from neo-classical economics conceives of space as a neutral container, at most effecting transportation costs that influence the equilibrium state(s) of the retail system. Political economic work, by contrast, has a more sophisticated understanding of the *reciprocal* nature of the relations between space and corporate retail activity. Wrigley (1989: 288), for example, has characterized retail change over space in terms of a number of phases of 'capital switching' operating at, and thereby helping to define, different spatial scales. The term 'capital switching' has an ambiguous status here; it is not, I think, intended to be read as synonymous with the use of the term in the Cambridge capital controversies (see Harcourt, 1972), though this reading may have some mileage. Rather it refers more readily to an identifiable series of intrinsically geographical changes in the operation of retailing activities, occurring at particular spatial scales.

Post-war out-of-town retail movements, for instance, have been characterized as a first phase of capital switching, effectively operative at the urban scale. Hallsworth (1991) has suggested that the dynamics of retailing's built environment may be linked to changes in the wider condition of the capitalist economy (cf Harvey, 1978). The idea of three post-war 'waves' of retail locational decentralization (Schiller, 1986) and subsequent inner city revitalization carries clear resonances with Harvey's (1989b) idea of the landscape of capitalism being made in capitalism's own image, with bouts of 'creative destruction' forming a necessary part of that mode of production. Beyond the observation that capital may be 'grounded' in retail property assets, however, this notion has remained underdeveloped.

A second phase of 'capital switching' has, according to Wrigley (1989), occurred within the *regional* arena, as corporate retailers have expanded geographically in order to meet increasingly unrealistic stock market expectations. In the British case, the overriding necessity of new store openings has resulted in the largest British retailers continuing to raise financial capital during the current recession (Wrigley, 1991). A third phase of 'capital switching' is also held to be in evidence, at the international scale (cf Treadgold and Davies, 1988). This is most notable in terms of transatlantic flows of capital towards the USA (Hallsworth, 1990; Wrigley, 1989) but pan-European retailing represents a further aspect of this scale of activity, following a capital logic similar to that explaining regional expansion.

Despite this understanding of the relations between space and retailing, it may be argued that this work represents 'medium level' theory, lacking an adequate *abstract* understanding of these relations. In an important paper, Ducatel and Blomley (1990) have attempted, from an orthodox Marxist perspective, to redefine the tenets in accordance with which the whole substantive topic of retail geography is to be understood. Their intervention is explicitly presented as a 'first attempt', deliberately side-stepping any real consideration of space (Ducatel and Blomley, 1990: 207). (Their paper does, though, range from international comparisons to the microgeographical scale of store design: Ducatel and Blomley, 1990: 223–4.) Rejecting out of hand the whole tradition of orthodox retail geography, Ducatel and Blomley (1990) provide an axiomatic formulation of 'retail capital' as the foundation for a new orthodox Marxist retail geography. Unfortunately, this theoretical strategy ultimately fails to deliver. As Fine and Leopold (1993b) have concluded, many of Ducatel and Blomley's empirical observations are not reliant on the category 'retail capital' and the theorization of the category itself seems to raise more problems than it solves: 'retail capital does *not* emerge as an appropriate abstract category to develop within Marxist theory ' (Fine and Leopold, 1993b: 274).

This argument is significant because, as Fine and Leopold readily admit, it does not deny the importance of retailing (no more than the lack of an abstract category of 'steelmaking capital' denies the importance of steelmaking). Rather, it questions the level of abstraction upon which Ducatel and Blomley (1990) pin their hopes and thereby partially supports the kind of theoretically informed empirical work characterizing much of the new retail geography discussed above. More importantly, however, Fine and Leopold provide a clarification of Ducatel and Blomley's analysis, raising a number of important theoretical points.

As Fine and Leopold (1993b: 283) note, Ducatel and Blomley (1990) jump between two equally inadequate definitions of retail capital as an abstract category: the first is based upon sale for final consumption; the second on sale for final consumption to workers. The former is problematic because the relevant abstract division is between commodities being sold as constant capital on the one hand, and as wage goods on the other – a division which is not empirically evident in retailing. (Both builders and DIY-enthusiasts shop at DIY superstores, for example.) The second definition is equally a contingent matter. The distinction between what workers and capitalists purchase and how they make those purchases cannot be seen to define an abstract category. Capitalist's 'luxury' consumption (out of surplus value) may take on particular qualities but this does not define an abstract category, locally excluding wages being used for such purchases. The overlaps between such categories of consumption are, therefore, potentially manifold. Thus,

> The boundaries of retail capital are not determined by the circulation of capital but by the circulation of revenue which ... is at a lower level of abstraction since it depends upon distributional struggle (and the potential divergence of the value of wages from the value of labour power, etc.) (Fine and Leopold, 1993b: 287)

As the positive aspect of their critique, Fine and Leopold (1993b) venture the view that Marx provided a comprehensive theory of capital in exchange which, unlike 'retail capital', can be justified analytically with reference to the circulation of capital. To detail this classification of capital in exchange: merchant capital represents a specialized subset of capital involved in the circulation of commodities; interest-bearing capital is also involved in the circulation of commodities, referring to that money capital lent to merchant capital where it is used to appropriate a portion of surplus value. These categories provide a hermetically sealed account of that portion of capital involved in exchange. While the detail of this more adequately defined Marxian model need not detain us here, its importance extends beyond the point that it has no room for 'retail capital'. As Fine and Leopold (1993b: 281) demonstrate, it also provides an important theorem suggesting a tendency towards the equalization of the rate of profit of merchant capital in relation to productive capital. While space limits a consideration of the full implications of this point, it may be noted that this not only creates difficulties for neo-Ricardian political economists dedicated 'to treating [commerce] as equivalent to productive activity ' but also presents problems for those wishing to argue that retail power emanating from capital concentration in the retail sector permits a greater appropriation of surplus value by retailers.

The debate between Ducatel and Blomley (1990) and Fine and Leopold (1993b) forms part of a wider disagreement between Marxists concerning the 'fractionation' of capital (see Jessop, 1982) and the degree to which 'it is possible to equate the expressions of the forms which social capital takes (i.e. its functional forms) with the concrete nature of capitalist institutions at a lower level of abstraction' (Tickell, 1992: 111). This debate can be read as outlining a need for a more rigorous political economic geography of commerce. My intention here, however, is to read this debate against the grain – and hence to break out of a set of arguments that could clearly found a new political economic geography of retailing to oppose the existing orthodoxy, in a polarized but glacial manner. The move I am making here is intended to take us out of this orbit and off on an entirely different tangent. It is not, however, a random move; it picks up on a particular aporia in Ducatel and Blomley's (1990) text. The most telling mark of this possibility is the problematic status of consumption which repeatedly makes itself felt. I am not alone in this reading. Although Fine and Leopold (1993b: 287) make relatively little of the point, they do suggest that Ducatel and Blomley (1990) have 'structured the role of demand' in a selective way to support their conceptualization of retail capital. Ducatel and Blomley allegedly characterize demand 'as something lying outside and confronting (retail) capital' (contra Marx's (1973) characterization of consumption in the Grundrisse as one of a number of 'distinctions within a unity' that equates to the circulation of capital). This, it is suggested, is evident in Ducatel and Blomley's (1990: 216) 'reference to the struggle of consumers to impose their use value logic as opposed to an exchange value logic' (Fine and Leopold, 1993b: 287). Use values are taken to be culturally constructed and hence extrinsic to the economy, though they may be taken to impinge upon class; for example, they signify class status for Bourdieu (1984).

What is revealed in Ducatel and Blomley's (1990) text, therefore, is an undercurrent that unwittingly escapes the capital-logic totality. It is perhaps no accident that the problematic character of the demands of final consumers begins to suggest an approach that parts company with the orthodox Marxian view at the very time when retailing itself is beginning to be transformed – at the point where it finds itself embracing a competitively driven need to become increasingly 'attentive' to consumers. The growth in retail marketing (treating the retailer itself as a *brand* rather than merely a stockist of manufacturer's branded goods) and in retail marketing management (McGoldrick 1990; Walters and White, 1987); in retail positioning (G J Davies and Brooks 1989); and in expenditure on store design, retail advertising and retail 'image' generally, signals a shift into a world of 'retail culture'. In some ways there is nothing new in this; J H Bird and Witherwick (1986) provide an interesting case study. In other ways, though, there is something of a marked sea-change in its importance. Again, a postmodern shift that has more than a little to do with capitalism but suggests a certain level of stress in that structure.

Whether these changes necessarily have anything to do with 'flexibility' (Gibbs, 1992; Harvey, 1989c) is a contentious point. It has been suggested, for instance, that the retail sector is at the leading edge in such logistical innovations as just-in-time systems, the implementation of information technologies and so on (Murray, 1988). The retail sector also provides clear examples of segmented labour markets with entry characteristics inviting a highly 'flexible', gender-specific secondary labour force. These points are of considerable empirical importance but this should not be taken too readily as implying a shift in the *economic* dynamic of capitalism toward the retail sector. Theoretical regard should be paid to the idea the 'far from retailers dominating productive capital, they are incorporating it in all but formal ownership' (Fine and Leopold, 1993b: 286).

One concern about the new economic geographies of retailing, therefore, must be that they may inherit from orthodox retail geography a continued emphasis on retailers and their store location activities – albeit in a manner far more appreciative of the economic context of the corporate retailer. This focus may misrepresent both the wider structure of the commodity channel and the status of consumption in shaping retail change. In fact these two aspects are increasingly related; for example, physical distribution management is linked to store layout and design via such techniques as direct product profitability (McKinnon, 1989). The problematic status of the consumption-retail nexus in particular, however, has increasingly provided a cultural dynamic to retail activity, though this is fuelled by, not separate from, the oligopolistic market structure of retailing.

One of the most important aspects of retailing relates to the fact that it creates a space where everyday life meets the machinations of capitalism. Such a conception begins to reveal something about consumption in relation to capitalism, while at the same time demonstrating the dependency of retailing and other forms of capital on a forceful and energized cultural logic.

From retail capital to general economy: a geography of exchange without reserve

Baudrillardians never make it past the shopping mall. (Massumi, 1992: 179)

In the previous section, some suggestion has been made as to the limits to 'retail *capital*' in relation to the growth of 'retail *culture*'. A parallel critique might have reversed this emphasis, placing the stress on the limits to *retail* capital. In other words, to understand the current historical geography of capitalism we may need not 'to theorize retailing', as Ducatel and Blomley (1990: 207) assert, but to theorize those aspects of capitalism which most directly attach to culture. The most obvious contender for such a critique would be advertising (though advertising is but the most high profile of a vast bank of marketing practices, and sometimes too easily becomes a scapegoat for more fundamental aspects of capitalism). Activities such as advertising have increased in importance, in part as a consequence of changes in the form taken by retailing. In the move from counter-service to self-service shopping, for instance, the 'sales push' of the shop assistant has largely given way to a 'sales pull', exemplified most clearly by the 'information' supplied to consumers by advertising (Porter, 1976). It would not prove too difficult to argue, without denying the increased importance of retailing, that forms of marketing such as advertising are also of a heightened importance.

The most significant feature of advertising – though many theorizations commit the violence of abstracting from this – is its peculiar cultural nature. 'If we stripped modern advertising of direct reference to the three themes of money, sex and power there would be very little left', writes Harvey (1989c: 287). And indeed many commentators have suggested that a key characteristic of consumer capitalism is its unprecedented reliance on an undercurrent of sex. While not wishing to imply that everything may thus be reduced to sex, this is a telling example. Although geography, like economics, has always eschewed the psychoanalytic notion of the unconscious, there can be little doubt that unconscious drives are at work in defining the contours of the economy. Thus, however much economists might theorize the fundamental rationality of the economy, 'something else' always seems to remain at work, beyond the sphere of rationality. This 'something', always to be explained away as a different category of concern, invariably falls under the heading of 'culture'. The idea that capitalism, in its present 'consumerist' guise, is driven by some manner of cultural logic is, therefore, of fundamental importance. An adequate account of this phase of capitalism would refuse those formulations which operate a restricted economy, which hold the suspended category 'culture' in reserve.

The most important line of argument to be taken up from cultural theory within geography concerns the constitution of the human subject. Work on the constitution of the *consuming* subject and the role of retail spaces in defining, as well as being defined by, the subject of consumption is certainly of relatively recent vintage as far as geography is concerned (Shields, 1992a). It should be acknowledged, though, that cultural studies have afforded attention to shopping in this manner for a far longer period of time (M Morris, 1988). This work provides an explicit recognition of the implications of the subject in spaces designed to valorize capital. Whilst this work has, perhaps, concentrated unduly on large shopping malls, it nevertheless indicates some important directions for geographical research – notably in recognizing (explicitly or implicity) that the spaces produced by consumer capitalism represent *hyperspaces* for the subject (cf Featherstone, 1991; Shields, 1989). This argument is, as yet, not well developed – or at least not well understood. It is not an easy argument. In my view it can best be conceived in terms which recognize three putative historical changes in the dialectical constitution of space and subjectivity. The space defined in Renaissance linear perspective constituted the subject at an externally positioned, all-seeing point of visual mastery (Cosgrove, 1985). However, tendencies evident in Modernist art (Lefebvre, 1991), the 'narrative space' of the cinema (Heath, 1981) and so on, modulated this subjectivity to a point where multiple vanishing points ultimately undermined the very notion of the vanishing point, thus paving the way for a postmodern 'hyperspace' (a new, virtual space) and new forms of subjectivity (D B Clarke, 1995).

Despite this highly important recognition of a fundamental change in space, however, there are some significant problems with existing cultural geographical work on consumption. In providing something like the antithesis to the kind of work discussed in the previous section – work which still owes a significant debt to structuralist Marxism, and therefore still insists on economic determination in the last instance – a focus on the *subject* of consumption will almost inevitably face the danger of being read as the other side of a structure–agency dualism. Although such a reading is fundamentally at odds with the tenor of the poststructuralism that influences much of this work, one cannot help but imagine that such a misrepresentation is actively at work in some such writing. (Evident, for examples, in work which presents culture as an economy (of meaning) which operates simply in parallel to the 'material' economy: cf Fiske, 1989a.) The solution to this problem is dependent as much upon a dismantling of the economistic view of structure as the agency-laden view of subjectivity. It is my contention here that this solution requires a deconstruction of the meaning of 'economic'. Such a task carries with it, however, profound implications for our understanding of capitalism. It cannot, therefore, avoid an engagement with Marxism.

A theoretical crisis has been facing Marxism for a long time now. Witness the optimistic conceptualization in the 1970s which labelled our era 'late capitalism' (Mandel, 1978). The term's dual implication of the 'last stages of' and the 'already dead' is now steeped in irony. This has seen a dramatic parodic reversal. Newer theorizations of 'early' or 'infantile' capitalism (Frisby, 1985; Jameson, 1984 respectively) – of a polymorphous perverse capitalism – cast a strange light over the traditions that constitute the theoretical edifice of late Marxism. Despite belated attempts to imbue untinged areas of geography – such as retail geography – with a dose of political economy, it is evident that this crisis has been working its way through geography. Harvey's (1989c) attempt to domesticate the flux and specificity of cultural change within the safety of an inadequate base-superstructure model is symptomatic of the threat culture is perceived to bear. It is precisely this point that makes the retheorization of retail geography – an insignificant enough sounding task to most outside the sub-discipline – an especially important one. For, as demonstrated above, it is in such areas that the cultural dynamic of contemporary capitalism can best be located.

The issues raised so far – especially the problems expressed in the (related) binary oppositions economic/cultural and structure/agency – finally point to the possibility of the economy manifesting not an unbounded (or even a bounded) rationality (as in mainstream economics and political economy) but an unbounded *irrationality*. (Here irrationality must be conceived of as eccentric to, not the binary opposite of, rationality.) This type of notion is most developed in Bataille's (1991) 'general economy'. The remainder of this section provides an explication of this line of thought, in a final move away from existing retail geographies and towards a far more expansive and potentially incisive geography of the consumer society.

The discussion of Bataille leads into an account of Baudrillard's conception of the consumer culture of the west. This, I would argue, offers a more politically charged indication of the theoretical strategies facing those with an interest in activities such as retailing and, of course, the spaces these activities define. While space limits any detailed explication of these ideas, a brief exposition of Baudrillard's position is provided together with a cursory critique in a brief commentary on the potential value of other approaches, including the works of Deleuze and Guattari and of Walter Benjamin. The general intention, though, is now to look forward to a new geography that no longer operates according to a restricted economy. This carries with it a political project that may be termed postmodern; it is, inevitably, incredulous towards meta-narratives and looks to analyse the cultural condition of the west without a renewed vision of progress. What will finally have proved important here is a new formulation of the 'economic' that recognizes the Hegelian essence of virtually all existing political-economy (D B Clarke and Purvis, 1994). Our future view of 'economy' will have been found to have required a deconstructive move.

Bataille's (1991) notion of 'general economy' rests on a reading of Mauss's (1966) Gift as an anti-economic principle – a reading diametrically opposed to Lévi-Strauss's development of the concept (Pefanis, 1991). Bataille sought to bring to prominence the irrationalist notion of the *parte maudite*, the 'accursed share'. The concept refers to a surplus, an excess – a radical expenditure that western culture has carefully repressed in order to preserve the myth of reason as the essence of (economic) progress. The concept carries with it a nihilistic danger, perhaps a nihilistic *telos*. It is a virulent destructive energy linked to all situations characterized by pure expenditure, loss or wastage: sacrifice, death, the loss of the self in the extremes of sexual ecstasy, all manner of discharges.

Derrida (1978) has spelled out the difference between the Hegelian 'restricted economy' and the 'general economy' of Bataille. While removing some of the surrealistic threat from Bataille's concept he does push the concept to its *logical* conclusion – literally, in relation to reason. The Hegelian dialectic took resort in an *accumulation*: Hegel went beyond the metaphysical binary opposition of identity/exclusion. But he reserved within the dialectic a progression – the third synthetic term accumulating a final greater value than that of the original thesis and antithesis. The general economy, by contrast, is without reserve. There is no third term gathering up the investment of the other two: there is only a spillage; a flooding caused by the breaching of binary oppositions; a sacrifice of two clear rational terms for a loss that is neither a total absence not a renewed presence; a transgression of two binding limits.

Bataille's (1991) use of 'general economy' took on a concrete appearance. Whole societies could be analysed from afar by mobilizing this concept, by tracking the surpluses of energy that inform a new kind of political economy. Bataille's direct task Baudrillard (1993) inherited in *Symbolic Exchange and Death*. Contrasting the multiplicitous primitive 'symbol' (the life-giving and life-destroying Aztec sun) with the simplistic univalent western 'sign' (the tourist sun of the modern sun-worshipper), the foreboding richness of the primitive with the facile clarity of western communication, Baudrillard seeks to analyse symbolic exchange: exchange that breaks the rules of equivalence; that accepts the anti-economic principle of Mauss's Gift; that mobilizes the *parte maudite*. The symbolic value of the Gift presents within itself the possible murder of the rationalist values of capitalist exchange. (While Baudrillard's primitivism may seem nostalgic, it is not a naive appeal to Nature. The symbolic is a different, not a prior order of signification.) This principle informs Baudrillard's perspective on consumer capitalism.

Baudrillard (1983b) has linked to this perspective an analysis of the dominance of the electronic mass media in western culture. His line, akin to McLuhan's, is that the media do anything but mediate: they block all response. (Again the suggestion is that the contemporary west holds superficiality in place of profundity.) The 'masses', the 'silent majority' – Baudrillard (1983a) parodies the utopianism of Marxism – reveal a transpolitical strategy in the face of such a situation. A society composed of empty signs is countered by the masses, who adopt the strategy of a black hole, manifesting a strength of inertia that absorbs everything and radiates back nothing. The strategy Baudrillard (1983a; 1990) observes and exposes is the acceleration of this extreme passivity, especially in relation to consumption:

> a system is abolished only by pushing it into hyperlogic, by forcing it into an excessive practice which is equivalent to a brutal amortization. 'You want us

to consume – O.K., let's consume always more, and anything whatsoever; for any useless and absurd purpose.' (Baudrillard, 1983a: 46)

Consumer capitalism thrives on signs functioning as the alibis for use values. Baudrillard suggests a mode of cultural analysis capable of pushing this system beyond its limits. It is a nihilism, a death drive. It is a thankful way to the abyss, to the end of consumption. Baudrillard's (1988b) *America* provides one possible model geography of the consumer society (see D B Clarke and Doel, 1994): revel in hyperspace and embrace the end of the world. Baudrillard's (1990) most recent *fatal* theory of the consumer society suggests the impossibility of anything other than joining the logic of the object.

This is not, of course, the only course. For Massumi (1992: 179) Baudrillard's strategy is simply inadequate. One of Massumi's points seems to refer to the Lyotardian mercantalization of data: 'in an "information economy" signs cost money' asserts Massumi (1992: 178). Thus Massumi interprets the Baudrillardian surrender to the seduction of signs as a form of *sophisticated* cynicism – mobilized along class lines. This does not accurately attack the fundamentals of Baudrillard's position. It does, though, suggest one of several underdeveloped areas of Baudrillard's theory of consumerism.

A more important point that Massumi (1992: 179) raises is that 'Baudrillard's "hyperspace" is eccentric but not exorbital. He fails to go off on a tangent.' 'Stealing away from the shopping mall on an exorbital path tangent to identity *and* undifferentiation is called schizophrenia . . . a breakaway into the unstable equilibrium of continuing self-invention' (Massumi, 1992: 92). Massumi thus suggests the importance that Deleuze and Guattari (1983; 1988) might hold for understanding the identifications associated with consumerism (see also Lieberman, 1993).

From a quite different tradition, the work of Walter Benjamin might offer a further alternative. Benjamin's 'Arcades project' presents a geography of consumer capitalism (see Buck-Morss, 1989). I do not feel competent to comment on this but Benjamin is certainly deserving of attention from geographers interested in conceiving of the spaces defined by the culture of consumer capitalism.

There is, therefore, no existing adequate exploration of the (postmodern) geography of hyperspace. In my view, this is the key theoretical task towards which we should move. The lack of recognition of the overthrow of perspectival space – a failure to recognize that hyperreality functions according to a video logic (Baudrillard, 1976) – ironically gives rise to a string of pointless concepts. Philosophers are now according an importance to the spaces of postmodernity. Geographers must recognize that this is also their fortune.

These words have given a flavour of what lies ahead – a vertiginous task, to be sure: its epistemology has left the mirror stage; its ontology embraces irrationality; its poetics instil a sense of the textuality of the world. As consumer research itself begins to view consumption as text (E C Hirschman and Holbrook, 1992), as the application of neuro-computing in market research begins to generate new consumption classes and, indeed, create virtual consumers (Horizon, 1993), there can be little doubt that the exploration of hyperspace is in imminent need of a new improved brand of geographical imagination.

Conclusions

As a theoretical intervention, this chapter has assumed the importance of a diversion of our concerns. P Jackson (1991c: 194) warns of the danger in the 'common reduction of consumption to advertising and retailing' in geography. Geography has, until quite recently, had little to say about advertising, much about retailing. It is certainly true that, in the case of retailing, consumption has received a grossly reductionist treatment.

There is an inherent problem, though, in identifying consumption *either* culturally *or* economically. This is especially true when this takes the (Hegelian) form of assuming an economy of meaning – a 'circuit of culture' – operating in parallel to the capitalist economy. It is vital that we look beyond any such restricted economies that assume an easy latch on the world.

If we are prepared to accept the Baudrillardian view of western culture as a loss of the symbolic, we face a daunting task. Maybe it is a task of theoretical terrorism. We ought to create a fatal theory capable of accelerating consumer culture to the abyss – the ironic ring of the 'new retail geography', as it takes on the air of an advertising slogan, forms part of a fragmenting *fin-de-millennium* human geography.

If we reject Baudrillard's nihilism, we should certainly not neglect the examination of the consumerism of everyday life. We need to be capable of saying something of the hyperspaces of the consumer society which takes us a considerable way beyond existing retail geographies.

References

Abelson E S 1989 *When ladies go a-thieving: middle class shoplifters in the Victorian department store.* Oxford, Oxford University Press

Akehurst G 1983 Concentration in retail distribution: measurement and significance. *Service Industries Journal* 3: 161–79

Akehurst G 1984 'Checkout': the analysis of oligopolistic behaviour in the UK grocery retail market. *Service Industries Journal* 4(2): 198–242

Amin A and **Malmberg A** 1992 Competing structural and institutional influences on the geography of production in Europe. *Environment and Planning A* 24: 401–16

Amin A and **Robins K** 1990 The re-emergence of regional economies? The mythical geography of flexible production. *Society and Space* 8: 7–34

Appadurai A 1986 Introduction: commodities and the politics of value. In A Appadurai (ed.) *The Social Things.* Cambridge, Cambridge University Press

Arce A and **Marsden T K** 1993 The social construction of international food: a research agenda. *Economic Geography* 69: 293–312

Arrow K 1969 The organisation of economic activity. In US Congress, Joint Economic Committee, *The analysis and evaluation of public expenditures.* Washington, DC, US Government Printing Office

Asanuma B 1989 Manufacturer–supplier relationships in Japan and the concept of relation-specific skill. *Journal of the Japanese and International Economies* 3: 1–30

Ashton D and Snug J 1992 The determinants of labour market transition: an exploration of contrasting approaches. *Work, Employment and Society* 6: 1–21

Ashton D, Maguire M and Garland V 1982 *Youth in the labour market.* Research Paper no 34, Department of Employment, London, HMSO

Atkinson J 1984 *Flexibility, uncertainty and manpower management.* Institute for Management Studies, University of Sussex, Report 89

Atkinson J 1985 Flexibility: planning for an uncertain future. *Manpower Policy and Practice*, 1, Summer, 26–9

Atkinson J and Meager N 1986 *Changing working patterns: how companies achieve flexibility to meet new needs.* London, NEDO

Auerbach P 1988 *Competition: the economics of industrial change.* Oxford, Blackwell

Barley S R 1992 Semiotics and the study of occupational and organisational culture. In P J Frost, L F Moore, M R Louis, C C Lundberg and J Martin (eds) *Reframing Organizational culture.* London, Sage: 39–54

Barnes T J 1988 Rationality and relativism in economic geography: an interpretive review of the *homo economicus* assumption. *Progress in Human Geography* 12: 473–96

Barnes T J 1989 Structure and agency in economic geography and theories of economic value. In A Kobayashi and S Mackenzie (eds) *Remaking human geography.* London, Unwin Hyman: 134–48

Barnes T J 1992a Reading the texts of theoretical economic geography: the role of physical and biological metaphors. In T J Barnes and J S Duncan (eds) *Writing worlds: discourse, text and metaphor in the representation of landscape.* London, Routledge: 118–35

Barnes T J 1992b Postmodernism in economic geography: metaphor and the construction of alterity. *Society and Space* 10: 57–68

Barnes T J and Duncan J S 1992 (eds) *Writing worlds: discourse, text and metaphor in the representation of landscape.* London, Routledge

Barrier M 1988 Walton's Mountain. *Nation's Business* April 18–26

Barron R D and Norris G M 1976 Sexual divisions and the dual labour market. In D L Barker and S Allen (eds) *Dependence and exploitation in work and marriage.* London, Tavistock: 47–69

Barth G 1980 *City people*. New York, Oxford University Press

Bataille G 1991 *The accursed share: an essay on general economy. Volume I Consumption*. New York, Zone Books

Baudrillard J 1976 *The evil demon of images*. Sydney, Power Institute of Fine Arts

Baudrillard J 1979 *Seduction*. London, Macmillan

Baudrillard J 1983a *In the shadow of the silent majorities*. New York, Semiotexte

Baudrillard J 1983b *Simulations*. New York, Semiotexte

Baudrillard J 1988a *Jean Baudrillard: selected writings*. Cambridge: Polity Press

Baudrillard J 1988b *America*. London, Verso

Baudrillard J 1990 *Fatal strategies*. London, Pluto

Baudrillard J 1993 *Symbolic exchange and death*. London, Sage

BDP Planning and Oxford Institute of Retail Management 1992 *The effects of major out-of-town retail development*. London, HMSO

Beaverstock J, Leyshon A, Rutherford T, Thrift N and **Williams P** 1992 Moving houses: the geographical reorganization of the estate agency industry in England and Wales. *Transactions of the Institute of British Geographers* NS17: 166–82

Beck U 1992a *Risk society: towards a new modernity*. London, Sage

Beck U 1992b From industrial society to risk society: questions of survival, social structure and ecological enlightenment. *Theory, Culture and Society* 9: 97–123

Bell D 1988 *Models of power: politics and economics in Zola's Rougon-Macquart*. Lincoln, University of Nebraska Press

Belussi B 1987 *Benetton: information technology in production and distribution: a case study of the innovative potential of traditional sectors*. SPRU Occasional Paper 25, University of Sussex

Belussi F 1992 Benetton Italy: beyond Fordism and flexible specialization: the evolution of the network firm model. In S Mitter (ed.) *Computer-aided manufacturing and women's employment: the clothing industry in four EC countries*. London, Springer-Verlag

Benetton L 1993 High interest: the unravelling of Benetton. *Channel 4* 18 April

Benson S P 1986 *Counter cultures: saleswomen, managers and customers in American* department stores 1880–1914. Urbana, IL, University of Illinois Press

Bernstein I 1990 *The New York City draft riots: their significance for American society and politics in the age of the civil war.* New York, Oxford University Press

Berry B J L 1967 *Geography of market centres and retail distribution.* Englewood Cliffs, NJ, Prentice Hall

Berry B J L and **Parr J D** 1988 *Market centres and retail location: theory and applications.* Englewood Cliffs, NJ, Prentice Hall

Best M H 1990 *The new competition: institutions of industrial restructuring.* Oxford, Blackwell

Best M 1992 The firm and the market: the dynamic perspectives of Schumpeter and Penrose. *Social Concept* 6: 3–24

Bienefeld M 1989 The lessons of history and the developing world. *Monthly Review* July–August 9–41

Bird J H and **Witherick M E** 1986 Marks and Spencer: the geography of an image. *Geography* 71: 305–19

Birkin M F and **Foulger F** 1992 Sales performance and sales forecasting using spatial interaction modelling: the W. H. Smith approach. Working Paper 92/21, School of Geography, University of Leeds

Block F 1990 *Postindustrial possibilities: a critique of economic discourse.* Berkeley, CA, University of California Press

Blomley N K 1986 Regulatory legislation and the legitimisation crisis of the state: the enforcement of the Shops Act (1950) *Society and Space* 4: 183–200

Bluestone B, Hanna P, Kuhn S and **Moore L** 1981 *The retail revolution: market transformation, investment, and labor in the modern department store.* Boston, MA, Auburn House

Blumin S 1989 *The emergence of the middle class: social experience in the American city, 1760–1900.* Cambridge, Cambridge University Press

Boden D and **Molotch H L** 1994 The compulsion of proximity. In R Friedland and D Boden (eds) *Now/here: time, space and modernity.* Berkeley, University of California

Bourdieu P 1984 *Distinction: a social critique of the judgment of taste.* London, Routledge

Bowlby R 1985 *Just looking: consumer culture in Dreiser, Gissing and Zola.* New York, Methuen

Bowlby R 1987 Modes of modern shopping: Mallarmé at the *Bon Marché.* In N Armstrong and L Tennenhouse (eds) *The ideology of conduct: essays on literature and the history of sexuality.* New York, Methuen: 185–205

Bowlby S R, Foord J and **Tillsley C** 1992 Changing consumption patterns: impacts on retailers and their suppliers. *International Review of Retail, Distribution and Consumer Research* 2: 133–50

Bowlby S R, Foord J and **Tillsley C** 1993 *Changing retailing–manufacturing links: a study in the geography of employment.* Final report to the ESRC, Grant no. R000231588

Boyer M C 1985 *Manhattan manners: architecture and style 1850–1900.* New York, Rizzoli

Boyle C, Cathro J, Comber L and **Emmett S** 1990 The UK ready meals report. *Industry and Market Reviews* 3, Leatherhead Food RA

Brennan B 1991 Managing through hard times. *Retail Control* 596: 3–9

Brewer J and **Porter R** (eds) 1993 *Consumption and society in the seventeenth and eighteenth centuries.* London, Routledge

Brittan A 1989 *Masculinity and power.* Oxford, Basil Blackwell

Broadbridge A 1993 *Female and male earnings differentials in retailing.* Paper presented at ESRC Research Themes in Retailing Seminar 'Theme 2: Operational Issues in Retailing', MPS/UMIST, May

Broadbridge A and **Davies K** 1993 Management education at a distance and its effect on career progression: the case of MBA in retailing and wholesaling students. *Distance Education* 14(1): 6–26

Bromley R D F and **Thomas C J** 1993 The retail revolution, the carless shopper and disadvantage. *Transactions of the Institute of British Geographers* NS18: 222–36

Brown S 1987 Institutional change in retailing: a geographical perspective. *Progress in Human Geography* 11: 181–206

Buck-Morss S 1989 *The dialectics of seeing: Walter Benjamin and the Arcades Project.* Cambridge, MA, MIT Press

Bukharin N 1966 *Imperialism and world economy.* New York, Fertig

Bureau of National Affairs 1993 Sears announces major restructuring, loss of 50 000 jobs, end to catalogs. *Daily Report for Executives,* 26 January

Burgoyne C B and **Routh D A** 1991 Constraints on the use of money as a gift at Christmas: the role of status and intimacy. *Journal of Economic Psychology* 12: 47–69

Burns J A, McInerney J and **Swinbank A** 1983 *The food industry: economics and policies.* London, Heinemann

Burrell G and **Hearn J** 1989 The sexuality of organization. In J Hearn, D L Sheppard, P Tancred-Sherriff and G Burrell (eds) *The sexuality of organization.* London, Sage: 1–28

Burt S L 1989 Trends and management issues in European retailing. *International Journal of Retailing* 4: 1–97

Burt S L and **Sparks L** 1994 Structural change in grocery retailing in Great Britain: a discount re-orientation? *International Review of Retail Distribution and Consumer Research* 4: 195–217

Carr R 1993 In the family way. *Drapers Record* 13 February

Catephores G 1994 The imperious Austrian: Schumpeter as bourgeois Marxist. *New Left Review* 205: 3–30

Cerny P 1991 The limits of deregulation: transnational interpenetration and policy change. *European Journal of Political Research* 19: 173–96

Chain Store Age Executive 1985 Progressive change pays off at Montgomery Ward. *Chain Store Age Executive* February: 30–6

Chain Store Age Executive 1988 Store and deliver: retailers rely on hygrade. *Chain Store Age Executive* May: 273–4

Chaney D 1983 The department store as a cultural form. *Theory, Culture and Society* 1: 22–31

Cheal D 1988 *The gift economy.* London, Routledge

Christopherson S 1989 Flexibility in the US service economy and emerging spatial divisions of labour. *Transactions of the Institute of British Geographers* NS14: 131–43

Christopherson S 1990a Emerging patterns of work. In T Noyelle (ed.) *Skills, Wages and Productivity in the Service Sector.* Boulder, CO, Westview Press

Christopherson S 1990b The spatial dimension of the restructuring of consumer services, paper presented at Fulbright Colloquium 1990, Buying Back America: UK Capital in the US Service Economy, Miskin Manor, Vale of Glamorgan, 10–11 December

Christopherson S 1993 Market rules and territorial outcomes: the case of the United States. *International Journal of Urban and Regional Research* 17: 274–88

Clark G L 1989 Remaking the map of corporate capitalism: the arbitrage economy of the 1990s *Environment and Planning A* 21: 997–1000

Clark G L 1992 Real regulation: the administrative state. *Environment and Planning A* 24: 615–27

Clark G L 1993 Costs and prices, corporate competitive strategies and regions. *Environment and Planning A* 25: 5–26

Clark G L 1994 Strategy and structure: corporate restructuring and the scope and characteristics of sunk costs. *Environment and Planning A* 26: 9–32

Clark G L and **Wrigley N** 1995a Sunk costs: a framework for economic geography. *Transactions of the Institute of British Geographers* NS20: 204–23

Clark G L and **Wrigley N** 1995b The rudiments of corporate geography: sunk costs and the spatial structure of production. Paper presented at the Annual Conference of the Institute of British Geographers, Newcastle-upon-Tyne, 3–6 January

Clarke D B 1995 On the dialectic of the consuming subject in space. Working Paper, School of Geography, University of Leeds

Clarke D B and **Doel M** 1994 The perfection of geography as an aesthetic of disappearance: Baudrillard's America. *Ecumene* 1: 317–21

Clarke D B and **Purvis M** 1994 Dialectics, difference, and the geographies of consumption. *Environment and Planning A* 26: 1091–109

Clarke M and **Wilson A G** 1985 Dynamics of urban spatial structure: the progress of a research programme. *Transactions of the Institute of British Geographers* NS10: 427–51

Clarke G P and **Wilson A G** 1986 Performance indicators within a model–based approach to urban planning. Working Paper 446, School of Geography, University of Leeds, Leeds

Clarke P 1993 A decade of growth: but what about the next 10 years? *The Grocer* 8 May: 45–6

Clive Lewis and Partners 1988 *Midsummer retail report.* Mimeo, Clive Lewis and partners, 8 Stratton Street, London, WX1 5FD

Cocks J 1989 *The oppositional imagination: feminism, critique and political theory.* London, Routledge

Coelho J D and **Wilson A G** 1976 The optimum size and location of shopping centres. *Regional Studies* 10: 413–21

Coelho J D, Williams H C W L and **Wilson A G** 1978 Entropy maximising submodels within overall mathematical programming frameworks: a correction. *Geographical Analysis* 10: 195–210

Cohen P C 1992 Safety and danger: women on American public transport, 1750–1850. In D O Helleby and S M Reverby (eds) *Gendered domains: rethinking public and private in women's history.* Ithaca, NY, Cornell University Press: 109–22

Connell R W 1987 *Gender and power: society, the person and gender politics.* Cambridge, Polity

Cook I 1994 New fruits and vanity: symbolic production in the global food economy. In A Bonanno, L Busch, W H Friedland, L Gouveig and E Mingiovie (eds) *From Columbus to Conagra: the globalization of agriculture and food.* Kansas, University Press of Kansas

Cooke P 1988 Flexible integration, scope economies, and strategic alliances: social and spatial mediations. *Society and Space* 6: 281–300

Cooke P and **Morgan K** 1986 Flexibility and the new restructuring: locality and industry in the 1980s. Papers in Planning Research, no 94, Department of Town Planning, University of Wales, Institute of Science and Technology, Cardiff

Corfield P J 1990 Walking the city streets: social role and social identification in the towns of eighteenth-century England. *Journal of Urban History* 16: 132–74

Cosgrove D 1985 Prospect, perspective and the evolution of the landscape idea. *Transactions of the Institute of British Geographers* NS10: 45–62

Couch D 1992 Retailing, organisational structure and personnel management. In W S Howe (ed.) *Retailing management.* Basingstoke, Macmillan: 187–211

Cowe R 1991 Dixons look for quality performer in bad times. *Guardian* 11 July

Cowling K and **Sugden R** 1987 *Transnational monopoly capitalism.* Brighton: Wheatsheaf

Cox N and **Cox J** 1985–6 Valuations in probate inventories. *Local Historian* 19: 20–30; 20: 30–40

Crang P 1993 Re-thinking and re-teaching economic geography. Paper presented to the Annual Conference of the Institute of British Geographers, London, January

Crang P 1994 It's showtime: on the workplace geographies of display in a restaurant in South-East England, *Society and Space* 12: 675–704

Crang P and **Martin R L** 1991, Mrs Thatcher's vision of the New Britain and the other sides of the Cambridge Phenomenon. *Society and Space* 9: 91–116

Crawford P 1992 The challenges to patriarchalism: how did the Revolution affect women? In J Morrill (ed.) *Revolution and restoration: England in the 1650s.* London, Collins and Brown

Crewe L 1994 Consuming landscapes: designing desire in the Nottingham Lace Market. *East Midland Geographer* 17:22–7

Crewe L and **Davenport E** 1992 The puppet show: changing buyer–supplier relationships within clothing retailing. *Transactions of the Institute of British Geographers* NS17: 183–97

Crewe L and **Forster Z** 1993a Markets, design, and local agglomeration: the role of the small independent retailer in the workings of the fashion system. *Society and Space* 11: 213–29

Crewe L and **Forster Z** 1993b A Canute policy fighting economics? Local economic policy in an industrial district: the case of Nottingham's lace market. *Policy and Politics* 21: 275–88

Crewe L and **Lowe M S** 1995 Gap on the map? Towards a geography of consumption and identity. *Environment and Planning A* 27

Crompton C, Hautrais L and **Walters P** 1990 Gender relations and employment. *British Journal of Sociology* 41: 329–50

Czarniawska-Joerges B 1992 Culture is the medium of life. In P J Frost, L F Moore, M R Louis, C C Lundberg and J Martin (eds) *Reframing organizational culture.* London, Sage: 285–97

Davidoff L and **Hall C** 1987 *Family fortunes: men and women of the English middle class, 1780–1850.* Chicago, University of Chicago Press

Davidson M 1992 *The consumerist manifesto: advertising in postmodern times.* London, Routledge

Davies B K and **Sparks L** 1989 Superstore retailing in Great Britain 1960–1986. *Transactions of the Institute of British Geographers* NS14: 74–89

Davies G 1990 Marketing to retailers: a battle for distribution? *Long Range Planning* 23: 101–8

Davies G and **Brooks J M** 1989 *Positioning strategy in retailing.* London, Chapman

Davies K, Gilligan C and **Sutton C** 1985 Structural changes in grocery retailing: the implications for competition. *International Journal of Physical Distribution and Materials Management* 15: 3–48

Davies K, Gilligan C and **Sutton C** 1986, Development of own-label product strategies in grocery and DIY retailing in the United Kingdom. *International Journal of Retailing* 1: 6–19

Davies R L 1976 *Marketing geography: with special reference to retailing.* London, Methuen

Davies R L 1984 *Retail and commercial planning.* London, Croom Helm

Davies R L 1986 Retail planning in disarray. *The Planner* 72(7): 20–2

Davies R L and **Howard E** 1988 Issues in retail planning in the United Kingdom. *Built Environment* 14: 7–21

Davis D 1966 *A history of shopping.* London, Routledge

Davis E and **Kay J** 1990 Assessing corporate performance. *Business Strategy Review,* Summer: 1–16

Dawson J A 1979 *The marketing environment.* London, Croom Helm

Dawson J A (ed.) 1980 *Retail geography.* London, Croom Helm

Dawson J A 1983 *Shopping centre development.* London, Longman

Dawson J A and **Broadbridge A M** 1988 *Retailing in Scotland 2005.* Institute for Retail Studies, University of Stirling

Dawson J A and **Shaw S** 1989 Horizontal competition in retailing and the structure of manufacturer–retailer relationships. In L Pellegrini and S Reddy (eds) *Retail and marketing channels: economic and marketing perspectives on producer–distributor relationships*. London, Routledge: 49–72

Dawson J A and **Shaw S A** 1990 The changing character of retailer–supplier relationships. In J Fernie (ed.) *Retail distribution management: a strategic guide to developments and trends*. London, Kogan Page

Dawson J A and **Sparks L** 1985 *Issues in retailing*. Edinburgh, Scottish Development Department

Dawson J A, Findlay A M and **Sparks L** 1987a Employment in British superstores. Working Paper 8701, Institute for Retail Studies, University of Stirling

Dawson J A, Findlay A M and **Sparks L** 1987b The impact of scanning on employment in UK food stores: a preliminary analysis. *Journal of Marketing Management* 23: 285–300

Dawson J A, Shaw S and **Harris G** 1989 *The impact of changes in retailing and wholesaling on Scottish manufacturers*. ESU Research Paper, Institute for Retail Studies, University of Stirling

Defoe D 1721 *The fortunes and misfortunes of Moll Flanders*. London

Deleuze G and **Guattari F** 1983 *Anti-Oedipus: capitalism and schizophrenia*. London, Athlone

Deleuze G and **Guattari F** 1988 *A thousand plateaux: capitalism and schizophrenia*. London, Athlone

Denison D R 1984 Bringing corporate culture to the bottom line. *Organizational Dynamics*, 13: 5–22

Denison D R 1990 *Corporate culture and organizational effectiveness*. New York, Wiley

Derrida J 1978 *Writing and difference*. London, Routledge

Derrida J 1994 Spectres of Marx. *New Left Review* 205: 31–58

Dicken P and **Thrift N** 1992 The organization of production and the production of organization: why business enterprises matter in the study of geographical industrialization. *Transactions of the Institute of British Geographers* NS17: 279–91

Diefenbach J 1987 The corporate identity as the brand. In J M Murphy (ed.) *Branding: a key marketing tool*. Basingstoke, Macmillan: 156–64

Discount Merchandiser 1988 Why we lose $25 billion a year. *Discount Merchandiser* 285: 86–90

DJK 1869 Shopping at Stewart's. *Hearth and Home* 9 January: 43

Doel C 1991 Corporate strategies in a dynamic sector: the case of the food industry. MSc dissertation, University of Sussex

Doel M 1992 In stalling deconstruction: striking out the postmodern. *Society and Space* 10: 163–79

Doeringer P and **Piore M** 1971 *Internal labour markets and manpower analysis.* Lexington, MA, D C Heath

Doogan K 1992 Flexible labour? Employment and training in new service industries: the case of retailing. Working Paper 105, School for Advanced Urban Studies, University of Bristol Working Paper 105

Douglas A 1977 *The feminization of American culture.* New York, Doubleday

Dowling R 1991 Shopping and the construction of feminity in the Woodward's Department Store, Vancouver, 1945 to 1960. MA thesis, Department of Geography, University of British Columbia

Dowling R 1993 Femininity, place and commodities: a retail case study. *Antipode* 25: 295–319

Driver S 1990 Beyond markets and hierarchies: a study of manufacturers and retailers in the UK clothing sector. DPhil thesis, University of Sussex

DTI 1992 *Abuse of market power: a consultative document on possible legislative options.* Cm 2100, Department of Trade and Industry, London, HMSO

Ducatel K and **Blomley N** 1990 Rethinking retail capital. *International Journal of Urban and Regional Research* 14: 207–27

Du Gay P 1992 Numbers and souls: retailing and the de-differentiation of economy and culture. Paper delivered at the Employment Research Unit Annual Conference, Cardiff Business School, University of Wales College of Cardiff

Economist Intelligence Unit 1992a Market report 2: chilled foods. *Retail Business* 410: 30–46

Economist Intelligence Unit 1992b Grocery retailers. *Retail Business Quarterly Trade* Reviews 24: 3–24

Economist Intelligence Unit 1992c *Retail Business Quarterly Trade Review: Annual Review of Retailing*. London, EIU

Economist Intelligence Unit 1993 *Europe's top retailers*. London, EIU

Edmondson B 1988 Hot spots. *American Demographics* January: 25–30

Emerson R M 1962 Power–dependence relations. *American Sociological Review* 27: 31–41

Employment Gazette 1992 Employment Statistics, Historical Supplement no 3. *Employment Gazette*, 1006: 1–58 Supplement

Featherstone M 1991 *Consumer culture and postmodernism*. London, Sage

Federal Reserve Bank of Chicago 1989 After big gains, challenges for small business. *Chicago Fed Letter* 19: 1–3

Ferguson H 1992 Watching the world go round: atrium culture and the psychology of shopping. In R Shields (ed.) *Lifestyle shopping: the subject of consumption*. London, Routledge: 21–39

Fernie J 1989 Contract distribution in multiple retailing. *International Journal of Physical Distribution and Materials Management* 19: 1–35

Fine B 1993 Modernity, urbanism, and modern consumption: a comment. *Society and Space* 11: 599–601

Fine B and **Leopold E** (eds) 1993a *The world of consumption*. London, Routledge

Fine B and **Leopold E** 1993b Relocating retail capital. In B Fine and E Leopold (eds) *The world of consumption*. London, Routledge: 274–95

Firat A F, Dholakia N and **Bagozzi R P** (eds) 1987 *Philosophical and radical thought in marketing*. Lexington, MA, Lexington Books

Fiske J 1989a *Reading the popular*. London, Unwin Hyman

Fiske J 1989b *Understanding popular culture*. London, Unwin Hyman

Fitch R and **Knobel L** 1990 *Fitch on retail design*. Oxford, Phaidon

Florida R and **Kenney M** 1990 High-technology restructuring in the USA and Japan. *Environment and Planning A* 22: 233–52

Florida R and **Kenney M** 1991, Transplanted organizations: the transfer of Japanese industrial organization to the US. *American Sociological Review* 56: 381–98

Florida R and **Kenney M** 1992 Japanese investment, production organisation and the geography of steel. *Economic Geography* 68: 146–73

Flynn A and **Marsden T K** 1992 Food regulation in a period of agricultural retreat: the British experience. *Geoforum* 23: 85–93

Flynn A, Marsden T K and **Ward N** 1994 Retailing, the food system and the regulatory state: constructing the consumer interest. In P Lowe, T K Marsden and S Whatmore (eds) *Regulating agriculture: critical perspectives on rural change vol. 5*. London, David Fulton

Food Safety Act 1990 *Public general acts – Elizabeth II, 1990*. London, HMSO, Chapter 16

Foord J, Bowlby S R and **Tillsely C** 1992 Changing relations in the retail-supply chain: geographical and employment implications. *International Journal of Retail and Distribution Managment* 20: 23–30

Foucault M 1977 *Language, counter-memory, practice*. Ithaca, NY, Cornell University Press

Fox B 1994 Brand erosion potential: retailers seek gains in private label *Chain Store Age Executive* 70: 28–37

Francis P 1994 *The president's message*. East Bridgewater, MA, Shaw's Supermarkets, January

Freathy P 1993 Developments in the superstore labour market. *Service Industries Journal* 13: 65–79

Freathy P and **Sparks L** 1993 *Sunday working in the retail trade*. Institute for Retail Studies, University of Stirling

Freathy P and **Sparks L** 1995a Flexibility, labour segmentation and retail superstore managers: the effects of Sunday trading. *International Review of Retail, Distribution and Consumer Research, 5*

Freathy P and **Sparks L** 1995b The employment structure of the Sunday labour market in retailing. *Environment and Planning A* 27: 471–87

Friedman A 1977 *Industry and labour: class struggle at work and monopoly capitalism*. Basingstoke, Macmillan

Friedman B 1988 Productivity trends in department stores, 1967–1986. *Monthly Labor Review* March: 17–21

Frisby D 1985 *Fragments of modernity: theories of modernity in the work of Simmel, Kracauer and Benjamin*. Cambridge, Polity

Fuller L and **Smith V** 1991 Consumers reports: management by customers in a changing economy. *Work, Employment and Society* 5: 1–6

Galbraith J K 1952 *American capitalism: the concept of countervailing power.* Boston, MA, Mifflin

Gardner C and **Sheppard J** 1989 *Consuming passion: the rise of retail culture.* London, Unwin Hyman

Gardner D S 1984 'A paradise of fashion': A.T. Stewart's department store, 1862–1875. In J M Jensen and S Davidson (eds) *A needle, a bobbin, a strike: women needleworkers in America.* Philadelphia, PA, Temple University Press: 60–80

Garner J 1992 Body matters. *DR The Fashion Business* 27 June

Gascoigne R 1992 Entry of the European limited line discounters into the UK. Paper presented at the Annual Conference of the Institute of British Geographers, Swansea, January

Gay J 1716 *Trivia: or the art of walking the streets of London.* London

Gebhardt R 1988 Strategies for store design. *Discount Merchandiser* 285: 95–104

Gereffi G 1993 The organization of buyer-driven global commodity chains: how US retailers shape overseas production networks. Working Paper Number 175, Papers in International Political Economy, Duke University, Durham, NC

Gertler M S 1988 The limits to flexibility: comments on the post Fordist vision of production and its geography. *Transactions of the Institute of British Geographers* NS13: 419–32

Gertler M S 1992 Flexibility revisited: districts, nation-states, and the forces of production. *Transactions of the Institute of British Geographers* NS17: 259–78

Gertler M 1995 Manufacturing culture: the spatial construction of capital. Paper presented at the Annual Conference of the Institute of British Geographers, Newcastle upon Tyne, 3–6 January

Gibbs D 1987 *Changing relationships between manufacturers and retailers in the British clothing industry: the impact of new technology.* Department of Environmental and Geographical Studies, Manchester Polytechnic

Gibbs D 1991 The role of consumption in the flexibility debate. Working Paper, Centre for Employment Research, Manchester Polytechnic

Gibbs D 1992 'The main thing today is shopping': consumption and the flexibility debate. SPA Working Paper 15, Spatial Policy Analysis, School of Geography, University of Manchester

Giddens A 1987 *Social theory and modern sociology*. Cambridge, Polity

Giddens A 1991 *Modernity and self-identity: self and society in the late modern age*. Cambridge, Polity

Giddens A 1992 *The transformation of intimacy*. Cambridge, Polity

Glennie P D and **Thrift N J** 1992 Modernity, urbanism and modern consumption. *Society and Space* 10: 423–43

Glennie P D and **Thrift N J** 1993 Modern consumption: theorising commodities *and* consumers. *Society and Space* 11: 603–6

Godkin E L 1876 Untitled piece in *The Nation* 22: 259

Goffman E 1959 *The presentation of the self in everyday life*. New York, Doubleday

Goss J 1992 Modernity and post-modernity in the retail landscape. In K Anderson and F Gale (eds) *Inventing places: studies in cultural geography*. Melbourne, Longman Cheshire

Goss J 1993 The 'magic of the mall': an analysis of form, function and meaning in the contemporary retail built environment. *Annals of the Association of American Geographers* 83: 18–47

Granovetter M 1985 Economic action and social structures: the problem of 'embeddedness'. *American Journal of Sociology* 91: 491–510

Grant R 1987 Manufacturer–retailer relations: the shifting balance of power. In G Johnson (ed.) *Business strategy and retailing*. London, Wiley: 43–58

Gregory A 1991 Patterns of working hours in large scale grocery retailing in Britain and France: convergence after 1992? *Work, Employment and Society* 5: 497–514

Gregory D 1978 *Ideology, science and human geography*. London, Hutchinson

Gregson N and **Crewe L** 1994 Beyond the high street and the mall: car boot fairs and the new geographies of consumption in the 1990s. *Area* 26: 261–67

Guha P 1993 Littlewoods shakes up supply network. *Drapers Record* May

Gupta H 1991 F&N employees vote to picket over scheduling. *Seattle Times*, 16 January: D4

Guy C 1980 *Retail location and retail planning in Britain*. London, Gower

Guy C 1988 Information technology and retailing: the implications for analysis and forecasting. In N Wrigley (ed.) *Store choice, store location and market analysis*. London, Routledge

Guy C M 1994 *The retail development process*. London, Routledge

Guy C M 1995a Retail store development at the margin. *Journal of Retailing and Consumer Services* 2: 25–32

Guy C M 1995b Corporate strategies in food retailing and their local impacts: a case study of Cardiff. *Environment and Planning A* 27

Hall C 1992a *White, male and middle-class: essays in feminism and history*. Oxford, Polity

Hall C 1992b 'The tale of Samuel and Jemima': gender and working-class culture in nineteenth-century England. In H J Kaye and K McClelland (eds) *E P Thompson: critical perspectives*. Philadelphia, PA, Temple Press: 78–102

Hallsworth A 1990 The lure of the USA: some further reflections. *Environment and Planning A* 22: 551–8

Hallsworth A G 1991 The Campeau takeovers: the arbitrage economy in action. *Environment and Planning A* 23: 1217–24

Hallsworth A G 1992 *The new geography of consumer spending*. London, Belhaven

Hamm L G 1982 Retailer–manufacturer relationships in the food sector: some observations from the USA. NC Project 117 Working Paper Series WP-64, ERS, US Department of Agriculture

Hampden-Turner C 1992 *Creating corporate culture: from discord to harmony*. New York, Addison Wesley

Hancher L and **Moran M** 1989 Organising regulatory space. In L Hancher and M Moran (eds) *Capitalism, culture and economic regulation*. Oxford, Clarendon Press:

Harcourt G C 1972 *Some Cambridge controversies in the theory of capital*. Cambridge, Cambridge University Press

Harrison G and **Hill P** 1989 Acquisitions to continue. *Discount Merchandiser* 295: 86–8

Harvey D 1973 *Social justice and the city.* Oxford, Blackwell

Harvey D 1978 The urban process under capitalism: a framework for analysis. *International Journal of Urban and Regional Research 2: 551–8*

Harvey D 1982 *The limits to capital.* Oxford, Blackwell

Harvey D 1989a From models to Marx: notes on the project to 'remodel' contemporary geography. In B Macmillan (ed.) *Remodelling geography.* Oxford, Blackwell

Harvey D 1989b *The urban experience.* Oxford, Blackwell

Harvey D 1989c *The condition of postmodernity.* Oxford, Blackwell

Haugen S 1986 Employment expansion in retail trade, 1973–1985. *Monthly Labor Review* August: 9–16

Hearn J 1992 *Men in the public eye.* London, Routledge

Heath S 1981 *Questions of cinema.* London, Macmillan

Henderson Crosthwaite 1992 'Three plus one'. Food retail report no. 10. Henderson Crosthwaite Institutional Brokers Ltd, 32 St Mary-at-Hill, London, EC3P 3AJ

Hirschman A 1970 *Exit, voice, loyalty.* Cambridge, MA, Harvard University Press

Hirschman E C and **Holbrook M B** 1992 *Postmodern consumer research: the study of consumption as text.* London, Sage

Hodgson G 1988 *Economics and institutions: a manifesto for a modern institutional economics.* Cambridge, Polity

Hogarth T and **Barth M** 1991 *Age works: a case study of B & Q's use of older workers.* Institute of Employment Research, University of Warwick

Hooks B 1991 *Yearning: race, gender and cultural politics.* London, Turnaround

Hopkins J 1990 West Edmonton Mall: landscapes of myth and elsewhereness. *Canadian Geographer* 34: 2–17

Hopkins T K 1957 Sociology and the substantive view of the economy. In K Polanyi, C M Arensberg and H W Pearson (eds) *Trade and market in the early empires: economies in history and theory.* Glencoe, Illinois, Free Press: 270–306

Horizon 1993 Suggers, fruggers and data-muggers: text adapted from the programme transmitted 15 February 1993. London, British Broadcasting Corporation

Huat Chua B 1992 Shopping for women's fashion in Singapore. In R Shields (ed.) *Lifestyle shopping: the subject of consumption.* London, Routledge

Hudson R, Schech S and **Krongsgaard Hansen L** 1992 Jobs for the girls? The new private sector service economy of Derwentside District. Occasional Paper no 28, Department of Geography, University of Durham

Hyman R 1993 Take it from the top. *Drapers Record* 9 January

Investment Property Databank 1991 *IPD Annual Review,* London, IPD

Jackson M P, Leopold J W and **Tuck K** 1993 *Decentralization of collective bargaining.* Basingstoke, Macmillan

Jackson P 1991a The cultural politics of masculinity: towards a social geography. *Transactions of the Institute of British Geographers* NS16: 199–213

Jackson P 1991b Social geography and the cultural politics of consumption. *Nordisk samhällsgeografisk tidskrift* 14: 3–16

Jackson P 1991c Repositioning social and cultural geography: comments on the papers by David Clarke and Michael Keith. In C Philo (ed.) *New words, new worlds: reconceptualising social and cultural geography.* Lampeter, Social and Cultural Geography Study Group of the Institute of British Geographers: 193–5

Jackson P 1993 Towards a cultural politics of consumption. In J Bird, B Curtis, T Putnam, G Robinson and L Tickner (eds) *Mapping the futures: local cultures, global change.* London, Routledge

Jackson P 1994 Consumption and identity: a theoretical agenda and some preliminary finding. Paper presented at the Annual Conference of the Institute of British Geographers, Nottingham, January

Jackson P and **Holbrook B** 1995 Multiple meanings: shopping and the cultural politics of identity. *Environment and Planning A* 27

Jackson P and **Thrift N** 1995 Geographies of consumption. In D Miller (ed.) *Acknowledging consumption*. London, Routledge

Jameson F 1984 Postmodernism, or the cultural logic of late capitalism. *New Left Review* 146: 53–93

Jeffreys J 1954 *Retail trading in Britain 1850–1950*. Cambridge, Cambridge University Press

Jessop B 1982 *The capitalist state: Marxist theories and methods*. Oxford, Martin Robertson

Johnson P and **Rahtz N** 1992 Meadowhall: new international employment practices? Paper presented at Aston/Umist Tenth Annual International Conference on Organisation and Control of the Labour Process, Aston University, 1–3 April

Jones K and **Simmons J** 1990 *The retail environment*. London, Routledge

Joseph J 1993 Welcome to the pleasure dome, at a price. *The Times*, 8 November: 9

Judd E 1994 Signs of the times: a study of the production and consumption of the spaces of the supermarket. Unpublished dissertation, Department of Geography, University of Lancaster

Kahn A 1992 Filling every Gap. *New York Times* 23 August

Kaplan E A 1992 *Motherhood and representation: the mother in popular culture and melodrama*. London, Routledge

Kasson J F 1990 *Rudeness and civility: manners in nineteenth-century America*. New York, Hill and Wang

Katz B 1987 *How to manage customer service*. Aldershot, Gower

Kenney M and **Florida R** 1993 *Beyond mass production: the Japanese system and its transfer to the US*. Oxford, Oxford University Press

Kerr C 1954 The Balkanisation of labour markets. In E W Bakke (ed.) *Labour mobility and economic opportunity*. New York, Wiley

Key Note 1992 *A market sector overview: ready meals*. London, Key Note Publications Ltd

King R 1990 Architecture, capital and the globalization of culture. *Theory, Culture and Society* 7: 397–411

Kirby D 1993 Working conditions and the trading week. In R D F Bromley and C J Thomas (eds) *Retail change: contemporary issues*, London, UCL Press: 192–207

Knopp L 1992 Sexuality and the spatial dynamics of capitalism. *Society and Space* 10: 651–69

Knox P 1991 The restless urban landscape: economic and sociocultural change and the transformation of metropolitan Washington, DC. *Annals of the Association of American Geographers* 81: 181–209

Kotter J P and **Heskett J L** 1990 *Corporate culture and performance.* New York, Free Press

Kransdorf A 1993 Making acquisitions work by the book. *Personnel Management* May: 39–43

Lacan J 1977 *Ecrits: a selection.* London, Tavistock

Laermans R 1993 Learning to consume: early department stores and the shaping of the modern consumer culture 1860–1914. *Theory, Culture and Society* 10: 79–102

Landes J B 1988 *Women and the public sphere in the age of the French Revolution.* Ithaca, NY, Cornell University Press

Lang T and **Wiggins P** 1985 The industrialisation of the UK food system: from production to consumption. In M Healy and B Ilbery (eds) *The industrialisation of the countryside.* Norwich, Geo Books

Lash S 1993 Reflexive modernisation: the aesthetic dimension. *Theory, Culture and Society* 10: 1–23

Lash S and **Urry J** 1993 *Economies of signs and space: after organized capitalism.* London, Sage

Lawrence J C 1992 Geographical space, social space, and the realm of the department store. *Urban History* 19: 64–83

Lazonick W 1991 *Business organisation and the myth of the market economy.* Cambridge, Cambridge University Press

Leach W R 1980 *True love and perfect union.* Middletown, CT, Wesleyan University Press

Leach W R 1984 Transformations in a culture of consumption: women and department stores, 1890–1925. *Journal of American History* 71: 319–42

Leahy T 1987 Branding: the retailer's viewpoint. In J M Murphy (ed.) *Branding: a key marketing tool.* Basingstoke, Macmillan: 116–24

Lefebvre H 1991 *The production of space.* Oxford, Blackwell

Lemire B 1988 Consumerism in pre-industrial and early industrial Britain: the trade in secondhand clothes. *Journal of British Studies* 27: 1–24

Lemire B 1991 *Fashion's favourite: the cotton trade and the consumer in Britain, 1660–1800.* Oxford, Clarendon Press

Lester R 1952 A range theory of wage differentials. *Industrial and Labour Relations Review* July: 483–500

Lesthaeghe R 1983 A century of demographic and cultural change in western Europe: an exploration of underlying dimensions. *Population and Development Review* 9: 411– 35

Levitt T 1983 The globalization of markets. *Harvard Business Review* 61(3): 92–102

Lieberman R 1993 Shopping disorders. In B Massumi (ed.) *The politics of everyday fear.* Minneapolis, MN, Minneapolis University Press: 245–65

Little I M D 1950 *A critique of welfare economics.* Oxford, Oxford University Press

Litwak D 1987 The nation's top grocery corporations. *Supermarket Business* 42: 92–6

Longmore A 1994 Football puts its skill on profit. *The Times,* 19 December: 27

Lovering J 1989 The restructuring debate. In R Peet and N Thrift (eds) *New models in geography: the political-economy perspective Vol. 1.* London, Unwin Hyman: 198–223

Lovering J 1990 Fordism's unknown successor: a comment on Scott's theory of flexible accumulation and the re-emergence of regional economies. *International Journal of Urban and Regional Research* 14: 159–74

Lowe M 1991 Trading places: retailing and local economic development at Merry Hill, West Midlands. *East Midland Geographer* 14: 31–48

Lowe, M 1993 Local Hero! An examination of the role of the regional entrepreneur in the regeneration of Britain's regions. In G Kearns and C Philo (eds) *Selling places: the city as cultural capital, past and present.* Oxford, Pergamon: 211–30

Lowe M 1995 Design innovation in UK fashion retailing: towards manufacturer-retailer-designer business partnerships. Research Proposal to the ESRC Research Grant Scheme

Lowe M and Crewe L 1991 Lollipop jobs for pin-money? Retail employment explored. *Area* 23: 344–7

Lunt P K and Livingstone S M 1992 *Mass consumption and personal identity: everyday economic experience.* Buckingham, Open University Press

Lynch J E 1990 The impact of electronic point of sale (EPoS) on marketing strategy and retailer–supplier relationships. *Journal of Marketing Management* 6: 157–68

Lyotard J-F 1984 *The postmodern condition.* Manchester, Manchester University Press

McCabe J D Jr 1971 *Lights and shadows of New York life; or, the sights and sensations of the great city.* London: André Deutsch Ltd. A facsimile edition from the 1872 original

McDowell L 1989 Women, gender and the organisation of space. In D Gregory and R Walford (eds) *Horizons in human geography.* London, Macmillan: 136–51

McDowell L 1994 The transformation of cultural geography. In D Gregory, R L Martin and G Smith (eds) *Human geography: society, space, and social science* Minneapolis, University of Minnesota Press: 146–73

McGoldrick P J 1990 *Retail marketing.* London, McGraw-Hill

McKinnon A C 1985 The distribution systems of supermarket chains. *Service Industries Journal* 5: 226–38

McKinnon A C 1989 *Physical distribution systems.* London, Routledge

McKinnon A C 1990 The advantages and disadvantages of centralised distribution. In J Fernie (ed.) *Retail distribution management.* London, Kogan Page

McMillan J 1990 Managing suppliers: incentive systems in Japanese and US industry. *California Management Review* 33: 38–55

MacRobbie A 1989 *Zoot suits and second-hand dresses: an anthology of fashion and music.* Basingstoke, Macmillan

MAFF 1974 *Food from our own resources.* Ministry of Agriculture, Fisheries and Food, London, HMSO

MAFF 1979 *Farming and the nation*. Ministry of Agriculture Fisheries and Food, London, HMSO

Maffesoli M 1991 The ethic of aesthetics. *Theory, Culture and Society* 8: 7–20

Maffesoli M 1992 *The time of tribes*. London, Sage

Mandel E 1978 *Late capitalism*. London, New Left Books

Marchington M and **Harrison E** 1991 Customers, competitors and choice: employee relations in food retailing. *Industrial Relations Journal* 22: 286–99

Marden P 1992 Real regulation reconsidered. *Environment and Planning A* 24: 751–67

Margolis J 1995 Wheels of fortune. *Sunday Times*, Style, 1 January: 6

Marsden T K 1993 Globalisation, the state and the environment: the limits and options of state activity. Paper presented at conference entitled Concepts of the state in a changing global agricultural food system, The Agricultural University, Wageningen, The Netherlands, August

Marsden T and **Wrigley N** 1995 Regulation, retailing and consumption. *Environment and Planning A* 27

Marsden T K, Murdoch J, Lowe P, Munton R and **Flynn A** 1993 *Constructing the countryside*. London, UCL Press

Marshall N 1992 Broad horizons. *DR The Fashion Business* 11 January

Martin J 1992 *Cultures in organisation: three perspectives*. New York, Oxford University Press

Martin R L 1990 Flexible futures and post-Fordist places: comments on pathways to industrialisation and regional development in the 1990s – an international conference. *Environment and Planning A* 22: 1276–80

Marx K 1973 *Grundrisse*. Harmondsworth, Penguin

Marx K 1976 *Capital: a critique of political economy I*. Harmondsworth, Penguin

Massey D 1989 Foreword. In R Peet and N Thrift (eds) *New models in geography: the political economy perspective*. London, Unwin Hyman: ix–xi

Massey D and **Meegan R** 1982 *The anatomy of jobs*. London, Methuen

Massumi B 1992 *A user's guide to capitalism and schizophrenia: deviations from Deleuze and Guattari*. London, Swerve

Mata J 1991 Sunk costs and entry by small and large plants. In P A Geroski and J Schwalback (eds) *Entry and market contestability: an international comparison*. Blackwell, Oxford: 49–62

Mathias P 1967 *Retail revolution*. London, Longman

Mauss M 1966 *The gift*. London, Cohen and West

May M 1994 Talking shop turns to shop talk. *The Times* 16 December: 29

Meisenheimer J, Mellor E and **Rydzewski L** 1992 Job market slid in early 1991, then struggled to find footing. *Monthly Labor Review* February: 3–17

Meyrowitz J 1985 *No sense of place: the impact of electronic media on social behaviour*. Oxford, Oxford University Press

Michon F 1987 Segmentation, employment structures and production structures. In R Tarling (ed.) *Flexibility in labour markets*. London, Academic Press: 23–58

Millar A 1993 Wheels of fortune. *Drapers Record* 26 June: 25

Miller D 1987 *Material culture and mass consumption*. Oxford, Basil Blackwell

Miller D 1990 Fashion and ontology in Trinidad. *Culture and History* 7: 49–77

Miller M B 1981 *The Bon Marché: bourgeois culture and the department store, 1869–1920*. Princeton, NJ, Allen & Unwin

Miller T G 1986 Goffman, positivism and the self. *Philosophy of Social Science* 16: 77–95

MINTEL 1985/6 Own brands. *Retail Intelligence* Winter: 109–43

Mitchell R 1992 Inside the Gap. *Business Week* 9 March

MMC 1981 *Discounts to retailers*. Monopolies and Mergers Commission, London, HMSO

Mohun S 1977 Consumer sovereignty. In F Green and P Nore (eds) *Economics: an anti-text*. London, Macmillan: 57–75

Moir C 1990 Competition in the UK grocery trades. In C Moir and J A Dawson (eds) *Competition and markets: essays in honour of Margaret Hall*. London, Macmillan: 91–118

Moir C and **Dawson J A** 1992 Distribution. In M C Fleming (ed.) *Reviews of United Kingdom Statistical Sources* (Volume XXIX). London, Chapman and Hall

Morgan K and **Sayer A** 1988 A 'modern' industry in a 'mature' region: the remaking of labour-management relations *International Journal of Urban and Regional Research* 9: 383–404

Morgenson G 1993 The death of the salesman. *Forbes* 15111: 106–12

Morris J L 1988 New technologies, flexible work practices and regional socio-spatial differentiation: some observations from the United Kingdom. *Society and Space* 6: 301–19

Morris J L and **Imrie R** 1992 *Transforming Buyer-Supplier Relations: Japanese-style industrial practices in a western context*. Macmillan, Basingstoke

Morris M 1988 Things to do with shopping centres. In Sheridan S (ed.) *Grafts: feminist cultural criticism*. London, Verso: 193–223

Morris M 1993 Things to do with shopping centres. In S During (ed.) *The cultural studies reader*. London, Routledge

Mort F 1989 The politics of consumption. In S Hall and M Jacques (eds) *New times: the changing face of politics in the 1990s*. London, Lawrence and Wishart: 160–72

Mort F 1995 Topographies of taste: commercial culture, masculinity and spatial relations in 1980s London. *Society and Space* 13

Moylan P 1991 Retailers review sourcing. *Drapers Record*, 28 September

Mui H C and **Mui L H** 1989 *Shops and shopkeeping in eighteenth-century England*. London, Routledge

Murray F 1983 The decentralisation of production: the decline of the mass collective worker. *Capital and Class* 19: 74–99

Murray R 1988 From Fordism to flexibility: the place of retailing. Paper presented at the Symposium on the Microelectronics Revolution and Regional Development, Labour Organisation and the Future of Post-industrial Society, Milan, Italy

Murray R 1989 Fordism and post-Fordism. In S Hall and M Jaques (eds) *New times: the changing face of politics in the 1990s*. London, Lawrence and Wishart

NatWest Securities 1993 *US food retailing: the European connection*. London, NatWest Securities

Nava M 1992 *Changing cultures: feminism, youth and consumerism*. London, Sage

NEDO 1988 *Part-time working in the distributive trades*. Distributive Trades Economic Development Committee, London, NEDO

Nelson R and **Winter S** 1982 *An evolutionary theory of economic change*. Cambridge, MA, Harvard University Press

Newby P 1993 Shopping as leisure. In R D F Bromley and C J Thomas (eds) *Retail change: contemporary issues*, London, UCL Press: 208–28

Norkett P 1985 Stack 'em high, sell 'em fast: the key to supermarket success. *Accountancy* 96: 74–9

Norris S 1990 The return of impact assessment: assessing the impact of regional shopping centre proposals in the United Kingdom. *Papers of the Regional Science Association* 69: 101–19

Noyelle T 1987 *Beyond industrial dualism: market and job segmentation of the new economy*. Boulder, CO, Westview

OFT 1985 *Competition and retailing*. Office of Fair Trading, Field House, Bream Buildings, London EC4 1PR

Ogbonna E and **Wilkinson B** 1988 Corporate strategy and corporate culture: the management of change in the UK supermarket industry, *Personnel Review*, 17 (6): 10–14

Olsson G 1980 *Birds in egg/eggs in bird*. London, Pion

Olsson G 1992 Lines of power. In T J Barnes and J S Duncan (eds) *Writing worlds: discourse, text and metaphor in the representation of landscape*. London, Routledge: 86–96

Openshaw S 1988 Building an automated modelling system to explore a universe of spatial interaction models. *Geographical Analysis* 20: 31–46

Ouchi W G 1981 *Theory Z*. New York, Wesley

Outram Cullinan and Company 1991 Private label: the branded manufacturer challenge. London, OC&C Strategy Consultants

Parkes C 1988 Brand new thinking. *Financial Times* 1 February

Peck J 1989a Reconceptualising the local labour market: space segmentation and the state. *Progress in Human Geography* 13: 42–61

Peck J 1989b Labour market segmentation theory. *Labour and Industry* 2: 119–44

Peck J and **Tickell A** 1991 *Regulation theory and the geographies of flexible accumulation: transistions in capitalism, transitions in theory.* Working paper no 12. Manchester, University of Manchester, School of Geography

Pefanis J 1991 *Heterology and the postmodern: Bataille, Baudrillard, and Lyotard.* London, Duke University Press

Penn R and **Worth B** 1993 Employment patterns in contemporary retailing: gender and work in five supermarkets. *Service Industries Journal* 13: 252–66

Penny N J and **Broom D** 1988 The Tesco approach to store location. In N Wrigley (ed.) *Store choice, store location and market analysis.* London, Routledge: 106–19

Pickholz J 1988 The end of the world as we know it. *Direct Marketing* November: 42

Piore M 1975 Notes for a theory of labour market stratification. In R Edwards, M Reich and D Garden (eds) *Labour market segmentation.* Lexington, MA, Lexington Books: 125–50

Piore M and **Sable C** 1984 *The second industrial divide.* New York, Basic Books

Pipe P 1992 Money's too tight. *DR The Fashion Business* 11 July

Pipe P 1993 Are they being served? What's selling in the States is customer care and British retailers could learn a few things from their North American counterparts. *Drapers Record* 3 April: 21–3

Podgursky M 1992 The industrial structure of job displacement, 1979–1989. *Monthly Labor Review* 115(9): 17–25

Polanyi K 1944 *The great transformation.* Boston, MA, Beacon

Polanyi K 1957a Aristotle discovers the economy. In K Polanyi, C M Arensberg and H W Pearson (eds) *Trade and market in the early empires: economies in history and theory.* Glencoe, Illinois, Free Press: 64–94

Polanyi K 1957b The economy as instituted process. In K Polanyi, C M Arensberg and H W Pearson (eds) *Trade and market in the early empires: economies in history and theory.* Glencoe, Illinois, Free Press: 243–70

Polhemus T 1994 *Streetstyle*, London, Thames and Hudson

Porter M E 1976 *Interbrand choice, strategy and bilateral market power.* Cambridge, MA, Harvard University Press

Porter M E 1980 *Competitive strategy: techniques for analysing industries and competition.* New York, Free Press

Porter M E 1985 *Competitive advantage: creating and sustaining superior performance.* New York, Free Press

Poston T and Wilson A G 1977 Facility size vs. distance travelled: urban services and the fold catastrophe. *Environment and Planning A* 9: 681–6

Preston E 1992 MANA member identifies compelling reason for Wal-Mart action. *Agency Sales Magazine* 224: 27–30

Prichett P 1987 *Making mergers work.* Homewood, IL, Dow-Jones Irwin

Progressive Grocer 1994 *Marketing Guidebook.* Stamford, CT

Rainnie A 1984 Combined and uneven development in the clothing industry: the effects of competition on accumulation. *Capital and Class* 22: 141–56

Rainnie A 1991 Just in time, sub-contracting and the small firm. *Work, Employment and Society* 5: 353–75

Rajan A 1987 *Services: the second industrial revolution.* London, Portersworth

Ramshaw J 1993 A source subject. *Drapers Record* 6 February

Rawlinson R 1991 Retailers review sourcing. *Drapers Record* 28 September

Ray C A 1986 Corporate culture: the last frontier of control. *Journal of Management Studies* 23: 287–98

Reekie G 1992 Changes in the Adamless Eden: the sexual and spatial transformation of a Brisbane department store 1930–90. In R Shields (ed.) *Lifestyle shopping: the subject of consumption.* London, Routledge: 170–93

Reekie G 1993 *Temptations: sex, selling and the department store.* St Leonard's, Australia, Allen & Unwin

Resseguie H E 1964 A.T. Stewart's marble palace: the cradle of the department store. *New York Historical Society Quarterly* 48: 131–62

Reynolds J 1983 Retail employment change: scarce evidence in an environment of change. *Service Industries Journal* 3: 334–62

Richards T S 1991 *The commodity culture of Victorian England: advertising and spectacle, 1851–1914.* London, Verso

Richardson G 1972 The organisation of industry. *Economic Journal* 82: 883–96

Roberts A and **Smith G** 1983 The cut-throat brands war. *Campaign* 29 April: 32–3

Roberts M 1985 'Words they are women, and deeds they are men': images of work and gender in early modern England. In L Charles and L Duffin (eds) *Women and work in pre-industrial England.* London, Croom Helm: 122–80

Robins K 1989 Global times. *Marxism Today* December

Roddick A 1991 *Body and soul.* London Ebury Press

Rubery J 1988 Employers and the labour market. In D Gallie (ed.) *Employment in Britain.* Oxford, Blackwell: 251–80

Rutherford B A and **Waring R T** 1987 *Cases in company financial reporting.* London, Harper and Row

Sack R 1988 The consumers world: place as context. *Annals of the Association of American Geographers* 78: 643–64

Saloman Brothers Inc 1991 Food retailing: heading for a discount. 5 November, London, Saloman Brothers

Sansolo M 1994 Battle of the brands (continued). *Progressive Grocer* 73: 65–6

Saunders P and **Harris C** 1990 Privatisation and the consumer. *Sociology* 24: 57–75

Sayer A 1984 *Method in social science.* London, Hutchinson

Sayer A 1986 New developments in manufacturing: the just-in-time system. *Capital and* Class 30: 43–71

Sayer A 1989 Post-fordism in question. *International Journal of Urban and Regional Research* 13: 666–95

Sayer A and **Walker R** 1992 *The new social economy: reworking the division of labour*. Oxford, Blackwell

Schein E C 1992 The role of the founder in the creation of organizational culture. In P J Frost, L F Moore, M R Lovis, C C Lundberg and J Martin (eds) *Reframing organizational culture*. London, Sage: 14–25

Schiller R 1986 Retail decentralisation: the coming of the third wave. *The Planner* 72: 13–15

Schlosberg J 1988 Sitting pretty. *American Demographics* May: 24–8

Schoenberger E 1988 From Fordism to flexible accumulation: technology, competitive strategies and international location. *Society and Space* 6: 245–62

Schoenberger E 1994a Corporate strategy and corporate strategists: power, identity and knowledge within the firm. *Environment and Planning A* 26: 435–51

Schoenberger E 1994b What is strategic about strategy? *Environment and Planning A* 26: 1010–12

Schor N 1978 *Zola's crowds*. Baltimore, MD, Johns Hopkins Press

Schwartz H and **Davis S M** 1981 Matching corporate culture and business strategy. *Organizational Dynamics* 10: 30–48

Scobey D 1992 Anatomy of the promenade: the rise of bourgeois sociability in nineteenth-century New York. *Social History* 17: 203–27

Scott A J 1983 Industrial organisation and the logic of intra-metropolitan location: theoretical considerations. *Economic Geography* 59: 233–50

Scott A J 1988a *New industrial spaces*. London, Pion

Scott A J 1988b Flexible production systems and regional development: the rise of new industrial spaces in North America and Europe. *International Journal of Urban and Regional Research* 12: 171–86

Scott A J and **Storper M** (eds) 1986 *Production, work, territory: the geographical anatomy of industrial capitalism*. London, Allen and Unwin

Segal L 1990 *Slow motion: changing masculinities, changing men.* London, Virago

Self P and **Storing H** 1962 *The state and the farmer.* London, Allen and Unwin

Semlinger K 1991 New developments in subcontracting: mixing market and hierarchy. In A Amin and M Dietrich (eds) *Towards a new Europe: structural change in the European economy.* Aldershot, Edward Elgar: 96–115

Senker J 1986 Retail influence on manufacturing innovation. DPhil thesis, Science Policy Research Unit, University of Sussex

Senker J 1989 The development of private brands and the balance of power between food manufacturers and food retailers: the case of the UK. Paper delivered to Forum Provendor Management Seminar, Malmo, 19 April

Sennett R 1977 *The fall of public man.* New York, Alfred A Knopf

Shackleton R 1994 Corporate strategy and market entry: British food retail investment in the US. Paper presented at the Association American Geographers, San Francisco, 1 April

Shackleton R 1995 Collisions of corporate culture: UK food retail investment in the US. PhD thesis, Department of Geography, University of Southampton

Shammas C 1990 *The pre-industrial consumer in England and America.* Oxford, Clarendon Press

Shaw G 1987 Retail development strategies and the British shopping hierarchy. In G Johnson (ed.) *Business strategy and retailing.* Chichester, Wiley: 257–73

Shaw S A, Nisbet D J and **Dawson J A** 1989 Economies of scale in UK supermarkets: some preliminary findings. *International Journal of Retailing* 4: 12–26

Shaw S A, Dawson J A and **Blair L M** 1991 *Opportunities for British food suppliers: product sourcing in the food chain.* Institute for Retail Studies, University of Stirling

Sheffield City Council 1987 *The retail revolution: who benefits?* Department of Employment and Economic Development Sheffield City Council, Sheffield

Shields R 1989 Social spatialisation and the built environment. *Society and Space* 7(2): 147–64

Shields R 1991 *Places on the margin: alternative geographies of modernity.* London, Routledge

Shields R (ed.) 1992a *Lifestyle shopping: the subject of consumption.* London, Routledge

Shields R 1992b The individual, consumption cultures and the fate of community. In R Shields (ed.) *Lifestyle shopping: the subject of consumption.* London, Routledge: 99–113

Shiret T 1991 Tesco PLC: a company capitalising too much interest. Credit Lyonnais Laing, November, Broadwalk House, 5 Appold Street, London EC2A 2DA

Shiret T 1992a How much hot air do you like in your accounts? Food retailer property valuations and their effect on the P & L. Credit Lyonnais Laing, 22 April, Broadwalk House, 5 Appold Street, London EC2A 2DA

Shiret T 1992b Putting a price-tag on the property of the food retailers. *The Times* 28 May

Shiret T 1992c Property again. Credit Lyonnais Laing, 29 May, Broadwalk House, 5 Appold Street, London EC2A 2DA

Shuttleworth S 1990 Female circulation: medical discourse and popular advertising in the mid-Victorian era. In M Jacobus, E Fox Keller and S Shuttleworth (eds) *Body/politics: women and the discourses of science.* New York, Routledge: 47–68

Silverstone R and **Hirsch E** 1992 *Consuming technologies: media and information in domestic spaces.* London, Routledge

Simmel G 1908 *On individuality and social forms.* Chicago, IL, Chicago University Press

Simmel G 1950 *The sociology of George Simmel,* ed. K Wolff. New York, Free Press

Simons J 1986 Culture, economy and reproduction in contemporary Europe. In D Coleman and R Schofield (eds) *The state of population theory.* Cambridge, Cambridge University Press: 256–78

Skipworth M 1992 Safeway accused of demanding unfair payments from suppliers. *Sunday Times* 13 September

Slichter S 1950 Notes on the structure of wages. *Review of Economics and Statistics* 32: 80–91

Smith D L G and Sparks L 1993 The transformation of physical distribution in retailing. *International Review of Retail, Distribution and Consumer Research* 3: 35–64

Smith M A 1974 John Snook and the design for A.T. Stewart's store. *New York Historical Society Quarterly* 58: 18–33

Smith N 1989 Uneven development and location theory: towards a synthesis. In R Peet and N Thrift (eds) *New models in geography: the political-economy perspective vol. 1.* London, Unwin Hyman: 142–63

Smith P 1988 Visiting the Banana Republic. In A Ross (ed.) *Universal abandon? The politics of postmodernism.* Edinburgh, Edinburgh University Press

Smith S 1988 How much change at the store? The impact of new technologies and labour processes on managers and staff in retail distribution. In D Knights and H Wilmott (eds) *New technology and the labour process.* Macmillan, Basingstoke: 143–62

Snell K D M 1985 The family. In *Annals of the labouring poor: social change and agrarian England 1660–1900.* Cambridge, Cambridge University Press: 320–73

Sparks L 1983 Employment characteristics of superstore retailing. *Service Industries Journal* 3: 63–78

Sparks L 1986a Employment characteristics of food superstores. PhD thesis, University of Wales

Sparks L 1986b The changing structure of distribution in retail companies: an example from the grocery trade. *Transactions of the Institute of British Geographers* NS11: 147–54

Sparks L 1987 Employment in retailing: trends and issues. In G Johnson (ed.) *Business strategy and retailing.* Chichester, Wiley: 239–55

Sparks L 1990 Spatial–structural relationships in retail corporate growth: a case study of Kwik Save Group PLC. *Service Industries Journal* 10: 25–84

Sparks L 1991a Retailing in the 1990s: differentiation through customer service? *Irish Marketing Review* 5: 28–38

Sparks L 1991b Employment in DIY superstores. *Service Industries Journal* 11: 304–23

Sparks L 1992a Restructuring retail employment. *International Journal of Retailing and Distribution Management* 3: 12–19

Sparks L 1992b Customer service in retailing: the next leap forward. *Service Industries Journal* 12: 165–84

Sparks L 1993 The rise and fall of mass marketing? Food retailing in Great Britain since 1960. In T L S Tedlow and G Jones (eds) *The rise and fall of mass marketing*. London, Routledge: 58–92

Stallybrass P and **White A** 1986 *The politics and poetics of transgression.* Ithaca, NY, Cornell University Press

Standard and Poor's Industry Surveys 1987 The velocity of assets. 22 January: 79–86

Stansell C 1987 *City of women: sex and class in New York, 1789–1860.* Chicago, University of Illinois Press

Storper M and **Scott A J** (1986) Production, work, territory: contemporary realities and theoretical tasks. In A Scott and M Storper (eds) *Production, work and territory: the geographical anatomy of industrial captialism*. Boston, Allen and Unwin: 3–15

Storper M and **Scott A J** 1989 The geographical foundations and social regulation of flexible production complexes. In J Wolch and M Dear (eds) *The power of geography: how territory shapes social life*. Boston, MA, Unwin Hyman: 21–40

Storper M and **Walker R** 1989 *The capitalist imperative: territory, technology and industrial growth.* Oxford, Blackwell

Strasser S 1989 *Satisfaction guaranteed: the making of the American mass market*. New York, Pantheon

Styles J 1993 Manufacture, consumption and design in eighteenth-century England. In J Brewer and R Porter (eds) *Consumption and society in the seventeenth and eighteenth centuries*. London, Routledge: 527–54

Styles J 1994 Clothing the north of England, 1600–1800. *Textile History* 25: 139–66

Swyngedouw E 1992 The Mammon quest. 'Glocalization', interspatial competition and the monetary order: the construction of new scales. In M Dunford and G Kafkalas (eds) *Cities and regions in the new Europe*. London, Belhaven

The Gap, Inc. 1991 *Annual Report*. San Francisco, CA, The Gap Inc.

The Gap, Inc. 1991 *A brief history of The Gap, Inc.* San Francisco, The Gap, Inc.

Therrien L 1988 Trying to make cooking as convenient as eating out. *Business Week* 11 January: 86

Thorpe D 1991a The development of British superstore retailing: further comments on Davies and Sparks. *Transactions of the Institute of British Geographers* NS16: 354–67

Thorpe D 1991b The changing geography of British shopping and retailing, 1944–1991: an agenda for research and an overview. Paper presented to the Annual Conference of the Institute of British Geographers, Swansea, January

Thrift N J and **Glennie P D** 1993 Historical geographies of urban life and modern consumption. In G Kearns and C Philo (eds) *Selling places: the city as cultural capital, past and present*. London, Pergamon: 33–48

Tickell A 1992 The social regulation of banking: foreign banks in Manchester and London. PhD thesis, School of Geography, University of Manchester

Tickell A and **Peck J A** 1992 Accumulation, regulation and the geographies of post-Fordism. *Progress in Human Geography* 16: 190–218

Tilly C 1991 Reasons for the continuing growth of part-time employment. *Monthly Labor Review* 114(3): 10–18

Tonnies F 1957 *Community and society: gemeinschaft and gesellschaft.* London, Harper

Totterdill P 1990 *Retail restructuring: changing patterns of consumption and their implications for public policy*. Research Study Series no 7, Centre for Local Economic Strategies, London

Townsend A 1986 Spatial aspects of the growth of part-time employment in Britain. *Regional Studies* 20: 313– 30

Treadgold A and **Davies R L** (eds) 1988 *The internationalisation of retailing*. London, Longman

Tse K K 1985 *Marks and Spencer: anatomy of Britain's most efficiently managed company*. Oxford, Pergamon

Turnbull P, Oliver N and **Williamson B** 1992 Buyer–supplier relations in the UK automotive industry: strategic implications of the Japanese manufacturing model. *Strategic Management Journal* 13: 159–68

Urry J 1985 Social relations, space and time. In D Gregory and J Urry (eds) *Social relations and spatial structures*. London, Macmillan: 20–48

USDAW 1990 Retailing in the 1990s: ADN Executive Council Statement. Manchester, USDAW

US Department of Commerce (Bureau of the Census) 1972, 1977, 1982, 1987 and 1992 *Census of retail trade*. Washington DC, Bureau of the Census

US Department of Commerce 1988 *US Industrial Outlook* 61: 1–7. Washington, DC, International Trade Administration

US Department of Labor (Bureau of Labor Statistics) 1988 *Occupational Projections and Training Data* April. Washington, DC, Bureau of Labor Statistics

US Small Business Administration 1987 *The State of Small Business: A Report to the President*. Washington DC, US Small Business Administration

Van Maanen J and **Barley S R** 1985 Cultural organization: fragments of a theory. In P J Frost, L F Moore, M R Louis, C C Lundbergh and J Martin (eds) *Organizational culture*. London, Sage: 31–53

Verdict Research 1991 *Verdict on Grocers and Supermarkets 1991*. Verdict Research, 112 High Holborn, London, WC1V 6JS

Vickery A 1993 Women and the world of goods: a Lancashire consumer and her possessions, 1751–81. In J Brewer and R Porter (eds) *Consumption and society in the seventeenth and eighteenth centuries*. London, Routledge: 274–301

Wachter M L 1974 Primary and secondary labour markets: a critique of the dual approach. *Brookings Papers on Economic Activity* 3: 637–93

Walker C 1991 What's in a name? *American Demographics* February: 54–6

Walker P 1985 *Zola*. London, Routledge and Kegan Paul

Walker R 1988 The geographical organisation of production systems. *Society and Space* 6: 377–408

Walker R 1989 A requiem for corporate geography. *Geografiska Annaler* 71B: 43–68

Wall Street Journal 1988 US apparel suppliers getting squeezed. 3 August: 22

Walters D and **White D** 1987 *Retail marketing management*. London, Macmillan

Warkentin J 1992 Grinning and bearing up. *Guardian* 27 April

Watkins S C 1991 From local to national communities: the transformation of demographic regimes in Europe. *Population and Development Review* 16: 241–72

Watson G 1993 Sunday working in Britain. *Employment Gazette* 101: 503–12

Weatherill L 1986 A possession of one's own: women and consumer behaviour in England, 1660–1740. *Journal of British Studies* 25: 131–56

Weatherill L 1988 *Consumer behaviour and material culture in Britain 1660–1760*. London, Routledge

Webb I R 1994 Green machine. *The Times* 23 November: 19

Webber M J, Clark G L, McKay J and **Missen G** 1991 Industrial restructuring: definitions, WP-91-3. Monash-Melbourne Joint Project on Comparative Australia–Asian Development, Development Studies Centre, Monash University, Clayton, Australia

Weeks J 1986 *Sexuality*. Chichester, Ellis Howard

Weiner E, Foust D and **Yang D** 1988 Why Made-In-America is back in style. *Business Week* 7 November: 116–20

Weisman W 1954 Commercial palaces of New York: 1845–1875. *Art Bulletin* 36

Whitmore M 1990 The influence of management in controlling labour retention in Tesco stores. MBA dissertation, University of Stirling

Whystall P 1981 Retail competition and the planner. *Retail and Distribution Management* 9: 44–7

Willen D 1992 Women in the public sphere in early modern England: the case of the urban working poor. In D O Helleby and S M Reverby (eds) *Gendered domains: rethinking public and private in women's history*. Ithaca, NY, Cornell University Press: 183–98

Williams C forthcoming Feminism, subjectivity and psychoanalysis: towards a corpo real knowledge. In K Lennan and M Whitford (eds) *Objectivity difference and the knowing subject: feminist perspectives on epistemology*. London, Routledge

Williams H C W L, Kim K S and **Martin D** 1990 Location-spatial interaction models: benefit maximising configurations of services. *Environment and Planning A* 22: 1979–1989

Williams K, Cutler T, Williams J and **Haslam C** 1987 The end of mass production? *Economy and Society* 16: 405–39

Williams R 1982 *Dream worlds: mass consumption in late nineteenth century France.* Berkeley, CA, University of California Press

Williamson J 1992a I–less and gaga in the West Edmonton Mall: towards a pedestrian feminist reading. In D H Currie and V Raoul (eds) *The anatomy of gender: women's struggle for the body.* Ottawa, Carleton University Press: 97–115

Williamson J 1992b Notes from Storyville North: circling the mall. In R Shields (ed.) *Lifestyle shopping: the subject of consumption.* London, Routledge: 216–32

Williamson O 1975 *Markets and hierarchies: analysis and anti-trust implications.* New York, Free Press

Williamson O 1985 *The economic institutions of capitalism: firms, markets, relational contracting.* New York, Free Press

Williamson O and **Ouchi W** 1981 The markets and hierarchies and visible hand perspectives. In A Van den Ven and W Joyce (eds) *Perspectives on organisation design and behaviour.* New York, Wiley

Willis P 1978 *Profane culture.* London, Routledge and Kegan Paul

Willis P, Jones S, Canaan J and **Hurd G** 1990 *Common culture: symbolic work at play in the everyday cultures of the young.* Milton Keynes, Open University Press

Willis S 1991 *A primer for daily life.* London, Routledge: 160–86

Wilson A G 1976 Retailer's profits and consumer's welfare in a spatial interaction shopping model. In I Masser (ed.) *Theory and practice in regional science.* London Papers in Regional Science, vol. 6. London, Pion

Wilson A G 1978 Spatial interaction and settlement structure: towards an explicit central place theory. In A Karlquist, L Lundquist, F Snickars, and J W Weilbull (eds) *Spatial interaction theory and planning models.* Amsterdam, North-Holland: 137–56

Wilson A G 1981 *Catastrophe theory and bifurcation: applications to urban and regional systems.* London, Croom Helm

Wilson A G 1985 Structural dynamics and spatial analysis: from equilibrium balancing models to extended economic models for both perfect and imperfect markets. Working Paper 431, School of Geography, University of Leeds

Wilson A G 1988 Store and shopping centre location and size: a review of British research and practice. In N Wrigley (ed.) *Store choice, store location and market analysis*. London, Routledge

Wilson A G 1991 'Author's response' Classics in human geography revisited: Wilson A G 1967 A statistical theory of trip distribution models. Transportation Research 1: 253–6. *Progress in Human Geography* 15: 433–6

Wilson A G and **Clarke M** 1979 Some illustrations of catastrophe theory applied to urban retailing structures. In M Breheny (ed.) *Developments in urban and regional analysis*. London, Pion: 5–27

Wilson A G and **Oulton M J** 1983 The corner shop to supermarket transition in retailing: the beginnings of empirical evidence. *Environment and Planning A* 15: 265–74

Wilson E 1985 *Adorned in dreams: fashion and modernity*. London, Virago

Wilson E 1989 These new components of the spectacle: fashion and postmodernism. In R Boyne and A Rattansi (eds) *Postmodernism and society*. London, Macmillan

Wilson E 1991 *The sphinx in the city: urban life, the control of disorder and women*. Berkeley, CA, University of California Press

Wilson E 1992 The invisible flâneur. *New Left Review* 191: 90–110

Wood D 1990 *Philosophy at the limit*. London, Unwin Hyman

Wood S 1989 The transformation of work. In S Wood (ed.) *The transformation of work*. London, Unwin Hyman: 1–43

Woodward D 1985 'Swords into ploughshares': recycling in pre-industrial England. *Economic History Review* 2nd series 38: 175–91

Wrigley N 1987 The concentration of capital in UK grocery retailing. *Environment and Planning A* 19: 1283–8

Wrigley N (ed.) 1988a *Store choice, store location and market analysis*. London, Routledge

Wrigley N 1988b Retail restructuring and retail analysis. In N Wrigley (ed.) *Store choice, store location and market analysis*. London, Routledge: 3–34

Wrigley N 1989 The lure of the USA: further reflections on the internationalisation of British grocery retailing capital. *Environment and Planning A* 21: 283–8

Wrigley N 1991 Is the 'golden age' of British grocery retailing at a watershed? *Environment and Planning A* 23: 1537–44

Wrigley N 1992a Antitrust regulation and the restructuring of grocery retailing in Britain and the USA. *Environment and Planning A* 24: 727–49

Wrigley N 1992b Sunk capital, the property crisis and the restructuring of British food retailing. *Environment and Planning A* 24: 1521–27

Wrigley N 1993a Retail concentration and the internationalization of British grocery retailing. In R D F Bromley and C J Thomas (eds) *Retail change: contemporary issues*. London, UCL Press: 41–68

Wrigley N 1993b Abuses of market power? Further reflections on UK food retailing and the regulatory state. *Environment and Planning A* 25: 1545–52

Wrigley N 1994 After the store wars: towards a new era of competition in UK food retailing? *Journal of Retailing and Consumer Services* 1: 5–20

Wrigley N 1995 Retailing and the arbitrage economy: market structures, regulatory frameworks, investment regimes and spatial outcomes. In T J Barnes and M S Gertler (eds) *Regions, institutions and technology*. Toronto, McGill–Queens University Press

Yeung H W 1994 Critical reviews of geographical perspectives on business organizations and the organization of production: towards a network approach. *Progress in Human Geography* 18: 460–90

Yip G 1982 *Barriers to entry*. Lexington, MA, Lexington Books

Zola É 1883; 1992 *The ladies' paradise*. Berkeley, CA, University of California Press with an introduction by Kristin Ross

Zukin S 1991 *Landscapes of power: from Detroit to Disney World*. Berkeley, CA, University of California Press

Zukin S and **Dimaggio P** (eds) 1990 *Structures of capital: the social organisation of the economy*. Cambridge, Cambridge University Press

Author Index

Subject Index